# THE KAISER'S PIRATES

# THE KAISER'S PIRATES

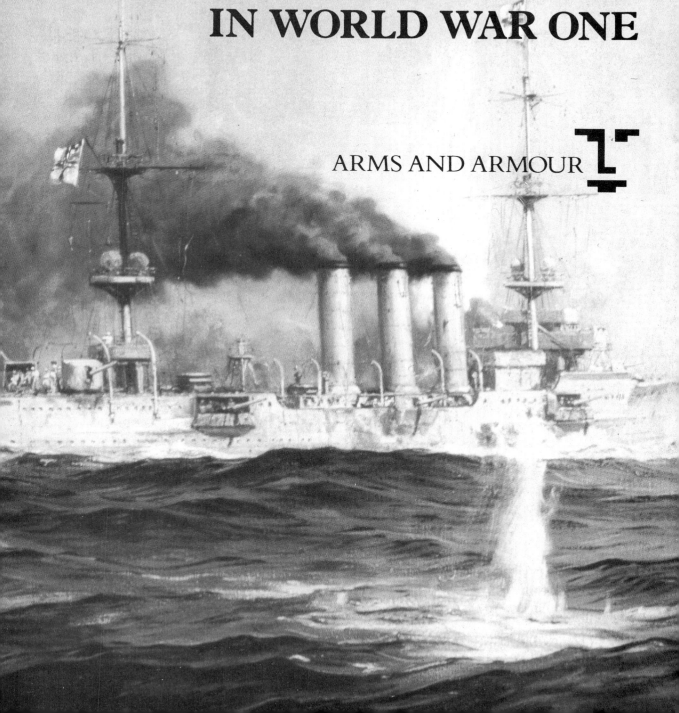

# JOHN WALTER

# GERMAN SURFACE RAIDERS IN WORLD WAR ONE

ARMS AND ARMOUR

Arms & Armour Press
*A Cassell Imprint*
Villiers House, 41–47 Strand, London WC2N 5JE

Distributed in Australia by
Capricorn Link (Australia) Pty. Ltd,
2/13 Carrington Road, Castle Hill, New South Wales 2154

© John Walter, 1994

**British Library Cataloguing in Publication Data**
A catalogue record for this book is available from the British Library

ISBN 1–85409–136–0

*For Alison and Adam, with love*

**Notes**

Every effort has been made to credit sources of illustrations accurately, though some prints give no clear indications of their origins. Unintentional infringement of copyright will be acknowledged, if appropriate, in future editions.

Place-names are usually given in their original form. Consequently, some names are given in a less familiar manner—e.g., *Habana* for 'Havana' or *Atol de Rocas* for 'Rocas Reef'. In cases where long-established usage has led to two differing names being used locally, the English version is preferred. This is particularly true of islands, bays and channels in the southern extremities of Chile and Argentina.

Pre-1918 German naval-officer ranks included Fähnrich z.S. (midshipman or ensign), Leutnant z.S. (sub-lieutenant or lieutenant, junior grade), Oberleutnant z.S. (lieutenant), Kapitänleutnant (lieutenant-commander), Korvettenkapitän (commander) Fregattenkapitän (captain with less than three years seniority), Kapitän z.S. (captain with greater than three years seniority), Konteradmiral (rear-admiral), Vizeadmiral (vice-admiral) and Admiral. The suffix 'z.S.' ('zur See') was used to distinguish naval personnel from army officers of the same rank.

**Title-page illustration**

'The Last Battle' by Claus Bergen, depicting *Emden* vainly duelling with *Sydney*. By courtesy of Fregattenkapitän d.R. Meinrad, Prinz von Hohenzollern-Emden. Photograph by courtesy of Fregattenkapitän Walter Reichenmiller, FGN.

Designed and produced by John Walter
Typesetting by the Typesetting Bureau, Wimborne, Dorset
Camerawork by Service Twenty-Four Ltd, Brighton, East Sussex
Printed and bound in Great Britain by The Bath Press, Bath, Avon

# CONTENTS

# FOREWORD

The creation of *The Kaiser's Pirates* and author's acknowledgements

*The Kaiser's Pirates* grew out of work undertaken on *Emden: The Last Cruise of the Chivalrous Raider*, which I produced for The Lyon Press Ltd in 1988–9. This book attempted to present a racy and most interesting memoir in a form which would be palatable to modern readers, many of whom could not be expected to visualise a typical pre-1914 merchant ship without the assistance of photographs.

*Emden* was a great critical success, excepting that, oddly, most reviews did not appear in print until it was a year old. Amongst all the praise, however, one particular magazine dismissed the project tersely—opining that no-one really wanted to read about British ships being sunk. This struck me as strange; the skippers of the pre-1918 German surface raiders, by and large, behaved as honourably as could have been expected in the circumstances. This was true even of the men sent out in the second half of the war, when the general tenor of hostilities had become cynical. It was also clear from modern shipping magazines that survivors often sought reunions with the men that had sunk them.

Gradually, therefore, I began to look in detail at raiders other than *Emden*. I became determined to rehabilitate the reputation of Erich Köhler of *Karlsruhe*, killed when his ship spontaneously exploded in November 1914. And there were so many colourful personalities—especially Felix von Luckner, commander of the sailing-raider *Seeadler*. The converted tramp steamer *Wolf* had even used a seaplane as a reconnaissance tool.

The project was initially conceived on a year-by-year basis, but attempting to interweave so many strands of detail made this approach difficult to justify. Thus I reverted to a concise ship-by-ship record, simplifying the narrative even though the movements of the raiders in relation to each other are less easily deduced.

I was greatly helped in framing my manuscript by Keble Chatterton's *The Sea Raiders*, published in the early 1930s; Chatterton was a well-versed writer on maritime history and his many books are still worth reading. Inspired by him, therefore, I elected to eschew detailed strategic analysis of the raiding campaigns and attempt to tell the story of the raiders against a background of the development of the imperial navy, the headlong rush into colonialism, Anglo-German industrial/mercantile rivalry, and the development of the wireless telegraph.

Interestingly, I found that detail varied from memoir to memoir. Time-scale could be questionable, as it was not always clear whether British or German chronology was being used: at the Battle of the Falkland Islands, for example, there was a half-hour difference. Thus care was necessary in the assessment of maps, some of which mixed systems of time indiscriminately.

Hours spent checking Lloyd's Registers of Shipping revealed that some reminiscences persistently mis-spelled ship names. Others sometimes gave displacement figures instead of gross registered tonnage, helping to inflate the perceived importance of a victim or the 'total bag'.

The greatest problem concerned the affairs of Felix von Luckner and *Seeadler*. The Sea Devil was a most skilled teller of tales even before the First World War began, and it is difficult to avoid the conclusion that figments of his vivid imagination were occasionally woven into his post-war memoirs as fact. Three different accounts give three differing versions of the mark he cut into the stern-rail of his erstwhile ship *Pinmore*, and the names selected to camouflage *Seeadler* as Norwegian are also subject to fluctuation. And should we believe von Luckner's account of the end of his ship . . . ? Work is undoubtedly still to be done.

I must thank the many people who have contributed information—often during work on *Emden*, little knowing that the project would continue beyond the confines of the original book. I owe particular debts to Fregattenkapitän a.D. Meinrad, Prinz von Hohenzollern-Emden, for the great enthusiasm with which he embraced the reprinting of his father's memoirs; to Fregattenkapitän Walter Reichenmiller, formerly commanding FGS *Emden* (F210), for forwarding information; to Laurence Dunn, for supplying many of the merchant-ship illustrations; to Ray Burt, for his help with illustrations of British warships; to Fregattenkapitän a.D. Alfred Nitzschke of the Deutscher Marinebund; to Joachim Görtz, for countless hours spent in pursuit of illustrations and documents in the Bundesarchiv; to Günter Huff, for photographs from his archives and copies of Aust's and von dem Borne's 'Karlsruhe' memoirs; to Jonathan Minns and Susan Wadbrook of the British Engineerium, Hove, for access to the museum library; to Alex. Hurst, for his matchless knowledge of the dying years of sail; to Mrs Dorothy Owston and Mrs Rosemary Matthews, sister and daughter of Laurence Prosser (whose recollections are reproduced in the *Emden* chapter); to John L. Glossop, nephew of the captain of HMAS *Sydney*, for supplying Bennet Copplestone's account of the duel with *Emden*; to Frau Elfriede Hennig, elder daughter of Karl von Müller (whom most British accounts paint as a childless batchelor!), for details of her father's life; to Mrs Barbara Jones of the Information Library, Lloyd's Register of Shipping; to Paul Kemp of the Imperial War Museum; to David Lyon of the National Maritime Museum; to the Bundesarchiv, Koblenz; to the Bayerisches Hauptstaatsarchiv, Stuttgart; and to the Australian War Memorial, Canberra.

But nothing would have been possible without the love of my wife Alison and son Adam, who have supported me through the periods of writer's block that inevitably attend the creative process. I hope that, therefore, *The Kaiser's Pirates* is as interesting to read as it was to write.

*John Walter, Hove, 1994*

# SELECT BIBLIOGRAPHY

——◆◆◆——

ASSMANN, Konteradmiral a.D. Kurt: *Der Krieg zur See 1914–1918* ('Die Kämpfe der Kaiserlichen Marine in den Deutschen Kolonien'). E.S. Mittler & Sohn, Berlin, 1935.

AUST, Kapitänleutnant Hubert: *Die Kriegsfahrten S.M.S. 'Karlsruhe'*. Braun'sche Hofbuchdruckerei u. Verlag, Karlsruhe, c.1925.

BENNETT, Geoffrey: *Coronel and Falklands*. B.T. Batsford Ltd, London, 1962.

BURT, R.A.: *British Battleships, 1889–1904*. Arms & Armour Press, London, and Naval Institute Press, Annapolis, Maryland, 1988.

CHARLEWOOD, Commander Clement J.: *Channels, Cloves and Coconuts*. The Western Press, undated (1935?).

CHATTERTON, E. Keble: *The "Königsberg" Adventure*. Hurst & Blackett, London, 1932.
—*The Sea Raiders*. Hurst & Blackett, 1931.

CORBETT, Sir Julian: *History of the Great War: Naval Operations*. Longmans, Green & Co. Ltd, London, five volumes, 1920–31.

DOHNA-SCHLODIEN, Nikolaus Burggraf und Graf zu: *The Cruise of "Moewe"*. Gotha, 1917.
—*Der Möwe Fahrten und Abenteur*. Friedr. Andreas Perthes, Berlin, 1927.

FAYLE, C. Ernest: *Seaborne Trade*. Longmans, Green & Co. Ltd, London, three volumes, 1920–4.

FIKENTSCHER-EMDEN, Fregattenkapitän d.R. Erich: *Erinnerung an unsere 'Emden' Zeit*. München, 1964.

FRIEDAG, B.: *Führer durch Heer und Flotte*. E.S. Mittler & Sohn, Berlin; eleventh edition, 1914. Reprinted by Jürgen Olmes, Krefeld, c.1981.

GARDINER, Robert (ed.): *Conway's All the World's Fighting Ships 1860–1905*. Conway Maritime Press, Greenwich, London, 1979.
—*Conway's All the World's Fighting Ships 1906–1921*. Conway Maritime Press, Greenwich, London, 1985.

GRÖNER, Erich: *Die deutschen Kriegsschiffe 1815–1945*. Bernard & Graefe Verlag, München, 1982–9. A six-volume revision by Dieter Jung and Martin Maass of a classic work (Lehmanns, München, 1966/8).

HANSEN, Hans Jürgen: *Die Schiffe der deutschen Flotten 1848–1945*. Urbes-Verlag Hans Jürgen Hansen, Gräfelfing vor München, 1973.

HAWS, Duncan: *Merchant Fleets*. A series of books by TCL Publications, East Grinstead. They include 'Blue Funnel Lines' (1988); 'British India S.N. Co.' (1987); 'Cunard Line' (1987); 'Ellerman Lines' (1989); 'Thos. & Jas. Harrison' (1988); 'New Zealand Shipping & Federal S.N. Co.' (1985); 'Pacific Steam Navigation Company (P.S.N.C.)' (1986); 'Royal Mail Line & Nelson Line' (1982); and 'Shaw, Savill & Albion' (1987).
—*Merchant Fleets in Profile*. Earlier versions of the 'Merchant Fleets' series, by Patrick Stephens Ltd, Cambridge. They included 'The ships of the Cunard, American, Red Star, Inman, Leyland, Dominion, Atlantic Transport and White Star Lines' (1978); 'The ships of the Hamburg America, Adler and Carr Lines' (1980); 'The ships of the P&O, Orient and Blue Anchor Lines' (1977); and 'The ships of the Union, Castle & Union-Castle, Allan and Canadian Pacific Lines' (1979).

HEATON, Paul M.: *Tatems of Cardiff*. Privately published, Pontypool, Gwent; 1987.

HILDEBRAND, Hans H.; ROHR, Albert; and STEINMETZ, Hans-Otto: *Die deutschen Kriegsschiffe* ('Biographien. Ein Spiegel der Marinegeschichte von 1815 bis zur Gegenwart'). Koehlers Verlagsgesellschaft, Herford; six volumes, 1979–89.

HOCKING, Charles, FLA: *Dictionary of Disasters at Sea during the Age of Steam*. The London Stamp Exchange, 1990.

HOHENZOLLERN-EMDEN, Oberleutnant z.S. a.D. Prinz Franz Joseph von: *Emden—Meine Erlebnisse auf SM Schiff Emden*. Richard Eckstein Nachfolger, Leipzig, 1925. Translations included *Emden. The Story of the Famous Raiding Cruiser* by Herbert Jenkins Ltd, London, 1928; and *L'Emden* (by 'François-Joseph de Hohenzollern') by Librarie Payot, Paris, 1929.
—[Fregattenkapitän a.D. Meinrad, Prinz von Hohenzollern-Emden, and John Walter, editors]: *Emden. The last cruise of the Chivalrous Raider, 1914*. The Lyon Press Ltd, Eastbourne, 1989. A modernised version of the previous book.

HOUGH, Richard: *The Pursuit of Admiral von Spee*. Allen & Unwin, London, 1969.

HOYT, Edwin Palmer: *Defeat at the Falklands* ("Germany's East Asia Squadron 1914"). Robert Hale Ltd, London, 1981.
—*The Last Cruise of the Emden*. André Deutsch, London, 1966.

HURD, Archibald S.: *The Merchant Navy*. Longmans, Green & Co. Ltd, London, three volumes, 1921–9.

KING-HALL, Admiral Sir Herbert: *Naval Memories and Traditions*. Hutchinson, 1926.

LAUTERBACH, Schiffskapitän Julius: *1000 Pf Sterling Kopfpreis—tot oder lebendig* ('Fluchtabenteuer des ehemaligen Prisenoffiziers SMS Emden'). August Scherl, Berlin, 1917.

LOCHNER, R.K.: *Die Kaperfahrten des Kleinen Kreuzers Emden*. Heyne Verlag, München, 1979.
—[Thea and Harry Lindauer, editors]: *The Last Gentleman of War* ('The Raider Exploits of the Cruiser Emden'). Naval Institute Press, Annapolis, Maryland, 1988. A translation of the preceding book.
—*Kampf im Rufiji-Delta* ('Das Ende des Kleinen Kreuzers "Königsberg". . .'). Heyne Verlag, München, 1987.

LOOFF, Vizeadmiral a.D. Max: *Kreuzerfahrt und Buschkampf*. Neudeutsche Verlags- und Treuehand-GmbH, Berlin, 1927.

MANTEY, E. von: *Der Kreuzerkrieg*. Three volumes. E.S. Mittler & Sohn, Berlin, 1933.

MARDER, Arthur J.: *From Dreadnought to Scapa Flow—The Royal Navy in the Fisher Era*. Oxford University Press; five volumes, 1961–70.

MIDDLEMAS, Keith: *Command the Far Seas*. Hutchinson & Co. Ltd, London, 1961.

MIDDLEMISS, Norman L.: *Gathering of the Clans* ('History of The Clan Line Steamers Ltd'). Shield Publications Ltd, Newcastle upon Tyne; 1988.

MILLER, Charles: *Battle for the Bundu* ('The First World War in East Africa'). Macdonald and Jane's London 1974.

MILLER, William H.: *German Ocean Liners of the 20th Century*. Patrick Stephens Ltd, Wellingborough, 1989.

MÜCKE, Kapitänleutnant Helmuth von: *Ayesha*. August Scherl, Berlin, 1915; and Langerhuysen, Amsterdam, 1917. A revised edition was published by Scherl in 1926.
—*Die Abenteuer der Emden-Mannschaft*. Verlag Ensslin, Reutlingen, 1921.
—*Die Taten der Emden und anderer Kreuzer*. Hessisches Volksbucherei, Leipzig, 1915.
—*Emden*. August Scherl, Berlin, 1915; and Ritter & Co., London, 1917.
—[J.G. Lockhart, editor] *The Ayesha. A Great Adventure* ('The Escape of the Landing Squad of the Emden'). Phillip Allan & Co. Ltd, London, 1930.

NERGER, Fregattenkapitän Karl August: *The Cruise of the "Wolf"*. Berlin, 1918.

PITT, Barrie: *Coronel and Falklands*. Cassell & Company, London, 1960.

PRAGER, Hans Georg: *Blohm + Voss. Ships and Machinery for the World*. Koehlers Verlagsgesellschaft mbH, Herford, 1977.

PRETORIUS, Major Pieter, DSO: *Jungle Man*. Dutton & Co., New York, 1948.

RAEDER, Admiral Dr Phil. h.c. Erich: *Der Kreuzerkrieg in den ausländischen Gewässern*. Three volumes. E.S. Mittler, Berlin, 1934–5.

SMITH, Engineer-Captain Edgar C., OBERN: *A Short History of Naval and Marine Engineering*. Babcock & Wilcox Ltd, 1937.

SPENCER-COOPER, Commander Henry E.H., MVORN: *The Battle of the Falkland Islands. Before and After*. Cassell & Company Ltd, London, 1919.

STEINBERG, J.: *Yesterday's Deterrent: Tirpitz and the Birth of the German Battle Fleet*. Macdonald & Company, London; 1965.

THOMAS, Lowell: *Lauterbach of the China Sea*. Hutchinson & Company, London, 1929.

THOMAS, P.N.: *British Ocean Tramps* ('Volume 1. Builders & Cargoes'). Waine Research Publications, Wolverhampton, 1992.

VAN DER VAT, Dan: *The Last Corsair* ('The Story of the Emden'). Hodder & Stoughton, Dunton Green, Sevenoaks, 1983.

WALDEYER-HARTZ, Hugo von: *Der Kreuzerkrieg 1914–1918*. Gerhard Stalling Verlag, Oldenburg, 1930.
—*Ran der Feind*. Verlag Jugendhort Walter Bloch Nachf., Berlin, 1915.
—*Von Tsingtau zu den Falklandinseln* ('Eine Erzählung von den Heldenkämpfen um Tsingtau und der ruhmreichen Fahrt des deutschen Kreuzergeschwaders in Weltkrieg 1914'). E.S. Mittler & Sohn, Berlin, 1917.

WALKER, Fred M.: *Song of the Clyde* ('A history of Clyde shipbuilding'). W.W. Norton & Company, London and New York, 1985.

WITTHOEFT, Korvettenkapitän Robert: *Unsere Emden* ('Erlebnisse auf den Kaperfahrten im Jahre 1914'). Reimar Hobbing, Berlin, 1916.
—[Heinz Oskar Wuttig, editor] *Unsere Emden* ('Kaperfahrten im Indischen Ozean'). Ernst Steiniger, Berlin, 1938.

# INTRODUCTION

Anglo-German maritime rivalry, the rise of the Kaiserliche Marine,
advances made prior to 1914 in naval and engineering technology, and the
value of a war against British seaborne trade.

—◆◆◆—

IN the early summer of 1889, Wilhelm II, the 'All-Highest', newly crowned Emperor of Germany and King of Prussia, was invited to the review of the Royal Navy at Spithead by his maternal grandmother, Queen Victoria. It was the first time that he had attended in such an august role, having succeeded his father Friedrich III only in June 1888. The event was scheduled for 2 August, but bad weather caused a three-day postponement.

The Royal Navy was the world's most powerful fleet, by any yardstick and by some way; only the French had pretensions to rivalry. However, the effects of industrialisation had been felt much more acutely in Britain—the cradle of what was later to be called the 'Industrial Revolution'—and Britain's shipbuilding industry reigned supreme. Even in 1889, there were many yards capable of building the ships with which the Royal Navy protected a far-flung colonial empire.

As Wilhelm II was conveyed down the lines of warships, the British fleet must have impressed its imperial guest. The largest of the warships were the representatives of the Admiral Class, the last of which, *Camperdown* and *Howe*, were only then completing. Four ships of the Victoria and Trafalgar classes authorised in 1885–6 had been launched, but none had been finished.

Typical of these leviathans was HMS *Anson* of the Admiral class, a product of the government-owned dockyard in Pembroke. Completed in May 1889 and displacing 10,600 tons at deep load, Anson was 330ft long between perpendiculars, with a beam of 68ft 6in. Her principal weapons were four 13·5-inch Mark I guns, each weighing 67 tons and capable of firing a 1,250lb shell to a maximum range of 14,500 yards. Secondary armament comprised six 6-inch, twelve 6-pdr and two 3-pdr guns, plus five 14-inch torpedo tubes below the waterline. The crew mustered 460 men, many of whom were required to stoke or tend the boilers powering two 3-cylinder Humphreys compound steam engines.

Service speed was 16 knots on 7,500ihp, though this could be raised to seventeen by the use of forced draught. The ship had two funnels in tandem, with a single pole mast and fighting top placed abaft the funnels. Variations on this curious layout were perpetuated as late as 1910, simply because the mast could be combined with a boom to handle the small boats efficiently. In practice, the fighting top was regularly enveloped in smoke.

Though many of the lesser Royal Navy warships of 1889 were relics of the sail-and-steam era, modernisation had begun in almost every category.

**Below** The British battleship *Benbow*, among the most advanced designs of the 1880s. Courtesy of R.A. Burt.

**Above:** the ironclad battleship *Friedrich der Grosse* pictured prior to 1890. Built in the Kiel dockyard, she was commissioned in November 1877 and hulked in 1906. The vessel displaced 7,718 tonnes, carried four 26cm and two 17cm guns, and could make fourteen knots. By courtesy of the Trustees of the Imperial War Museum, negative no. Q22320.

The newest ships were the acme of naval design, more than capable of outclassing any champion forwarded by rival navies. Frenchmen cast envious glances towards the British ships. For much of the preceding two centuries, France and Britain had vied with one another for supremacy. Each country had acquired a colonial empire which could only be served through open sea lanes; each navy, consequently, was charged with a broadly comparable task. The French had generally been bested in large-scale engagements, the most recent being Trafalgar in 1805, but the eclipse of the French navy in the second half of the nineteenth century owed more to industrialisation than battle. Though the French had created the first steam-powered ironclad battleship, the *Gloire* of 1858, the Royal Navy had countered with HMS *Warrior* and the facility with which the British shipyards could build ensured that there would only be one winner in any new naval race.

By 1889, the French navy had been weakened by the catastrophic Franco-Prussian War of 1870–1 and a lengthy period of political turmoil. French industry was efficient, but small and comparatively limited in scope. The ships, therefore, were powerful on paper but often technically deficient.

Though *Hoche* and three ships of the Marceau class had been laid down, the newest ships in 1889 were *Amiral Baudin* and *Formidable*. Crewed by about 625 men, the ships displaced 11,905 tonnes, measured

101m on the waterline, and had a beam of 21·3m. Their guns included three 37cm, four 16·3cm and eight 13·9cm breech-loaders, plus four 4·7cm quick-firers and a selection of Hotchkiss revolver cannon. Six 40cm torpedo tubes were carried below the waterline. The weakness of the design lay principally in the engines—two vertical compound steam engines that developed about 8,400ihp (in *Amiral Baudin*) and gave a speed of only fifteen knots. Bunkering of merely 800 tonnes of coal also restricted operational radius.

The obsolescence of these ships arose from their protracted building; laid down in the autumn of 1879, they were not completed until December 1888 (*Amiral Baudin*) and February 1889 (*Formidable*). The British Admiral-class ships, in contrast, took an average of six years to reach service. At a time when development of warships was progressing in leaps and bounds, protracted building times often ensured that a line-of-battle ship was outmoded almost as soon as it had been commissioned.

By contrast with the fleets of her two illustrious neighbours, which were breathtaking in quantity whatever their qualititative deficiencies, Germany had little to offer. The imperial navy had a short history—the German Empire itself dated back only to the beginning of 1871—and had progressed little farther than a coastal defence force. By 1889, Wilhelm II had had little opportunity to realise his ambitions; though German prestige had grown as a result of the largely unexpected outcome of the Franco-Prussian War, colonial expansion had yet to become much more than a few tracts of land in Africa and a handful of Pacific islands.

Industrialisation had begun to permeate the fabric of the German states comparatively early in the nineteenth century, but fragmented political structure ensured that growth had been patchy. A financial crisis in the Zollverein ('Customs Union') in 1857 had been followed by a partial economic collapse that had not been entirely reversed by the outbreak of the war against Denmark in 1864, when Prussia had been forced to enlist the aid of Austria to assure victory. However, just two years later, the Prussians crushed the Austrians and their allies in the brief Seven Weeks War. This astonished many commentators, who had expected the Habsburg troops to brush aside the Prussian challenge relatively easily.

The victory was ascribed to good fortune, the Dreyse breech-loading infantry rifle, efficient field artillery, or better leadership. The underlying cause, however, was more effectual industrialisation in Prussia than Austria. When the confederated German states defeated France in 1871, surprise was all but universal; even though resolve had been undermined by political unrest for many years, the French army had been reckoned as a match for any combination of the German forces.

As the industrial influence of France declined, so the star of united Germany rose. In spite of a crisis of economic confidence, which affected many sales markets adversely in 1874–5, concerted efforts to establish the

new empire as a major power were made throughout the 1870s. Signs of greatness could be detected in the success of the first Mauser rifles and Krupp guns, or the export orders gained by German railway-locomotive builders.

This success was not initially shared by the embryo German shipbuilding industry. There had been a strong maritime tradition in northern Germany for many years, particularly in the Hanseastädte (Free Towns), along the North Sea coast and in the Baltic margins. Yet only the Vulcan shipyard in Stettin could claim to have any real international significance in 1889. The first ships of the Kaiserliche Marine had been purchased from Britain or France whilst the state-owned shipyards were being created. The ironclad *Friedrich Carl*, for example, had been built in Toulon by Société Nouvelles des Forges et Chantiers La Seyne and *König Wilhelm* had come from the Thames Iron Works & Ship Building Company of Blackwall in London. The oldest of the German yards was the former Prussian establishment in Danzig, which had been created prior to the Franco-Prussian War. The first ship to be begun in the Kiel yard was the turret ship *Friedrich der Grosse* of 1871, her sister *Grosser Kurfürst* being the second ship to be laid-down in Wilhelmshaven.

As the sea-loving Wilhelm II gazed at the ranks of British ships, he must have mused on the standing of his own navy. The four most powerful German ships were the central-battery ironclads of the Sachsen class, work on which had been divided equally between the imperial dockyard in Kiel and the privately-owned Vulcan yard in Stettin. Laid down in 1877–8 (*Sachsen*,

**Below:** the battleship *Bayern* (7,742 tonnes) in her original four-funnel pre-1895 form. Built in the Kiel dockyard and given six 26cm guns, the ship was commissioned in April 1882. *Bayern* was ultimately reduced to the status of a target ship in 1911. By courtesy of the Trustees of the Imperial War Museum, negative no. Q22313.

*Bayern* and *Württemberg*) and 1880 (*Baden*), the ships were completed with astonishing rapidity; the first was commissioned in 1881 and all were in service by the end of 1883. Technically, however, they were unremarkable. Displacing 7,635 tonnes (*Baden*), they were 98·2m overall and had a beam of 18·4m. They were armed with six 26cm breech-loading guns, a pair appearing on the fore-deck and one at each corner of a squared central citadel. Secondary armament amounted to six 8·7cm guns and six 3·7cm Hotchkiss revolver cannon. Manned by 317 officers and men, the ships were driven by two horizontal simple-expansion steam engines developing 5,000ihp; service speed was only about 13·5 knots.

A central-battery ironclad christened *Oldenburg* had been completed in 1886, but was little more than a Sachsen-class ship emasculated by the limited availability of funds. The first of the more effectual Siegfried-class coastal battleships had been laid down in the Krupp'sche Germaniawerft (Kiel) shipyard in 1888, but was not commissioned until April 1890.

Excepting Britain and France, few other navies had much to offer. The Russian fleet was substantial on paper, but was qualitatively poor and riddled by corruption; Austria-Hungary, land-locked excepting for the Adriatic sea-coast, had a few small coastal battleships and protected cruisers; the US Navy was only beginning to emerge from its post-Civil War lethargy; whilst Spain protected remnants of a once-powerful colonial empire largely with antiquated sail-and-steamships.

Only in Italy—like the German Empire, a recent creation—was there headway. Catastrophic defeat by the Austrians in the great sea-battle of Lissa (1866) had had a dramatic effect. Thereafter, the Italians built ships that were almost always interesting technically and, at their very best, the equal of anything produced elsewhere. In 1889, the Regia Marina had the largest and fastest battleships in Europe. The two ships of the Italia class were 124·6m overall, displaced 15,897 tonnes (*Lepanto*) and carried a main armament of four 43·2cm guns. Driven by four vertical compound steam engines, *Lepanto* was credited with 18·4 knots on 15,797ihp.

Considering the strength of his own fleet against that of the rival European powers, therefore, Kaiser Wilhelm II had reason to be downcast.

## The rise of the German mercantile marine

The eye of the Kaiser was taken by the appearance in the Spithead Review of the brand-new *Teutonic*, built in Belfast by Harland & Wolff for the White Star Line. The elegant black-hulled passenger steamship was bigger than even the largest of the British ironclad battleships, being 565ft long, 57ft 6in in the beam and displacing about 12,000 tons (9,686grt). Driven by two triple-expansion engines with 43-, 68- and 100-inch diameter cylinders and a 60-inch stroke, she had attained 19,500ihp and 21 knots on her trials.

If the Kaiserliche Marine of 1889 was deficient by comparison with its European peers, much the same could be said of the German merchant navy. Though criticism could not be made of the business acumen of the Hansa towns, in particular, it could certainly be aimed at the German shipbuilding industry's inability to meet demands made on it.

The people of Hamburg had become so strongly Anglophile that they habitually ordered new ships from the yards of the Clyde or north-east England. Hans Georg Prager, in his classic history of Blohm & Voss, quoted a contemporaneous account of life in Hamburg:

'Many . . . homes, in fact the majority of those of the better class, are so thoroughly anglicised that when in them one entirely forgets that one is on German soil. One could swear that this is a house in Fleet Street, at Charing Cross or in Soho Square. The dress is English; the yawns and curses are English. Ask for a newspaper and one gets the *Star*, the *Morning Chronicle* or *The Times*. One sits on black English horsehair at a table laid only with English china, eating roast beef and plum pudding, and drinking porter and ale from London or Burton'.

Many Hamburgers were mortified when the policies of Bismarck rudely interrupted their free-trade economy in the 1880s.

The German mercantile marine in 1889, even though ranking second in registered tonnage, scarcely troubled Britain—possessor of the largest fleet not only in Europe but also in the world. Statistics published in 1890 revealed that Britain owned 55 per cent of the 9,638 vessels known to have registered tonnages in excess of a hundred.

Though merchantmen had been built locally—notably by Stettiner Maschinenfabrik AG 'Vulcan'—most of the largest German passenger ships had emanated from Britain; *Normannia* and *Lahn*, for example, had both been built on the Clyde by the Fairfield Ship Building & Engineering Company. Was it not time, mused the Kaiser, for German industry to compete with, or preferably surpass the British?

Among the principal pioneers was the Hamburg–Amerikanische Packetfahrt Actien-Gesellschaft (also known as the Hamburg–Amerika Linie, 'HAL' or 'Hapag'), formed in May 1847 by a group of merchants seeking to run sailing ships between Hamburg and New York. The rival Norddeutscher Lloyd ('NDL') was formed in 1848 by the amalgamation of several small steamer companies in the Bremen area.

The first four NDL steamships were built on the Clyde in the yard of Caird & Company of Greenock, but success awaited the rapid growth of the emigrant trade after the end of the American Civil War in 1865. The 2,752grt steamer *Amerika*, built by Caird in 1863, was followed by a series of comparable vessels from the same yard. NDL's business was greatly helped by the acquisition of the German–American mail service, and by the selection of an English Channel port—Southampton—as a base for transatlantic services.

British commentators often expressed surprise that the only two major steamship companies to use the Southampton facilities prior to 1900 were both German. Cunard, White Star and other indigenous shipping companies preferred Liverpool or Queenstown, which were respectively nearer the Welsh coalfields and several hundred miles closer to America. However, the approach to Liverpool was guarded by the dreaded Mersey Bar, over which deep-draught ships could pass only at high tide, whilst disembarking at Queenstown necessitated a train journey across Ireland and the services of a steamer across the Irish Sea to reach the British mainland.

By the beginning of the 1880s, the profitability of Hamburg–Amerika and NDL Atlantic services had been threatened by the introduction of newer and faster British-flag ships. Sharpening of competition hastened the introduction of NDL's 4,500grt *Elbe*, built by John Elder & Company; *Werra* and *Fulda*, 5,000grt apiece, followed in 1881 from the same yard. The Fairfield-built *Ems* and *Eider* (5,129grt, 1884) were then followed by *Aller*, *Trave* and *Saale* (5,381grt, 1886). *Aller* had the distinction of being the first liner on the Britain–New York route to be fitted with triple-expansion engines.

The Fairfield shipyard completed the NDL steamer *Lahn* in 1888. With a registered tonnage of 5,661, a length of 448ft and a speed of eighteen knots, *Lahn* was capable of competing as an equal with the best of her British rivals. She was the first transatlantic liner to be fitted with the special Fairfield-pattern triple expansion engine, in which two high-pressure cylinders exhausted into a single intermediary and thence to a pair of low-pressure units. This design was credited to Andrew Laing, manager of the Fairfield engineering department.

Contemporaneously with the delivery of *Lahn* from Clydeside, Norddeutscher Lloyd accepted its first large German-made ships, *Spree* and *Havel*—products of the Vulcan yard in Stettin, each of 6,963grt and 147·8m overall. Their four cylinder triple-expansion steam engines developed about 13,600ihp, propelling the ships at a little under twenty knots. The sisters were roundly criticised in the British technical press for retaining a single screw instead of the more advanced and allegedly safer twin-screw design; excepting the Cunarders *Umbria* and *Eturia*, built in 1885, all the leading British ships of this period had twin screws. However, the German vessels soon proved successful enough in service.

The 7,363grt steamship *Columbia* was delivered to the Hamburg–Amerika Linie by Laird & Company of Birkenhead in the summer of 1889, leaving Hamburg on her maiden voyage on 18 July. Powered by two triple-expansion steam engines, developing 13,800ihp on trials, she proved to be capable of 19·1 knots. In the Spring of 1890, *Columbia* took the eastbound Blue Riband.

In the Spring of 1890, the Fairfield Ship Building & Engineering Company delivered *Normannia* to the Hamburg–Amerika Linie. The elegant three-funnelled ship measured 500ft between perpendiculars, had a beam of 57ft 3in, and displaced about 10,500 tons; her registered tonnage was originally listed as 8,242. Twin three-cylinder triple-expansion engines—developing 16,352ihp on trials run in the Clyde estuary—gave a maximum of 20·78 knots. *Normannia* soon took the eastbound Blue Riband from *Columbia*, but in turn lost it to the Vulcan-built *Fürst Bismarck*.

*Normannia*, however, was the last large German liner to be built in Britain; after being tested by the Kaiserliche Marine in 1895 as a 'Hülfkreuzer', she was sold to the Spanish navy in 1898 to serve as the auxiliary cruiser *Patriota*. She subsequently passed to Compagnie Générale Transatlantique in November 1899, plying the

---

**Below:** a painting of 6,963grt *Spree*, completed in 1889 for Norddeutscher Lloyd by the Vulcan yard in Stettin. Artist unknown. Author's collection.

**Above:** the 14,281grt *Saxonia*, completed for Cunard by John Brown & Co. of Glasgow in 1900. From an 'Oilette' postcard in the 'Celebrated Liners' (no. 9126) published by Raphael Tuck & Sons. Artist unknown. Author's collection.

Atlantic as *L'Aquitaine* until sent to the breakers in 1906.

*Columbia* and *Normannia* each had a near-sister (*Augusta Victoria* and *Fürst Bismarck* respectively) from the Stettiner Maschinenfabrik AG 'Vulcan' yard. Launched in the winter of 1890, *Fürst Bismarck* departed from Hamburg on her maiden voyage on 8 May 1891. Measuring 153·2m between perpendiculars, with a beam of 17·6m, the three-funnelled steamer displaced 10,362 tonnes (8,430grt). Her two three-cylinder triple expansion engines developed 16,412ihp on trial, corresponding to a speed of 20·7 knots.

*Fürst Bismarck* had an interesting career. Sold to the Russian navy during the crisis of 1904, and renamed *Don*, she passed into the hands of the Russian Volunteer Fleet in 1906 (as *Moskva*) and thence to the Austro-Hungarian navy in 1909. Armed with four 12cm and four 6·6cm guns, she served as the torpedo depot ship *Gäa* throughout the First World War. Ceded to Italy after the Armistice, she was refitted and traded as *San Giusto* on the Trieste–Napoli–New York route until severely damaged by heavy seas. The vessel was stricken in 1923.

## The quest for the Blue Riband

By the 1890s, public interest in the performance of the transatlantic passenger ships had grown to the point at which the speediest crossing—for the mythical 'Blue Riband'—became a contest in which shipping lines could gain immense prestige, and national pride could be staked. Ships grew ever larger and faster, though not until 1899 did any of them exceed Brunel's legendary *Great Eastern* in length.

The Fairfield-built Cunard sisters *Campania* and *Lucania* were typical of the British response to *Lahn* and *Normannia*. With an overall length of 622ft and a beam of 65ft 3in, they were the largest ships in service. Displacement was about 18,000 tons (12,950grt) and their twin five cylinder triple-expansion steam engines, designed to produce 30,000ihp in service, allowed *Campania* to reach 23·18 knots on trial.

*Campania* took the Sandy Hook–Queenstown record on her second voyage in May 1893. Her fastest crossing occurred in August 1894, an average of 21·59 knots being obtained from an eastward passage of 5 days, 9 hours and 21 minutes.

Retired shortly before the First World War began, the ship was acquired by the Admiralty on 27 November 1914 from the breakers Thomas W. Ward & Company. Eight 4·7-inch guns were installed by Cammell Laird, but the aged machinery was deemed too unreliable for *Campania* to serve as an armed merchant cruiser and she was transformed instead into a primitive aircraft carrier. She sank in the Firth of Forth in November 1918 after colliding with the battleship *Revenge*.

*Lucania*, marginally faster than her sister, took the Atlantic record in October 1894 with an average speed of 21·75 knots and held it until beaten by *Kaiser Wilhelm der Grosse* in 1897. *Lucania* served Cunard until 1909, when she burned out alongside the dock in Liverpool and was sold to Thomas W. Ward for breaking.

Burgeoning Teutonic competition became evident in the mid 1890s, when the first German-built fast transatlantic steamship was ordered. The situation had been created partly from a government-led broadening of trade routes—Norddeutscher Lloyd, for example, had ordered five new ships simultaneously in the mid 1880s to trade with India, the Far East and Australia—and also by the placing of lucrative mail contracts in the early 1890s. It was easy to ensure that mail was carried only by shipping lines that ordered German-made ships. Consequently, though freighters were still ordered from British yards in considerable numbers, very few ships larger than 10,000grt were bought outside Germany.

Concentrating resources on the lucrative passenger traffic, which also attracted great prestige, ensured that the major German shipping lines grew powerful in a way that few of their British rivals could match. Thus, though the British merchant fleet still eclipsed its arch-rival numerically, the German merchant marine was perceived as having established a technological lead. This became particularly evident when, in November 1897, *Kaiser Wilhelm der Grosse* took the Blue Riband for the fastest Atlantic crossing from *Carmania* with an eastbound run of 22·35 knots.

The British, believing in free trade, rarely offered subsidies or grants to industries in the same way in which the German government encouraged national maritime growth. It was widely believed in Britain that the creation of a competitive shipbuilding industry and merchant marine in Germany owed much to 'unfair' mail subsidies and governmental 'encouragement' of the emigrant trade, as well as to the short-term or temporary recruitment of British workmen from whom skills could be copied.

Movement of people proved to be a great boon to the German shipping industry in the late nineteenth century. Once consisting largely of central Europeans sailing to find a better future in North America (the annual average had reached 113,000 immediately after the end of the American Civil War), it subsequently became concerned largely with the transport of the poorer classes of European Russia—which at that time included Poland and Finland—to the USA. By 1913, annual emigration of Germans to the USA had dropped to 34,000. The numbers leaving Russia, however, had increased from 2,000 per annum in 1865–74 to nearly 200,000 by 1912.

Eastward migration, by way of Vladivostok, was extremely difficult for European Russians. Though the Trans-Siberian railway had been finished by 1903, a loop around Lake Baikal was not completed until 1905 and reliance on eleven hundred kilometres of the Chinese Eastern Railway through Manchuria did not end until 1915. Thus the capacity of the railway to move huge quantities of people was very limited prior to the First World War. This left Russians with no option but to proceed westward. As they travelled west, they came to Germany; the Alps blocked the route that might otherwise have taken them into France. Thus they were automatically directed not to the French Atlantic ports but to those on the northern coast of Germany in general, and Hamburg and Bremerhaven in particular.

In 1894, citing a terrible cholera epidemic that had affected Hamburg in the early 1890s and the need to prevent the spread of infectious diseases, the German government built clearance stations along the eastern

**Below:** the 19,361grt Norddeutscher Lloyd liner *Kaiser Wilhelm II*, completed in 1903 by AG 'Vulcan' of Stettin. Author's collection.

border with Russian Poland. The supervision of these centres was given to the Hamburg–Amerika Linie and Norddeutscher Lloyd, greatly helping emigrants by simplifying their trip across Germany from railheads on the border between Ostpreussen (East Prussia) and Russian Poland. Berthing these Russian emigrants almost exclusively in German steamers was not only economically sensible, but also contributed greatly to the rise of the shipping lines and the construction of new ships.

*Kaiser Wilhelm der Grosse*, a product of the ubiquitous AG 'Vulcan' shipyard in Stettin, was easily distinguished by four funnels grouped in separated pairs. The ship was 197·5m overall, had a beam of about 20·1m, and displaced 21,210 tonnes (14,349grt). Powered by twin four-cylindered triple expansion engines, she could attain 22·5–23 knots in service on about 30,000ihp. Each engine had a single high-pressure cylinder, one intermediate cylinder and two low-pressure cylinders, the diameters being 132cm, 225cm and 245cm respectively; the piston stroke was 175cm. *Kaiser Wilhelm der Grosse* was the largest ship in the world at the time of her completion.

Launched on 4 March 1897 in the presence of thirty thousand people, *Kaiser Wilhelm der Grosse* was an immediate success. Her maiden voyage returned an average of 21·39 knots outbound and 21·94 knots on the return, figures that were improved on her third trip to 22·35 and 22·83 knots respectively.

A second German four-funnel ship, *Deutschland*, was launched from the Vulcan yard in January 1900 for the Hamburg–Amerika Linie. Virtually the same length as the contemporary 685ft White Star liner *Oceanic*, the first ship to exceed *Great Eastern* in both length and displacement tonnage, she was somewhat leaner than her British rival in pursuit of speed. Thus her registered tonnage was 16,502 instead of 17,274, and displacement was merely 24,300 tonnes instead of about 27,500. Propelled by two six-cylinder quadruple expansion engines, *Deutschland* attained 23·5 knots on trial. The engines were technically very interesting, with cylinder diameters increasing from two 93cm (high pressure) by way of single 187cm and 264cm patterns to two 270cm low-pressure units. The piston stroke was 185cm. Completed in the summer of 1900, *Deutschland* immediately captured the Blue Riband with a westbound passage of 22·42 knots.

However, the powerful engines vibrated so badly that a smooth passage could not be guaranteed and the ship never performed consistently in service. In common with all the large Vulcan-built ships of this period, she was lightly built, prone to structural weakness, and expensive to maintain.

*Deutschland* was followed by 14,908grt *Kronprinz Wilhelm*, completed for Norddeutscher Lloyd by AG 'Vulcan' in 1901. This ship was 202·1m overall, had a 20·1m beam and two six-cylinder quadruple expansion

engines developing 36,000ihp. The speed of *Kronprinz Wilhelm* was comparable with that of her immediate predecessor, averages on her maiden voyage being 19·74 knots out and 23·01 knots back. These were improved in 1902 to 23·09 knots westbound and 23·47 knots eastbound.

*Kaiser Wilhelm II* (Vulcan, 1903) was larger—216·6m overall, 21·9m in the beam, 19,361grt—and developed about 38,000ihp from four four-cylinder quadruple-expansion steam engines. The distinctive feature was a third mast immediately abaft the fourth funnel. Maximum speed remained at 23·5–24 knots, suggested by experience to be the most that could be extracted from reciprocating engines, but was just sufficient to regain the Blue Riband in June 1904 with an average of 23·58 knots eastbound.

Engineering limitations also restricted the speed of *Kronprinzessin Cecilie*, built by AG 'Vulcan' for Norddeutscher Lloyd in 1907. This ship was 217·2m overall, had a 21·9m beam and a gross registered tonnage of 19,360, but was unable to exceed 23·5 knots even though the four-cylinder quadruple expansion engines developed more than 40,000ihp. Her maiden voyage returned a disappointing 21·8 knots outbound from Cherbourg to New York, but a more encouraging 22·65 on the return voyage. Even though the outbound average was improved to 23·21 knots in the summer of 1908, *Kronprinzessin Cecilie* was unable to compete with the turbine-driven Cunarders.

The largest German passenger liners could serve as armed merchant cruisers if the need ever arose. This intention was always an open secret. Charles Lee, writing in his book *The Blue Riband* in the 1930s, recorded that:

"As an auxiliary cruiser, the vessel [*Kronprinzessin Cecilie*] was designed with her rudder and steering gear well below the waterline, and it was intended that in war-time she should carry eight 5·9's, four 4·1's, two 3·4's, and 16 light quick-firers and machine guns. In addition, she was fitted to hoist two small torpedo boats with 16 torpedoes in dropping gear . . ."

Painstaking care was taken to ensure that the fittings of these great ships, whatever operational deficiencies they may have had, matched the popular esteem in which they were held. Norddeutscher Lloyd proclaimed that—

"no-one, be he multi-millionaire or working man, can complain. The splendid 'suites deluxe' and cabins, designed and decorated under the direction of Johann Poppe, the German architect, are as dainty and comfortable as the boudoir of the wealthiest woman in the land. But it is in the grand dining saloons, in the ladies', children's and smoking rooms, the cafés and libraries that the splendour of Poppe shines . . . The most lavish expressions of paintings and plastic arts are found, the subjects ranging from the allegorical fantasies of the artists, to the portraits of the rulers and greatest public men of the two nations that are so closely linked together by Lloyd—Germany and the United States.

"Poppe's work reached its pinnacle in the decoration of the famous quartet. Above the dining saloon of the *Kaiser Wilhelm II*, the light-well rises three stories and is surrounded by

**Above:** the Grand Staircase (Haupttreppe) of the 52,117grt Hamburg–Amerika liner *Imperator*, built by AG 'Vulcan' of Stettin. From the postcard series 'An Bord des Vierschrauben-Turbinen-Schnellpostdampfer "Imperator"...', published by NPG, Berlin, in 1913. Author's collection.

magnificent decorations. The four large paintings on the ceiling represent the seasons. The panels of the walls in this saloon, as well as on the *Kaiser Wilhelm der Grosse*, are decorated with embossed leather designs. The allegorical figures in the great light-well of the *Kronprinz Wilhelm* rank with the work of the most famous artists ..."

The advent of these large steamships immeasurably boosted the reputation of the shipping companies and, by extension, that of Germany. A notable growth of prosperity occurred as a direct result of increased influence, and many of the largest shipowners paid impressive dividends to their shareholders. In the decade 1896–1905, Deutsch-Dampfschiffs-Gesellschaft 'Kosmos' of Hamburg paid an average dividend of 10·65 per cent, never once falling below 7·5 per cent; the Hamburg–Südamerikanische line paid an average of 8·6 per cent, despite paying nothing at all in 1902, whilst the Hamburg–Amerika Linie managed 7·65 per cent. A few of the smaller lines fared badly—the Deutsche Levante Linie did not pay any dividends in 1903–6—but were exceptions to the general rule.

In 1906, the Hamburg–Amerika Linie increased its capital to 120 million Marks, with extra debentures amounting to fifty million Marks and reserves of 27 million. The aggregate gross registered tonnage of the fleet stood at 811,943 at the end of 1905, whilst revenue for the 1905/6 financial year amounted to a staggering 38 million Marks. Norddeutscher Lloyd capital amounted to 125 million Marks in this period, reserves being 26·88 million. The fleet comprised 86 ocean-going steamships

totalling 577,912grt; 48 coasting vessels of 68,853grt; and fifty river craft of 5,849grt.

Increases in size were reflected in improvements in port facilities. By 1906, for example, the 72km stretch of the Elbe leading to Hamburg had been dredged to a navigable depth of eight metres at low water, though only at a cost of 700,000 Marks per annum to keep the channel open. The area of thirteen tidal basins and the part of the river accessible to ocean-going steamships amounted to 220 hectares, with 30km of quayside.

The aggregate value of Hamburg shipping trade— the sum of imports and exports alike—reached 5,570 million Marks in 1906, a twelve per cent increase on the previous year. Europe accounted for 1,368 million Marks export and 1,244 million Marks import, most of the trade being undertaken with Britain and (to a lesser extent) other German ports. The export trade with British India was also substantial, reaching 87 million Marks in 1906 compared with 76 million in 1905; the value of imports, 273 million marks in 1906, was also appreciably greater than the 228 million recorded a year earlier.

Yet still the British merchant navy continued to outstrip all German attempts to compete. In mid 1890, the British had possessed 5,302 steamships of 5,106,581grt; by 1895 the figures had risen to 8,386 ships of 9,952,211grt. Gross registered tonnage had reached 14,883,594 by 1906, and 20,431,543 at the outbreak of the First World War. Though the largest German ships were luxuriously appointed, with well-trained crews, fine lines, and engines of impeccable quality, they were not unqualified successes in service. *Kaiser Wilhelm der Grosse* was renowned for very poor stability, being nicknamed 'Rolling Billy' in many Anglo-American circles; and the replacement of triple- with quadruple expansion engines in later ships was accompanied by discomfiting vibrations at high speed.

Even as *Kronprinzessin Cecilie* was being prepared for service, therefore, the initiative was being wrested back to Britain by the Cunard liners *Lusitania* and *Mauretania*. The secret of their great success lay in a gamble on the potential of the turbine. But where Britain led, of course, others could follow.

## The steam turbine

The development of a turbine effectual enough for maritime use was largely due to the Honourable Sir Charles Parsons, sixth son of the Earl of Rosse. The essence of the perfected Parsons turbine, derived from his generators of electricity, was a housing containing a central propeller shaft fitted with a series of blade-bearing discs. High-pressure steam was admitted at the front of the casing, where it could be guided through angled vanes integral with the inner surface of the turbine casing to strike the first row of disc-blades. This imparted a rotary motion to the propeller shaft. However, the steam, which had only lost a small part of its velocity, passed out of the rear of the rotating disc, though another series of guide vanes and onto the blades of another disc.

This continued until the steam had lost so much velocity that it had little use. Residual low-pressure steam was then led back into the condenser to revert to water, then returned to the boiler to be used again.

Most turbines were essentially compound engines in which several rotor discs of increasing diameter replaced the multiple cylinders of the conventional triple- and quadruple expansion units. Turbines had no need for the pistons, cranks and valve gear of reciprocating engines, ran much more smoothly, and were generally simple in design; savings in weight were particularly attractive. To be offset against these advantages, however, were uneconomic low-speed performance and great initial expense—the fitting of the many blades and vanes was especially critical. In addition, unlike conventional steam engines, a direct-drive turbine could not be reversed.

Charles Parsons formed the Parsons Marine Steam Turbine Co. Ltd in January 1894 to build a suitable ship. The result was *Turbinia*, famed for her dash down the lines during the Spithead Diamond Jubilee navy review of 1897 at a speed far in excess of what was expected from even the contemporaneous 'Thirty Knotter' torpedo-boat destroyers. Success had not come easily. The earliest turbine installation, a single-shaft unit developing the equivalent of 1,500ihp, propelled *Turbinia* at little more than eighteen knots. Dynamometer trials indicated that the turbine was capable of generating power effectually enough, but also that output was limited by the single shaft and a poorly shaped propeller.

*Turbinia* promptly gained a three-shaft system—high pressure engine to starboard, intermediate to port and low-pressure in the centre. A separate reversing turbine was fitted on the low-pressure shaft, the propelling machinery and associated coal-fired boilers contributing half the displacement tonnage of 44. Trials revealed that the little vessel could attain 34·5 knots on 2,300shp, performance being limited largely by the rate at which

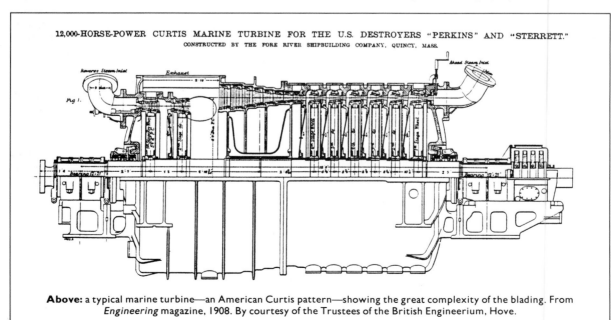

**Above:** a typical marine turbine—an American Curtis pattern—showing the great complexity of the blading. From *Engineering* magazine, 1908. By courtesy of the Trustees of the British Engineerium, Hove.

the furnaces could be stoked in the cramped conditions of the boiler room.

The Admiralty, aware of the potential of the turbine even before *Turbinia*'s dash into history, saw the new power-plant as a suitable replacement for the triple-expansion engines fitted in torpedo-boat destroyers. Reciprocating engines were capable of vibrating even the largest liners unless carefully balanced, and could shake lightweight warships so badly that the integrity of their hulls was affected.

Experiments undertaken in 1896–7 had led to the three '33 Knotter' torpedo-boat destroyers—*Albatross* (Thornycroft), *Express* (Laird) and *Arab* (Thomson)—but none reached the contract speed despite protracted experimentation with engines and propeller profiles. Each ship was characterised by excessive vibration and, particularly in *Arab*, unacceptable mechanical reliability. Development of high-speed warships with reciprocating engines had reached its apogee.

On 4 March 1898, therefore, the Admiralty ordered a turbine-engined destroyer from the Parsons Marine Steam Turbine Co. Ltd, the hull being sub-contracted to Hawthorn, Leslie & Co. Ltd. HMS *Viper* was launched in September 1899 and completed early in 1900.

Though large by the standards of torpedo-boat destroyers, and far larger than *Turbinia*, the new warship was still comparatively small: 210ft 3.5in long, with a beam of 21ft and a displacement tonnage of 344 at light draught. The outer pair of four shafts was coupled directly to the high-pressure turbines, the inner shafts serving the low-pressure and reversing units; two propellers were fitted to each shaft.

Trials undertaken without armament returned an encouraging 36.58 knots, making *Viper* the fastest ship in the world.* The experiments also showed that she could maintain speed with little of the vibration that had bedevilled the reciprocating engines of the unsuccessful '33-Knotters'. Even after one 12-pdr gun, five 6-pdr guns and two 18-inch torpedo tubes had been fitted, 33.75 knots were still attainable. However, before *Viper* could show her true capabilities, she was run onto Renonquet rocks off Alderney in the Channel Islands on 3 August 1901 and became a total loss.

The Royal Navy soon lost its only other turbine destroyer. HMS *Cobra* had been built by Armstrong, Whitworth & Co. Ltd to the company's own account. Fitted with turbines purchased from Parsons, the vessel was 213ft 7.5in long, had a beam of 20ft 6in, and displaced 375 tons at light draught. Trials run shortly after launching at the end of June 1899 recorded a speed of 34.9 knots, but completion was delayed by a collision and the vessel was not sold to the Admiralty until the Spring of 1901. By this time she had been fitted with the same armament as *Viper* and speed had dropped to a

little over thirty knots. The problems were traced to the failure of the stoking rate to match the potential output of the turbines during continuous periods of high speed.

However, before remedial action could be taken, *Cobra* foundered off Outer Dowsing Shoal, Flamborough Head, on 18 September 1901 with the loss of all but twelve of the 79 people aboard. The dead included the captain, Lieutenant Alan Bosworth Smith, together with Magnus Sandison, the Chief Engineer of Armstrong, Whitworth & Co. Ltd, and Robert Barnard of the Parsons Marine Steam Turbine Co. Ltd; but for fortune, and the pressures of work, Sir Charles Parsons himself might have been aboard.

The Court Martial called to ascertain the loss of *Cobra* concluded that it had been due to "the structural weakness of the ship, that she was weaker than other Destroyers, and that it is to be regretted that she was purchased into His Majesty's service . . . [as she was] the climax of a form of construction in which safety had been perilously sacrificed to lightness and speed". Several survivors testified that a blow had been felt immediately before the ship broke in two in heavy seas, but the implication that a derelict mast or spar had been at least partly responsible for the sinking was rejected.

The loss of *Viper* and *Cobra* in rapid succession was countered by the purchase of *Velox*, built as a speculative venture by Hawthorn, Leslie. The new warship was more robust than her predecessors, displacing about 400 tons at light draught, and had two propellers on each of four shafts. The problems of uneconomic performance at slow speed, which bedevilled early direct-drive turbines, were solved by coupling triple-expansion engines to the inner or low-pressure turbine shafts to facilitate cruising and reversing. The multi-engine installation was never particularly successful, restricting service speed to a disappointing 27 knots; not until geared turbines were substituted in 1906 did performance improve appreciably.

In spite of the vicissitudes of early turbine-powered destroyers, the British naval authorities were convinced of the virtue of the engines. The opportunity was taken to compare one turbine ship authorised under the 1901–2 programme with an otherwise identical sister-ship with reciprocating engines. Prior experience suggested that Hawthorn, Leslie & Co. Ltd should build the two ships of the River Class. *Derwent* (triple-expansion engines) and *Eden* (three-shaft Parsons turbines) were laid down in June 1902, launched in February and March 1903 respectively, and completed within a month of each other in the summer of 1904.

The two destroyers were much more robust than preceding British warships of the type, measuring 225ft 6in overall and displacing 550 tons at light draught. The quest for speed had been subordinated to improving sea-keeping qualities, so the ships were designed to attain little more than 27 knots. *Eden* proved no faster

* An 'Admiralty Mean' of six runs made off the mouth of the Tyne on 13 July 1900. The maximum speed, made on two of the runs, was 37.11 knots.

**Above:** the 580-tonne Germaniawerft-built torpedo-boat destroyer *G137*, running trials in 1907. From a postcard published by Gebr. Lempe of Kiel ('Neptun' series, no. 27). Author's collection.

than *Derwent*, but was vibration-free and considerably more economical at high speed. She set the pattern; almost all subsequent destroyers were turbine powered.

However, progress was not without its hazard. Seduced by the lure of the turbine, the Admiralty soon returned to the quest for speed. This was partly due to experimentation with turbine-driven ships in Germany, from where, in September 1907, it was reported that—

'some extraordinary results have been obtained with the turbine torpedo-boat destroyer *G137*... With some recent destroyers... fitted with reciprocating engines, it has ... proved impossible to obtain the contract speed, though several different propellers were fitted in succession. With the *G137*, however, fitted with Parsons turbines, a speed of no less than 33·9 knots was obtained on the first trial, the contract requirements being 30 knots only. The trials were run with full load on board, the displacement being 580 tons. On the measured mile the speed was 33·9 knots, as stated, and over a run of five hours at full power a speed of 33 knots was maintained. We are unable to explain the large margin of power provided, but the fact that the introduction of the Parsons turbine into the German Navy has met with a most determined opposition in certain quarters has presumably had its influence in causing the designers to provide a very ample margin for contingencies.'

The British destroyers of the Tribal class, the first five of which were ordered under the 1905–6 Estimates, were to be oil fired and capable of maintaining 33 knots for eight hours. As the details were once again left to the builders, profiles and fittings varied even though Parsons turbines driving three shafts were common to all. Normal displacements varied between 850 and 1,090 tons, whilst overall lengths ranged from 250 to about 280ft.

Trials revealed that the destroyers—appreciably larger than *G137*—were very fast under favourable conditions. HMS *Tartar*, a product of the Woolston

(Southampton) yard of John I. Thornycroft & Co. Ltd, recorded a mean of 35·672 knots from six runs undertaken at the mouth of the Thames in December 1907; *Mohawk*, built by J. Samuel White & Co. Ltd of East Cowes on the Isle of Wight, recorded a mean of 34·511 knots during the course of six runs in the vicinity of the Maplin Sands. The fastest runs had been 37·037 (*Tartar*) and 35·019 knots (*Mohawk*), speeds the Admiralty believed to give sufficient margin of superiority over rivals such as the German *G137*. Though Tribal-class ships soon proved to be uneconomical in service, the efficacy of the turbine was clear. All subsequent British destroyers were powered in this way, though perfection awaited the general adoption of geared turbines during the First World War.

## The first large turbine-drive warships

Four Third-Class Cruisers were ordered for the Royal Navy in 1902–3, constituting what became known as the Gem class. *Diamond*, *Sapphire* and *Topaze* all had conventional two-shaft triple expansion engines whilst *Amethyst* was given Parsons steam turbines driving three shafts. Each ship displaced 3,000 tons, measured 373ft 9in overall and had a 40-foot beam; armament comprised twelve 4-inch and eight 3-pdr quick-firers, four machine-guns and two 18-inch torpedo-tubes.

Comparative trials were undertaken at the end of 1904 between three of the warships, before they had been armed. *Amethyst* was eventually completed in the Tyneside shipyard of Armstrong, Whitworth & Co. Ltd in March 1905, with engines supplied by Parsons. Her reciprocating-engined sisters *Topaze* and *Sapphire* were completed in the Birkenhead yard of Laird & Co. Ltd and the Jarrow yard of Palmer's Ship Building & Iron Co. Ltd in November 1904 and February 1905 respectively.

The contract speed of 21·75 knots at 9,000ihp, with forced draught, was easily exceeded; *Topaze* recorded 22·1 knots on 9,868ihp; *Sapphire* attained 22·34 knots on 10,200ihp; and *Amethyst* returned 23·63 knots on 14,002shp. Experience showed that, with a standard load of 750 tons of coal, the reciprocating-engined *Topaze* had an endurance of 7,300 nautical miles at ten knots compared with only 5,570 for her turbine rival; at fourteen knots the figures were very similar—about 5,100 and 4,950 miles respectively. At twenty knots, however, *Amethyst* could travel 3,160 nautical miles: half as far again as her conventionally engined sisters.

The success of the turbine cruiser persuaded the Director of Naval Construction to specify turbines for the new 'big gun' battleship *Dreadnought*. Though the two-shaft installation was restricted to 24,700shp and a service speed of about 21 knots, the new ship was an instantaneous success and rendered every other battleship obsolescent. This great advance is generally attributed to the vision of Admiral Sir John Fisher, but owed more to the Director of Naval Construction and his staff—who had wanted to arm the preceding 'Lord Nelson' class exclusively with 12-inch guns—and to the development by Charles Parsons of effectual turbines.

Turbines did not raise speed by more than a couple of knots above that of earlier battleships, but the weight saved (compared with reciprocating engines) allowed better armour protection to be used without substantially increasing displacement. Even by 1914, however, her role fulfilled by ships that were more advanced technically, *Dreadnought* was approaching obsolescence.

## The naval races

Grand advances in battleship design have often eclipsed their contemporaries at a stroke. The British Admiral class could have defeated any predecessor in a ship-to-ship engagement; and it has even been claimed that a single 'Admiral' could defeat all the ironclads built prior to 1881 in the same engagement, yet still emerge comparatively unscathed.

The Majestic-class ships of the 1890s represented another progression, though not as markedly. A single ship of this type could not have defeated a squadron of Admirals, but an engagement between fleets of equal size would have had only one result. However, the value of each individual advance lasted only until a potential rival built ships of better type. In Britain, at least, superiority could usually be prolonged simply by building more ships than anyone else. But this was valid only as long as the technical superiority remained with the Royal Navy, forcing others to chase the lead; if the technical advantage passed abroad, the British had much to lose. Squadrons could be made obsolescent at a stroke.

Important re-equipment programmes of 1888–9 and 1893–4 were intended primarily to re-establish the 'Two

Power Standard'—that the Royal Navy would match, or preferably exceed the sum of the strength of the next two most powerful of the world's navies. The first crisis was inspired by a report by three highly respected admirals casting doubts on the efficacy with which Britain had achieved the requisite strength, suggesting that a whole fleet of new battleships was needed instead of the five individual ships that had been commissioned. The second crisis arose when the brand-new *Victoria* sank in the Mediterranean after colliding with *Camperdown*.

The advent in France of an effectual smokeless propellant then made guns firing British Prismatic Brown Powder—a form of gunpowder—obsolescent almost overnight. Finally, Sir W.G. Armstrong & Co. Ltd of Elswick developed an effectual quick-firing ('Q.F.') gun. Capable of discharging fifteen 6-inch shells per minute, this weapon revolutionised naval warfare. Unfortunately for Britain, reliance placed by Armstrong on export of warships soon spread the secret worldwide.

The potential of the submarine and the mine were largely ignored in Britain until the lessons were learned at great cost during the First World War, but neither had progress been made elsewhere by 1914.

Even though the Royal Navy was often hamstrung by political indecision and lack of funds, the fleet was still strong enough to dissuade Germany or the Dual Alliance—weak maritime powers—interfering in the Second South African War of 1899–1902. The success of *Dreadnought* and the universal acceptance of turbines, however, made it easy for lesser nations to design bigger and better ships in the knowledge that the Royal Navy's great superiority in numbers had been severely compromised by technological advances. Progress was amazingly rapid. During trials run in the autumn of 1914, the British battle-cruiser *Tiger* attained 29·07 knots on a staggering 104,635shp—more than four times the power of *Dreadnought* a mere seven years earlier—but even this failed to meet the contract requirements.

The Germans, most notably, elected to challenge the Royal Navy. Admiral Fisher himself realised the danger, pressing for the scrapping of many old craft on the grounds that they were no longer capable of performing roles of any value. However, a reduction in the quantitative strength of the Royal Navy could not be countenanced by the British government, whatever qualitative shortcomings existed in individual ships. The goal was still the 'Two Power Standard'.

The French navy was the first in continental Europe to experiment with turbine power, fitting an experimental Rateau unit in the torpedo-boat *Libellule*, ordered from Forges et Chantiers de la Méditerranée in March 1898 but not completed until early in 1904. Unfortunately, the installation soon proved ineffectual, maximum speed being only fifteen knots. Greater success was found in the torpedo-boat *293* (39·5m overall, 94 tonnes), ordered from the Normand yard in October 1902, which reached 27·3 knots with three-shaft Parsons turbines in 1904; and the similar *294* (39·45m, 100 tonnes), ordered in March 1903, which recorded 25·14 knots with two-shaft Bréguet-Laval turbines in 1905. However, the French navy had endured many years of neglect and was in no position to extend the use of turbines. The failure of the earliest Laval-pattern engine to develop enough power was a great disappointment to its promoters.

The German navy was assured of better funding than the French and had a much higher professional standing. Rapid progress was made with turbine drive, beginning with the torpedo-boat destroyer *S125*—a 1904-vintage product of the Schichau yard in Elbing—and the small cruiser *Lübeck*, completed in April 1905.

Elsewhere, few navies launched turbine-powered warships prior to the completion in Britain of HMS *Dreadnought*. Yet the first challenge had been made. The Germans were well aware that the British shipbuilding industry could easily outstrip them, but realised that British political will was not always in favour of wholesale naval expenditure—and that production was spread among a large number of shipyards of variable efficiency. Thus the Admiralstab determined to rely on a few highly mechanised shipyards, and a series of Flottengesetze ('Fleet Laws'), culminating in the programme of 1909, to lay down guidelines for rapid development of the Kaiserliche Marine. Admiral von Tirpitz, to whom the transition from a coast-defence force to the second most powerful navy in the world could be

attributed, was well aware of the risk that was being taken. The new ships were even called the Risiko-Flotte, or 'Risk Fleet'. The theory was that the Germans could build sufficient ships to outnumber, in the North Sea at least, a Royal Navy stretched by colonial duties; and that, therefore, the British would not dare to attack what considered in total was a weaker opponent.

The British viewed the growth of the German navy with considerable apprehension, though little was done excepting to maintain construction. In 1909, however, Kaiser Wilhelm II gave the *Daily Telegraph* a disparaging view of the British in general and the Royal Navy in particular. A sharpening of public opinion then forced the government of the day to sanction ever-increasing numbers of new warships. But where was the race to end . . . ?

## The turbine-engined passenger ship

The success of installations in the earliest British destroyers, even though it was not shared by the warships themselves, persuaded Sir Charles Parsons and his backers that similar machinery could be applied to passenger steamships. His enthusiasm was not shared by their operators, who were satisfied with perfected reciprocating engines. Paddle steamers driven by tandem compound diagonal engines were still favoured for the intensive estuarine passenger services undertaken in many parts of Britain. Among the most frenetic services ran on the Clyde, where hot competition had developed between the independent railway companies operating in

**Below:** HMS *Dreadnought* 'under weigh at Spithead'. From a photograph by S. Cribb, Southsea, published by The Rapid Photo Printing Co. Ltd of London. Author's collection.

**Above:** the 10,629grt turbine liner *Victorian*, completed in 1905 by Workman, Clark & Co. of Belfast. She is shown in the colours of the Allan Line prior to the First World War. From an 'Oilette' postcard published by Raphael Tuck & Sons in the 'Celebrated Liners' series (no. 9213); artist unknown. Author's collection.

the Glasgow area. Parsons realised that, to convince sceptics, a turbine ship would have to be introduced to the Clyde to compete with the established paddlers.

A syndicate was formed by the Parsons Marine Steam Turbine Co. Ltd, shipbuilders William Denny & Brothers and mariner Captain John Williamson to make and then operate a turbine-engined steamer for at least a year. The result was *King Edward*, Denny yard no. 651, launched in May 1901. Measuring 250ft 6in overall, with a beam of 30ft 2in, the ship had a three-shaft turbine unit. The centre shaft, with a single propeller, was driven by the high-pressure turbine whilst low-pressure and reversing turbines were coupled to wing shafts with two propellers apiece. Unlike the preceding warships, *King Edward* had conventional double-end boilers operating at the modest pressure of 150lb/sq.in. The vessel was also designed for rapid conversion to a paddler if the turbines failed to meet expectations.

The worries proved to be groundless when, after experimentation with differing propellers, the new ship achieved a mean of 20·48 knots on the Skelmorlie Mile in June 1901. The best speed had been 20·57 knots, more than two knots faster than the most effectual of the paddle steamers. *King Edward* proved to be a great success, lasting fifty years even though manoeuvrability and reversing were inferior to paddle-driven rivals.

The success of the trail-blazing Clyde steamers was enough to persuade others that the turbine had merit.

Among the first to commission a channel packet was the South Eastern & Chatham Railway, which ordered the 310ft 1,676grt *Queen* in 1903. The first turbine-drive German passenger ship was the 563grt *392*, later the Hamburg–Amerika Linie *Adler*, which was built as a speculative venture by Howaldtswerke of Kiel and launched in October 1904. A 1,200shp Zoelly turbine driving a single screw gave a speed of 15·5–16 knots.

Where smaller companies led, larger businesses soon followed. Cunard decided to build a turbine steamer of prodigious size to compete against a sister-ship with reciprocating engines, but the lesser known Allan Line, subsequently bought by the Canadian Pacific Navigation Company, became the first to introduce ocean-going turbine steamships with the *Virginian* (10,757grt) and *Victorian* (10,629grt) of 1905. Built by A. Stephen & Sons of Glasgow and Workman, Clark & Co. Ltd of Belfast respectively, they had three-shaft Parsons turbines delivering 12,000shp and were designed to achieve an optimal service speed of seventeen knots— below which, as Parsons and Denny had found with *King Edward*, reciprocating engines were often equally economical. On trials, *Victorian* recorded an encouraging mean of 19·8 knots.

Built by John Brown & Company of Clydebank, the Cunarders *Caronia* (19,687grt) and *Carmania* (19,524grt) were sisters in all respects but their engines. The former was completed in February 1905, to be followed by the latter in December; each was 675ft overall, with a beam of 72ft 3in, and displaced about 30,000 tons. *Caronia* had two four-cylinder quadruple expansion engines rated at 21,000ihp, designed to give a service speed of eighteen knots though 19·5 were achieved on the Skelmorlie Mile. *Carmania* had three shafts, with a high-pressure Parsons turbine in the centre. The low-pressure and reverse turbines were coupled to the wing shafts.

Trials showed that the turbine-engined ship was capable of a little over twenty knots, though this was subsequently attributed more to the modified contours of the stern than the engines. The consensus was that the quadruple expansion engines of *Caronia* were cheaper and less problematical to maintain, but that the turbines of *Carmania* ran more smoothly.

Commissioned as an armed merchant cruiser at the outbreak of the First World War, *Carmania* is best known for destroying the German liner *Cap Trafalgar* (q.v.) off the Ilha da Trindade in 1914.

The loss of the Atlantic Blue Riband to *Kaiser Wilhelm der Grosse*, even though Cunard had never officially recognised the title, was a keen national disappointment. In 1903, conscious of the severe effects of German primacy on the British share of the North Atlantic trade, the government of the day advanced Cunard a loan of £2·6 million at 2·75 per cent interest to build a turbine liner to regain the Blue Riband. The only proviso was that the ship should be fitted to act as an armed cruiser when required.

The returns from the North Atlantic services for 1904 suggested that the move was long overdue. Norddeutscher Lloyd had carried 135,547 passengers, followed by the Hamburg–Amerika Linie with 120,323. Cunard had carried merely 82,851, whilst the White Star Line, British-registered though largely American owned, had contributed 82,332. Then came Compagnie Générale Transatlantique ('The French Line') with 50,609, the Belgian-flag Red Star Line with 48,586 and the American Line with 37,251. On a basis of loading per voyage, the German ships had still proved triumphant; Hamburg–Amerika Linie vessels had averaged 1,256 fare-paying passengers, followed by Norddeutscher Lloyd with 1,201. The figures for the Cunard and White Star lines were 906 and 869 respectively.

The results of governmental intervention were the magnificent half-sisters *Lusitania* and *Mauretania*. Launched on 7 June 1906, *Lusitania* was a product of John Brown & Company of Clydebank. Measuring 790ft overall, with a beam of 87ft 10in and a gross registered tonnage of 31,550, she was then the largest British ship afloat. Driven by direct-acting Parsons turbines on four propeller shafts, *Lusitania* reached 26·45 knots on trials with none of the terrible vibration that had affected some of her reciprocating-engined German rivals.

Much to the delight of her owners and the British people, *Lusitania* took the westbound Blue Riband from *Kaiser Wilhelm II* on her second voyage. The average speed was the merest fraction below 24 knots.

*Mauretania*, built on Tyneside by Swan, Hunter & Wigham Richardson, was essentially similar to *Lusitania* excepting that her registered tonnage was initially given as 31,938. After exchanging the Blue Riband with *Lusitania*, the acquisition of improved propellers in 1909 conferred a considerable advantage. *Mauretania* regained the Blue Riband with a 25·69-knot crossing and held the record for twenty years.

Though the Germans continued to produce large ships, none matched *Lusitania* and *Mauretania* in the years before the First World War. Cunard ordered an even larger vessel, *Aquitania*, whilst the White Star Line countered initially with *Olympic*, ill-fated *Titanic* and *Britannic*. White Star's designers resolved the perceived weaknesses in direct-drive turbines—comparatively poor slow-speed economy and an innate inability to reverse—by fitting additional reciprocating engines. The favoured method, successfully tested in the torpedo-boat destroyer *Velox* in 1906, was to exhaust high-pressure steam from reciprocating engines into a low pressure turbine. This arrangement was used in both *Olympic* and *Titanic*, conventional engines driving the outer shafts and the turbines the inner pair.

A better answer was eventually found in the geared turbine produced by Parsons in 1909. The steamship *Vespasian*, powered by a triple-expansion steam engine, was purchased from her owners and thoroughly tested. The engine was then replaced by a standard turbine geared down 20:1, the original boilers and propeller being retained to validate comparison. The reduction in fuel consumption was found to be about twenty per cent. Thereafter, geared turbines were fitted to most high speed warships and in many cross-channel steamers.

The effectual direct-drive turbine had done much to re-establish the waning dominance of the British shipping industry by 1910. Regaining the Blue Riband, even if Cunard and others did not officially recognise its existence, was a great boost to morale; and the eclipse of the vibration-prone German ships irked the Kaiser as much as it annoyed Albert Ballin and fellow directors of the Hamburg–Amerika line. The only answer was to produce ships of even greater magnitude, accepting that they would be driven by steam turbines instead of the massive reciprocating engines with which German builders had previously excelled.

The new passenger liners offered simply breathtaking dimensions—*Imperator*, built by the new AG 'Vulcan' shipyard in Hamburg, and *Vaterland* by Blohm & Voss. The registered tonnages of these colossi were 52,117 and 54,282 respectively; each was the largest ship in the world at the time of its completion. Both were more than 275m long. There would have been a third leviathan, *Bismarck* (56,551grt, 291·3m overall), but the advent of war delayed completion until 1922.

**Above:** the 52,117grt Hamburg–Amerika liner *Imperator*, pictured when new—with the eagle on the prow and the original tall funnels. **Below:** the banqueting room ('Festsaal') aboard *Imperator*, from a postcard published in the 'An Bord des Vierschauben-Turbinen-Schnellpostdampfers "Imperator". . .' series by NPG of Berlin in 1913. Author's collection.

*Imperator* and *Vaterland* were record breakers only in size, however, service speed being listed as merely 23 knots. Despite the grandeur of their furnishings, it is arguable whether they would have eclipsed the British queens of the Atlantic. *Imperator*, in particular, was very tender. Unsteadiness manifested itself so badly on her maiden voyage that radical reconstruction had to be undertaken; the funnels were lowered by three metres, most of the heavy marble panelling was removed from the upper deck in favour of light cane furniture, and a substantial quantity of concrete was poured into the bilges in an attempt to correct tendencies to list and roll.

Neither of the German super-liners played any part in hostilities, *Imperator* being laid up in Hamburg and *Vaterland* in New York. Ironically, their successful post-war careers were pursued under the British and American flags respectively.

Excepting the loss of 'unsinkable' *Titanic*, ascribed variously to ill fortune, reckless navigation or—most recently—the brittleness of the plating in cold waters, the greatest tragedy of these magnificent ships was the sinking on 7 May 1915 of *Lusitania*. This was made all the more poignant by the loss occurring within sight of land. However, the demise of such a large ship to a single torpedo fired by the submarine *U20* has been questioned on many occasions. There seems little doubt that it was actually due to an additional internal explosion—the detonation of munitions, perhaps, or ignition of coal dust—which blew out a large section of the hull.

Far greater than the loss of the ship was the effect of the sinking on international affairs. Skilfully manipulated by British propagandists, it did much to swing American opinion against the Germans. In addition, though less directly, it also ended the days of the surface raiders in favour of the submarine menace.

## Maritime trade

The distances involved in the shipping industry were often prodigious. To reach a typical West African port—Freetown in Sierra Leone—required an outward journey of three thousand miles from the Pool of London; Cape Town lay 6,100 miles away. One of the nearest North American ports, Halifax in Nova Scotia, was 2,480 miles distant from Southampton; there were roughly 3,060 miles between Southampton to New York, and 4,065 miles to Kingston in Jamaica.

A voyage from Southampton to Port Stanley in the Falkland Islands was about 7,310 miles, whilst the distance to Valparaiso by way of Rio de Janeiro, Buenos Aires and Cape Horn amounted to 8,460.

To reach Pernambuco in Brazil from Southampton necessitated a voyage of 3,960 miles, then 1,065 more to Rio de Janeiro. Buenos Aires was about 6,300 miles from London. A journey to Bombay from London encompassed 6,400 miles, or 8,300 to Calcutta, whilst Hong Kong was about 9,900 miles distant. The longest routes were to Australia: e.g., 9,800 miles from London to the West Australian port of Fremantle. A journey from Port Said to Melbourne encompassed 7,915 miles, then an additional 575 to Sydney and 1,745 more to reach Fiji. Wellington in New Zealand was 12,600 miles away from London by way of Suez.

The length and duration of prospective voyages were particularly important to steamers, in perpetual need of fuel; sailing vessels obviously relied on a natural, if often capricious force for their propulsion and were not as dependent on supplies. Advent of steamships led to the establishment of bunkering facilities in once-obscure places, and nations often haggled to the brink of war over land that had seemed valueless.

The British Empire was the most influential colonial aggregation prior to the First World War and also the most diverse geographically. Owing to the great reliance Britain laid on maritime trade, it was vitally important that British ships could coal from British-owned stations virtually anywhere in the world. Excepting in South America, this had been accomplished by 1914.

Britain's economy had been at its strongest in the 1870s, when many benefits of industrialisation were already being reaped. Germany had only just been formed from an aggregate of states, principalities and minor duchies; France was suffering in the wake of the Franco-Prussian War; and the USA, though making enormous strides, was still handicapped not only by poor communications but also by a concentration of people on the eastern seaboard.

However, the balance of British trade had been severely affected by the rise of protectionism at the end of the nineteenth century. Restrictive regulations had been passed in Germany, beginning in 1879; in Russia from 1881; in France and Austria-Hungary from 1882 onward. The USA had passed the McKinley and Dingley Acts in 1890 and 1897 respectively to hinder the importation of goods from abroad. Even the outposts of the Empire were not immune from the practice, Canada passing legislation in 1879 and the Commonwealth Act of 1900 forcing the last bastion of Free Trade in Australia, New South Wales, to toe the confederacy line.

Consequently, sales of some manufactured goods declined appreciably in the late nineteenth century, whereas the trade in British coal, machinery, ships, railway locomotives and similar equipment boomed. In the long term, however, sales of this type would clearly succeed only in allowing competitors to produce goods of their own in larger quantities . . . and then distribute them with ever-increasing facility.

According to the *Fiscal Blue Book* of 1903, the aggregate value of British-made cotton goods had declined from £75,564,000 in 1880 to £69,751,000 by 1900; conversely, the output of coal, coke, iron, steel and other metals increased from £40,373,000 to £76,258,000, whilst the assessments of machinery and machine-work rose from £9,264,000 in 1880 to £19,620,000 twenty years later. Shipbuilding in 1899 was worth £9,897,000 alone.

The USA overhauled Britain as the world's leading producer of coal in 1899, having achieved primacy in the production of steel in the early 1880s; in 1895, Germany had reduced Britain to third place in the world steel-making league, achieving the same with pig-iron in 1903. In addition, German coal production increased by 159 per cent in 1893–1913, compared with only 75 per cent in Britain; figures for the output of crude steel were 522 and 136 per cent respectively, whilst those for exports of manufactured goods were 239 and 121 per cent.

By 1908, German steel output of 10·9 million tons was double that of Britain. However, levels of production of this magnitude ultimately presented a threat. In the beginning, much of the steel was sold to Britain at comparatively low rates to make the ships that then earned money for the British economy. German yards, whose needs were far smaller, had to buy the same steel at a higher price; ultimately the British gained, as their ships were cheaper to build and, therefore, also cheaper to operate.

The excessive production of steel in Germany was beneficial in the opening phases of the First World War, as it enabled the output of the shipyards to increase with comparatively little trouble whilst simultaneously applying pressure to manufacturers in Britain which had previously relied on steel from the Ruhr. However,

owing to the limited capacity of the few major German shipyards, production could not rise as far as it did in Britain and was ultimately seriously compromised by a shortage of raw material.

The British blockade, which was far more effectual than the escape of a very few raiders suggested, also did much to reduce the capacity of Germany to win the war—even though the unrestricted use of submarines in an attempt to destroy the ability of Britain to feed her population provided brief hope in 1917.

By 1914, Britain's share of the world production of manufactured goods had declined from 32 per cent in 1870 to only fourteen per cent, though the trends were hidden by a rise in output. It was simply that British production had risen more slowly than had the world's.

Cargoes still stayed in British bottoms, even if shipowners were forced by the reduction in European trade to expand markets in Asia, the Far East, the Levant and, to a lesser extent, South America. This in turn increased national dependence on maritime trade and kept the British shipbuilding and marine-engineering industries in a position of dominance until the First World War began. Production figures rose satisfyingly; the average gross registered tonnage built annually in British yards increased from 463,500 in 1870–4 to 769,750 in 1895–9. The division in 1870 had been roughly 86 per cent for home use and 14 per cent for export. By the end of the century, it had altered only slightly to 77:23.

**Below:** the 1,907grt freighter *Patmos* of the Deutsch-Levante Linie (AG 'Neptun', Rostock, 1902), leaving Hamburg. Author's collection.

Though the maintenance of a strong shipbuilding industry through a period of gradual recession could be hailed as an achievement, it allowed some countries—particularly Germany—to increase their maritime trade by buying British-built ships whilst simultaneously creating effectual industries of their own. By the end of the nineteenth century, very few major vessels were being ordered by German owners from shipyards outside Germany. By the early 1900s, German, French and Italian yards, often helped by subsidies, were even competing directly against British interests.

The production of merchant ships of more than 100grt amounted in 1900 to 1,442,471grt in Britain, 333,527grt in the USA and 204,731grt in Germany. By 1913, the relevant gross registered tonnage figures were 1,932,153, 276,448 and 465,226 respectively. Thus it will be seen that though British yards had increased output by 34 per cent and US production had temporarily fallen, Germany had raised its total by a staggering 127 per cent.

> Three typical pre-1914 merchant steamships.
>
> **Top:** 4,938grt *Tarantia* (formerly *Kirkfield*) of the Anchor Line, completed in 1911 for the Kirkfield Shipping Company by Russell of Port Glasgow. **Middle:** 6,757grt *Eisenach* of Norddeutscher Lloyd, built by Bremer Vulkan of Vegesack in 1908. **Bottom:** shown here as *Njegos* of Jugoslavenski Lloyd, this 4,746grt tramp was completed in 1908 by A. MacMillan & Sons Ltd of Dumbarton and named *Suruga*. Author's collection.

On 1 June 1913, according to Lloyd's Register of Shipping, the British merchant navy still comprised 43·5 per cent of the world's tonnage. The USA had 11·6 per cent, Germany had 10·8 per cent, Norway had 5·2 per cent and France had 4·7 per cent. However, British vessels were scattered among a variety of owners, some of whom had only a handful—perhaps even just one. The ships were often operated by specialist managers and owned by syndicates of individuals, their shares traditionally divided into 64ths.

Though the Merchant Navy possessed some of the biggest, fastest and most elegant ships in the world, more than six tenths of tonnage afloat in 1914 were represented by the 'tramp' steamer—so called because the vessel had to tramp the world in search of its cargo. Passengers were rarely carried in these ships.

The British tramp of 1914 was comparatively small, averaging only 3,650grt, but ran very economically. Typical of the breed in size—if not construction—was the 'turret' *Nonsuch*, launched from the Wearside shipyard of William Doxford & Sons Ltd in 1906 for Bowles Brothers & Company of London.* About 350ft

* Patented by Doxford in the early 1890s, this improved the ratio of deadweight to gross registered tonnage in a successful attempt to reduce the cost of a passage of the Suez Canal in relation to the amount of cargo carried. The topsides of the hull were turned inward to carry a notably narrow deck. Doxford made 176 turret-ships prior to 1914.

overall, with a beam of 50ft and a deep draught of 25ft 3in, *Nonsuch* had a gross registered tonnage of 3,826. Rated at 1,700ihp, her triple expansion engine had cylinder diameters of 24in, 41in and 68in, with a 45-inch stroke. Fuel consumption was about 2 cwt of coal per mile (1·3lb/ihp/mile) at ten knots.

Bunkerage depended on the voyage that was to be undertaken, as much space as possible being reserved for paying cargo. The fixed bunkers held 361 tons of coal, which promised a range of 3,600 miles. When the small bridge hold and reserve bunkers were filled, however, maximum coal capacity rose to 1,372 tons. Consequently, at least theoretically, *Nonsuch* could have sailed from London to the New Zealand port of Wellington without refuelling. This performance, typical of virtually all ships of this type, was a deciding factor in the success of the raiders *Möwe* and *Wolf* (qq.v.).

The German mercantile marine was dominated by a handful of companies that were far bigger than anything the British could muster. In addition, a much larger proportion of ships was devoted either to passenger traffic or to a combination of passengers and cargo.

Nearly two thirds of the total German registered tonnage were owned by only eleven of the leading companies—Hamburg–Amerika Linie; Norddeutscher Lloyd; Hamburg–Südamerikanische Dampfschifffahrts-Gesellschaft; Roland Linie; Deutsch Levante Linie; Woermann Linie; Deutsche-Dampfschiffs-Gesellschaft 'Hansa'; Deutsch Ostafrika Linie; Hamburg–Bremer–Afrika Linie; the Deutsch Australische Dampfschiffs-Gesellschaft; and Deutsche-Dampfschiffs-Gesellschaft 'Kosmos'. With the exception of Norddeutscher Lloyd (Bremerhaven), DDG 'Hansa' (Bremen) and the Roland Linie (Bremen), all were based in Hamburg. Between them, they owned ships amounting to 3,349,000grt and received annual subsidies of more than 400,000 Marks.

In August 1914, the Hamburg–Amerika Linie fleet was the most powerful in the world—nearly five hundred ships, tugs and lighters totalling 1,093,000grt, running more than seventy services and carrying about 400,000 passengers annually. Norddeutscher Lloyd, whose first steamship had been built by Caird of Greenock in 1858, contributed an additional 716,000grt.

However, few perceptible changes in maritime trade had been noticed in Britain in the entire period between 1870 and 1914. British ships had represented seventy per cent or more of the total number entering and clearing British ports from 1870 until 1899 inclusively. The decline in shipping trades, therefore, was far less noticeable than it had been in some other industries.

## The value of a war against commerce

In 1914, the Merchant Navy provided a lifeline for Britain and the Empire. Excepting Africa and Asia, where there was a modest export surplus, the balance of trade on the eve of the First World War favoured imports. Figures for

1913 showed that imports from North America amounted to £174·1 million compared with exports of British goods valued at only £54·4 million. The relevant figures for South America were £80·7 million and £55·8 million; for Europe, £317·9 million and £188·3 million. Even Australasia sent more to Britain than it received.

Clearly, a concerted attack on British shipping would strike at the very heart of national prosperity. Most of the exports were coal, machinery or similar manufactured goods. If these could be destroyed, no payments would be made and the economy would suffer. Many of the imports were food: rice came from Burma; wheat and grain from the USA, Canada and Australia; fruit from the Caribbean; meat from South America and New Zealand. If these could be destroyed, the British people would suffer and political instability might follow.

The maritime trades were often seasonal, but their patterns had been fixed by custom that ships followed time-honoured courses. The primary route to North America was straight across the Atlantic, whilst the Caribbean was reached either by way of a North American port or via the Canary islands (las Islas Canarias) and Cabo São Roque. Westward routes to the Pacific and the Far East skirted Cape Horn in the days before the Panama Canal was opened.

Alternatively, Southern Africa, the Indian Ocean, the Far East and the Pacific could be reached by an easterly route, with the options of heading south-eastward for the Cape of Good Hope or turning into the Mediterranean through the Pillars of Hercules and then heading east for the Suez Canal, the Red Sea and the Gulf of Aden.

The predictability of these routes created centres at which shipping automatically concentrated—off Cabo São Roque; in the Western Approaches to Britain; at the mouth of the Red Sea, where it flowed into the Gulf of Aden; in the vicinity of the Canary islands; around Cape Horn; and south of the Cape of Good Hope.

Attacks made in these areas would be bound to succeed. However, it was necessary not only to have sufficient ships to sustain a protracted campaign but also the ability to refuel them. These weaknesses ultimately proved to be the downfall of surface-raiding schemes involving German warships powered by reciprocating engines and turbines alike.

## The creation of the German empire

The German empire owed its foundation to the Franco-Prussian War of 1870–1, but comparatively late creation brought its share of problems. Time was needed to weld the constituents of the new empire together. Industrial potential was enormous, but success depended on communications and the railway systems of even the principal states needed rationalisation. Thus the global expansion of the Deutsches Reich, which was demanded in some quarters to compete with Britain and France by spreading German influence throughout the world, had to wait until a stable economic foundation had been laid.

As early as 1874, members of the Reichstag were tabling motions stressing that the acquisition of a colonial empire was of paramount importance. However, arguments that this would not only favour trade but also satisfy the ambitions of Germans with expansionist views—which could not prosper within the confines of central Europe—failed to convince Bismarck.

The ownership of much of the globe had already been settled by 1871. The great empires of Spain and Portugal had been dismantled, giving South American countries independence which was unassailable. Though the Spanish-American War of 1898 ended Spain's direct involvement in the New World, cultural domination of central and southern America remained everywhere excepting in Portuguese-orientated Brazil. Germany could do little in the Americas but encourage trade links, often astutely based around military supplies such as Krupp cannon or Mauser rifles. By 1914, therefore, surprisingly large expatriate German communities had been established in Argentina, Brazil and Chile.

The colonising impetus came from societies such as the Gemeinschaft für Deutsche Kolonialisation (the Society for German Colonialisation) and, particularly, from merchants keen to expand their markets into Africa. Prospects seemed bleak. Britain and France had carved most of the continent between them, though the Italians had footholds in the north and the Belgians managed to prolong ownership of the Congo.

The first German penetration of the so-called Dark Continent was based around settlements pioneered by missionaries in the middle of the nineteenth century. Acquisitions generally followed a common plan; most of the areas had no binding links with other trading agencies, and local chieftains were easily persuaded to sign treaties of friendship in return for gifts or minor concessions. Carl Peters, a leading coloniser, extended German influence over a large area of East Africa. He was able to persuade a reluctant Bismarck to grant a charter to the Deutsch Ostafrika Gesellschaft and then permit the occupation of Dar-es-Salaam in 1885; eventually, the government in Berlin recognised the colony in 1891.

The history of Deutsch Südwestafrika was similar, excepting that the prime mover was Bremen merchant Hans Lüderitz. British administrators in Cape Colony had concluded agreements with the local chieftains in 1876, hoping that the new territory would be claimed by the British government. However, London wanted only the small parcel of land around the settlement of Walvis Bay. Lüderitz and his associates landed at Angra Pequena in April 1884 to claim the area as a German protectorate.

Togo and Kamerun were seized in 1884, the latter after the Germans had occupied Duala. The initial colonisation of Kamerun was credited to another of the Hamburg businessmen, Gustav Nachtigal.

Above: taken from *The War Illustrated* for August 1914, this advertisement reflects the reliance placed by Britain on trade with her colonies. Author's collection.

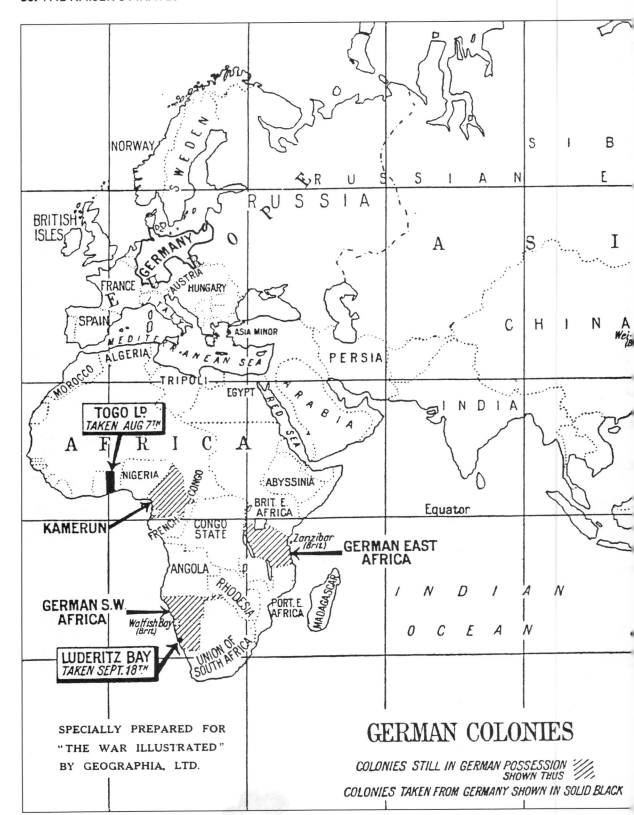

TOGO L^D
TAKEN AUG 7^TH

KAMERUN

GERMAN EAST
AFRICA

GERMAN S.W.
AFRICA

LUDERITZ BAY
TAKEN SEPT. 18^TH

SPECIALLY PREPARED FOR
"THE WAR ILLUSTRATED"
BY GEOGRAPHIA, LTD.

# GERMAN COLONIES

*COLONIES STILL IN GERMAN POSSESSION* ///
*SHOWN THUS*
*COLONIES TAKEN FROM GERMANY SHOWN IN SOLID BLACK*

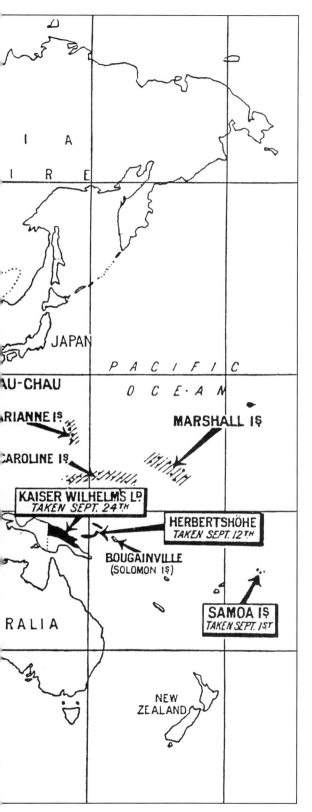

Incursions were made into the Pacific Ocean in the early 1880s, the islands in the Bismarck archipelago being seized in October 1884. German influence was extended in 1886 to the Ellice Islands and part of New Guinea ('Kaiser-Wilhelm-Land'); to the Marshalls in 1888; to the Marianas in 1889; to the Gilbert Islands in 1892; and to the Caroline Islands in 1899.

Citing as a pretext the murder of two Lutheran missionaries in Yen-chou-fu in November 1897, the Germans then staked their claim in China. The commander of the Ostasiatischen Kreuzerdivision, Vizeadmiral von Diedrichs, was immediately ordered northward to 'protect German interests' in the region of Tsing-tao, which was known from prior intelligence to be not only an excellent natural harbour but also an ideal point at which to exert influence on a crumbling empire.

On 13 November 1897, the ships *Kaiser*, *Prinzess Wilhelm* and *Cormoran* dropped anchor off the sleepy Chinese fishing village. At dawn the next morning, landing parties were sent ashore to subdue the garrison and demand the surrender of the local administrator. Wisely, the Chinese did not resist. At 14:30 on 14 November, therefore, a 21-gun salute was fired to honour the raising of the German flag over the new protectorate of Kiautschou.

By 1914, the Germans had created an empire of about a million square miles, with a population of fourteen million. However, the effectual protection of far-flung colonies required the creation of suitable naval units, particularly when there were so many small islands to police. The Westafrikanische Geschwader was formed by an imperial order of 1 October 1884, initially comprising *Bismarck* (flagship), *Gneisenau*, *Ariadne* and *Olga* under the command of Konteradmiral Eduard Knorr. The creation of East African and East Asian squadrons soon followed.

Eventually, the foundation of Kiautschou forced the enlargement of the naval forces in the Far East; on 23 November 1897, Admiral Prinz Heinrich von Preussen ordered the despatch of a second cruiser division, comprising *Deutschland* (flagship), *Kaiserin Augusta* and *Gefion*.

In March 1898, German and Chinese governments agreed a 99-year lease on the Kiautschou protectorate— just as the British had acquired Hong Kong fifty years earlier. On 5 May 1898, II. Kreuzer-Division arrived in Kiautschou bay to form the nucleus of the Kreuzergeschwader ('cruiser squadron') charged with maintaining German order in the Chinese protectorate and the 'Deutsche Schutzgebiet Südsee'.

The colonial stations of the Kaiserliche Marine were initially served by obsolescent warships, often converted from sail-and-steam vessels of the 1870s. These were usually acceptably seaworthy and carried sufficient weapons to deal with local squabbling. Neither the Chinese nor the Japanese fleets seemed much of a threat to European colonialism in the Far East until 1905, when the Japanese destroyed the Russian navy in the Straits of Tsushima and upset the balance of power.

By 1900, the Kreuzergeschwader was commanded by Vizeadmiral Bendemann, flying his flag in the brand-new armoured cruiser *Fürst Bismarck*, a product of the Kaiserliche Werft in Kiel (yard no. 23). Specifically designed for tropical service, with a wood-sheathed hull beneath the waterline to minimise corrosion in the tropics, *Fürst Bismarck* displaced 10,690 tonnes and was 125·7m long. Powered by triple expansion steam engines, driving two propellers, she had a service speed of eighteen knots and a range of about 4,560 nautical miles at ten knots. Armament comprised four 24cm, twelve 15cm, ten 8·8cm and four 3·7cm guns, in addition to six 45cm torpedo tubes. The crew mustered 697 officers and men, including eighty belonging to the admiral's staff.

By the standards of the Far East in 1900, the German cruiser was a very powerful warship indeed.

Bendemann was accompanied by the large cruisers *Hertha*, *Hansa* and *Kaiserin Augusta*, as well as the small cruisers *Irene* and *Gefion*. This gave sufficient strength to discourage interference in German affairs.

The American Station was protected by the large cruiser *Vineta*, the small cruiser *Geier* and the gunboat *Luchs*. The small cruisers *Cormoran* and *Seeadler* served the Australian Station, together with the survey ship *Möwe*, whilst *Loreley* was based in the Mediterranean ('Mittelmeer-Station'). The colonial cruisers *Bussard*, *Condor* and *Schwalbe* were on the East African Station, the gunboat *Habicht* and the survey ship *Wolf* sufficing to protect West Africa.

The East Asian Station (Tsingtau) mustered the new gunboats *Jaguar*, *Iltis* and *Tiger* in addition to providing a base for the Kreuzergeschwader.

The advent of effectual light cruisers in the first years of the twentieth century allowed the Germans to muster a squadron of comparatively fast and powerful ships in the Far East, forcing the British to keep a fleet of at least equal strength stationed at Hong Kong and Wei-hai-wei.

## The wireless telegraph

Among the greatest of the difficulties faced by naval high commands at the beginning of the twentieth century was communicating with individual warships. Co-ordinating supplies of coal relied on good fortune; so did ensuring

**Below:** the iron-hulled corvette *Gneisenau* (2,843 tonnes) was built by the imperial shipyard in Danzig and commissioned into the Kaiserliche Marine in October 1880. She was lost in a storm off Malaga in December 1900. By courtesy of the Trustees of the Imperial War Museum, negative no. Q22324.

that messages from central command were transmitted efficiently to detached naval units, or securing the arrival of replacement crewmen. Thus the submarine cable and the wireless telegraph, in particular, were tremendously useful to planners.

The father of the wireless telegraph is widely regarded as the Italian-born Guglielmo Marconi—who sought his first British patents in June 1896—but the basic principles of 'spark telegraphy' had been known for many years. As early as 1866, the American inventor Mahlon Loomis had successfully transmitted simple messages from Catochin Ridge to Bear's Den in the Appalachian Mountains in Virginia. A US Patent for 'Improvements in Telegraphing' was granted to Loomis in July 1872, but shortage of capital prevented the Loomis Aerial Telegraph Company prospering.

In July 1897, Marconi and his backers formed the Wireless Telegraph & Signal Co. Ltd and a permanent station was installed on the Isle of Wight in November. In the summer of 1898, realising that the system would facilitate the reporting of shipping movements, Lloyd's ordered a Marconi transmitter/receiver to connect Rathlin Island lighthouse with a shore station in Ballycastle in County Antrim. The success of the experiments soon persuaded Lloyd's to instal Marconi equipment in all its signal stations.

By 1901, Marconi had successfully bridged the North Atlantic when a message sent from Poldhu, in Cornwall, was detected by a receiver in St John's, Newfoundland. The earliest successful transmission directly from Britain to Australia—made from the Carnarvon long-range station—occurred in 1918.

In a presidential address to the Institution of Civil Engineers in November 1907, Sir William Matthews noted that the length of submarine cables had grown from 19,263 nautical miles (state-owned) and 145,154 nautical miles (private) in 1897 to 44,988 and 216,116 respectively by 1907. "Although it is but a few years ago that the method of signalling by Herzian waves was brought to a practical stage by Mr. Marconi," he continued, "there were at the beginning of the present year in connection with this system no fewer than 195 stations, either wholly or partially devoted to commercial work, in all parts of the world, and 147 stations provided for purely naval, military or . . . lighthouse purposes. The range has gradually increased up to 1500 miles, and has recently culminated in Mr. Marconi's great achievement in enabling messages to be conveyed from this country to America and Canada, independent of ocean cables."

This success persuaded many inventors to seek differing forms of wireless telegraphy. The success of patent suits hinged largely on whether protection granted to Marconi was sufficient to prevent others using the principle of wireless telegraphy, or simply enshrined a means by which it could be achieved. The Wireless Telegraph & Signal Co. Ltd—later Marconi's Wireless Telegraphy Ltd—had established a near-monopoly in Britain, negotiating licences with the Admiralty in June 1903 and the Postmaster-General in August 1904, but courts elsewhere were often less tolerant; in the USA, for example, the precedent of the 1872-vintage Loomis patent was crucial.

By 1914, the leading German manufacturer was the Gesellschaft für Drahtlose Telegraphie of Berlin, better known as 'Telefunken', which had been formed in 1903 by amalgamating the systems of Friedrich Braun of Strassburg and the Arco-Slaby partnership of Berlin; these had previously been promoted by Siemens & Halske ('Braun-Siemens Gesellschaft für Drahtlose Telegraphie') and Allgemeine Elektrizitäts-Gesellschaft respectively, each manufacturer having a substantial stake in the Telefunken organisation.

Among the most important of the early Telefunken installations was at Scheveningen in the Netherlands, with a guaranteed range in 1906 of 350 kilometres and occasional successes up to 800km; duplicates were installed in Batavia (now Djakarta) and Cheribon (Tjeribon) in Java, in the Netherlands Indies.

The aggression with which Telefunken systems were marketed—often as accompaniments to German weaponry—ensured that they spread rapidly. By 1906, stations had been erected for the Cuban government at Mariel, near Habana, and on the Isla de Pinos off the southern coast; and, on behalf of the Ottoman Empire, at Derna in Cyrenaica and Patara on the southern coast of Asia Minor. Work had also begun on stations in Argentina, Brazil, Mexico, Siam and China. It is no coincidence that the armies of these states were all equipped with German rifles, machine-guns and cannon.

The Telefunken station outside the old town of Nauen, 40km to the west of Berlin, was opened in the summer of 1907. On 3 October 1907, communication was maintained with the steamship *Bremen*, 2,500 kilometres away in the Atlantic. This great success had been achieved only by building a large and expensive installation; the iron lattice tower of the parasol antenna, for example, was 100 metres high. However, Telefunken was also offering a transmitter/receiver weighing a mere 400kg. This used a 15-metre mast and had a range of 50km; a larger version with a range of 300km weighed 1,500kg and required a 30-metre mast. Yet these units were sufficiently portable by the standards of the day to extend the use of wireless telegraphy with surprising rapidity.

The Kaiserliche Marine viewed the development of the new wireless telegraph with great enthusiasm, realising the part that it could play in the control of warships on colonial service. Even by the end of 1906, thirteen Slaby-Arco or Telefunken stations had been built on the Baltic and North Sea coasts, and every major German warship was being fitted with transmitter/receivers. In October 1907, the magazine *Engineering* had reported that—

**Above:** the Kaiser-Wilhelm-Kanal linking the North Sea with the Baltic was of great importance to Germany. Here the cruiser *Cöln* is making an eastward passage. In the distance is the Rendsburger Hochbrücke. Author's collection.

"the number of stations equipped with the apparatus of the . . . Slaby-Arco [i.e., original Slaby-Arco and Telefunken types] system of wireless telegraphy is now 641, or 41 per cent of the entire list of existing wireless telegraph stations, now numbering 1550. The 641 stations are scattered over the territory, or vessels, of thirty-one different countries. Of these, some 174 are situated on land. They usually command a radius of 125 miles, but in several cases this is extended to 310 miles, 435 miles, or even greater distances. Germany's own quota of stations is thirty-six mostly located on the coasts of the Baltic and the North Sea. It includes a great experimental station at Nauen, which commands a radius of 1860 miles. In the United States are twenty stations; including Fire Island, Washington, New Orleans, San Francisco, and San Juan. Russia has seventeen stations. That of Vladivostock is the most prominent, commanding, as it does, a range of 620 miles. Austria-Hungary has ten stations; Denmark and Spain, seven each; Holland, six (that of Scheveningen reaches 435 miles); and Norway and Sweden, five each. In non-European countries the system has four stations in Argentina, six in Brazil, five in China, eight in Cuba (that of Habana commanding 930 miles), six in Mexico, two in the Philippines, and one in the Sandwich Islands (at Honolulu). The majority of these land stations are Government property, and are under the control of the postal, naval, or lighthouse services. Most of the installations are on ocean vessels. Of these, 22 are on Dutch and German steamers, while 389 are on warships. They include vessels of the following nationalities:– German, 140; Russian, 126; American, 43; Swedish, 19; Austrian, 17; Dutch, 10; Norwegian, 8; Argentine, 6; Brazilian, 5; Spanish, 5; Danish, 5; Greek, 3; and Indian, 2. Some 54 mobile military stations have been installed in various countries. In France, Great Britain, and Italy the German system is unable to meet the competition of systems under local control."

Even the most primitive wireless-telegraph unit was capable of revolutionising the pattern of maritime trade—or, when necessary, the conduct of war. One 1906-vintage report confided that:

the 'influence of atmospheric conditions is also well established . . . Some extraordinary long ranges, twice the average range and more, have been temporarily been covered on the eastern coast of the United States, while in the Tropics apparatus sometimes fails to come up to half their [sic] normal capacity. Fog seems to stop the waves . . . owing to this uncertainty, radiotelegraphic stations have to be built with ample reserve power'.

However, there were still major problems. The range of transmissions was comparatively low, clarity was unpredictable, and the effects of interference were often serious enough to prevent messages being received in comprehensible form. As the concept of radio-direction finding was largely unknown in this era, the ease with which ships could disappear into the expanse of the Atlantic, Indian or Pacific oceans is understandable.

The limited range of pre-1914 sets required the assistance of relay stations to transmit messages over long distances. And whilst the fitting of transmitters and receivers in a few hundred ships may have impressed the readership of *Engineering* in 1907, it represented a tiny fraction of the world's seagoing vessels. Britain alone possessed ten thousand steamships and only the biggest or most progressive owners could be bothered with wireless telegraphy. When war came, this conservative attitude was a boon to the German raiders; attacks could often be made in the knowledge that the victim could neither call for help nor pinpoint the position of the raider with a distress signal.

A few enthusiasts had used transmitting/receiving equipment as a direction finder, with some success at short range, and had also tried to monitor signal strength as a guide to distance. However, atmospheric conditions could alter the strength of reception so greatly that experiments often ended in failure. Misunderstanding of wireless telegraphy equipment did eventually account for one raider: though the operators aboard *Emden* intercepted messages prior to the arrival of HMAS *Sydney*, their weakness was taken as a sign that the

Australian cruiser was several hundred miles away. What the Germans did not know was that *Sydney* was transmitting on half-power, and that every minute that *Emden* passed hove-to off Direction Island was vital to her survival. Von Müller and his crew were trapped, the subsequent destruction of their ship owing much to a simple miscalculation.

## The Etappe system

The wireless telegraph also played a significant part in allowing the German raiders of 1914 to prolong their activities. The Admiralstab had always known that it would be difficult to supply fuel to warships on colonial stations, particularly if Tsingtau fell to the British or Japanese and the sea lanes were swept by hostile forces.

The solution was found in the so-called Etappe system, the word being borrowed from French to mean 'base' or 'zone'. The oceans were divided into areas centred on a communications bureau under the control of a naval officer, often in a major city where the Germans maintained diplomatic representation. This system enabled messages transmitted from Nauen and elsewhere in Germany to be relayed either directly to the appropriate ships or, if the local transmitters were not powerful enough, by way of intermediaries. The vessels of all the major German shipping lines were fitted with transmitter/receiver equipment, and their masters had sealed orders to be opened in case of war or national emergency. The information included details of the Etappe to which the merchant-ship had been allocated to serve on behalf of the Kaiserliche Marine.

The system was thoroughly overhauled from time to time, and was at a peak of readiness when the opening shots of the First World War were fired. Unfortunately, encirclement of the globe by German wireless-telegraphy stations had not been completed by August 1914. The intention had been for messages to be transmitted from Nauen and relayed by a few powerful intermediaries.

Relay stations had been built at Kamina in Togo, Windhuk in Deutsch Südwestafrika, and Yap in the south Pacific, but the major installations in Tabora (Deutsch Ostafrika) and Sumatra, in the Netherlands Indies, had not been completed. Lesser transmitters sited in Duala (Kamerun), Bukoba, Muansa and Dar-es-Salaam (Deutsch Ostafrika), Tsingtau, Angaur, Rabaul, Nauru, and Apia (Samoa) could often extend the signal range when necessary, but there were areas in the Indian Ocean and the southern Pacific where communication was possible only when atmospheric conditions were ideal.

The distance from Nauen to the unfinished Tabora station was 5,700km, which represented a considerable transmitting feat in itself, but Yap was 11,250km away from Tabora. Even the addition of a station in Sumatra would only have reduced the maximum to 7,200km. Tsingtau and Apia were roughly 3,500km and 6,000km from Yap respectively, though the station at Nauru (3,400km from Yap) could relay messages when required.

When the First World War began, large numbers of colliers were immediately despatched to pre-arranged stations or to meet with warships in mid-ocean. The Germans gambled that most South American states would take a benevolent view of the neutrality laws, and thus that no action would be taken to prevent colliers fulfilling their prescribed roles. Argentina, Brazil and—particularly—Chile had sizeable German communities and had benefited greatly from German investment.

Organisational centres included Tsingtau, China, Japan, Manila, Batavia ('Südetappe'), San Francisco ('Etappe Nordwest Amerika'), Valparaiso ('Etappe Südwest Amerika'), Callao (Peru), La Plata, Rio de Janeiro ('Etappe Brasilien'), the Caribbean ('Etappe Westindien'), New York ('Etappe Nord Amerika'), Duala ('Etappe West-Afrika'), Dar-es-Salaam ('Etappe Ostafrika') and even in the Mediterranean ('Etappe Mittlemeer').

So many merchant ships were chartered that it is impossible to give a detailed list, the interested reader being directed to the fourth volume of *Die deutschen Kriegsschiffe 1815-1945* by Gröner, Jung and Maass, where copious information will be found.

Typical were the affairs of La Plata section, under whose control nine steamers fell in August 1914—*Santa Isabel* (5,199grt, 1914) of Hamburg–Südamerikanische Dampfschifffahrts-Gesellschaft; *Pontos* (5,703grt, 1900) and *Silvia* (6,580grt, 1901), belonging to the Hamburg–Amerika Linie; *Josephina* (1,295grt, 1899), managed by Jos de Poorter of Rotterdam; *Sierra Cordoba* (8,226grt, 1912) and *Gotha* (6,653grt, 1907) of Norddeutscher Lloyd; *Eleonore Woermann* (4,624grt, 1902) of the Woermann Linie; *Mera* (4,798grt, 1900) of Deutsche-Dampfschiff-fahrts-Gesellschaft 'Kosmos'; and *Muansa* (5,408grt, 1911) of the Deutsche–Ostafrika Linie.

*Santa Isabel* was sunk on 8 December 1914, during the Battle of the Falkland Islands, by the Royal Navy cruiser *Bristol*; *Eleonore Woermann* was sunk by the battle-cruiser HMS *Australia* in the Straits of Magellan (Estrechos de Magellanes) in January 1915; and *Josephina* was captured by the British cruiser *Carnarvon* in the Straits of Magellan soon afterward. The others were eventually interned once local authorities had been convinced by the destruction of the Kreuzergeschwader that a stricter interpretation of neutrality was advisable.

Eventually, all the principal countries in South America declared war on Germany and the last vestiges of the Etappe system disappeared. The difficulty of coaling the surface raiders in 1914–15, particularly small cruisers, was to be a strong argument in favour of economical ships such as *Möwe* and *Wolf*.

## The growth of the German navy

Though the completion of *Dreadnought* materially altered the balance of naval power, the influence was not immediately obvious in 1907, when an editorial in

*Engineering* entitled 'Battleship Strength and Relative Value' summarised the popular view.

"With October comes the intersessional political oratory, and this year we are promised a more than usually vigorous campaign. Two questions of interest to all connected with industry will be brought to the front . . . [including] naval strength and Admiralty administration.

"We shall, as ever, be confronted with lists which state that Great Britain possesses so many battleships, that France, Germany, the United States of America, &c., possess so many; and starting from this hypothesis, articles will be written to prove that either now, or at some date in the comparatively near future, the first-named Power will be overtaken and passed, and that the sea supremacy, which none deny to her in the present, will then be dangerously jeopardised. But the writers and speakers who merely count units—units which are described as battleships—do not always analyse, and lay before the public which they address, the data concerning the vessels mentioned in these lists.

"If a comparison is to be of any value, it must take into account not only the number of ships, but also their fighting capacity. As an example, let us see in what way the Channel Fleet, under the command of Lord Charles Beresford, will be constituted in the immediate future. It will consist of eight ships of the King Edward VII type, and six of the Formidable type, fourteen battleships, forming the most powerful and also the homogeneous force, which is an all-important matter, in the whole world. Of the first type mentioned, the oldest was launched in 1903, the youngest—the *Hibernia*—in 1905. These eight ships each carry four 12-in., four 9·2-in., and ten 6-in. guns, as well as small guns and five submerged torpedo tubes; their armour is 9-in. Krupp amidships, tapering to 6-in. and 2-in.; their horsepower is 18,000, and their speed nearly 19 knots, their tonnage being 16,350 tons. The Formidables are older, November 1898 being the date of the oldest of the class, and their size is smaller, being 15,000 tons, carrying four 12-in., twelve 6-in., besides small guns and four submerged tubes; horse-power is 15,000, and speed 18 knots.

"These details are given in order that comparisons may be instituted between this, the principal British Fleet, and the ships of foreign powers . . ."

The article then harshly, but accurately, wrote that the "importance of the French navy has been always reckoned as one of the most potent factors in keeping the balance of European armaments; but it cannot be said of late years that the great Republic has kept up her ancient fame in this respect . . . [and] enormous mischief [has been] wrought at the hands of a Socialist Minister of Marine." It was said of the Germans that—

"Their fleet, both war and mercantile, is among those things of which [they] are the most proud—and with reason. The Kaiser on a memorable occasion declared that 'the future of Germany is on the sea,' and to do him justice, he has never ceased, in season and out of season, to do his best to ensure that

**Below:** the 13,208-tonne pre-dreadnought *Elsass* (Schichau, Danzig, 1904) enters harbour. Author's collection.
**Above right:** the Aviso *Wacht* (1,475 tonnes), built by AG 'Weser' of Bremen and commissioned in August 1888. She was sunk in a collision with the battleship *Sachsen* in September 1901. By courtesy of the Trustees of the Imperial War Museum, negative no. Q22332. **Right:** the 4,564-tonne cruiser *Breslau* (AG 'Vulcan', 1912) in Kiel harbour. From a photograph by Gebr. Lempe, published in postcard form by NPG, Berlin ('Neptun' series, no. 85). Author's collection.

that future shall be prosperous. Germany, like every other nation, piles ship upon ship and gun upon gun, protesting loudly all the while that nothing is further from her thoughts than war; this, of course, is all part of the game, and nobody minds, because we all do and say the same thing. But it may be permissible to doubt whether Germany does not view the development of 'mastodonte' in warships with greater dismay than any other nation. The Fatherland was really getting along very nicely in the naval way until the arrival of the *Dreadnought* put all her plans astray. There is one thing that neither King, Kaiser, nor Republican President can alter, and that is the physical configuration of the land in which they dwell, and Nature has ensconced Germany behind one of the most intricate and tortuous labyrinths of sandbanks which exist in the world. Very useful are such natural defences against a potential maritime enemy, but when a nation wishes to develop into a great maritime Power, they embarrass it almost as much as they would do its foe. As at present constituted, the German navy possesses no battleship of over 13,200 tons, and has afloat no gun of a greater calibre than 11-in. There are five of the Braunschweig class, dating from 1902–3, and five of the Deutschland class, dating 1904–6, of this tonnage, carrying four 11-in. and fourteen 6·7-in. guns; horse-power, 16,000; speed, 18 knots. There are also five Wittelsbachs, of 11,830 tons, and five of the Kaiser class, of 11,150 tons, carrying four 9·4-in. and eighteen 6-in. guns, 15,000 and 14,000 horse-power, and speed 18 knots. The Brandenberg [sic] class, of four ships, date from 1891, and are of 10,060 tons.

"If we compare these ships, of which the German high sea fleet is composed, with the Channel Fleet alone, we need not fear the comparison, But Germany has further ambitions, and the 'mastodons' which she has projected are the *Sachsen*, *Baiern* [sic], *Baden*, and *Wurtemburg* [sic]. They are to have a tonnage, it is reported, of 17,170 tons, possibly 19,000 tons—but apparently nothing definite has been settled—and are to carry sixteen 11-in. guns . . ."

The article concluded that 'for the present, England is in

a satisfactory position. But the pace is being forced all along the line, and our rivals are striving to ... surpass us. If this fact is kept in mind by our politicians, we need not fear our supremacy, for we can build faster than any other nation, and certainly quite as well. The danger is that we may presume on our abilities, and defer our preparations too long. Fortunately, all parties are agreed that the British Navy must always remain supreme on the seas.'

The introduction of *Dreadnought* was not seen in Germany as the catastrophe the British had assumed. Tirpitz and his advisers were aware that the turbine powered big-gun battleship rendered all the earlier vessels obsolete, but also realised that this applied as much to the British King Edward VII class as it did to the Kaiserliche Marine's Deutschlands. If the German shipyards could produce modern warships sufficiently quickly, parity would be maintained if the British government failed to vote enough funds in the annual Naval Estimates to replace ships that were only a few years old.

The Germans knew that the British shipbuilding industry could easily outstrip indigenous production, but also that this could only happen if the appropriate political will existed.

## The earliest German small cruisers

The origins of the ships of the First World War lay in specialised torpedo-cruisers or Avisos, beginning with 1,101-tonne *Zieten* of 1875 and progressing by way of *Blitz* and *Pfeil* to the 2,050-tonne *Greif* of 1887. This three-funnel vessel had the most to offer for patrol duties, where range and seaworthiness outweighed offensive power. Though *Greif* ultimately proved wanting in North Sea service, reliance on twin shaft simple-expansion steam engines rather than less effectual sail-and-steam combinations was the key to future developments.

The 'cruiser corvette' *Gefion*, displacing 3,746 tonnes on a waterline of about 109 metres, was the first German warship to mount 10·5cm Schnellade-Kanone C/88 ('SK C/88') in what became the classical layout—paired fore-and-aft, with three additional midship guns on each beam. Built in the Schichau yard in Danzig, *Gefion* was commissioned on 27 June 1894 and could make nearly twenty knots. Triple-expansion steam engines rated at 9,000ihp were contained in an iron hull, sheathed in wood to facilitate service in the tropics. After serving the Kreuzergeschwader loyally for many years, being greatly rebuilt at Wilhelmshaven in 1901–3, *Gefion* became an accommodation ship during the First World War.

In all respects excepting armament, however, *Gefion* was a precursor of the Viktoria Luise-class armoured cruisers; *Hela*, built by AG 'Weser' and commissioned in May 1896, was closer to a true light cruiser. With a single funnel, a lightly armoured deck, a ram bow and a puny armament of four 8·8cm guns, *Hela* displaced 2,027 tonnes on a waterline measuring nearly 105 metres. Though triple-expansion engines of 6,000ihp gave a speed of only about twenty knots, service abroad showed *Hela* to be a good seaboat. She was modernised in 1903–6 and again in 1910, acquiring a second funnel and the general appearance of the later Gazelle class.

The naval construction programmes of the late 1890s called for small cruisers to be built to what became the 'Gazelle' design. The first vessel—*Gazelle* herself—was laid down in the Friedr. Krupp'sche Germaniawerft shipyard in Kiel in 1897, though the first representatives to be commissioned were *Niobe* and *Nymphe*, on 25 June and 20 September 1900.

Though the ten ships differed in detail, they all measured about 105m on the waterline. *Gazelle* and *Niobe* each displaced 2,643 tonnes; *Nymphe*, *Thetis*, *Ariadne*, *Amazone* and *Medusa* displaced 2,659 tonnes; whilst *Frauenlob*, *Arcona* and *Undine* (2,706 tonnes) carried ten additional crewmen. Nine of the class could make about 21·5 knots from triple-expansion engines nominally rated at 8,000ihp, the principal exception being the 19·5-knot *Gazelle*, with a distinctive charthouse between two slender widely-spaced funnels. *Ariadne* proved to be the fastest on trials, attaining 22·23 knots on 8,827ihp. Armament remained ten 10·5cm SK C/88, reinforced by six 3·7cm revolver cannon and two torpedo tubes.

The ships of this group were very successful and long-lived, excepting war-losses *Undine* and *Frauenlob*. The authorities were sufficiently impressed to order essentially similar vessels under the 1902 programme, merely enlarging the basic design to displace 3,278 tonnes on a waterline of 110·6 metres. The increase in size allowed better armour protection, more boilers, and the additional power necessary to attain 22 knots on an anticipated 10,000ihp.

The first of the new three-funnel vessels to enter service was *Hamburg*, built in the AG 'Vulcan' yard in Stettin-Bredow and commissioned on 8 March 1904. She was followed by *Bremen*, built by AG 'Vulcan' and commissioned on 8 March 1904. Then came *München* from AG 'Weser' of Bremen, commissioned on 10 January 1905; *Berlin* (Kaiserliche Werft, Danzig, 4 April 1905); *Lübeck* (AG 'Vulcan', Stettin, 26 April 1905); *Leipzig* (AG 'Weser', 20 April 1906; and finally *Danzig* (Kaiserliche Werft, Danzig, 1 December 1907).

The first turbine-engined German warship to enter service had been the torpedo-boat destroyer *S125*, completed in the Elbing yard of Friedr. Schichau in 1904. She displaced 447 tonnes, measured about 64·7m overall, and was powered by two Parsons turbines. Trials returned 27·8 knots on 6,600ihp. Comparisons with near sisters of the S120 class, all of which had reciprocating engines, revealed the customary greater economy at high speed and an absence of vibration.

The authorities were sufficiently impressed by *S125* to fit one of the Bremen-class cruisers with turbines.

Above: the 3,278-tonne cruiser *Hamburg* (AG 'Vulcan', Stettin, 1904) running trials. From a postcard by Hermann Ch. Büsing, Oldenburg (1904, no. 374). Author's collection.
**Right:** bow-shields were a useful identification feature. Drawings by John Walter.
**Below:** the 3,265-tonne turbine-engined cruiser *Lübeck* (AG 'Vulcan', Stettin, 1905), from a postcard published by Gebr. Lempe, Kiel ('No. 103 Rö.'). Author's collection.

LEIPZIG

STRALSUND

S. M. Kleiner Kreuzer Lübeck

*Lübeck* was laid down in the AG 'Vulcan' yard in Stettin in 1903, launched in March 1904 and completed in April 1905—only a few weeks after HMS *Amethyst*, the world's first turbine-driven warship of cruiser size. *Lübeck* displaced 3,265 tonnes, measured 111·1m overall, and was driven by Parsons engines purchased from Britain.

Trials gave a maximum of 23·1 knots on 14,035shp. Though four of *Lübeck*'s reciprocating-engined sister ships achieved 23·3 knots on trial, on power ranging from 11,582ihp (*Hamburg*) to 12,205ihp (*München*), the turbine installation ran more smoothly at high speed. *Lübeck* was initially fitted with four propellers on each shaft, but these were subsequently replaced by two apiece.

The Kleine Kreuzer *Königsberg* was ordered in the 1903/4 fiscal year. Built by the Kaiserliche Werft, Kiel (yard no. 31), she displaced 3,390 tonnes, measured 114·8 metres on the waterline and attained 24·1 knots on trials (13,918ihp). Armed with ten 10·5cm SK L/40 and ten 3·7cm revolver cannon, *Königsberg* had been extensively rebuilt at Danzig in 1911–13 before being sent to Dar-es-Salaam shortly before the First World War began.

The ships of the Stuttgart class—*Stuttgart*, *Stettin* and *Nürnberg*—were authorised in 1904/5. They were slightly larger than the otherwise similar *Königsberg*, displacing 3,469–3,480 tonnes and measuring 116·8m on the waterline, but were readily identified by a notable gap between the second and third funnels. *Stettin* was driven by Parsons turbines coupled with four shafts, making 25·2 knots on the measured mile (21,670shp), whilst her twin-screw sister ships had vertical triple-expansion machinery driving two shafts. *Stuttgart* returned 23·9

knots on trials, whereas *Nürnberg* developed marginally greater power (13,154ihp). Main armament remained ten SK L/40, though the secondary battery was increased to eight 5·2cm SK L/55.

The ships of the 3,664-tonne Dresden class were authorised in the 1905/6 financial year. Commissioned on 14 November 1908, *Dresden* was the work of Blohm & Voss of Hamburg, whilst *Emden* (10 July 1909) was built in the Kiel dockyard. The two ships were externally similar; internally, however, *Dresden* had four-shaft turbines and *Emden* had conventional twin-shaft vertical triple-expansion machinery. Trials showed that *Dresden* was appreciably faster, attaining 25·2 knots (18,880shp) compared with 24 knots (16,350ihp) for her sister.

The earliest turbine-driven Kleine Kreuzer were all fitted with Parsons-type turbines licensed from Britain, but the Germans were aware that they could not place long-term reliance on a potential adversary. The obvious answer was for leading German firms to establish commercial links with the principal non-German turbine manufacturers, something that the British, supremely confident in their ability to outbuild anyone else, did little to discourage. The lack of indigenous capacity was emphasised by the dreadnoughts of the Nassau and Helgoland classes, all eight of which had conventional triple-expansion engines.

The first German capital ship to be fitted with turbines was the 19,370-tonne battle-cruiser *Von der Tann*, completed in the Hamburg yard of Blohm & Voss in February 1911 with four-shaft Parsons-type engines. This ship caused consternation in British naval circles by

---

**Below:** SMS *Stettin* (3,480 tonnes, AG 'Vulcan', Stettin, 1907), showing the characteristic gap between the second and third funnels. From a postcard published by Gebr. Lempe, Kiel ('No. 99 Rö.'). Author's collection.

S. M. Kl. gesch. Kreuzer Stettin

**Above:** the 4,570-tonne cruiser *Stralsund* (AG 'Weser', Bremen, 1912), from an anonymous postcard sent from Cuxhaven in January 1915. The title misleadingly suggests that the ship is *Karlsruhe*, which the presence of funnel bands and the design of the bow-shield refutes! Author's collection.

returning 27·4 knots on her trials in the autumn of 1910 from 79,007shp. Even though the extent to which the boilers had been forced was not clear, the Admiralty knew full well that the 'leaked' 29–30 knots attributed to the seaworthy but weakly protected battle-cruisers of the Indefatigable class was a considerable overstatement—*Von der Tann*, therefore, presented a real threat.

## The perfected German small cruisers

The ships of the 4,362grt Kolberg class, authorised in 1906–7, all had turbine drive. A product of the Schichau shipyard in Danzig, *Kolberg* had Melms-Pfenninger engines; *Mainz*, built in Stettin by AG 'Vulcan', had American Curtis-type units made under licence by Allgemeine Elektrizitäts-Gesellschaft; *Cöln*, from the Krupp'sche Germaniawerft yard in Kiel, had proprietary turbines; and *Augsburg*, built in the Kiel navy yard, apparently had Parsons patterns supplied from Britain.

The cruisers all had four shafts excepting *Mainz*, which had two. Trial speeds ranged from 26·3 to 26·8 knots on 22,040–31,033shp. Interestingly, though the power-output range of the turbines varied greatly, speeds were surprisingly similar. Main armament was twelve 10·5cm guns and two 45cm torpedo tubes submerged on the beam.

The four small cruisers of the 1908–9 programme, laid down in 1910, were all completed in 1912. With a design displacement of 4,535–4,570 tonnes and a waterline length of 136 metres, they were the first to feature a protective armour belt built integrally with the hull. Though this delayed their construction, the result was a group of four-funnelled warships whose sea-keeping qualities bettered those of any previous Kleine Kreuzer. *Magdeburg* (AG 'Vulcan', Stettin) and *Stralsund* (AG 'Weser', Bremen) had Bergmann turbines driving three shafts; *Breslau*, by AG 'Vulcan' of Stettin, had twin

paired AEG-Vulcan turbines driving four shafts; and *Strassburg*, built by Wilhelmshaven dockyard, had two turbines designed by the navy engineering department. Trial speeds ranged from 27·5 knots on 33,482shp (for *Breslau*) to 28·2 knots on 35,515shp (*Stralsund*). *Magdeburg* recorded the poorest power output—merely 29,904shp—but was a tenth of a knot faster than *Breslau*.

The result of the experimentation was that the cruisers authorised in 1910, *Karlsruhe* (by Krupp'sche Germaniawerft, Kiel) and *Rostock* (Howaldtswerke, Kiel) each had two-shaft navy turbines. These units had proved to be as effectual as any of those tested prior to 1912 and had been designed specifically to meet the requirements of the Kaiserliche Marine. In addition, no licensing fees were necessary. All post-1912 cruisers were powered by them.

Karlsruhe-class cruisers had a design displacement of 4,900 tonnes and measured 142·2 metres overall. Their engines were intended to give 26,000shp in ordinary service, equivalent to 27 knots, but substantially greater outputs were recorded on trial; *Rostock*, the faster of the pair, attained 29·3 knots on 43,628shp.

Commissioned on 10 August 1914 and 3 January 1915 respectively, the 4,912-tonne *Graudenz* and *Regensburg* were built under the 1911 programme. The last small cruisers to be completed in Germany before the First World War began, these three-funnel turbine-powered ships, measuring about 142·7m overall, achieved more than 29 knots in shallow water acceptance trials and were undoubtedly capable of exceeding thirty in favourable conditions. They initially carried twelve 10·5cm and two 5cm guns, plus two submerged torpedo-tubes.

## The balance of power, 1914

The rapidity with which the Germans built warships raised the status of the Kaiserliche Marine from an insignificant coastal-defence force in 1900 to the second most powerful navy afloat in 1914. The aggregate naval displacement tonnage constructed in 1900–13 provides confirmation. In this period, Britain contributed 1,781,420 tons, followed by Germany (978,629), the USA (734,697), France (604,044), Russia (469,789) and Japan (373,636). On the basis of tonnage alone, Britain had managed to maintain the desired 'Two Power Standard', as the aggregate of even the USA and Germany together did not surpass the Royal Navy. But it was arguable whether the lead had been maintained qualitatively.

The ships of the Kaiserliche Marine were at least the equal of their Royal Navy equivalents, though the Germans still could not build vessels fast enough to overtake their greatest rival numerically. After the Kaiser had given a damning interview to the *Daily Telegraph* in 1909, however, fear of German intentions caused the naval race to accelerate. Truth was often obscured by politicking in this period—particularly when the great navies were compared in government statistics.

In 1909, for example, Britain's Liberal government was confidently predicting a balance of dreadnoughts of about twenty to seventeen in British favour by 1912, assuming the four 'contingency ships' authorised in 1908 were not begun; Conservative opposition claimed that the Germans would be leading 20:21.

Early in 1914, the British government published a paper estimating the strengths of the principal navies of the world on the preceding 1 January. Disregarding most of the ships that were more than twenty years old, on the realistic premise that they had no fighting merit, the inventory of battleships of all types was deduced as—Britain, 58 and fourteen building; Germany, 35 plus six; France, 21 plus ten; and the USA, 30 plus six. In addition, Britain had ten battle-cruisers, one of which was still incomplete, and Germany had seven (four of which were building). Britain was credited with 47 armoured and protected cruisers, eight of which were more than twenty years old but regarded as suitable for colonial patrol duties; Germany had nine; France 24; and the USA seventeen (three more than twenty years old).

Britain also had 65 light cruisers and another twenty in various stages of completion; Germany had 49, six of which were building; France had only eight ships; and the USA had eighteen. The inventory of destroyers concluded that the British strength stood at 201 plus 36 building; Germany had 132 plus twelve; France had eighty plus seven; and the USA had 52 plus fourteen. The lesser category of torpedo-boats favoured Germany, with 153, ahead of Britain (106), France (80) and the USA (21).

The Royal Navy had the most submarines—69, plus another 29 building. Curiously, in view of the prominence to which the U-Boat had risen within a few years, the Kaiserliche Marine total of only 38 (fourteen of which were building) was inferior to that of France (a total of 76) and the USA (fifty).

What these figures did not show in detail, however, was that the Royal Navy was spread thinly around the entire globe; excepting the Kreuzergeschwader and the few ships on lesser colonial outposts, the Kaiserliche Marine was concentrated exclusively in the North Sea and the Baltic.

By the end of 1914, according to one summary, the balance of power, suitably adjusted to account for impressments and losses, still showed a balance in favour of the Royal Navy at the expense of the Kaiserliche Marine in virtually every category. These included a ratio of 73:42 in battleships of all types; though the British total included nearly forty obsolescent pre-dreadnoughts, the German figures included sixteen ships of this type as well as eight old coast-defence ships of practically no fighting value. The inventory of cruisers was assessed at 114:47, that of destroyers and torpedo-boats as 372:190, and submarines as 72:34.

Yet even these impressive totals could not prevent commerce raiding across the trade routes.

## The surface raiders

When the *Rangliste der Kaiserliche Marine* was published in the summer of 1914, most of Germany's small cruisers were stationed in home waters. The greatest concentration was in the Aufklärungsschiffe or Scouting Division, commanded by Konteradmiral Franz Hipper. In addition to several battle-cruisers, Hipper had *Cöln* (commanded by Fregattenkapitän Meidinger), *Mainz* (Kapitän z.S. Wilhelm Passchen), *Stralsund* (Kapitän z.S. Karl Harder), *Kolberg* (Fregattenkapitän Widenmann), *Rostock* (Fregattenkapitän Thilo von Trotha), *Dresden* (Fregattenkapitän Erich Köhler), *Breslau* (Fregattenkapitän Kettner) and *Strassburg* (Fregattenkapitän Retzmann). The obsolescent *Hela*, under the command of Fregattenkapitän Paul Wolfram, acted as a tender.

*Breslau* was acting as part of the Mittelmeer Division (Mediterranean squadron), whilst *Strassburg* had been seconded to the independent 'Detached Division'. The Inspektion des Unterseebootwesens (inspectorate of submarine affairs) had *Hamburg*—commanded by Korvettenkapitän von Gaudecker—and *Stettin*, then under the temporary command of Kapitänleutnant von dem Hagen pending the arrival of Korvettenkapitän Karl August Nerger in the summer. Nerger subsequently achieved fame as the skipper of the raider *Wolf* (q.v.).

The Inspektion der Schiffsartillerie (inspectorate of naval gunnery) had the cruisers *Augsburg*, *Stuttgart* and *Danzig*, commanded by Kapitän z.S. Andreas Fischer, Fregattenkapitän Friedrich Richter and Fregattenkapitän Reiss respectively. The Inspektion des Küstenartillerie und des Minenwesens (inspectorate of coastal artillery and mine warfare) had *Arcona*, under the command of Korvettenkapitän Wilhelm von Hippel, in addition to the cruiser-like minelayers *Albatross* and *Nautilus*.

The Torpedoversuchskommando had *Magdeburg* and *München*, commanded by Korvettenkapitän Habenicht and Kapitän z.S. von Studnitz respectively. The other small cruisers, mostly obsolescent, were held in reserve.

Once the First World War began, the inventory depleted rapidly. *Cöln*, *Mainz* and *Ariadne* were blown to pieces during the Battle of Heligoland Bight on 28 August 1914, facing British battle-cruisers against which their light armour and puny guns gave little protection; *Magdeburg* was destroyed after running aground on the Baltic island of Odensholm on 26 August; *Hela* was sunk by the British submarine *E9* on 13 September.

As described in detail in the relevant chapters, *Karlsruhe* succumbed on 4 November 1914 to an internal explosion; *Emden* was comprehensively outgunned by HMAS *Sydney* and destroyed on 9 November; *Leipzig* and *Nürnberg* were lost during the Battle of the Falkland Islands on 8 December. *Dresden* was finally cornered in neutral Chilean waters off Más Afuera in the Juan Fernández islands and scuttled on 14 March 1915. *Königsberg* was blockaded in the Rufiji Delta and destroyed on 11 July 1915.

By 1915, however, it was obvious that the small cruisers made poor commerce raiders; though they had speed and adequate offensive power, they lacked the endurance needed to tramp many thousands of miles in search of prey. In addition, they had to rely greatly on accompanying colliers and the efforts of the Etappe system to organise supplies of fuel throughout the world. As German colonies fell to Allied forces and neutrality was imposed with ever-increasing rigidity by uncommitted countries, supplying good-quality coal to warships became increasingly problematical. Hard steam coal was essential, otherwise tell-tale smoke was emitted by the funnels, furnace-hearths clogged, the efficiency of boilers declined, and speed dropped appreciably.

The Kaiserliche Marine, like the Royal Navy, was keen to impress large merchant ships as armed cruisers. Promising experiments had been undertaken with the Hamburg–Amerika liner *Normannia* during large-scale fleet manoeuvres as early as 1895. By the early twentieth century, reinforced decks were being built into selected ships, and secret documents were being issued to instruct the captains in an emergency.

In Britain, an agreement between Cunard and the Admiralty in 1903 had a similar effect. The Cunard ships had mountings built into their decks onto which naval guns could be fitted when required. Plans of *Aquitania*

**Below:** the wreck of *Emden* lies beached on North Keeling Island after the epic duel with HMAS *Sydney* on 9 November 1914. By courtesy of the Australian War Memorial, Canberra, negative no. EN 401.

published in marine- and general engineering magazines in 1914 clearly showed that eight guns could be mounted on the shelter deck—four on the forecastle, the remainder aft—in addition to four on the bridge deck.

Merchant cruisers could carry large quantities of fuel, increasing their endurance far beyond that of the regular warships, and were increasingly favoured for duties in the South Atlantic. They could not compete with cruisers in ship-to-ship duels, but the chances of such a contest occurring were remote. The British knew that the Germans would commission as many converted liners as they could, to eke out meagre supplies of Kleine Kreuzer, but believed that British ships—which often carried the armament of a small protected cruiser—would prove superior if the test ever came.

Experience of war soon showed that the largest liners were too clumsy to make effectual auxiliary warships, but that fast ships of medium size could render good service. In the North Sea, the British armed merchant cruisers proved more successful than obsolescent Royal Navy protected cruisers, which were withdrawn from patrol duties after severe gales revealed their limitations. The passenger ships invariably proved more seaworthy in adverse conditions.

Unfortunately for the Kaiserliche Marine, the German merchant navy could muster far fewer large passenger ships than Britain, an imbalance that mirrored the shortage of German light cruisers. Many of the largest

liners (*Vaterland*, for example) were abroad on the outbreak of war. Some were unfortunate enough to be caught in unfriendly ports and were promptly interned. Others were too far away from home to be readily armed.

Though some of the ships were very fast—*Kaiser Wilhelm der Grosse* and *Kronprinz Wilhelm* had each once held the Blue Riband—they consumed fuel profligately, presented immense targets and mustered large crews. In the absence of suitable fast passenger ships with gross registered tonnages of 10,000–15,000, therefore, the Germans decided to convert selected cargo ships for commerce raiding. By selecting modern vessels of this comparatively plentiful type, the navy gained strength, small size, extraordinarily economical steam engines, and thoroughly anonymous appearance. The ships were fast enough to overhaul many British merchantmen and sufficiently powerful to compete against small unarmoured warships with a chance of success. Thus the exploits of *Möwe* and *Wolf*, under the command of Nikolaus zu Dohna-Schlodien and Karl August Nerger respectively, owed much to the 'Emden Tradition'.

The earliest cruises in 1914—particularly by *Emden* and *Karlsruhe*—successfully dislocated British seaborne trade. However, the effects were soon forgotten once the first group of raiders had been hunted down.

Yet the exploits of *Emden* excited such interest that von Müller and his crew were as well known throughout

the British Empire as they were in Germany. Many Britons were genuinely saddened when the final battle with *Sydney* cost the lives of so many of *Emden*'s crewmen. *The Times* recorded—

"...that the *Emden* finally found her inevitable end was received in this country with great relief... Since the first September days when the *Emden* appeared in the Gulf of Bengal, her daring and enterprising actions have shown her to possess attributes which people with England's naval tradition must admire. Cut off from all logistical support and with poor prospects of gathering supplies, the *Emden* travelled alone on the wide oceans of the world. Her destiny was an honourable fight for existence. She lead it with a daring which friend and foe alike had to acknowledge. If she ran out of coal, she caught a coal ship; if she required provisions, she fetched them from merchant ships on the high seas. Nevertheless, there is no charge of violence that can be held against her. As reported, Commander von Müller treated the crews of his captured ships nobly and even-handedly. At no time did he destroy human life unnecessarily. As far as is known, he strictly obeyed and observed the code of international law. At Madras, he let his crew fire only on oil tanks and the fort... We are pleased that the cruiser *Emden* was finally destroyed, but we acknowledge Commander von Müller as a valiant and chivalrous adversary. We hope that his life was spared, for should he come to London, we would prepare for him a rousing welcome. Our sea-faring nation knows how to admire a daring and resourceful seaman, and there are few events in the new history of sea warfare which are more remarkable than the bright career of the little *Emden*."

Raiders were sent out again at the end of 1915, the most famous being *Möwe*, but the sporting attitude that had greeted the rampages of *Emden* had been replaced by a grimmer outlook. Though Nikolaus zu Dohna-Schlodien undertook two very successful cruises in *Möwe*, the tonnage of shipping destroyed being second to none at the cost of comparatively few lives, his activities drew only scorn from sections of the British Press hardened to the ritual slaughter on the Western Front. One periodical drew attention in May 1916 to the issue of decorations to the crew of *Möwe*, under the headline 'Pirates One and All! Officers and Men of the Notorious German Raider *Moewe* Decorated with the Iron Cross', stating that—

'It is paradoxical that while the German military authorities have commandeered church bells, door handles, kettles, and even copper coin... to transmute into the inevitable bullet, Iron Crosses for valour, more or less, are still rained upon whole battalions of soldiers and sailors. The officers and men of the notorious German raider *Moewe*... all... appear to have been decorated with the emblem of Christianity, for piracy on the high seas. It will be recalled that the *Moewe* was alleged by the Germans to have sunk no more that fifteen allied steamers before finding its way back to home waters.'

The protracted cruise of Karl August Nerger and *Wolf*, which was particularly interesting for the imaginative use of a reconnaissance seaplane, was overshadowed by the colourful exploits of Felix von Luckner in the sailing ship *Seeadler*, which enjoyed a less successful voyage before coming to grief on a reef in the Pacific Ocean. However, by 1917, annihilation of merchantmen by submarines was applying more effectual strangulation to mercantile trade than the solitary raider.

It can be said, on balance, that the achievements of the surface raiders scarcely repaid the effort and ingenuity invested in them. However, most of the raider-captains adhered to the spirit of the Cruiser Rules (if not always the detail) and were chivalrous men. And though the sinking of more than a hundred ships was a severe blow to British pride, particularly in 1914–15, the cost in human terms ultimately greatly favoured the Allies.

It can never be said that the story of the surface raiders lacks drama.

The pages that follow are divided into sections dealing with each of the major raiders individually. Criteria for selection, however, are often somewhat subjective. The principal yardstick is simply that at least one merchantman should have been taken during the course of a protracted ocean cruise. Thus, major warships such as *Scharnhorst* and *Gneisenau* have been omitted— whereas the small cruiser *Nürnberg*, which was sent specifically to wreck the wireless-telegraphy and cable station on Fanning Island, is included. Details of lesser raiders will be found in Appendix One.

> **Left:** Karl August Nerger ('x') of *Wolf*, after his investiture with the Pour le Mérite. Bayerisches Hauptstaatsarchiv, Staudinger Sammlung.
>
> **Below:** Karl von Müller of *Emden*. Author's collection.

**Above:** Summer 1914. The brand-new cruiser *Karlsruhe* departs from Germany for Port-au-Prince, Haiti. This ship was the most successful of the cruiser-raiders excepting *Emden*, but was destroyed by an internal explosion on 4 November 1914. Photograph by courtesy of the Bundesarchiv, Koblenz, negative no. 134–B307.

**Below:** typical of the large British armoured cruisers involved in the search for the raiders were the ships of the Devonshire class, one member of which—HMS *Hampshire*—was prominent in the chase of *Emden*. Author's collection.

# CAP TRAFALGAR

31 August–14 September 1914; no victims.
This converted passenger liner was destroyed in a classic ship-to-ship engagement
before embarking on her raiding career.

**Type:** Hilfskreuzer. Also known as *Hilfskreuzer B.*
**Builder:** AG 'Vulcan', Hamburg (yard no. 334). Equipped at sea
by the gunboat *Eber*, August 1914.
**Owner:** Hamburg–Südamerikanische Dampfschifffahrts-
Gesellschaft, Hamburg.
**Launch date:** 31 July 1913.
**Maiden voyage:** March 1914.
**Commissioned:** 31 August 1914.
**Crew:** approximately 20 officers and 310 men.

**Dimensions**
Registered tonnage (grt): 18,805.
Design displacement: 23,640 tonnes.
Full-load displacement: about 25,700 tonnes.
Overall length: 186·0 metres.
Waterline length: 179·8 metres.
Beam: 21·9 metres.
Full-load draught: about 8·5 metres.

**Weapons**
Guns: two 10·5cm SK C/88 L/40.
Maximum range of main armament: 12,200 metres.
Lesser guns: six 3·7mm automatic cannon and small arms.
Munitions: 300 10.5cm shells.
Armour protection: only on gun shields.

**Performance**
Powerplant: two vertical four-cylinder triple expansion steam
engines and a low-pressure exhaust turbine, supplied by
fourteen boilers. Three propeller shafts.
Boiler pressure: 15at (221psi).
Coal bunkerage: 5,100 tonnes.
Speed, trials: 17·8 knots (15,900ihp).
Speed, service maximum: 17 knots (15,000ihp).
Range: 7,100 nautical miles at 15 knots.

Typical of the many large German passenger liners
trading at the outbreak of the First World War was the
Hamburg–Südamerikanische *Cap Trafalgar*, a new ship
built by AG 'Vulcan' of Hamburg. After making her
maiden voyage in March 1914, she had enjoyed barely
five months of service before the hostilities began.

The liner was immediately interned in Buenos Aires,
but the Argentine authorities could find nothing
untoward in her cargo. After unloading, *Cap Trafalgar*
sailed for Montevideo at 17:00 on 17 August amidst
rumours that she had taken on large quantities of extra
coal and timber baulks to reinforce her gun positions. A
careful search failed to find any trace of the suspicious
load, so the liner took on 1,600 tonnes of coal and sailed
for home on 23 August.

Though the intent had been declared to travel by way
of Las Palmas, this was pure fiction; instead, the liner met
the gunboat *Eber* and 4,570grt Hamburg–Amerika Linie
steamship *Steiermark* (AG 'Vulcan', Stettin, 1911), which
had travelled westward from Lüderitz bay in Deutsch
Südwestafrika. The gunboat, old and slow, had no
fighting value; consequently, her two 10·5cm and six
3·7cm guns were transferred to *Cap Trafalgar* and the
captain of the gunboat, Korvettenkapitän Wirth, assumed
command of the converted liner. To aid deception, the
dummy third funnel was removed. The British had
plenty of large two-funnel ships, but very few with three.

The new warship cruised off the eastern coast of
South America for ten days without success, then hove-to
off Ilha da Trindade with her two colliers. The 4,624grt
steamship *Eleonore Woermann*, owned in peacetime by
the Woermann Linie but seconded to the La Plata Etappe,
had been built by Blohm & Voss of Hamburg in 1902;
*Berwind*, an 1893-vintage product of Blumer & Company
of Sunderland, had a gross registered tonnage of 2,589
and was owned in 1914 by the New York & Porto Rico
Steamship Company.

At about 10:55 on 14 August, lookouts aboard *Cap
Trafalgar* made out the smoke of an approaching ship.

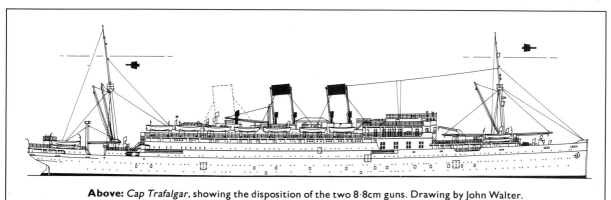

**Above:** *Cap Trafalgar*, showing the disposition of the two 8·8cm guns. Drawing by John Walter.

**Above:** the liner *Cap Polonio*—later, slightly larger but otherwise comparable with *Cap Trafalgar*. The black funnels indicate that this photograph was taken prior to 1920. Author's collection.

As large ships were rarely encountered off Trindade, Wirth assumed that the newcomer was most probably British and likely to be a man-of-war. He immediately ordered his colliers to cast off and telegraphed the engine room to raise power as quickly as possible. *Berwind* steamed off north-westward, whilst *Eleonore Woermann* made off to the south east.

The newcomer was *Carmania*, a Cunarder which had been hastily converted into an armed merchant cruiser. She had arrived in Liverpool on 7 August 1914, three days after Britain had declared war on Germany. No sooner had the passengers disembarked than the ship was docked. The cargo was unloaded, coal was substituted, and eight old 4·7-inch guns were fitted into mounting-plates on the shelter deck; all that was required was to cut away part of the bulwarks to allow the guns the maximum arcs of fire. A Barr & Stroud range-finder and searchlights were fitted on the bridge, whilst makeshift magazines were added in the holds. Thin armour plate and woven-rope matting protected vital areas; much of the flammable panelling in the cabins, public rooms and between-decks was removed. A speaking-tube system was installed to improve communications from the bridge to the gun positions, engine room, and an auxiliary steering room

aft. The pristine white upper works were hastily painted grey, and the red-bodied funnels were given a coat of black. By 14 August, the new armed merchant cruiser was ready for service.

*Carmania* had been commanded in peacetime by Captain John Barr of the Cunard Line, who was now given the rank of Commander in the Royal Naval Reserve. The new skipper was Captain Noel Grant RN, assisted by Lieutenant Edmund Lockyer RN. Grant retained as many of the liner's engine-room crew as possible—they, after all, were most familiar with the machinery—whilst men of the Royal Naval Reserve and the Royal Fleet Reserve arrived to man the guns. A party of Royal Marines formed a boarding party.

The merchant cruiser left the Mersey early in the morning of 16 August 1914, coaled in Bermuda on 22 August, and came under the command of Rear-Admiral Sir Christopher Cradock.

On 11 September, *Carmania* and the cruiser HMS *Cornwall* were sent to intercept the German collier *Patagonia*, which was known to have been working in league with *Karlsruhe* and was reportedly about to leave either Pernambuco or Bahia Blanca. The first sweeps revealed nothing suspicious, so Grant and *Carmania* were despatched to inspect Ilha da Trindade.

Soon after 05:30 on 14 September, lookouts aboard *Carmania* saw the outline of the island. At 11:03, they reported that a large two-funnelled merchant ship was apparently lying at anchor. It was *Cap Trafalgar*. As the British ship bore down on the island, two colliers made off rapidly in opposite directions. Grant determined on caution; he had no way of knowing whether *Karlsruhe* or some other warship lurked around the other side of the island waiting for *Cap Trafalgar* to lure him into a trap. *Carmania* steered straight for the centre of the island, until Grant decided to keep his quarry to starboard and turned to pass Trindade on its south-western side.

*Cap Trafalgar*, meanwhile, had backed out from land, came about and then made off after *Berwind*, which had already disappeared over the horizon. The scene was set for a historic action. One of the participants subsequently recorded that the duel—

'was unique, because the combatants were not men-of-war in the proper sense of the word, and the first of its kind on record, as it [had] never been known before that a floating hotel fitted with miniature artillery should meet and engage on the high seas a similar adversary similarly armed'.

The British ship gave chase. *Cap Trafalgar* was powered by triple-expansion steam engines driving three propeller shafts and had a service speed of about seventeen knots; the British ship, marginally larger, had the first set of Parsons turbines to have been fitted in a vessel of her size. Her service speed was generally listed as about

sixteen knots by 1914, though Grant hoped that eighteen could be raised when required; twenty knots had been recorded on her measured-mile trials in the Clyde in 1905.

In peacetime, the German ship had a black hull, white uppers, and red-topped white funnels; now she was painted grey, with red-topped black funnels, and presented the general appearance of a British Union-Castle vessel. However, the disguise was not good enough to fool the experienced officers aboard *Carmania*. *Cap Trafalgar* still had the characteristic lines that marked a product of a German shipyard. The removal of the third funnel persuaded Grant and Barr, after some debate, to tentatively identify *Cap Trafalgar* as *Berlin* of Norddeutscher Lloyd. They were agreed that the mystery ship was hostile.

Suddenly, *Cap Trafalgar* swung to starboard and headed across *Carmania*'s bow. At 12:00, Grant sent his men to general quarters, simultaneously hoisting the White Ensign to both mast-heads as well as on the jack-staff at the stern. *Carmania* was then sailing south-west by south, whilst *Cap Trafalgar* set a course roughly west south-west. At 12:03, at a range of 8,500 yards, the forward port gun on the British ship put a single shell across the bows of the German ship; *Cap Trafalgar* ran up the German ensign and joined battle. The first shells from her starboard gun fell short and ricochetted over *Carmania*. The next overshot, but only by fifty yards.

The ships were now on converging courses and the

**Below:** the Cunard liner *Carmania*, from a postcard produced prior to 1914. Artist: Charles Turner. Author's collection.

range had come down to about 4,500 yards by 12:10. The 4·7-inch guns on the port side of *Carmania* obtained hit after hit. But so did the 10·5cm gun of the Germans. A British officer reported that—

'of the first few shells that hit the *Carmania* on the port side, three made holes, large and small, at and above the waterline; one tore through the stewards' quarters and embedded itself in the protective sandbags outside the engine-room; another made havoc in the galley on the lower deck and carried away the fire-main leading to the fore part of the ship and bridge, with well-nigh disastrous results . . .'

Another account captured the tenor of the action:

'. . . we turned into demons, in a scene that had turned diabolical. Screaming shrapnel, returned by salvos of common shell; splinters everywhere; lumps of iron; patches of paint; a hurricane of things flying; hoarse shouting and unintelligible sounds from dry throats. Men discarding garments, and laughing with delirium—over all a white pall [of smoke] hiding the ghastly work. What matter that a shot cannoned down the after-companion and laid low three of the whip party? Volunteers were not wanting to close in the breach and keep up a brisk supply of ammunition to the hungry guns. Or that a shot glanced off the shield of No.I gun, past the officer in charge, and blew away the neck of a corporal of Marines passing projectiles along the deck . . . ?'

The German ship was making eighteen knots at this juncture, whereas *Carmania* could raise only about sixteen owing to serious condenser problems. As *Cap Trafalgar* closed to less than 4,000 yards, she began to use her lighter guns, deliberately raking *Carmania*'s bridge. One 10·5cm shell then destroyed the British fire-control position, forcing the guns to revert to local operation. Ventilators, rigging and boats were shot away by accurate fire.

Seeing that *Cap Trafalgar* had developed a slight list to starboard, Captain Grant ordered all the guns that could be brought to bear to concentrate on holing the enemy on the waterline. Korvettenkäpitan Wirth continued to hammer away at *Carmania*'s bridge in an attempt to interrupt the chain of command. Soon the British ship was on fire beneath the bridge, which had to be abandoned in favour of the after steering position whilst the damage-control parties worked frantically to extinguish the flames.

Mindful of the damage being done to his ship by an enemy almost directly off his port beam, Grant turned sharply to starboard, momentarily enabling him to bring all four starboard guns and the aftermost port gun to bear on *Cap Trafalgar* as *Carmania* circled away to neutralise the effect of the 3·7cm cannon. At 12:28, having completed the circle to run before the wind and thus prevent the conflagration in the bridge spreading aft before it could be contained, *Carmania* cut through the course of *Cap Trafalgar*. The German ship was now ahead and to starboard of the Cunarder, but had suffered badly in the preceding ten minutes. A fire had begun forward, steam was issuing skyward from severed pipes, and the list to starboard had become more obvious.

*Cap Trafalgar* then turned slightly to port to run parallel with *Carmania*, allowing the port-side 10·5cm gun to bear. The range lengthened to about 5,500 yards by 12:30, and had become 6,900 yards by 13:00. By 13:30, *Cap Trafalgar* was outside the 9,300-yard maximum range of the British guns. It seemed as though she was getting away. Her gunners continued to fire sporadically.

Then the German ship ceased firing altogether and turned back towards Ilha da Trindade. Her list had increased markedly; speed suddenly slackened. Soon the engines had stopped altogether and boats were being lowered. *Carmania* also stopped firing, allowing as many men as could be spared to fight the fires that still raged beneath the bridge.

Boats lowered from the German steamship began to pull hard for *Berwind*, which had returned to stand by; eighteen officers and 292 men, some of whom were seriously injured, were subsequently transferred to *Eleonore Woermann* and landed in Buenos Aires on 15 September. At 13:50, *Cap Trafalgar* capsized to starboard and sank in 20°10′S 29°51′W. An eye witness—believed to have been Lieutenant M.F. Murray RNR—described how the—

'wounded ship, distant from us about five miles, suddenly lurched over on the starboard beam ends, looking for all the world as if she were about to turn turtle. Lower and lower she went, until her huge funnels were level with the water . . . and dense clouds of smoke and steam escaped from all parts of her as from a volcano in a high state of activity. As quickly again, the mammoth righted herself; down, down went her bows; up, up her stern till quite one-third of the hull stood upright to the sky, then with a majestic plunge she slid beneath the waves, game to the end, for the last to disappear was the German flag'.

Sixteen of her crew, including Korvettenkapitän Wirth, had been lost with her.*

Captain Grant and his men, after raising three cheers for their own deliverance and the gallantry of their foe, took stock of their situation. *Carmania* had been hit nearly eighty times and there were holes everywhere. Five of her crew had been killed outright, four were dying of wounds, and 27 others had injuries of varying severity. The bridge was a total shambles; virtually all navigational equipment had been destroyed, whilst communications depended on megaphones, whistles, voices and runners.

A course was set for the Arquipélago dos Abrolhos (Abrolhos Rocks) with the help of a few instruments which had been salvaged from the fire. Requests for assistance were transmitted to any Royal Navy ships in the vicinity. Finally, escorted by the cruisers *Bristol* and *Cornwall*, the battered merchant cruiser entered the Abrolhos anchorage at about 08:00 on 15 August 1914.

Engineers from *Cornwall* managed to repair the worst of the damage, navigation instruments were obtained, and *Carmania*—escorted by the merchant

* As claimed in German literature. The ferocity of the action and the extent of casualties aboard *Carmania* suggest that they are understated.

cruiser *Macedonia*—headed out for Gibraltar on 17 September. There Grant and his crew were feted as heroes, as the action was soon compared with the most famous ship-to-ship engagements in history. Noel Grant himself subsequently stated that the duel—

'was the only one throughout the war in which an equal, or as a matter of fact a slightly inferior, vessel annihilated the superior force ... *Cap Trafalgar* was a faster ship and [her guns] outranged ours by 2,000 yards.

I am therefore very thankful that the German Captain came in towards me and put up a perfectly fair fight, instead of taking advantage of these two great assets ...'

One of the most important results of the action was that the coaling station on Ilha da Trindade was thereafter denied to German raiders. A message was soon transmitted from the Nauen wireless-telegraphy station warning the German raiders active off South America that all existing coaling stations had been compromised, adding appreciably to the difficulties faced by *Karlsruhe* and *Dresden* in particular.

*Carmania* and *Cap Trafalgar* were not quite as evenly matched as contemporaneous British claims suggested. Indeed, it is worth pondering why Wirth pressed the fight at all if he knew *Carmania* to be the slower ship. He must

also have known, though Grant did not, that the British ship was better armed—her eight 4·7-inch guns, four on each beam, were more than a match for *Cap Trafalgar's* two 10·5cm guns, one of which was mounted on the port side of the forecastle ahead of the foremast and the other in an embrasure cut in the starboard side of the main deck ahead of the mainmast.

Wirth also had six 3·7cm automatic cannon, but these were only useful at ranges of less than 4,000 metres.

The German skipper had had two alternatives: to run if he had the speed, or to fight at extreme range in the knowledge that his two 10·5cm guns outdistanced the old British 4·7-inch type by nearly 3,000 metres. In the event, by pursuing a converging course, he was drawn into combat at a range that initially favoured *Carmania*; by the time *Cap Trafalgar* had closed to a range at which the 3·7cm cannon could be effectual, sufficient waterline damage had apparently already been done to the German ship to cause her subsequent loss.

A theory was subsequently advanced that failure to secure the starboard coaling ports hastened *Cap Trafalgar's* sudden demise by allowing water to enter unchecked when the list to starboard became critical, but remains unproven.

**Below:** the epic duel between *Cap Trafalgar* (background) and *Carmania*, from a painting by Charles Turner. By courtesy of Trafalgar House plc.

# DRESDEN

I August 1914–14 March 1915; four victims (12,960grt).
A conventional light cruiser, remembered more for protracted evasion of the Royal Navy
than for the efficacy of her raiding career.

●◆●

Type: Kleine Kreuzer.
Authorisation: as 'Ersatz Pfeil', 1906.
Builder: Blohm & Voss, Hamburg (yard no. 195).
Laid down: 1906.
Launch date: 5 October 1907.
Commissioned: 14 November 1908.
Crew: 18 officers and 343 men.
**Dimensions**
Design displacement: 3,664 tonnes.
Full-load displacement: 4,268 tonnes.
Overall length: 118·3 metres.
Waterline length: 117·9 metres.
Beam: 13·5 metres.
Full-load draught: about 5·5 metres.
**Weapons**
Guns: ten SK 10·5cm C/88 L/40.
Maximum range of main armament: 12,200 metres.
Lesser guns: eight 5·2cm SK L/55 (see text below).
Torpedo tubes: one submerged on each beam.
Munitions: 1,470 10·5cm high-explosive and thirty 10·5cm
shrapnel shells; five 45cm C/03 torpedoes.
Armour protection: deck 20–30mm, conning tower 100mm,
gun-shields 50mm.
**Performance**
Powerplant: two sets of Parsons direct-drive turbines, supplied
by twelve boilers. Four propeller shafts.
Boiler pressure: 16at (235psi).
Coal bunkerage: 400 tonnes normal, 860 tonnes maximum.
Speed, trials: 25·2 knots (18,880shp).
Speed, service maximum: 24 knots (15,000shp).
Range: 3,600 nautical miles at 14 knots.

*Dresden*, only the third turbine-powered light cruiser to be accepted by the Kaiserliche Marine, was a sister-ship of the more famous *Emden*. Manufacturers Blohm & Voss had obtained a sub-licence from Deutsche Parsons Marine AG 'Turbinia' of Mannheim, a subsidiary of Brown, Boveri & Co. The decision to rely on the Parsons-type turbines instead of rivals such as the Curtis variety produced by AEG and AG 'Vulcan' proved to be correct; ultimately, the Blohm & Voss machinery proved more effectual than most German-made rivals.

The principal weakness of steam turbines was their complexity—those in *Dresden* had no fewer than 605,000 blades ranging in length from 14mm to 220mm—and the skill required during construction. *Dresden* had two sets of machinery driving four propeller shafts, with the high pressure turbines coupled to the outer shafts. The low pressure and reversing units were placed inboard. The cruiser was also the first large ship to combine turbine propulsion with the use of superheated steam.

Trials were run in the Spring of 1907 in Eckenförde bay. Unfortunately, during a run on the measured mile, a brick-laden wherry cut across *Dresden*'s bows as the

cruiser was working up to full speed. The ram bow of the cruiser scythed into the port side of the sailing ship, which sank to leave the mast, sails and rigging draped over the warship's bow. Before the engines could be braked by counter-pressure, the propellers entangled in the flotsam of the sinking wherry and the starboard outer propeller bracket was bent backward. *Dresden* had to be returned to Blohm & Voss for repairs to the propeller, shaft and stern.

Though the crew of the wherry had been rescued, *Dresden* gained a temporary reputation as a jinxed ship. However, the turbines had run surprisingly freely and, apart from the difficulties of reversing, which was basically a handling problem, no untoward experiences had occurred. The cruiser soon showed herself to be handy and manoeuvrable.

The upper section of the forecastle breakwater folded in *Dresden* but was fixed in the otherwise similar-looking *Emden*. The latter ship lacked an external steam pipe on her middle funnel, and the pipe on the side of the forefunnel was cranked rather than upright.

The searchlight platform on *Dresden*'s mainmast was two metres higher than that aboard *Emden* and, at least until the beginning of 1910, *Dresden* had only a single searchlight on the mast platforms instead of two.

*Dresden* was despatched to the South American station, where she remained on duty in the summer of 1914 under the command of Erich Köhler. In June, however, the brand-new cruiser *Karlsruhe* (q.v.) was sent out under Fregattenkapitän Lüdecke as a replacement.

Born in Dirschau in Westpreussen on 5 February 1873, Fritz Lüdecke had entered the navy in April 1890. After serving with III. Matrosen-Abteilung in the fortress of Helgoland (1896–1903), he was promoted Kapitänleutnant and posted to the battleship *Wettin* as gunnery officer. Promotion to Korvettenkapitän then followed in 1908, whereupon Lüdecke returned to administrative duties as a member of the staff of I. Geschwader. On 25 April 1912, he was appointed to the command of SMS *Dresden* as Fregattenkapitän.

In December 1913, however, Lüdecke exchanged command of *Dresden* with Fregattenkapitän Erich Köhler—who had been supervising trials of the new cruiser *Karlsruhe* since June. Once the new warship had been commissioned, Fritz Lüdecke was instructed to hone the efficiency of her new crew and oversee the voyage to the South Atlantic Station; there he was to regain his old command, *Dresden*, and bring her home for a refit.

**Above:** the starboard midships of *Dresden*. Note the embrasured gun abaft the bridge and the stupefying complexity of the rigging. By courtesy of the Bundesarchiv, Koblenz, negative no. 134–C132.

On 25 June 1914, the two warships exchanged captains in Port-au-Prince, capital and principal seaport of Haiti. On 28 June, *Dresden* left Port-au-Prince bound for the Danish island of St Thomas. There Lüdecke would find one of the best natural harbours in the Caribbean, administration offices of the Hamburg–Amerika line, and a communications centre for Etappe operations in times of war. St Thomas was far more than a routine port-of-call.

Lüdecke left St Thomas on 31 July, steaming north eastward for the Ilhas dos Açôres (Azores), the English Channel and a home port. However, after travelling only a few miles, a message was relayed to *Dresden* from Puerto Rico. Owing to the deteriorating political situation in Europe, the German captain was ordered to abandon his homeward voyage and await further instructions. Realising that this would involve attacking merchant shipping, Lüdecke turned around and headed for the sea lanes off the eastern seaboard of South America.

Here, off the Brazilian port of Pará (now Belém) on 6 August 1914, he stopped the 4,072grt British steamship *Drumcliffe*, built on Wearside in 1905 and managed by Joseph Chadwick & Sons for the Steam Ship 'Drummond' Co. Ltd. Registered in Liverpool, she was bound in ballast for Trinidad from Buenos Aires. Though it was obvious

from her height out of the water that *Drumcliffe* was not heavily laden, Lüdecke sent over a boarding party.

Discovering that Captain Evans was accompanied by his wife and small child, and mindful of the absence of cargo, Lüdecke decided to allow the British ship to proceed once her wireless-telegraphy installation had been destroyed. He had no tender in which prisoners could be accommodated, and the presence of British prisoners—particularly a woman and child—would be a great inconvenience aboard the warship.

Eighty minutes after dismissing *Drumcliffe*, the Germans came across 4,252grt *Lynton Grange*, completed in 1912 by the Northumberland Ship Building Co. Ltd of Newcastle upon Tyne, owned by the Houlder Line and registered in West Hartlepool. Bound for Barbados and Britain in ballast, she had little to offer *Dresden* and was released; so, too, was 3,325grt *Hostilius* of the British & South American Steam Navigation Co. Ltd, which hove into sight just as *Lynton Grange* was getting underway.

Captain Jones and crew of *Hostilius* steadfastly refused to sign a declaration that, as a condition of their parole, they would take no further part in the war; others amongst the German raider commanders would have taken this as a personal insult and scuttled the offending ship on the spot, but not the phlegmatic Lüdecke.

*Hostilius* was released at 19:30, leaving *Dresden* to continue south-eastward to the Atol dos Rocas. The cruiser was now desperate for coal. However, the Etappe system provided *Corrientes* of the Hamburg–Südamerikanische Dampfschifffahrts-Gesellschaft; the 3,775grt steamship, built by Blohm & Voss of Hamburg in 1894, had been waiting in Maranhão harbour for summons to a rendezvous. On the afternoon of 8 August, in the little harbour of Jericocoara, *Dresden* took on 570 tonnes of coal before proceeding northward of Atol de Rocas and the tiny island of Fernando Noronha. Off the latter, best known for its prison colony and a wireless-telegraphy station, Lüdecke called up the 7,676grt Hamburg–Amerika Linie steamer *Baden*, built by Bremer Vulkan of Vegesack in 1913, which had been waiting patiently in Pernambuco harbour with a 12,000-tonne cargo of good-quality steam coal.

The steamship arrived off Atol dos Rocas on 13 August, lashed to the cruiser and began transferring coal. No more than a few hundred tonnes had been shipped when the keeper of the Rocas lighthouse asked the identity of the warship. The Atol dos Rocas was neutral territory, and the keeper's duties were clear; if *Dresden* was a belligerent, she was entitled to take on only sufficient coal to take her to the nearest friendly harbour. Lüdecke bluffed that his command was the Swedish cruiser *Fylgia*—which *Dresden* superficially resembled— in need of some urgent repairs to her engines. The ruse worked very well; it was too much to expect a mere light-house keeper to be able to distinguish between the two warships. However, Lüdecke immediately sent *Corrientes* into Pernambuco to recruit *Prussia* (3,557grt) and *Persia* (3,554grt). Owned by the Hamburg–Amerika Linie, the sister-ships had been built by Flensburger Schiffbau-Gesellschaft in 1912 and 1914 respectively.

On 21 August, *Dresden* headed south from Atol dos Rocas in company with *Baden* and *Prussia*. Now that he was accompanied by suitable tenders, Lüdecke could sink any British ship he encountered. The first victim was 3,352grt *Hyades*, encountered about 180 nautical miles north-east of Pernambuco bound under Captain James Morrison for Las Palmas with a cargo of grain. The ship—a near-sister of *Hostilius*—was owned by the British & South American Steam Navigation Co. Ltd and had been completed by Blumer & Co. of Sunderland in 1900. The crew of the British ship was transferred to *Prussia*, and *Hyades* was promptly scuttled.

Later the same day, *Dresden* came across 4,847grt *Siamese Prince* of the Prince Line Ltd (Sunderland Shipbuilding Co. Ltd, 1911) but, surprisingly, for reasons that are still not clear, Captain Anderson was allowed to proceed after an examination of his papers. *Prussia* was despatched southward to Rio de Janeiro to land the crew of *Hyades*, whilst Lüdecke steered a false course until the tender had finally disappeared over the horizon.

His true destination was Ilha da Trindade, reached on 19 August. There *Dresden* met the old gunboat *Eber* (which had wisely left Cape Town on 30 July to avoid meeting Royal Navy patrols) and the merchantman *Steiermark*, which had steamed across the Atlantic from

**Below:** the Houlder Line tramp *Lynton Grange*. By courtesy of Laurence Dunn.

**Above:** *Katharine Park*, with her engines aft, was regarded as a very advanced ship in her time. By courtesy of Laurence Dunn.

Lüderitz bay in Deutsch Südwestafrika. The Etappe La Plata 5,199grt *Santa Isabel*, built by Bremer Vulkan of Vegesack in 1914 for the Hamburg–Südamerikanische Dampfschifffahrts-Gesellschaft, had also arrived with a cargo of bullocks, oil, shovels and coal sacks. The merchantman had left Buenos Aires on 9 August on the pretext of sailing for Togoland.

The gathering of colliers allowed *Dresden* to replenish fuel and supplies at leisure. On 22 August, the cruiser began the run southward to the sea lanes leading to the Rio de la Plata. On 26 August, the 4,223grt 1912-vintage British steamship *Holmwood*, owned by F.S. Holland of London, sailed blithely into the trap and was taken 160 nautical miles south south-west of Cabo Santa Maria Grande. *Holmwood* was carrying coal from Newport to Bahia Blanca, but *Dresden* had more fuel than she needed and sank the collier with explosive charges once the crew had been transferred to *Baden*.

By the time the cruiser had reached the southern margins of Brazil, she encountered the 4,854grt *Katharine Park*, built by Napier & Miller of Glasgow in 1903 and owned in 1914 by the Park Steam Ship Co. Ltd. Captain William Paterson was heading his ship for New York with an American-owned cargo, which Lüdecke could not destroy without making his masters in Berlin liable for its value. Consequently, the crewmen of *Holmwood* were rowed over from their incarceration in *Baden*, and *Katharine Park* was despatched with orders to land the Britons at her first port of call. This proved to be Rio de Janeiro, gained on 30 August.

*Dresden*, meanwhile, headed farther south. On 31 August, she hove-to in Gill Bay to coal and attend to

the turbines. Work was completed by 2 September, whereupon the leisurely voyage southward in company with *Santa Isabel* resumed. The tender was sent into Punta Arenas harbour on 4 September to transmit information to Berlin, Buenos Aires and Valparaiso. On 7 September, the Punta Arenas wireless-telegraph station received a coded cable from Berlin telling Lüdecke to round Cape Horn to disrupt British trade along the western seaboard of South and Central America in collusion with the cruiser *Leipzig*, which would proceed southward from Guaymas in the Golfo de California. *Santa Isabel* immediately left Punta Arenas to pass the news to Lüdecke.

*Dresden* battled gamely around Cape Horn as the weather deteriorated and the bleak landscape assumed its most forbidding mantle. On 10 September, Lüdecke dropped anchor in Orange Bay (Bahia de Nassau) on Hoste Island. Crewmen were allowed ashore in groups, though there was little to do other than stretch legs and leave the customary calling cards. Discovering a board proudly bearing a list of ships' names, the men of *Dresden* could not resist the temptation to add their own ship to the list. This natural reaction was a grave mistake; even though the officers accompanying the men realised what had been done and erased the evidence as best they could, traces of the visit remained.

On 16 October 1914, *Dresden* left her anchorage in Orange Bay in company with *Baden*, seeking to join the ships of the Kreuzergeschwader. On 18 October the Germans encountered the 8,075grt mail steamer *Ortega* of the Pacific Steam Navigation Company, homeward bound around the Horn from Valparaiso under

**Above:** *Ortega* of the Pacific Steam Navigation Company, renowned for escaping the clutches of *Dresden*. By courtesy of Laurence Dunn. **Below:** *Dresden* running trials in 1908. Note that she still has only a single searchlight on each mast, subsequently altered to two apiece. By courtesy of the Bundesarchiv, Koblenz, negative no. 134–B286.

the command of Captain Douglas Kinneir. Lüdecke immediately gave chase, but the liner—completed by Harland & Wolff Ltd of Belfast in 1906—made off at speed into the uncharted Nelson Strait. Though *Ortega*'s nominal maximum speed was only fourteen knots, superhuman efforts by her stokers, aided by the prevailing currents, raised nearer eighteen from her twin quadruple expansion steam engines.

Lüdecke set off in pursuit, firing his forward guns ineffectually. However, mindful of his orders to join von Spee and fearful of damaging or—worse still—losing his ship in the uncharted waters, the German captain soon abandoned the chase.

*Ortega* disappeared into the mist to steam cautiously along the channel to landward of Queen Adelaide Archipelago, preceded by ship's boats taking soundings. Emerging unscathed into the Straits of Magellan by way of Smyth Channel, Captain Kinneir found the Chilean destroyer *Almirante Lynch* searching for survivors of what local authorities had presumed to be a disaster.

*Dresden* and *Baden* steamed northward to Bahia San Quentin in the Golfo de Penas, where a coaling stop was made. Finding no British shipping in the area, Lüdecke then steered out toward the island of Más Afuera. There, on 3 October, effectual wireless communications were established with von Spee. Lüdecke was immediately summoned to a rendezvous off Easter Island.

Easter Island—it had been discovered on Easter Day in 1722—was populated by about 250 people in 1914, including an Englishman and a German, managers of the only ranch and the solitary tobacco plantation respectively. Nominally a Chilean possession, nowadays also known as the Isla de Pascua, Easter Island was so remote from the civilised world that the outbreak of war had passed unnoticed. The last visit of a large ship had occurred in June 1913, when a schooner named *El Dorado* had put in for repairs. The yacht *Mana* had arrived in March 1914, bringing British archaeologist Scoresby Routledge and his wife, but had already left to collect provisions from Chile when the Kreuzergeschwader arrived in the morning of 12 October 1914.

Easter Island had never seen such an assembly of men-of-war: *Scharnhorst, Gneisenau, Nürnberg* and their colliers, reinforced by the arrival of *Dresden*—being unceremoniously towed by *Baden* to conserve fuel. Finally, *Leipzig* arrived from her cruise off the American coast. Von Spee had calculated correctly that news of war had not filtered through to his remote port of call. Mrs Scoresby Routledge gave letters to be posted back to England, and Mr Edmunds, manager of the ranch, sold the Germans a large quantity of fresh meat.

The secret was not kept for as long as the German admiral had hoped. The poor state of the ships was notable, and the native population soon detected the absence of the gifts and bonhomie customarily dispensed by visitors. Eventually, the truth was imparted to the German tobacco planter by German crewmen. But there was nothing the Britons could do.

On 18 October, having flouted Chilean neutrality for a week, the warships raised their anchors and headed away south-eastward for Más Afuera. Reaching the island on 26 October, von Spee coaled hurriedly and headed for Valparaiso on the next day.

The presence off the western seaboard of Chile of *Dresden*, at least, was now known to the Royal Navy. Rear-Admiral Sir Christopher Cradock K C V O C B, flying his flag in the armoured cruiser *Good Hope*, had been ordered by the Admiralty to patrol the area between Punta Arenas and Valparaiso. Cradock's protestations that his ships were not powerful enough to defeat von Spee were ignored back in London. By 5 October, therefore, Cradock had visited Orange Bay twice. Though no German ships had been encountered, British shore parties found the evidence thoughtlessly left by *Dresden*.

Cradock was determined to settle an old score and assembled his squadron about three hundred miles north of Valparaiso, just as, on 26 October, von Spee and the Kreuzergeschwader were coaling off Más Afuera. Cradock's fleet comprised his flagship, HMS *Good Hope*, under the command of Captain Philip Francklin M V O; the armoured cruiser *Monmouth*, Captain Frank Brandt; the light cruiser *Glasgow*, Captain John Luce; and the armed merchant cruiser *Otranto*, Captain Herbert Edwards.

In their wisdom, the Lords of the Admiralty had denied Admiral Cradock the reinforcements he had been seeking, preferring instead to form a new squadron to patrol the South Atlantic under the command of Rear-Admiral Archibald Stoddart, flying his flag in the armoured cruiser *Carnarvon*. The new formation included the powerful cruiser *Defence*, which had originally been ordered to join Cradock; all the luckless admiral would receive would be the obsolescent pre-dreadnought battleship *Canopus*, commanded by Captain Heathcoate Grant. Unfortunately, despite being armed with four 12-inch guns, *Canopus* was too slow to be of much use.

In the early afternoon of 26 October, Cradock sent *Glasgow* southward to Coronel with important despatches to be transmitted to London. As she passed Valparaiso, *Glasgow* picked up the distinctive signals of a German warship—*Leipzig*—at a range estimated from the strength of reception to be about 150 miles. Cradock intended to wait for his cruiser to return from Coronel, then assemble his squadron, including *Canopus* when the battleship eventually appeared, and head immediately for Más Afuera. At the very moment this plan was finalised, von Spee and the Kreuzergeschwader were themselves coaling at Más Afuera!

On her trip south to Coronel, *Glasgow* intercepted many messages that were clearly intended for German ships. Most were coded and had to be handed over to the British consulate in Coronel for transmission to London, where the code had been broken. However, Captain Luce of *Glasgow* informed Cradock of the volume of wireless traffic even though the individual messages could not be deciphered. Cradock in turn issued orders for a search to begin; *Glasgow* was to cruise off Coronel harbour, whilst awaiting replies from London, and *Otranto* was despatched to Puerto Montt. There she detected the presence of *Leipzig* in the vicinity of Coronel.

The die had been cast. Though a message had been despatched from London telling Cradock to wait for reinforcements—*Defence* was eventually ordered to join him without delay—the squadron was already at sea. Owing to the limited range of even the best and most powerful 1914-vintage transmitters, information had to be relayed from station to station. There is no evidence that Cradock ever received the last communications sent from London.

Cradock ordered *Glasgow* to meet *Good Hope* and the other British warships about fifty nautical miles west of Coronel on 1 November 1914. By 12:00, the squadron had assembled; at 14:05, Cradock ordered his ships to steam on slightly diverging courses, with *Glasgow* proceeding north-east by east—nearest the Chilean coast—and *Good Hope* steaming north-west by north at ten knots. But approaching from the north was von Spee.

The Kreuzergeschwader was sailing in line astern, *Scharnhorst* leading *Gneisenau* and *Leipzig*. *Dresden* trailed a few miles behind, whilst *Nürnberg*, which had been detached, was struggling to make up ground on *Dresden*. At 16:15, the lookout in the fore-top of *Scharnhorst* reported ships to westward; at 16:20, *Glasgow* spotted the Germans. Realising that he was outnumbered, Captain Luce ordered the three ships in his charge to reverse course whilst the flagship *Good Hope*, which had disappeared over the horizon, was recalled. Von Spee pursued a parallel course to the south of Luce until, at 17:47, the British warships regrouped around their flagship. By 17:50, the British were steaming south by east to the north of the Kreuzergeschwader, which was travelling south by west.

The courses of the squadrons gradually converged as each admiral sought to gain a tactical advantage. Cradock wished to join battle before the sun set, so that the German gunners would have the glare in their eyes; von Spee, conversely, attempted to postpone the action until the sun had disappeared entirely. This would leave Cradock's ships silhouetted by the afterglow whereas the German vessels would be hard to distinguish against the Chilean shore. As Cradock was limited by the speed of *Otranto*, which could manage little more than seventeen knots in the heavy seas, von Spee held the upper hand. At 19:03, by which time *Dresden* had reached station behind *Leipzig*, von Spee opened fire at a range of 11,000 metres.

*Scharnhorst* was soon engaging *Good Hope* whilst *Gneisenau* exchanged fire with *Monmouth*, leaving the smaller German cruisers to snipe at *Glasgow*. Cradock

had already ordered Captain Edwards of *Otranto*, whose offensive power was limited, to effect an escape.

The battle was one-sided. The German ships not only outnumbered their rivals, but their crews had been honed by two years of service and a concentrated programme of gunnery exercises on their way across the Pacific Ocean. By contrast, only *Glasgow* amongst the Royal Navy warships was crewed by professional sailors. *Good Hope* and *Monmouth* had both been commissioned at the beginning of the First World War, and were manned largely by a core of regulars supported by reservists or volunteers recruited amongst the fishermen of Scotland.

The parsimonious attitude of the Admiralty had ensured that virtually no gunnery practice had been undertaken; now the novice gunners had to learn their trade fighting for their lives. The fresh southerly wind gave a head sea, heavy enough to interfere with the fighting of the casemated main-deck guns of *Good Hope* and *Monmouth*, seaworthy ships though they both were in many other respects.

Unfortunately for Cradock, a single shell from the third salvo fired by *Scharnhorst* wrecked the forward turret of *Good Hope*. The two 9·2-inch guns of the British flagship had represented the principal threat to von Spee, but this had been halved virtually before Cradock had opened fire. The 6-inch guns of the British ships—*Good Hope* had six, *Monmouth* had fourteen and *Glasgow* had two—had neither the power nor the penetrating capabilities to damage the armour of the large German cruisers. As each of von Spee's armoured cruisers had eight 21cm guns, the disparity in offensive capability was greatly in German favour.

Systematically, *Scharnhorst* and *Gneisenau* soon inflicted tremendous damage on their rivals. *Glasgow*, meanwhile, had managed to shake off *Leipzig* and *Dresden*, both of whom were wary of the power of the British ship's two 6-inch guns, and was trying to engage the large German cruisers in a bid to protect the stricken *Monmouth*.

At about 19:50, the British flagship *Good Hope* exploded; when the smoke had cleared, no trace of her or her crew remained. *Monmouth* had also been ravaged; most of her guns were silent, fires raged internally. Yet still the battered cruiser showed the will to fight. As *Scharnhorst* and *Gneisenau* closed to pound her into submission, a sudden squall obscured *Monmouth*. When the weather cleared, she was nowhere to be seen.

By 20:00, realising that the battle was finally lost, John Luce had turned *Glasgow* northward. He had sustained only a half-dozen hits—none of particular significance—and determined to use his superior speed to escape to fight another day. Luce chanced upon the battered *Monmouth*, down by the head, listing, burning, but still under way. Ordering Captain Brandt to make his escape northward, Luce turned his warship north-west and then west north-west before heading off into the

**Above:** the ill-fated armoured cruiser *Good Hope*, lost with all hands during the Battle of Coronel. By courtesy of Ray Burt.

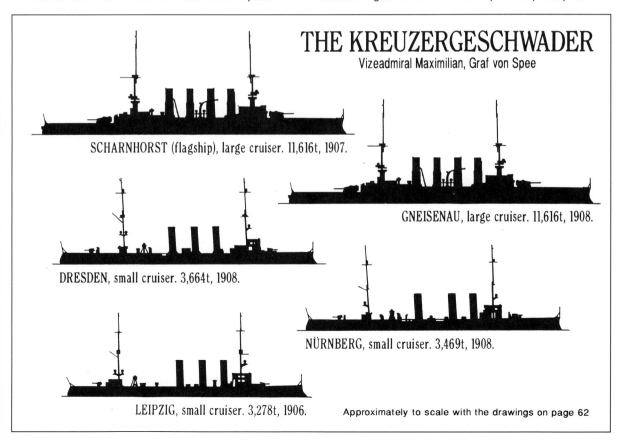

# THE KREUZERGESCHWADER
## Vizeadmiral Maximilian, Graf von Spee

SCHARNHORST (flagship), large cruiser. 11,616t, 1907.

GNEISENAU, large cruiser. 11,616t, 1908.

DRESDEN, small cruiser. 3,664t, 1908.

NÜRNBERG, small cruiser. 3,469t, 1908.

LEIPZIG, small cruiser. 3,278t, 1906.

Approximately to scale with the drawings on page 62

Pacific Ocean at top speed. *Glasgow* made a final signal to *Monmouth* at 20:30, but received no reply.

*Dresden* had played little part in the battle; neither Lüdecke nor Haun, commanding *Leipzig*, reported any damage. The German cruisers searched fruitlessly for *Glasgow* and *Otranto*, but both had escaped.

No survivors of *Good Hope* were ever found; the waters were bitterly cold, and the sweeps made by the German light cruisers were undertaken more with a view to locating *Glasgow* or *Monmouth* than a rescue mission.

Eventually, in the fitful moonlight, the laggardly *Nürnberg* found *Monmouth* heading slowly north by east with so great a list that the guns on the port side could not be brought to bear. Deliberately, *Nürnberg* shelled *Monmouth* until the armoured cruiser capsized slowly to port at 21:28. The White Ensign had flown to the last.

Though crewmen could be seen sliding down the overturning hull into the water, nothing was done aboard *Nürnberg* to help. This was partly due to the fact that the boats aboard the German cruiser had been filled with water as a precaution against fire and could not be launched quickly; in addition, however, Kapitän z.S. von Schönberg gave no specific orders to stop. Von Spee's despatch after Coronel suggested that lookouts on *Nürnberg* had sighted smoke and were expecting to face *Glasgow* or another enemy warship, but, like the British flagship *Good Hope*, *Monmouth* was lost with all hands.

The German ships returned to Más Afuera to coal from two captured sailing ships—one French, with 3,500 tonnes, and one Norwegian with 2,634 tonnes. The steamship *Sacramento* had brought additional supplies from San Francisco. *Dresden* and *Leipzig* were sent into Valparaiso on 11 November to replenish supplies, send despatches and give their crews a brief respite ashore. On Sunday 15 November, after Divine Service aboard the ships, the Kreuzergeschwader set course for Bahia San Quentin.

On 16 November, Lüdecke captured the steamer *North Wales* (3,691grt) of the North Wales Shipping Co. Ltd of Newcastle upon Tyne, built by Readhead of South Shields in 1905. Captain George Owens was outbound from the Tyne with a cargo of coal. After the crew had been transferred to the 6,982grt DDG 'Kosmos' tender *Rhakotis* (Blohm & Voss, 1907), supplied by the Etappe Südwestamerika station in Valparaiso, the tramp was sunk. A month later, the Britons were landed in Callao.

By 21 November, von Spee had concentrated his forces—five cruisers and five colliers—in Bahia San Quentin. Finally, on 26 November, a course was set to pass Cape Horn instead of taking the easier, but much more visible, passage through the Straits of Magellan. Accompanied by *Baden*, *Santa Isabel* and *Seydlitz*, judged the most seaworthy of the five supply vessels, the Kreuzergeschwader set off for the Atlantic Ocean and an attack on the Falkland Islands. On 2 December 1914, *Leipzig* (q.v.) captured the 1,844grt barque *Drummuir* and

the squadron hove-to off Picton Island whilst coal was transferred to supply ships. *Drummuir* was scuttled on 6 December, whereupon the Kreuzergeschwader resumed its homeward voyage. This unforeseen delay would ultimately prove fatal.

At 02:00 in the morning of 8 December 1914, lookouts in *Scharnhorst* spotted the Falkland Islands ahead and, at 05:00, *Gneisenau* and *Nürnberg* were detached northward to reconnoitre. Von Spee, aware that units of Stoddart's squadron might be in Port Stanley harbour, did not wish to be caught unaware.

The morning dawned clear and crisp, a beautiful day in a month in which, in the South Atlantic, rain squalls and mist were much more normal. However, if the German ships could see the Falkland Islands, then the islanders could see the German ships. The wife of a sheep farmer living at Port Pleasant, some twenty miles from Port Stanley, was the first to notice the approach of *Gneisenau* and *Nürnberg*. Realising that the vessels were a lighter shade of grey than Royal Navy warships, she sent her maid and houseboy to the top of the nearby hill to get a better view. When the boy reported that there were five ships, Mrs Felton telephoned the governor's house shortly after 07:45.

As the two warships approached Port Stanley, lookouts on *Gneisenau* saw wisps of smoke. Dismissed as the inhabitants burning sensitive material in the face of a German invasion, they were actually the warning signals of the Falkland Island Volunteers. Aboard *Gneisenau*, Kapitän z.S. Maerker regarded the sight of mastheads in harbour as proof that he had found *Otranto* and *Glasgow*.

Increasing speed to prevent the British warships escaping, Maerker headed for the harbour mouth. As he approached, to his surprise, several other masts were reported; then came a surprising amount of smoke, even though only two sets of masts seemed to be moving.

At 09:15 the forward turret of the battleship *Canopus*, which had been run aground on a mudbank and very carefully camouflaged, fired the first two rounds of the Battle of the Falkland Islands. Practice shells, loaded the previous night, landed a half-mile short of *Gneisenau* and skipped across the water towards the armoured cruiser. Almost immediately, two live rounds fell only a couple of hundred yards away, the colossal splashes shaking the Germans out of their leisurely progress. Then Maerker saw something that chilled his blood: the towering tripod masts of two very large warships.

*Gneisenau* frantically signalled the information to *Scharnhorst*, whereupon von Spee ordered Maerker to return. Had he only known what confusion existed in the harbour, the gallant German admiral may have decided that the best course of action was to attack immediately; most of the British ships had arrived merely two days previously, and only HMS *Kent*, acting as guard ship, was under way. The indolence had been such that Captain Luce, alerted by *Canopus*, had to fire a gun to attract the attention of the flagship *Invincible* to signals flying from *Glasgow*'s yard-arm.

Catching the British warships at anchor had been von Spee's only chance of inflicting such great damage that the Kreuzergeschwader could escape in the confusion. Instead, the German squadron turned to run, unaware of what would pursue it. As the British warships filed out of harbour, the worst fears of the most pessimistic German sailor were realised.

Mortified by the loss of Cradock and his men at Coronel, and by the effect it had had on public opinion in Britain, the Admiralty had sent the battle-cruisers *Invincible* and *Inflexible*. In addition to *Glasgow* and *Kent*, there were *Glasgow*'s sister-ship *Bristol*, *Kent*'s sister *Cumberland* and the large armoured cruiser *Carnarvon*. By 10:30, all the British ships excepting *Bristol* were forming in line off the harbour mouth. The chase was on.

Von Spee harboured no grand illusions about his plight. Just as he had been able to out-manoeuvre and out-gun Cradock at Coronel, so he was now inferior to Sturdee. Though *Scharnhorst* and *Gneisenau* were stoutly constructed and well-armed by armoured cruiser standards, their 21cm guns were no match for the 12-inch Mark X guns of the battle cruisers, which fired a 850lb shell to a distance of 20,750 yards. He also knew that the British ships had been designed to hunt down and destroy cruisers, and thus that they were not only fast but very seaworthy. Any hope he had entertained that his opponents would be slowed by high seas vanished with the beautiful weather.

*Invincible* and *Inflexible* were soon surging towards the Kreuzergeschwader at 25 knots. Sturdee slackened speed at 11:15 to allow *Carnarvon* to keep pace, giving the Germans respite. Shortly afterward, realising that von Spee was preparing to fight, the British admiral ordered his big ships to close with the enemy at full speed. Von Spee, his options limited, had decided to join battle in the slender hope of disabling at least one of his opponents. Captain Phillimore of *Inflexible* opened fire at 12:55 at a range of 16,000 yards, shells of the first salvo landing only about a hundred yards behind the straggling *Leipzig*. Von Spee realised that his light cruisers were vulnerable to even a single hit from such a large shell, ordering first *Leipzig* and then also *Nürnberg* and *Dresden* to flee independently as best they could.

The opening phases of the battle resolved into a contest between *Scharnhorst* and *Gneisenau* on one side and *Invincible* and *Inflexible* on the other. Von Spee opened fire at 13:30, but the outcome was predictable; though the German gunners shot with great accuracy and commendable courage, their shells were too light to harm the battle cruisers. The British 12-inch guns, meanwhile, wreaked havoc. By 16:00, the German flagship was a flaming wreck, still firing sporadically, but greatly down by the head and listing sharply to port. At 16:10 she rolled onto her beam ends, then sank at 16:17 in 52°40'S 55°51'W. There were no survivors.

The British battle-cruisers, joined by *Carnarvon*, switched their attention to *Gneisenau*. Eventually, after a spectacular pounding—Admiral Sturdee later suggested

---

**Below:** the battle-cruiser *Invincible*, flagship of Admiral Sturdee during the Battle of the Falkland Islands. From a coloured postcard (no. 1523) by Gale & Polden Ltd, c.1914. Author's collection.

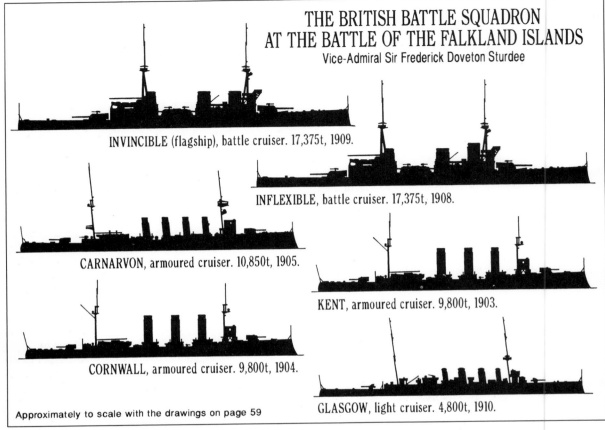

# THE BRITISH BATTLE SQUADRON AT THE BATTLE OF THE FALKLAND ISLANDS
## Vice-Admiral Sir Frederick Doveton Sturdee

INVINCIBLE (flagship), battle cruiser. 17,375t, 1909.

INFLEXIBLE, battle cruiser. 17,375t, 1908.

CARNARVON, armoured cruiser. 10,850t, 1905.

KENT, armoured cruiser. 9,800t, 1903.

CORNWALL, armoured cruiser. 9,800t, 1904.

GLASGOW, light cruiser. 4,800t, 1910.

Approximately to scale with the drawings on page 59

that the German ship had been hit at least fifty times by 12-inch shells alone—*Gneisenau* fired her last round at about 17:45. She heeled slowly over to starboard and sank at 18:02 in 52°40'S 56°20'W.

The light cruisers headed off at more than twenty knots, with *Dresden* in the lead, *Leipzig* to starboard and *Nürnberg* to port. They were pursued by *Glasgow*, *Kent* and *Cornwall*. Travelling at 27 knots, *Glasgow* began to overhaul her enemies and eventually opened fire from her forward 6-inch gun at a range of 12,000 yards in an attempt to force the German ships to change course. This challenge was initially refused, until the range shortened to 10,000 yards and *Glasgow* could use her forward 4-inch guns as well.

The captains of *Leipzig* and *Nürnberg* then turned their ships to bring their broadsides to bear, seeking to damage *Glasgow* but simultaneously losing way.

Straining boilers and machinery to breaking point, the two British armoured cruisers slowly closed the range. When *Leipzig* and *Nürnberg* finally regained their course, *Dresden* had pulled farther away and presented Captain Luce of *Glasgow*, the senior British officer, with a problem. *Glasgow* alone had the speed to pursue and perhaps even overhaul *Dresden*, but the weather was already deteriorating. If Luce set off in pursuit, there was

no guarantee that *Kent* and *Cornwall* would be able to catch *Leipzig* and *Nürnberg*. Reluctantly, he decided to harry the two slower German ships to delay them until the more powerful armoured cruisers could engage.

The destruction of *Leipzig* and *Nürnberg* is related in greater detail in the relevant chapters.

*Dresden*, true to form, was simply running away at top speed, proving capable of maintaining 25–26 knots. As even *Glasgow* would have been hard pressed to catch her, Luce's decision to let *Dresden* go was undoubtedly correct—but left a score that would take time to settle.

HMS *Bristol* and the merchant cruiser *Macedonia* pursued and then sank the supply ships *Baden* and *Santa Isabel*, but *Seydlitz* escaped with the crew of the sailing-ship *Drummuir*. The Britons were released when the steamship, running short of fuel, put into Bahia Blanca on 14 February and was interned by the Brazilian authorities.

The destruction of the Kreuzergeschwader, together with the contemporaneous loss of *Emden* and *Karlsruhe*, brought a perceptible change in the balance of power. German influence began to wane throughout South America in general, and in Chile in particular. Universal internment of German merchant shipping began; the interpretation of neutrality became stricter. No longer could the Etappe system function properly; in any case, only the ineffectual *Dresden* remained at large off South America by Christmas 1914. The only places where coal and assistance were forthcoming in quantity were Las Palmas and Tenerife in the Canary islands (Islas Canarias). In the days before German submarines wrought havoc, the Royal Navy had shown its value by restoring confidence in maritime trade.

The high-speed flight from the Falkland Islands had cost *Dresden* so much of her coal that Lüdecke became fretful. He considered setting course for Picton Island, where a Kreuzergeschwader rendezvous had been arranged should the warships become separated, but it had been obvious that von Spee would be fortunate to survive the battle and anxious wireless requests failed to raise a German collier. The obvious coaling station was Punta Arenas, but British warships were expected to be guarding the eastern entrance to the Straits of Magellan.

Lüdecke elected to inch his way through dangerous Cockburn Channel, anchoring on 10 December in Sholl Bay to the south of Punta Arenas. A shore party was despatched to find fresh water and cut as much wood as possible to eke out the coal supplies that had dwindled to little more than 150 tonnes.

A large warship was seen approaching in the morning of 11 December. Alarm that the four funnels signified a British cruiser abated when the shape materialised into a Chilean vessel coming to warn Fritz Lüdecke that transgressions of neutrality beyond the permissible 24 hours would not be tolerated. The German captain was not likely to risk antagonising his hosts; in addition, the threat posed by *Almirante Condell* was not to be taken lightly. Commissioned only a few months previously, the large British-built destroyer was not much smaller than the German cruiser. Measuring 320ft overall and capable of more than thirty knots, she also carried a potent punch in the shape of six modern 4-inch guns. At 10:00 on 12 December, therefore, *Dresden* raised steam and headed for Punta Arenas.

Fortunately for Lüdecke, news of the ultimatum presented by the captain of *Almirante Condell* had not reached the authorities in Punta Arenas. The 6,656grt collier *Minnesotan* had been chartered by the Etappe Nordamerika from the American-Hawaiian Steamship Company of New York, but her skipper refused to transfer fuel to a belligerent. Fortunately, the 5,152grt steamship *Turpin* of the Roland Linie, an 1899-vintage product of Furness, Withy & Co. of West Hartlepool, handed over 750 tonnes of coal briquettes. At 22:00 in the evening of 13 December, *Dresden* steamed out of Punta Arenas harbour. At 03:00 in the morning of 14 December, HMS *Bristol* arrived. Fritz Lüdecke's luck still held.

Though the cruiser had escaped from the Royal Navy once again—owing more to luck than judgement—shortage of fuel was causing concern. Destruction or capture of so many of the German merchantmen, and the

insistence of once-friendly authorities on increasingly strict implementation of neutrality, caused the Etappe system to deteriorate rapidly. In addition to the loss of *Baden* and *Santa Isabel* during the Battle of the Falkland Islands, *Memphis* was interned in Coronel, *Luxor* in Callao and *Mera* in Montevideo.

*Patagonia* had been seized by an Argentine warship for breaching neutrality, whilst *Josephina* had been caught by *Carnarvon* at the eastward entrance to the Straits of Magellan on 6 January 1915. Admiral Stoddart had sent her into Port Stanley under the supervision of the boarding party.

The steamship *Eleonore Woermann*, which had landed the survivors of *Cap Trafalgar* (q.v.), was discovered at 14:30 on 6 January by HMS *Australia*. Hampered by a damaged propeller, the battle-cruiser was unable to chase the fleeing freighter as effectually as she would have done in favourable circumstances; finally, still ten miles behind her quarry as sunset approached, *Australia* loosed off a single 12-inch shell. The proximity of the 150-foot splash caused *Eleonore Woermann*'s captain to heave-to immediately. His ship had been despatched southward from Buenos Aires to wait in the vicinity of Puerto Santa Elena for instructions from the Kreuzergeschwader, and had been seeking *Dresden*.

Admiral Patey decided to sink the ship and her cargo of coal once the crew had been taken off. But the Germans were nothing if not resourceful. Von Spee had previously sent the steamship *Amasis* to await instructions in Fox Bay, south south-east of Punta Arenas, and an attempt was to be made to tranship fuel from *Minnesotan*. In addition, *Sierra Cordoba* was travelling south from Montevideo to help *Dresden*.

Punta Arenas was the principal port and centre of trade in the tip of South America. So much of the town's population made a living from the shipping trades—often indirectly, by producing meat, wool or hides—that many German sympathisers were to be found. Some assistance took the form of provisions; often it was simply a matter of reporting movements of the British warships.

The Royal Navy conducted a meticulous search of many bays, channels and islands in a vain attempt to find the fugitive German cruiser. But *Dresden* seemed to have vanished into thin air. Not until after the war did the reason become clear. Many Admiralty charts were based on surveys undertaken by Charles Darwin and the crew of the *Beagle* during the nineteenth century. They provided a sound basis, but lacked detail. No survey had ever been made of Barbara Channel, which lay between the two largest islands west of Tierra del Fuego and the archipelago of islands stretching from Cape Horn to the western exit of the Straits of Magellan.

Yet Fritz Lüdecke, with uncharacteristic bravado, had simply steamed southward through Estrecho Magdalena and Cockburn Channel to Hewett Bay at the south western end of Barbara Channel. Here the cruiser finally encountered the collier *Amasis* of DDG 'Kosmos' and Etappe Peru. The 7,224grt steamship, completed by Flensburger Schiffbau-Gesellschaft in 1914, was loaded with good quality steam coal.

On 19 December, Lüdecke learned that the La Plata Etappe had despatched the 8,226grt *Sierra Cordoba* of Norddeutscher Lloyd (AG 'Vulcan', Stettin, 1912) with an additional 1,600 tonnes of coal. Realising that he could now risk sending *Amasis* to retrieve the coal in *Minnesotan*, Lüdecke ordered the steamer into Punta Arenas harbour on 20 December. Unfortunately, not only did the captain of *Minnesotan* maintain his neutral stance but the Chileans also detained *Amasis* as an auxiliary warship. When the British presence forced *Sierra Cordoba* to hide in Estrecho Magdalena, Lüdecke was again reduced to collecting firewood.

Then came bad luck. On 26 December, one of *Dresden*'s boats, despatched on a foray for wood and fresh water, chanced upon a French auxiliary yacht named *Galileo*. Tattoos had revealed the true nationality of the Germans, despite their protestations and denials. When the news was reported to Lüdecke. He knew that it would just as speedily reach the Royal Navy and elected to move *Dresden* immediately. On 27 December, guided by the steam pinnace, the cruiser entered what is now known as Christmas Bay or Seno Navidad—but was then, obligingly, marked as land on British charts.

By use of boats and ultimately by chartering the small Chilean steamer *Esplorador*, Lüdecke contrived to maintain his secret. The French hunter had reported *Dresden*'s position to the British consul in Punta Arenas, who had in turn informed both Admiral Stoddart and the

Admiralty. But the consensus was that no such location could exist. The Punta Arenas pilots denied it, though some Britons suspected them of pro-German sympathies; the Admiralty pointed to the misleading charts as proof that there could be no suitable anchorages. Though Stoddart searched Cockburn Channel with the cruisers *Carnarvon* and *Bristol*, he failed to proceed westward. This lack of vigilance enabled *Sierra Cordoba* to join *Dresden* on 19 January 1915.

Lüdecke was now in a stronger position, but well aware that it could only be a matter of time before he was discovered. Requests for assistance relayed back to Berlin brought forth only advice to proceed eastward into the Atlantic, coal off Lavendeira reef, and then set a homeward course for Germany. This overlooked the fact that *Dresden* could not reach Lavendeira without refuelling, and also that the Royal Navy now had a tight grip on the eastern entrance to the Straits of Magellan.

Weighing the odds as carefully as he could, Lüdecke decided to leave the southern tip of South America and journey westward across the Pacific Ocean. The plan made sense; with the destruction of *Emden*, the Pacific area had been largely denuded of British warships. Merchantmen would be plentiful, and there would be colliers amongst them. The voyage would be an ideal means of restoring the morale of the German crew, which had declined in the wake of the disaster off the Falkland Islands and subsequent self-imposed exile.

Encouraged, Lüdecke despatched a lengthy message to Berlin on 3 February, asking for a collier to be sent to the Netherlands Indies. No reply was received until 10 February. It simply noted that chances of supplying coal

**Below:** the cruiser HMS *Kent*, veteran of the protracted search for *Dresden*. By courtesy of Ray Burt.

anywhere in the Pacific were slim owing to the loss of the German colonies and the activities of British, Japanese and allied warships. Lüdecke was advised to use the sailing-ship routes and meet a collier in 5ºS 36ºW.

On 28 January, however, a German otter-hunter had appeared in Christmas Bay to be given secret instructions for *Esplorador*. Early in February, the small Chilean steamer arrived under the guidance of a German pilot. Once the provisions had been safely transferred, the steamer was despatched to find a new hideaway for *Dresden* and *Sierra Cordoba*. This proved to lie between Isla Santa Inés and William Island, where the German ships dropped anchors on 5 February.

The telegram from Berlin was a disappointment, but Lüdecke had determined on his course of action and was not to be deterred. At 17:30 on 14 February, after despatching a request to be met by a collier in 37ºS 80ºW, Lüdecke took his ships out into the Pacific. His intention was to plunder the sailing-ship routes, for which the innocent-looking *Sierra Cordoba* was sent a hundred miles ahead of the cruiser to relay information. Yet the sea lanes seemed empty.

Not until 27 February did a prize materialise, when the barley-laden 1,694grt British three-masted steel barque *Conway Castle*—an 1893-vintage product of W. Pickersgill & Company of Sunderland—was taken 560 miles south west by west of Valparaiso. Owned by the quaintly-named "The Ship 'Conway Castle' Co. Ltd", she was sunk off Isla Mocha in 37º21'S 76º15'W after the crew had been transferred to the cruiser; a week later, *Dresden* sent the crew into Talcahuano aboard the Peruvian barque *Lorton*.

As coal ran short, Lüdecke had to transfer some of his own fuel to *Sierra Cordoba* before despatching the steamship into Valparaiso. In spite of the flagrant breach of neutrality, the Chilean harbour authorities allowed the tender to take on 1,200 tonnes of coal and leave again. The fragmentary Etappe system prepared many ingenious schemes to coal *Dresden*, but, in the end, Lüdecke had been left to live on his wits alone.

Intercepted wireless messages told the Royal Navy that La Plata Etappe had despatched the 6,653grt *Gotha*, built by Bremer Vulkan of Vegesack in 1907 for Norddeutscher Lloyd. The steamship had left Montevideo on 20 February to proceed to an appointed spot—37ºS 80ºW—sometime between 5 March and 30 March 1915. As all the other German cruisers in the southern hemisphere had been eliminated, Admiral Stoddart theorised correctly that *Dresden* would be the recipient of the coal. Yet operations were still dogged by sloth.

The search for the elusive German cruiser had been proceeding for weeks. Starting from her last reported position in a corner of Stokes Bay in 54ºS 72º40'W, *Kent*, *Glasgow*, *Bristol* and *Orama* had spent the last days of 1914 and the first weeks of the New Year searching every bay and inlet along the Straits of Magellan. German ships were reported in the straits on 4 February; near Punta Arenas in the middle of the month; and in Last Hope Inlet (Seno Ultima Esperanza) on 22 February. Each and every report had to be investigated, even though most of them were either misleadingly false or deliberately spurious. On 25 February, British Consul Millward of Punta Arenas, still smarting at the rebuff by the Admiralty of his information concerning *Dresden*'s whereabouts, had even chartered the yacht *Galileo* and ventured southward under the guidance of an Anglophile Chilean pilot.

Captain John Luce of *Glasgow*, the senior officer of the searchers, decided in conference with his fellow captains that *Dresden* still lay somewhere to the south of the Straits of Magellan. To penetrate into the many channels and inlets denied to larger ships, the steam launch of *Kent* was promptly armed with two torpedoes, a Maxim machine-gun, small arms and ammunition, and equipped with a short-range radio transmitter/receiver. The launch was christened 'HMS *Gillingham*' and placed under the command of Lieutenant-Commander Eric Wharton.

Captain Luce decided that *Glasgow*, *Kent* and *Gillingham* should make a search of Barbara Channel in the hope of flushing *Dresden* northward onto the guns of *Bristol* and *Orama* waiting at the northern exit of the channel into the Straits of Magellan. At 04:30 in the morning of 3 March, the sweep began. The warships filed cautiously by way of Estrecho Magdalena, Cockburn Channel and Adelaide Passage into the southern mouth of Barbara Channel. *Gillingham* searched inshore, but nothing was found. The ships then received a message that the collier *Gotha* had been ordered to a rendezvous in the Pacific, two hundred nautical miles west of Más Afuera. Luce determined to send *Kent* as well.

Captain John Allen of *Kent* was presented with the thorny problem of getting out of Barbara Channel as quickly as possible. He elected to try a passage through the narrows at the northern entrance, two miles long but no more than a hundred yards wide and requiring a sharp turn at the mid-point. As soon as the morning light was sufficient, *Gillingham* was sent to examine the designated channel. Wharton reported that it was barely navigable but that attempting a passage seemed worth the risk.

Ironically, soon after the navy had abandoned the search of the Straits of Magellan, Consul Millward aboard *Galileo* found the anchorage off Isla Santa Inés. Felled trees and water chutes at last gave him the satisfaction of not only knowing he had been right—this he had known all along—but also of being able to prove it to the Admiralty.

Saving a day by the risky exit through the Barbara Channel narrows was vital, as *Kent* had to steam more than a thousand nautical miles before reaching the point at which the German collier was expected to meet *Dresden*. The British cruiser approached the appointed spot as the morning of 7 March dawned, slowing to twelve knots to minimise emission of smoke from the funnels. To Allen's disappointment, no hostile ships materialised. He knew that *Kent* outgunned *Dresden*; he also knew that his engineers had raised 25 knots whilst pursuing *Nürnberg* during the Battle of the Falkland Islands. A repetition of this speed—two knots greater than *Kent* had achieved on her trials in the early 1900s—would minimise the advantage *Dresden* was believed to hold. A boarding party was mustered; practices were held. Still the Germans declined to appear.

The morning of 8 March passed calmly, allowing the British seamen to scrape clean as much of the cruiser's bottom as possible to improve speed through the water. At 15:30, Leading Signalman Hill, a lookout stationed in the fore-bridge, spotted a three funnelled ship heading northward across *Kent*'s bow at a distance of about 15,000 yards. Allen immediately rang for full speed ahead and *Kent* burst into life.

Before the British cruiser could swing out to cut across the newcomer's bow, the quarry turned away and began to accelerate. The British ship closed to 16,000 yards, but could make no progress; as the range of the old 6-inch guns was only about 11,000 yards, Allen could do nothing except wring as much speed as possible from his old cruiser. Woodwork was broken up to feed the furnaces; the canvas dodgers around the bridge were removed, as they made effectual air brakes; and all off-duty sailors were ordered aft to trim *Kent* another few inches by the stern. The output of the engine was gauged to be 26,000ihp, 4,700 greater than *Kent* had achieved on her trials, but the speed through the water of only 21·5 knots was restricted by her foul bottom. The funnels glowed red-hot; showers of sparks blasted from their tops. Still *Dresden* pulled away, and Captain Allen reluctantly called a halt to his gallant pursuit.

The decipherment of coded signals subsequently revealed that *Dresden* had been cruising at fourteen knots, awaiting *Sierra Cordoba* and *Gotha*. The chase had, however, put *Kent* in an awkward position. She was more than three hundred nautical miles from Coronel with merely 260 tons of coal in her bunkers. The only realistic choice was to head for harbour at a most economical cruising speed. *Kent* made port in the nick of time, with little more that forty tons in her bunkers.

John Allen did not know that his chase after *Dresden* had brought heartening results. Lüdecke had pressed on at 23 knots long after *Kent* had let him go, but the effort had strained machinery which was already badly in need of a lengthy overhaul. Boiler tubes began to fail and turbine blades had been damaged; though the cruiser's engineers strove to make effectual repairs, they were forced to report that *Dresden* would not be able to raise more than twenty knots until she reached a dockyard. At a stroke, the ambitious plan to sail across the Pacific Ocean had been dashed. No colliers were to be seen, and the ship that had once hidden so successfully had been trapped by fate just as freedom beckoned.

The most obvious course open to Lüdecke was to intern *Dresden* in the nearest neutral port, the Chilean naval station in Talcahuano being favoured. However, after intercepting messages from British warships, he set a course for the lonely Islas Juan Fernández. Shortly after 08:30 on 9 March 1915, *Dresden* dropped anchor in Cumberland Bay on the north side of Más á Tierra. Administered by Chile, the little island was inhabited only by a few hundred hardy souls.

In Cumberland Bay, Lüdecke received dispensation from the Kaiser to intern *Dresden* if he wished to do so. Then the lighthouse keeper, in his role as governor of the island, came over to insist that *Dresden* observe Chilean neutrality and leave within 24 hours. The German captain promptly invoked the clause that allowed him to make his ship seaworthy. *Dresden*'s engines and boilers were genuinely in need of repair, but, more importantly, Lüdecke needed to buy time until a collier could arrive. After sending some of his officers away in a small trading schooner on 12 March, Fritz Lüdecke could do little but wait nervously. He was well aware that it would not be long before the British reappeared. He also knew that, barring a miracle, he would not be able to fight.

As Lüdecke pondered, Assistant Paymaster Lloyd Hirst of *Glasgow*, who enjoyed a challenge, had finally decoded a signal sent by *Dresden* but intercepted by *Kent* during the abortive chase of 9 March. The cyphers revealed that the rendezvous was to be Juan Fernández.

In the morning light of 14 March 1915, *Glasgow*, *Orama* and *Kent* appeared off Juan Fernández, the first two approaching from westward and *Kent* from the east in case *Dresden* made a break for freedom. Lüdecke elected to fight as best he could though, with less than eighty tonnes of coal remaining, he could raise only enough steam to power the auxiliary machinery.

Smoke began to pour from *Dresden*'s funnels, seen aboard the British ships as the prelude to an escape attempt. Captain Luce determined to end the contest as soon as possible. After an hour spent searching for positions from which his ships could fire without threatening the small houses that dotted the shore of Cumberland Bay, Luce ordered his squadron to open fire. Surgeon-Commander Thomas Dixon aboard *Kent* recorded the brief encounter:

"She had run up the German flag at her fore and was getting up steam. I dived below again and shortly afterwards heard the order come through, 'Open Fire'. The first salvo brought back the old smell of the Falklands Battle, even down to us below, and filled the passages with smoke. Salvo after salvo roared out above us but in four minutes it was all over. The *Dresden* had hoisted a white flag and the crew were leaving in boats and going ashore . . . She was on fire after and amidships. Her after guns were dismantled. There was a huge hole in her starboard waterline aft, and her casemates were blown to pieces in two places."

*Glasgow* immediately lowered a rowing boat carrying Lieutenant-Commander Wilfred Thompson and staff

**Top:** smoke rises from the stern of *Dresden*, lying stationary in Bahia Cumberland with white flags flying from her fore-mast. Author's collection. **Above:** punctures in the hull of *Dresden*, seen here from HMS *Glasgow*'s boat, testify to the efficacy of the British shelling. Author's collection.

surgeon Alexander Wysard. As the boat crew pulled towards *Dresden*, they passed the German steam pinnace heading for *Glasgow* under an enormous flag of truce. Leutnant z.S. Wilhelm Canaris claimed that *Dresden* had been interned and that, therefore, the British had no right to open fire. Captain Luce would have none of the protestations, demanding nothing less than unconditional surrender to stop the British ships rejoining the action. Chastened, Canaris and his men scurried back to their ship. The Imperial ensign was run back up to the mast-head; finally, according to Surgeon-Commander Dixon—

"there was a big explosion on the *Dresden* and smoke came from her port-side forward. Just previous to this a man had been seen to rush up on deck from below and, waving away a boat that was coming alongside for him, dive into the water and swim off to the boat. Evidently they had blown up the magazine."

*Dresden* immediately began to settle by the bow. At about 12:15, she listed slowly to port and then sank in

**Above:** the last moments of *Dresden*. Author's collection. **Below:** Leutnant z.S. Wilhelm Canaris, members of the crew of *Dresden* and the German community in Valparaiso honour the seven men killed aboard the cruiser at a memorial service. Courtesy of the Bundesarchiv, Koblenz, negative no. 134–B2918.

33°37′S 78°49′W. The British ships immediately sent their surgeons ashore to tend to German sailors hurt in the brief action. Seven men had been killed and 29 were wounded. Excepting the fifteen most seriously injured, the survivors were subsequently taken to Valparaiso for internment. The island governor came aboard *Glasgow* to protest that *Dresden* had been interned, but Luce reminded him that *Dresden* had been flying her battle ensign and had trained her guns on the British squadron. The matter was settled amicably when Luce paid for damage caused to a trading schooner by shell fragments, and for the death of a thousand lobsters which could be distributed amongst the British warships.

The Chilean government, relieved by the demise of a most unwelcome visitor, subsequently protested about the violation of Chilean neutrality and accepted a full apology proffered by the British. It was no secret that German warships and auxiliaries had been abusing the trust for many months.

*Sierra Cordoba* was interned in Callao on 17 March, and *Gotha* reached Valparaiso three days later. The collier *Alda* had been prevented from reaching *Dresden* by a Chilean official travelling aboard her, and *Bangor* had been taken in the Straits of Magellan by HMS *Bristol*. The southern seas had finally been cleared of the cruiser-raiders and their tenders.

# EMDEN

1 August–9 November 1914; fifteen mercantile and two warship victims (66,023grt plus 3,491td).
The most famous of all the warship-raiders, destroyed in an epic ship-to-ship engagement with
HMAS *Sydney* in the Cocos Islands on 9 November 1914.

———◆◆◆———

Type: Kleine Kreuzer.
Authorisation: as 'Ersatz Pfeil', 23 December 1905.
Builder: Kaiserliche Werft, Danzig.
Laid down: 1 November 1906.
Launch date: 26 May 1908.
Commissioned: 10 July 1909.
Crew: 18 officers and 343 men.

**Dimensions**
Design displacement: 3,664 tonnes.
Full-load displacement: 4,268 tonnes.
Overall length: 118·3 metres.
Waterline length: 117·9 metres.
Beam: 13·5 metres.
Full-load draught: about 5·5 metres.

**Weapons**
Guns: ten 10·5cm SK C/88 L/40.
Torpedo tubes: one submerged on each beam.
Maximum range of main armament: 12,200 metres.
Lesser guns: eight 5·2cm SK L/55 (see notes below); one 6cm
short-barrelled SK L/21 landing gun; four 8mm Maxim
machine-guns; small arms.
Munitions: 1,470 10·5cm high-explosive shells and thirty
10·5cm shrapnel shells; five 45cm C/03 torpedoes.
Armour protection: deck 20–30mm, conning tower 100mm,
gun-shields 50mm.

**Performance**
Powerplant: two three-cylinder triple expansion steam
engines, supplied by twelve boilers. Two propeller shafts.
Boiler pressure: 16at (235psi).
Coal bunkerage: 400 tonnes normal, 790 tonnes maximum.
Speed, trials: 24·0 knots (16,350ihp).
Speed, service maximum: 23·5 knots (13,500ihp).
Range: 3,760 nautical miles at 12 knots.

Authorised as the 'Kriegsschiff der IV.Rangklasse, des
Kleinen geschützten Kreuzer "Ersatz Pfeil"...', *Emden*
took a long time to build. Her sister ship *Dresden*,
from the privately owned Blohm & Voss yard, was
launched and commissioned first—even though the
Danzig fitting-out basin was needed to accommodate the
armoured cruiser *Hertha* for an overdue rebuild. Finally,
Bürgermeister Fürbringer, mayor of Emden, christened
the new warship at noon on 26 May 1908.

The cruiser followed the pattern set by previous ships
bearing 'town' names, especially the preceding three-ship
Stettin class. She had three tall funnels, all circular in
section, and carried ten 10·5cm guns. Only the bow, stern

**Below:** *Emden* during a passage.
Author's collection.

and midships guns were shielded, the other main deck guns being carried in sponsons.

*Emden* was also originally equipped with eight 5·2cm guns, paired on deck above the sponsons with additional 'chasers' at bow and stern. However, wartime reports make no mention of these guns, even though photographs of the ship on trial and departing for the Far East show them clearly. No 5·2cm weapons are visible in pictures of the wreck, which suggests that they were unshipped either during the last cruise or—more probably—left behind in Tsingtau. The bow and stern guns were useless in heavy seas, and the efficacy of those mounted directly above the sponsons would have been reduced in combat by blast and smoke from the 10·5cm guns. There is no evidence that the 6cm landing gun was being carried when *Emden* met her end.

The greatest difference between *Emden* and her near-sister *Dresden* was that the former had twin reciprocating triple-expansion engines driving two shafts whilst the latter had two sets of Parsons steam turbines driving four propeller shafts. The principal external differences are summarised in the *Dresden* section. The most obvious was the position of the bow shields.

In a six-hour forced draught run on 10 August 1909, *Emden* exceeded 23 knots on 15,683ihp. A top speed of 24·014 knots was reached on the Neukrug Mile on 20 August. The most economical speed was deduced to be eight knots, though optimal cruising speed was reckoned to be twelve. Twenty knots could be maintained for long periods, though speeds as high as 23·85 knots could be obtained for short spurts by forcing the boilers.

Trials were successfully completed by 21 August, after which the new warship was selected to escort the imperial yacht *Hohenzollern* to Swinemünde. After the 'Kaisermanöver', fitting-out continued until the end of the year. Owing to the delayed completion, *Nürnberg* was sent to the Kreuzergeschwader to replace *Niobe*.

*Emden* was to proceed to the China Sea in the Spring of 1910 by way of Buenos Aires, to mark the centenary of the founding of the Argentine Republic. On 1 April, *Emden* mustered the crew of *Arcona*, which had returned for lengthy repairs, and readied for sailing. In the morning of 12 April 1910, freshly painted in tropical white with buff superstructure, the cruiser entered the Holtenauer Schleuse under the command of Korvettenkapitän Waldemar Vollerthun; an epic journey around Cape Horn had begun. The warship would never return to Germany.

*Emden* anchored in Porto Grande harbour on 22 April. By 10 May 1910, she had moved to Montevideo Roads and thence—on 18 May—to Buenos Aires in company with SMS *Bremen*. At the end of May, *Emden* left Buenos Aires to sail round Cape Horn, reaching Punta Arenas in the Straits of Magellan on 3 June and Valparaiso on 11 June; 23 June found the warship coaling in the harbour of Talcahuano, ready for a voyage that passed close by

Easter Island and Pitcairn before ending in Tahiti on 12 July 1910.

From Tahiti, Vollerthun and his crew sailed to Apia and a rendezvous with SMS *Scharnhorst*, flying the flag of Konteradmiral Gühler, commanding the Kreuzergeschwader. Finally, on 17 September, *Emden* made a grand entrance into her new home port of Tsingtau, where her pristine appearance and elegant lines soon gained the nickname 'Swan of the East'.

Korvettenkapitän von Restorff replaced Waldemar Vollerthun as captain of *Emden* on 23 November 1911, and was himself relieved at the end of May 1913 by Korvettenkapitän Karl von Müller.

Karl Friedrich Max von Müller, son of an army officer, was born in Hanover on 16 July 1873. After transferring from the army to the Kaiserliche Marine in 1891, he was promoted to Leutnant z.S. and Oberleutnant z.S. in 1894 and 1897 respectively. Von Müller was posted in 1898 to the cruiser *Schwalbe*, departing for a tour of duty in East Africa. Returning to Germany in 1900, he was briefly adjutant of I. Matrosen-Division before becoming second gunnery officer aboard the battleship *Kaiser Wilhelm II*.

Promoted to Kapitänleutnant in March 1903, von Müller served aboard *Kaiser Friedrich III* and *Kaiser Wilhelm der Grosse* before being appointed to the staff of the fleet commander, Admiral Prinz Heinrich von Preussen. Raised to the rank of Korvettenkapitän early in

**Below:** the cruiser *Emden*. Drawing by John Walter.

December 1908, Karl von Müller was seconded to the Reichs-Marine-Amt in Berlin. There he attracted the eye of Admiral von Tirpitz before finally realising his ambition of an independent command and ultimately, in August 1913, the rank of Fregattenkapitän.

On 20 June 1914, Vizeadmiral Graf von Spee, who had succeeded von Krosigk in March 1913, took the Kreuzergeschwader on a cruise into the Pacific. The ageing gunboats and *Emden*, in need of attention, were left in Tsingtau. Von Müller, as senior officer, was charged not only with protecting the port but also with implementing the contingency plans if war should begin. In the absence of the ships of the Kreuzergeschwader, von Müller had little at his disposal other than the gunboat *Cormoran*, docked for extensive repair, together with two large gunboats of the Iltis class. He told the river gunboats in China to scuttle, and their crews to return to Tsingtau; two additional 'Iltis' vessels were ordered back, together with the obsolescent torpedo-boat *S90*. The antiquated Austro-Hungarian cruiser *Kaiserin Elisabeth* subsequently arrived in Tsingtau roads, but could offer little in the way of additional offensive power.

Ordering two of the gunboats and *S90* to remain in Tsingtau at the disposal of the governor, Kapitän z.S. Meyer-Waldeck, von Müller slipped *Emden*'s moorings at 19:00 on 31 July 1914 and headed warily north-eastward for the Straits of Korea and the Vladivostok–Nagasaki

shipping lanes. At 04:15 on 4 August—the day on which Britain declared war on Germany—lookouts spotted the outline of a steamer, though the conditions were too poor to allow a positive identification.

Von Müller ordered *Emden*'s helmsman to shadow the steamship. By 06:00 improved visibility had revealed that the target had a plain black hull, a distinctive flush deck, and two black-topped buff funnels. Oberleutnant z.S. d.R. Julius Lauterbach—who had previously commanded the Norddeutscher Lloyd steamer *Staatsekretär Kraetke* on the Tsingtau–Shanghai–Port Arthur run—recognised the silhouette as a Russian mail steamer based in Vladivostok.

Two blank rounds were fired, but smoke clouding from the funnels of the Russian ship showed that she was intent on running. Von Müller increased speed to seventeen knots, but it was soon obvious that the mail packet was faster than had been thought and was frantically transmitting distress signals; von Müller immediately ordered his wireless operators to jam the Russian messages, as *Emden* accelerated to nineteen knots. As the cruiser gradually overhauled her quarry, the gunnery officer, Kapitänleutnant Erich Gaede, began to fire live rounds at the fleeing vessel. The tenth shell fell within a few metres of the stern of the Russian ship, drenching those on deck, whereupon the quarry turned broadside to the cruiser and hove-to in 35°5'N 119°39'E.

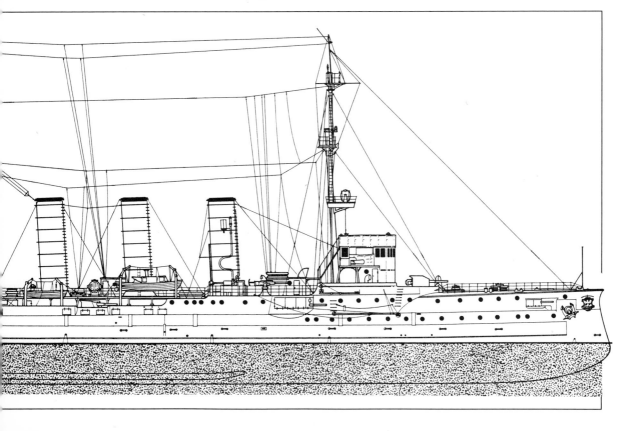

Julius Lauterbach and a boarding party of twenty armed men were hurriedly despatched to investigate.

*Emden* had taken the first prize to fall to the Kaiserliche Marine during the First World War.

The victim proved to be the 3,522grt *Ryazan*, the last of five sister-ships—the others were *Orel*, *Poltava*, *Simbirsk* and *Pensa*—ordered in October 1908 by the Russian Volunteer Fleet Association, ironically from Friedrich Schichau AG of Elbing.

Delivered from the German yard in November 1909, *Ryazan* was travelling from Nagasaki to Vladivostok with about eighty passengers, including women and children. The Russian ship had a British-born captain named Austin, who, only a few days previously, had been a drinking companion of the larger-than-life Lauterbach.

The protracted chase had shown that *Ryazan*, in spite of her single screw, was surprisingly fast. Her sister *Orel* had recorded 16·42 knots on a measured-mile run in August 1909, but had only been able to maintain 14·54 knots on a 24-hour trial; however, von Müller estimated that *Ryazan* had managed to maintain 16·5–17 knots in the desperate flight and could become a useful armed merchant cruiser. The Russian Volunteer Fleet Association, though basically a commercial operation, provided the Russian navy with transports in time of war—and so gun-mounting points were already built into the decks.

The German warship escorted her prize back to Tsingtau, narrowly missing a confrontation with the big French armoured cruisers *Montcalm* and *Dupleix*. Fortunately, the Frenchmen had mistaken *Emden* and *Ryazan* for *Scharnhorst* and *Gneisenau*, and turned back in fright.

Entering Tsingtau harbour on 6 August, *Ryazan* was subsequently fitted with eight 10·5cm guns and two searchlights taken from the colonial gunboat *Cormoran*. She was renamed *Cormoran II* and commissioned as an auxiliary cruiser with the Kreuzergeschwader. Her brief and ineffectual career is summarised in Appendix 1.

*Emden* left Tsingtau for the last time in the early evening of Thursday 6 August, heading for Pagan. There, as his ship was readied for coaling, von Müller attended a conference aboard *Scharnhorst*. Supported by some of his fellow commanders, Karl von Müller pressed Vizeadmiral Graf von Spee to allow one of the small cruisers to operate independently whilst the squadron voyaged across the Pacific, around Cape Horn and back to Germany. Otherwise, von Müller argued, the departure of the entire Kreuzergeschwader would free Allied warships on the China Station for offensive duties elsewhere.

On 14 August, as the squadron headed eastward, *Scharnhorst* ran up the signal 'Detached' and *Emden*, acknowledging the honour, hauled out of line. Von Müller

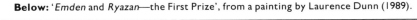

**Below:** '*Emden* and *Ryazan*—the First Prize', from a painting by Laurence Dunn (1989).

had been assigned the 4,505grt *Markomannia* of the Hamburg–Amerika Linie as a tender. Completed by Irvine's Shipbuilding and Dry-Dock Company of West Hartlepool in 1911, as *Nigarstan* for F.C. Strick, the collier had been sold to Germany in 1912. She was still quite new and could maintain twelve knots even when fully laden. *Emden* immediately headed south-westward for the Straits of Molucca and the Indian Ocean.

Nothing happened until the late evening of 9 September, when a merchant ship was brought to a halt after a short chase. She was black-hulled, but her funnel was much more colourful: buff, with a black top above a blue band displaying 'E' on a white circle superimposed on a white saltire. Over went a prize crew under the command of Julius Lauterbach. Soon the signalman flashed back bad news: *Pontoporos* had been completed in 1913 for National Steam Navigation Company of Greece by William Doxford & Sons Ltd of Sunderland. The steamship displaced about 7,480 tons (4,049grt) and could make nine knots.

Although theoretically neutral, *Pontoporos* was laden with 6,500 tons of Indian coal owned by the British Government. As Greek skipper Polemis cared little whether his paymaster was British or German, *Pontoporos* became part of the *Emden* convoy once Lauterbach and an armed guard had been put aboard to maintain discipline.

A black-hulled steamer with what appeared to be a black-topped buff funnel appeared at 09:00 on 10 September. Lookouts aboard *Emden* were puzzled; the ship had wireless antennae on her masts, and white box-like structures on deck. She was also flying a strange blue flag. As the distance between the ships closed, the flag resolved into a Blue Ensign. This could be flown by British merchant ships whose crews contained sufficient naval reservists. Was the stranger an auxiliary cruiser? Once the range closed, observers noted that the ensign was defaced with a circular emblem. Aboard *Emden*, brows furrowed; the ship did not seem to be armed, so what did the flag mean?

*Emden* ran up the imperial ensign, fired a blank and hoisted 'Stop. Do not use wireless', repeating the instruction in English by megaphone. The steamship stopped in 10°48'N 84°2'E to receive a boarding party led by Oberleutnant z.S. von Levetzow and Vizesteuermann d.R. Meyer. Owned by James Nourse Ltd of London, *Indus* had blundered straight into the German cruiser's path, steaming in ballast from Bombay to Calcutta under Captain Henry Swaridge. Built by Charles Connell & Co. Ltd of Glasgow in 1904, the 3,413grt *Indus* had been chartered by the Indian government at the beginning of the First World War to serve as a troop transport. This explained the flag; the strange white structures were simply stalls to hold cavalry horses.

By the late afternoon of 10 September, *Indus* had been plundered and arrangements were made to sink her. Sea cocks were opened and six 10·5cm shells were fired into the waterline from close range. The ship was reluctant to sink. R.K. Lochner recorded in *The Last Gentleman of War* that—

'for a long time she looked as if she were not sinking at all. Then the hull started slipping through the water's surface, slowly at first, the motion gradually accelerating. With a heavy plunge into the swells the ship took water over her railings and through her side portholes. After that she went quickly. Water rushed into the previously opened loading hatches. The steamer settled on her side. Escaping blasts of air forced large columns of water out of the openings on the port side. Then, finally, going bow first, the ship vanished . . .'

The destruction of the ship affected watchers aboard *Emden* and *Markomannia* almost as much as it did Captain Swaridge. Many sailors, tears in their eyes, stared silently at the sea in the knowledge *Emden* could be a victim as easily as a victor.

The following day proffered a large black-hulled ship with a black funnel displaying a single white band, and a Blue Ensign fluttering at the jackstaff. Stopped shortly after 14:00 by a warning shot, in 16°25'N 86°32'E, 6,102grt *Lovat* was owned by J. Warrack & Co. of Leith. The single-screw steamship had been delivered from the yard of Russell & Co. of Port Glasgow in April 1911. Under charter to the Indian government as a troop transport, she was seized whilst bound for Bombay from Calcutta under the command of Captain Richard Glegg. Though *Lovat* towered over *Emden*, she was unarmed. Thus no resistance was presented and, by nightfall, she had gone the way of *Indus*.

Von Müller considered destroying the Calcutta lightship, which would paralyse shipping in the Hooghly estuary until alternative arrangements could be made. He was still pondering the question when lights were seen in the distance. Shortly after 22:00 on 10 September 1914, the 4,657grt Ellerman & Bucknall steamship *Kabinga* was taken merely by ordering her by siren and signal lamp to heave-to. Built by Armstrong, Whitworth & Co. Ltd of Newcastle upon Tyne in 1907, *Kabinga* was one of four similar vessels ordered by the Bucknall Steamship Line. The single-screw freighter had been transferred to Ellerman & Bucknall on 1 January 1914. An unusual circlet of six white diamonds on her black funnel commemorated the discovery of gems in southern Africa.

*Kabinga* had been bound for New York from Calcutta, by way of the Suez Canal, under the command of Captain Thomas Robinson. Robinson had his wife and child aboard, whilst *Kabinga* held another unpleasant surprise for Julius Lauterbach, Leutnant z.S. Eugen Gyssling and the prize crew sent over from *Emden*: her cargo of jute was largely American-owned. Though von Müller could still have sunk the ship, the German government would have become liable for the neutral cargo. In addition, he was reluctant to risk the life of a woman and child during the risky transhipment of men from the captive. So *Kabinga* was ordered to follow in a convoy comprising a cruiser and three merchantmen, until released as a prison ship ('Lumpensammler') on 14 September.

No sooner had the little convoy mastered station keeping than *Emden* raced off in pursuit of a black hulled ship with a single black-topped red funnel. The British collier *Killin*, built in 1908 by Charles Connell & Co. Ltd for Connell Bros. Ltd of Glasgow, had been stopped in 17°55′N 86°24′E. A boarding party of sailors led by Oberleutnant z.S. Ernst von Levetzow and Leutnant z.S. Fritz Karl Zimmermann discovered that Captain J.K. Wilson was taking the 3,544grt single-screw steamer from Calcutta to Colombo with six thousand tons of Indian coal. Owing to the capture of *Pontoporos*, von Müller had more good-quality coal than he needed, so *Killin* was scuttled at 10:00 on 13 September by the combination of open sea-cocks and a few 10·5cm shells; heavily laden, she sank with unseemly haste.

*Emden*'s officers were finishing lunch in the wardroom when the cruiser hared off in pursuit of another smoke-cloud. The quarry was large and had four widely spaced masts. As *Emden* approached, the lofty black funnel was seen to be banded in white and red, and

a Red Ensign was run up the jackstaff. One of five similar vessels built in Glasgow in 1904–12, 7,615grt *Diplomat* had been completed in October 1912 by Charles Connell & Co. Ltd for the Charente Steam Ship Co. Ltd of London (managed by T. & J. Harrison). A single-screw twin-deck steamship driven by a quadruple-expansion engine, she could make about twelve knots.

*Diplomat* was the largest of *Emden*'s victims. She had just left Calcutta under the command of Captain Robert Thompson, laden with several thousand tons of tea bound for the Thames and Mersey. Owing to the great size of the captive steamship, von Müller was worried about the efficacy of the scuttling procedure used on previous victims. He ordered the torpedo officer, Oberleutnant z.S. Robert Witthoeft, to lay explosive charges in an effort to accelerate the process. However, the cargo was packed so tightly that Witthoeft could not set the scuttling charges below the waterline. They blew out a large portion of the hull on the port side, abaft the bow, but this was sufficient to encourage *Diplomat* to settle by the head and then sink amongst a maelstrom of tea chests in 18°1′N 86°24′E.

*Emden* then pursued smoke clouds only to find the steamers *Loredano* and *Dandolo* of Società Veneziana di Navigatori a Vapori—captained, coincidentally, by the brothers Giacopello. Italy was theoretically friendly with Germany, but there was good reason to believe that differences of opinion with neighbouring Austria-Hungary would be strong enough to bring the Italians into the war on the Allied side. Leutnant z.S. Franz Joseph, Prinz von Hohenzollern, who led the boarding party, reported to von Müller that he did not consider the captain of *Loredano* to be trustworthy even though Giacopello had given his solemn word that he would not reveal the whereabouts of the warship. The German lieutenant was astute; *Loredano* soon met the 6,603grt Hall Line steamship *City of Rangoon* and warned her of *Emden*'s presence. The master of *City of Rangoon* turned back to tell the British authorities, by so doing saving

*Itonus* (5,340grt) of the British India Steam Navigation Co. Ltd, the 'turret' steamer *Lotusmere* (3,911grt) of the Irismere Steam Shipping Co. Ltd, and *Rajput* (5,628grt) of the Asiatic Steam Navigation Company. All three were about to head in the direction of the raider.

*Emden*'s rampages had persuaded von Müller that, after accosting so many ships in such a short time, it was time he left the Calcutta–Colombo sea lanes for Madras–Calcutta. No sooner had station been taken—in the early evening of 14 September—than the Germans seized the Kyle Transport Co. Ltd collier *Trabboch* in 19°55′N 87°10′E. The black-funnelled 4,028grt British steamer, registered in Liverpool, had been completed by A. McMillan & Sons Ltd of Dumbarton in March 1910.

A boarding party led by Julius Lauterbach, Ernst von Levetzow and Erich Fikentscher discovered that the collier, commanded by Captain William Ross, was

Three of *Emden*'s many conquests.

**Above::** the Ellerman & Bucknall *Kabinga* (4,657grt), running trials off Tynemouth in 1907. The steamship was fortunate enough to be released as a prison-ship. Courtesy of the Trustees of the National Maritime Museum, Greenwich.

**Left:** the 3,544grt tramp *Killin*, owned by Connell Bros of Glasgow, running trials in the Clyde estuary in 1908. She was sunk in the Indian Ocean on 13 September 1914. Courtesy of Emden-Archiv Günter Huff.

**Below:** *Trabboch* (4,028grt) of the Kyle Transport Company, running trials in the Clyde estuary in 1910. The ship was sunk in the Indian Ocean on 14 September 1914. Courtesy of the Mitchell Library, Glasgow.

bound in ballast for Calcutta from Negabatam. After a cursory inspection revealed nothing of interest, von Müller decided to scuttle the collier immediately. The charges were laid and the scuttling party retreated to a safe distance to watch the ship slide slowly into the depths. But *Trabboch* went with a bang rather than a whimper: the scuttling charges ignited coal dust in the holds, producing a tremendous sheet of flame and an explosion that was audible for miles.

Just as *Kabinga* was being released, having offered three cheers for *Emden* and Fregattenkapitän von Müller, a light was detected in the gathering gloom and the cruiser set off in pursuit. Duly warned by the noisy destruction of *Trabboch*, the steamship piled on speed in

**Above:** the steamship *Clan Macintosh*, an identical sister of *Clan Mactavish*, pictured in the Mersey. Author's collection.
**Right:** the attack on Madras, from a contemporaneous painting by the German marine artist Willy Stöwer. **Below right:** oil tanks of the Anglo-Persian Oil Company burn after the attack. Author's collection.

an attempt to escape, defying siren signals and blanks fired by the pursuer until a live round made her captain see reason and heave-to in 19°55′N 87°11′E. 'What ship?', megaphoned *Emden*. 'Clan Matheson', replied the steamer. 'English?' queried *Emden*. 'BRITISH!' came the reply from a Scottish master and crew.

Completed by Furness, Withy & Co. Ltd of West Hartlepool in March 1906 for the Clan Steamship Line of London—managed by Cayzer, Irvine & Co. Ltd— the 4,775grt single-screw tramp *Clan Matheson* was commanded by Captain William Harris and had been travelling to Colombo from Liverpool.

Led by Julius Lauterbach and Leutnant z.S. Robin Schall, the boarding party discovered a valuable cargo which included railway locomotives, several Rolls-Royce motor cars, typewriters and a pedigree racehorse. However, as *Emden* needed very little, *Clan Matheson* was promptly sunk.

On 18 September, after coaling in the Andaman islands and attending to the boilers, the Germans apprehended a smart steamship with a black hull, white upperworks and a plain yellow funnel. The Norwegian steamer *Dovre* was neutral, but provided an ideal means of ridding the tender *Markomannia* of an accumulation of prisoners. The Norwegian captain subsequently dumped the Britons in Rangoon, where they sang the praises of their erstwhile captors whilst simultaneously giving as much information as they could to bring the hunt for *Emden* to a rapid and successful conclusion.

Wireless-telegraphy signals were intercepted in the night of 18/19 September from a British warship with

the call-sign QMD. This particular vessel had been a continual nuisance, and her captain had shown an almost telepathic ability to guess von Müller's next move. Eventually, a careless shore installation identified the mystery ship as the powerful British armoured cruiser *Hampshire*, commanded by Captain Grant. Fortunately for von Müller, the doggedness of the British pursuit was not equalled by good fortune.

As September 1914 progressed, the Germans had become past masters at seizing, plundering and scuttling merchantmen. Confidence had grown, so von Müller decided to strike at a land target. In the evening of Tuesday 22 September 1914, therefore, having raised her dummy fourth funnel to masquerade as British, *Emden* sailed straight into brightly-lit Madras harbour without so much as a challenge. The crew was sent to battle stations at 20:55 and Erich Gaede was ready to open fire by 21:45. *Emden* then stopped engines, turned southward, and, at 20:48, switched on searchlights to probe the target. At a range of 3,000 metres, the first shells crashed out of the five starboard guns.

The first salvo was a hundred metres too long, though one shot destroyed a gun in the Fort St George battery behind the oil-storage tanks of the Burmah Oil Company. A second salvo was a hundred yards short. The third landed on the fringes of the shore, too short by a few yards, but the fourth ignited the largest of the oil tanks. The second tank proved to be empty; then the third burst into flames. One shell hit the British India Steam Navigation Company's steamer *Chupra* at her mooring next to the mole—fatally wounding seventeen-year-old

cadet Joseph Fletcher—and a few stray shells landed in the margins of the town, killing seven Madrassi and wounding twelve before brightly lit *Emden* steamed off northward to attract attention. Lights were doused and then the warship doubled back past the harbour, unseen even by the light of the flames that licked the night sky.

Only a handful of shots had been fired by the shore batteries. One fell a hundred yards short of *Emden*, two had flown well over the ship and the remainder had not even fallen within spotting range.

The Madras Raid was sensational. Though the damage was far from serious, local morale suffered so badly that trade was dislocated exactly in the way von Müller had hoped. *Emden* had ridden her luck once again. Captain Grant aboard *Hampshire* had correctly predicted the attack and had decided to visit Madras shortly after 20 September. During the night of 18/19 September, however, when wireless operators aboard *Emden* were intercepting British signals sent in impenetrable code, Grant was being told of naval activity off the Burmese seaport of Akyab. He was ordered to investigate, though personally sceptical. In his absence, the observation of Madras was passed to *Chikuma*. But the Japanese cruiser had only just finished a leisurely coaling stop when *Emden* gleefully shelled the port.

The quest for more merchant victims then took *Emden* toward Ceylon. Friday 25 September 1914 proved to be busy. A steamer plodding unsuspectingly toward Calcutta from Alexandria was accosted early in the afternoon, obligingly revealing her nationality by hoisting the Red Ensign as *Emden* approached. *King Lud*

**Above:** *Emden* sinks the Bolton Steam Shipping Co. Ltd steamer *Ribera*—a picture that makes up in atmosphere what it lacks in accuracy. By courtesy of the Bundesarchiv, Koblenz, negative no. 134–C2331.

**Below right:** the dredger *Ponrabbel* running trials in the Clyde estuary in the summer of 1914. By courtesy of Emden-Archiv Günter Huff.

had been delivered to the King Line Ltd by J.L. Thompson & Sons Ltd of Sunderland in November 1906. The 3,650grt black-hulled ship had a black topped buff funnel and buff masts.

As she was travelling in ballast, and thus had little to offer her captors, *King Lud* was sunk at about 16:15 in 5°47'N 79°46'E by an effectual combination of open sea cocks and demolition charges.

A neutral Norwegian tanker was hailed at 20:00 but allowed to pass; and finally, at about 23:00, the sugar-laden tramp *Tymeric*—with a black hull and black topped buff funnel—was stopped in 7°10'N 79°21'E on a voyage from Samarang to Falmouth under the command of Captain John Tulloch. Built by Russell & Co. of Port Glasgow for the Steamship 'Tymeric' Co. Ltd, the 3,314grt single-screw tramp had been delivered in January 1901. A cursory inspection was made by Julius Lauterbach and Franz Joseph, Prinz von Hohenzollern, though von Müller had decided to search the prize thoroughly the following morning. The truculent attitude of the captain and chief engineer then forced von Müller to change his mind; once her crew had been hastily rowed over to *Markomannia*, the captive was sunk on the spot.

Next came the 4,437grt steamer *Gryfevale*. Delivered in April 1906 to the Gryfevale Steamship Co. Ltd by the Grangemouth & Greenock Dockyard Company, the single-screw tramp was registered in Glasgow. Out of Aden, bound for Colombo in ballast under the command of Captain J.W. Steel, she was seized by Lauterbach,

Zimmermann and the boarding party on 26 September and retained as a 'dump'.

The night of 26 September brought the lights of a large steamer, burning so brightly that they made identification in darkness very difficult. The presence of four masts convinced von Müller and lookouts aboard *Emden* that the vessel was the 5,300grt motor-ship *Fionia* of the neutral Danish Ostasiatiske Kompagni A/S, but Lauterbach and onlookers aboard *Gryfevale*—certain that they could see a tall thin funnel—insisted that she was a British Bibby liner. The German skipper elected to let the stranger pass, in case a serious mistake was made by stopping a passenger ship so close to land.

At about 02:30 on 27 September 1914, in 7°24'N 76°41'E, *Emden* captured the London-registered collier *Buresk*, travelling from Barry to Hong Kong under the command of Captain Frederick Tayler. As she carried more than six thousand tons of high-grade Welsh coal, von Müller had a prize beyond price. Completed in May 1914 by Richardson, Duck & Co. of Stockton on Tees for the Buresk Steam Ship Co. Ltd of London, the single-screw 4,337grt collier could make a mere ten knots at full speed.

Sunday 28 September should have been a rest day. No sooner had *Buresk* been manned by Germans and Divine Service held aboard *Emden* than Lauterbach reported fighting aboard his charge *Gryfevale*. Once the disturbance had been quietened and midday meals served aboard the cruiser—the officers enjoyed soup, corned beef and rice, then stewed fruit—a smoke cloud was spotted on the horizon.

The Bolton Steam Shipping Co. Ltd tramp *Ribera* had been built in 1904 by J.L. Thompson & Sons Ltd of Sunderland. With a registered tonnage of 3,500, the single-screw steamer was bound from Alexandria for Batavia (now Djakarta) under the command of Captain James Isdale. Bolton ships had black hulls and plain black funnels. Though *Ribera* was in ballast, she was provisioned on such a grand scale that many a delight was surrendered to *Emden*'s plunderers before the steamer was shelled to reinforce open sea-cocks and scuttling charges. She sank in 7°30′N 75°26′E.

At about 21:10, *Emden* took *Foyle* in 7°56′N 74°5′E. The vessel had been completed in April 1902 for the Mercantile Steamship Co. Ltd of London by J.L. Thompson & Sons Ltd of Sunderland. Captain William Gibson had been taking the single-screw 4,147grt steamship in ballast from Port Said to Rangoon by way of Aden and Colombo. Scuttling was then delayed whilst *Emden* chased a brightly-lit ship in the hope of seizing a rich mail packet. *Djocja* was indeed such a ship—but Dutch and, therefore, inviolably neutral.

The dump *Gryfevale* was released at noon on Monday 28 September, the captive Britons giving three cheers each for Karl von Müller, his officers and *Emden*, just as *Kabinga*'s contingent had done some days earlier. At 06:00 on 9 October, *Emden* dropped anchor off Diego Garcia so that the hull could be scraped, the upperworks repainted and the boilers cleaned. Diego Garcia was so remote that no-one there even knew war had been declared, so von Müller explained away the condition of his ship by a lengthy world cruise and severe storms. *Emden* left the harbour at noon on 10 October; two days afterward, *Hampshire* and the armed merchant cruiser *Empress of Russia* dropped anchor.

Out in the Indian Ocean, lookouts aboard *Emden* spotted lights at 23:00 on 15 October and *Clan Grant* was seized shortly after midnight in 8°10′N 73°11′N—Cayzer, Irvine & Company were the only business to lose two ships to the German cruiser. Built in 1902 for the Clan Steamship Line of London, by William Doxford & Sons Ltd of Sunderland, 3,948grt *Clan Grant* was a single-screw 'turret-deck' ship, designed to reduce the tariffs payable during the passage of the Suez Canal by minimising deck area. The tramp was travelling under the command of Captain Norman Leslie from Liverpool to Calcutta by way of Colombo, with a cargo which included porcelain, typewriters, livestock and food.

Whilst the unloading of *Clan Grant* was underway, *Emden* dashed off to investigate a smoke cloud over the horizon. As the range closed, the lookout in the crow's nest reported that he could see a single mast which was pitching very strangely. Concerned that he could be

about to face a destroyer, von Müller ordered the guns to be cleared for action.

Rolling inebriately in the ocean swell, the oddest of *Emden*'s victims wallowed into view in 8°21′N 72°24′E. Bought by the Marine Board of Launceston (Tasmania) from Ferguson Brothers of Port Glasgow, the 473grt twin-screw dredger *Ponrabbel* was making four knots through the seas that had already claimed a predecessor.

Led by the indefatigable Julius Lauterbach, the boarding party stepped aboard *Ponrabbel*, only to be confronted by the spectacle of Edwin Gore and his men packed and ready to go. Skipper Gore explained that everyone had been paid in advance, owing to the demise of the previous dredger, and were eagerly anticipating the safety promised by *Emden* and her entourage. *Ponrabbel* bowed to a few well-aimed shells, sinking after a brief inverted sulk. *Clan Grant* met her watery end shortly afterward.

More lights were sighted at 23:15 on 17 October, a large freighter being stopped by signal lamp—shortly after midnight—in 8°16′N 72°55′E, about sixty nautical miles north-west by west of Minicoy island. The 4,806grt single-screw tramp *Benmohr*, registered in Leith by William Thomson & Co. Ltd ('The Ben Line'), had been completed by Scott's Shipbuilding & Engineering Co. of Greenock in September 1912. One of the last of a dying breed, her clipper bow an elegant legacy of the era of sail, black-hulled *Benmohr* was hauling five thousand tons of cargo—including motor vehicles, bicycles and machine parts—from London to Penang and Yokohama under the command of Captain James Larchet. Soon she had joined twelve of *Emden*'s previous conquests on the sea bed.

After stopping a neutral Spanish mail packet in the Indian Ocean on 18 October. *Emden* had another run of luck on a Sunday. The officers had gathered after Divine Service for drinks in the wardroom, but no sooner had Fregattenkapitän von Müller arrived than a smoke-cloud was sighted away to starboard. Nothing could be seen of the ship as *Emden* hared off in pursuit. Then an enormous funnel appeared over the horizon, a splash of blue betraying an Alfred Holt vessel. The Germans were overjoyed, aware that Holt owned only impressive ships.

The newcomer was *Troilus*, delivered to the Ocean Steam Ship Co. Ltd of Liverpool (Alfred Holt & Co. Ltd) by Hawthorn Leslie & Co. Ltd of Newcastle upon Tyne only a few weeks before war had begun. Lauterbach went over with the boarding party to report that the 7,562grt single-screw steamer was on the return leg of her maiden voyage, conveying passengers and a valuable cargo of copper, rubber and zinc from Yokohama back to London under the command of Captain George W. Long. *Troilus* was one of ten sister-ships built for Holt in 1913–17 (including a replacement of the same name) and managed under the flags of the Blue Funnel Line, the Ocean Steamship Company or the China Mutual Steam Navigation Company.

As Lauterbach climbed aboard *Troilus*, he had been greeted warmly by a solitary female passenger: for once, *Emden*'s officers recalled with amusement, the voluble seadog had been rendered speechless. The lady had been a passenger on Lauterbach's command *Staatsekretär Kraetke* shortly before the war had begun; she had even sat at the Captain's Table to dine. Up on the bridge, meanwhile, Captain Long fumed impotently. His brand-new ship had been following a route guaranteed by the Royal Navy authorities in Colombo to be safe.

With *Troilus* following in convoy, *Emden* steamed away. At 21:00 on 18 October the Germans spotted a vessel showing no lights. When challenged by signal lamp, the shape metamorphosed into the Liverpool registered *Saint Egbert*, built by Russell & Co. of Port Glasgow for the British & Foreign Steamship Co. Ltd and managed by Rankin, Gilmour & Company. Stopped in 8°16′N 75°7′E, the 5,596grt 423ft single-screw freighter was the command of Captain William Barr. Unfortunately for the Germans, she was bound for New York out of Colombo with an American-owned cargo of sugar and piece goods.

Von Müller decided to use the newcomer as a dump, reducing the congestion aboard *Buresk*, and ordered *Saint Egbert* to follow. More lights were seen at 00:30 on 19 October. The Cardiff collier *Exford*, owned by the Tatem Steam Navigation Company and laden with 5,500 tons of Welsh coal bound from Britain to India under Admiralty charter, was stopped by siren and signal lamp in 8°39′N 75°7′E. *Exford* had been completed in 1911 by Craig, Taylor & Company of Stockton on Tees. The 4,542grt single-screw ship could make twelve knots.

Provisions were transferred from *Troilus* as soon as 19 October dawned, while *Emden* unsuccessfully sought the missing *Saint Egbert*. The errant collier had reappeared by 07:00, but another smoke cloud was spotted at 08:00 and the cruiser set off in pursuit.

As 10:00 approached, the cruiser returned with the British India Steam Navigation Company's *Chilkana*, bound for Calcutta from the Tees and London with a mixed cargo but taken in 9°22′N 75°4′E. Captain James Archdeacon had reason to be distraught: his command, newer even than *Troilus*, was also on her maiden voyage.

Possibly the unluckiest of *Emden*'s victims, the 5,146grt single-screw steamship was merely a few days old when seized and scuttled in Nine Degree Channel in the Arabian Sea. Built by William Gray & Co. Ltd of West Hartlepool, one of four similar vessels dating from 1912–14, *Chilkana* had only been delivered at the beginning of September. Her service speed was eleven knots, 12·75 being made on trial.

Whilst stores were being taken from the newcomer and distributed among the convoy, the scuttling party finished its work aboard the Holt steamship. The charges were fired, and *Emden*'s gunners contributed a few shells by way of practice. However, *Troilus* was sub-divided

more effectually than many of the victims and refused to sink quickly.

On 21 October 1914, Fourth Officer Laurence Prosser of *Chilkana* wrote to his father Thomas—

"You will no doubt have heard by this [time] of the sinking of the 'Chilkana' and I hope it did not give you a shock. I am writing this in a gentleman's bungalow in a small place called Cochin on the west coast of India. We arrived here last night on board the steamer 'St. Egbert', which the 'Emden' mercifully spared.

". . . After leaving Aden we set our course for Colombo and all went well for the first few days. We knew the 'Emden' was somewhere between us and Colombo and steamed at night with all lights out so that we might pass her in the dark, but no such luck, for on Monday morning about half-past seven, the Chief and I were on the bridge when we saw in the distance a cloud of smoke which, in about a quarter of an hour's time, turned out to be a bunch of steamers. The 'Old Man' came up and said it must be a convoy, but suddenly out of the bunch of vessels we saw a three funnel cruiser coming at us as hard as it could steam. The Skipper still thought it was one of our Men of War, and I casually remarked to him "The Emden has three funnels, hasn't she Sir?" at which he laughed. Anyway, in another few minutes she was quite close, and then we saw to our chagrin that she was hoisting the German colours. It was too late to run for it because we were at least 200 miles off land and already the 'Emden' had fired across our bows and had run up a signal telling us that if we used our wireless she would sink us. So the 'Old Man' thought discretion was the better part of valour and stopped the engines. The 'Emden' by this time had launched one of her boats and a boatload of men were pretty soon aboard. The young Lieutenant in charge marched up respectfully on the bridge and saluted our 'Old Man' and had the audacity to wish him 'Good morning, Sir!'.

"Of course the Captain knew jolly well it was no use making a fuss, so he and the Lieutenant went down into the saloon and had a tot of whiskey and a smoke, and talked matters over.

"By this time the Germans had taken charge of the ship and we were following in the wake of 'Emden' to her place of slaughter. We were told to pack up all our personal belongings as smartly as we could then put them in the lifeboats all ready for leaving. All our Coolies were packed off to one of the other ships lying near, together with most of the whites who, no doubt, were thinking they were going to sink us there and then by the rush among them. I stayed behind with the Chief Officer and the Skipper, and the German officer parted with a good natured smile. There's no doubt about it, the Germans behaved like gentlemen. They joked with us and offered us cigars, etc., and never opened their mouths about the war, or made an unpleasant remark. For example, one of our passengers had a motor cycle on board and was thinking of leaving it behind when one of the German officers ordered his men to sling it and put it on board a special boat so that it would not get smashed up. We were then sent aboard one of the five captured boats and then I saw a sight that will live in my memory as long as I live.

"First of all the 'Emden' approached within twenty yards [sic] of a great big Blue Funnel Liner and fired four shots into her, and it was a sickening sight to see her gradually sinking lower and lower in the water.

"She went down so far and then seemed to stop, so the 'Emden' let fly two more shots and she gradually got lower until she took a final lurch, keeled over on her side and went down bow first, her stern describing a semi-circle in the air and shot out of sight. Her cargo was worth one million pounds Sterling and she was a new boat, like 'Chilkana' on her maiden voyage.

"Then came the turn of the 'Chilkana' after they had taken all our stores. The operation was repeated, but she went down in 20 minutes, whereas the Blue Funnel boat stayed five solid hours. We had a Grand View of it all, as we were only 30 yards [sic] away. There were now only 3 ships left. Two of them had a cargo of coal for our Navy, and the other, the one on which we were stranded together with the officers and crews of seven other vessels which the 'Emden' had sunk in the last 2 days. Altogether we were 374, as you may know we were anything but comfortable, packed like sardines in a tin with nowhere to sleep and nothing to eat. The 'Emden' kept the other two vessels for her own use and took the Chinese crew off the Alfred Holt Liner to man them, but they are paying them wages. We were told to proceed to Cochin and were ironically wished a safe passage. Thank goodness it was only 24 hours run or perhaps I would not be alive to tell this tale, but I won't worry you with the details of my experience which are too miserable to quote. But anyway, I'm now ashore and just had a good bath and tuck in. All I want now is a good sleep and I'll be as fit as ever."

Though this letter captures the tension of the sinkings admirably, the ranges quoted are extremely suspect. Owing to the limited depression of the 10·5cm guns, it is very unlikely that *Emden* would have approached to within even two ships' length of a potential target if the gunners were expected to hit the waterline.

*Chilkana* had been *Emden*'s fifteenth victim. The flurry of sinkings off Ceylon, however, necessitated a change of base. After coaling from *Buresk* in False Bay in the Nicobar Islands on 26 October, von Müller decided to sail straight into Penang harbour and destroy whatever he found. The plan was daring; the harbour, something of a bottleneck, would contain warships in addition to choice merchantmen. It could only be reached by a narrow channel and von Müller had every reason to believe that the navigation buoys would be extinguished; a night attack, therefore, was fraught with many a hazard. He decided that the gains far outweighed the risks. The greatest danger would come from a British warship, but the limited intelligence he had been able to glean suggested that no Royal Navy ships of any great offensive power were in the vicinity.

A briefing was held in the wardroom on 27 October before the ship was thoroughly prepared for action. Extra ammunition was brought up to the guns, and the crewmen were ordered to don clean clothing to minimise infection should they be wounded. Owing to first-hand knowledge of Penang harbour, Julius Lauterbach was appointed navigating officer for the duration of the raid.

At 02:00 on Wednesday 28 October 1914, *Emden* appeared off Pulo Penang lighthouse with her dummy fourth funnel raised. At 04:50 she nosed into the brightly lit harbour, ready to face whatever threat materialised.

No sooner had the German cruiser entered the roadstead than the Russian cruiser *Zhemchug* was spotted. Comparable in size and power to *Emden*, though somewhat older, the protected cruiser—one of two ships of the Izumrud class—was originally distinguished by a combination of three funnels and three masts. By 1914, however, she had apparently been re-rigged with only a single mast between the second and third funnels.

Laid down in 1901 and completed in 1904, *Zhemchug* was a product of the Nevski shipyard in St. Petersburg. She displaced 3,103 tons at standard load draught, measured 364ft overall and had been able to reach 24 knots when new. By 1914 she mounted eight 12·2cm, six

5cm and two 3·7cm guns, plus three 45cm torpedo tubes. However, Captain Second Class Baron Cherkassov and his crew were caught totally unprepared; the guns were unmanned, and only a meagre harbour watch was being kept as the cooks departed in the ship's boats to purchase vegetables and fresh meat ashore.

*Emden* fired a single torpedo at 05:18, striking *Zhemchug* beneath the aftermost funnel; the engine room immediately flooded, extinguishing the fires in the boilers, as the German gunners raked their target—well aware that Russian seamen would berth in the forward flats. The stricken cruiser rapidly settled aft whilst her forward superstructure was being blasted away by a torrent of 10·5cm shells.

French warships in the inner harbour opened fire, but succeeded only in hitting nearby merchantmen. *Emden* then came about and raced out of Penang, launching a second torpedo as she passed *Zhemchug*. The missile struck home forward of the bridge at 05:28, igniting the magazine and blowing the fore-part of the Russian cruiser to pieces. Four minutes later, the wreck foundered beneath a cloak of yellow smoke. Casualties were high, despite the comparative ineffectiveness of the German 10·5cm shell; out of a complement of about 350, 91 Russians were dead and 108 had wounds of varying severity.

Mistaking a small government launch for a hostile torpedo-boat, *Emden* surged out to attack. When the mistake was apparent, von Müller chased after what appeared to be a large auxiliary merchant cruiser. All he found shortly after 07:00 was *Glenturret*, a simple tramp magnified by mirage. The 4,696grt steamer had been delivered in September 1896 to the Glen Line Ltd of London (McGregor, Gow & Co. Ltd) by the London & Glasgow Shipbuilding Co. Ltd. She was now laden to the gunwhales with explosives. Fortunately for Captain Jones and his crew, the proximity of the French torpedo-boat *Mousquet* persuaded von Müller to release the steamer to sail into Penang. Jones was to deliver an apology for shelling a pilot-boat and to explain that the presence of so many ships had prevented the Germans rescuing survivors of *Zhemchug*.

The boarding party was recalled from *Glenturret* as *Emden* replaced the dummy funnel and prepared to confront a new threat. Approaching was *Mousquet*, a 298-tonne torpedo-boat destroyer of the Arquebuse class built by Chantiers de la Loire of Saint Nazaire under the 1900 programme. Launched in August 1902, *Mousquet* measured about 58m on the waterline and had been capable of 28 knots when new; she carried a single 6·5cm and six 4·7cm quick-firing guns, plus two torpedo tubes.

Unfortunately, Lieutenant de Vaisseau Théroinne injudiciously turned away when he realised that he had been duped by the dummy funnel into approaching not HMS *Yarmouth*, as expected, but *Emden*. As the French torpedo-boat withdrew, the Germans let fly from the five starboard guns. The first salvo screamed over *Mousquet*; the second was short. But the third was a straddle. Away went the foremast and Tricouleur, then a hit amidships wrecked the boiler room. Wreathed in steam, *Mousquet* fired a torpedo harmlessly astern of her tormentor and wheezed to a halt.

Von Müller ordered Erich Gaede to cease firing after twelve salvoes, but the torpedo-boat showed no signs of surrendering even though the foremast and fore-funnel had been shot away, and the bridge had been blasted into a tangled mass of iron. Ten more broadsides enticed the shattered wreck to slide bow-first into the deep.

*Emden* then set about rescuing the survivors, retrieving 36 of the 76-man crew. One Frenchman swam ashore, but the others were lost and three of the twelve wounded men taken aboard *Emden* subsequently died.

The German warship steamed off at high speed, pursued by *Mousquet*'s sister-ship *Fronde*. The French torpedo-boat was eluded in a rain squall. The last prize should have been the Newcastle Steam Ship Company's 3,554grt single-screw tramp *Newburn*, built by Swan, Hunter & Wigham Richardson Ltd of Newcastle upon Tyne and delivered in June 1904. The steamship was seized on 30 October 1914 whilst bound from England to Singapore. However, but her papers revealed the cargo of salt to be German-owned. Captain William Richards was simply instructed to land the French sailors in Khota Raja or Sabang and *Newburn* was released.

By November 1914, the crewmen aboard *Emden* were in need of rest. Before this could be permitted, Fregattenkapitän von Müller elected to attack the sparsely populated Direction Island in the Cocos (Keeling) Group, an important wireless station and trans-oceanic cable relay.

At 06:00 on 9 November 1914, the German cruiser appeared off the northernmost of the Cocos islands and dropped anchor in Port Refuge at about 06:30. Command of the landing party was given to the First Officer, Kapitänleutnant Hellmuth von Mücke, who picked many of the best long-service men as a reward for their loyalty. Leutnant z.S. Fikentscher, who was Duty Officer, objected to the absence from *Emden* of the most experienced gunlayers, but was overruled by von Müller on the grounds that the men would soon return. At 06:33, the steam pinnace towed the two cutters toward Direction Island at high speed. In addition to Hellmuth von Mücke, Eugen Gyssling and Roderich Schmidt, there were fifteen technical personnel and 32 seamen. In anticipation of resistance, the Germans took the cruiser's four 8mm Maxim machine-guns and a selection of small-arms.

The wireless messages despatched by *Emden* to the collier *Buresk* had already been noted by the staff of Direction Island station. As *Emden*'s wireless operators failed to reply to a request for identification, the Britons had simply looked out to sea. Recognising that something was amiss, they began to transmit 'SOS. Strange ship

**Below:** the torpedo-boat *Fronde*, pictured in harbour prior to 1914. Photograph by Marius Bar, Toulon.

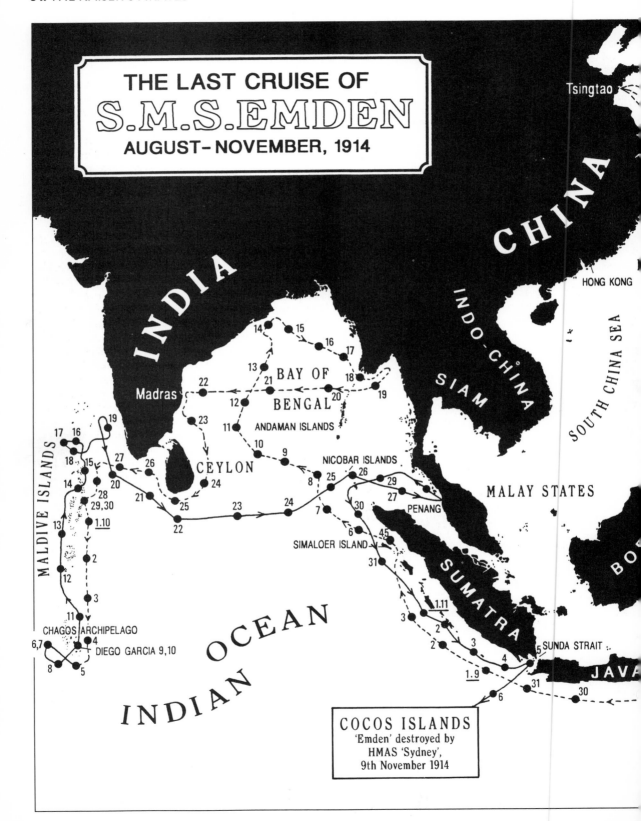

THE LAST CRUISE OF
S.M.S. EMDEN
AUGUST– NOVEMBER, 1914

CHINA

INDIA

Tsingtao

HONG KONG

INDO-CHINA

SIAM

SOUTH CHINA SEA

MALAY STATES

BORNEO

Madras

BAY OF BENGAL

ANDAMAN ISLANDS

CEYLON

NICOBAR ISLANDS

PENANG

SUMATRA

SIMALOER ISLAND

MALDIVE ISLANDS

CHAGOS ARCHIPELAGO

DIEGO GARCIA 9,10

INDIAN OCEAN

SUNDA STRAIT

JAVA

COCOS ISLANDS
'Emden' destroyed by
HMAS 'Sydney',
9th November 1914

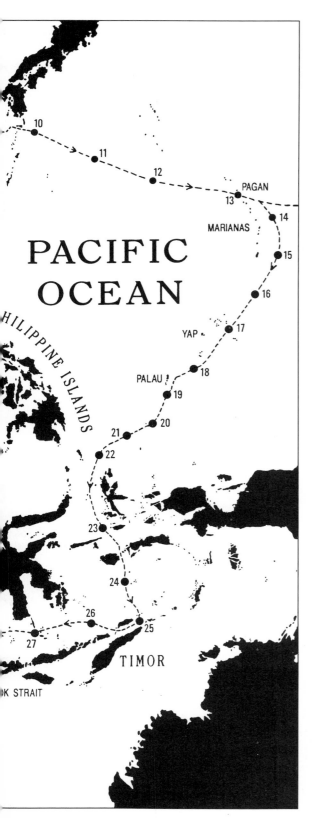

PACIFIC
OCEAN

PHILIPPINE ISLANDS

PAGAN

MARIANAS

YAP

PALAU

TIMOR

K STRAIT

in harbour' followed eventually by 'SOS. Emden here'. These the Germans strove to jam.

Before the German landing party could reach the transmitting station—the mast was toppled shortly after 07:00—messages had been received aboard HMAS *Melbourne* and the Bucknall steamship *Karoo*, part of the convoy of troopships that was less than sixty nautical miles from Direction Island.

Captain Silver of *Melbourne*, the senior naval officer of the escorts, immediately despatched the light cruiser *Sydney* to investigate. The cruiser attempted to raise Direction Island, but the transmission was detected aboard *Emden*. Its weakness suggested that the sender was two hundred miles away, so von Müller ceased worrying and resumed attempts to summon *Buresk*.

The stays supporting *Emden*'s tall funnels had been detached, as they got in the way of coaling. Shortly after 09:00, the masthead look-out reported a smoke cloud. The cloud became a ship with a single funnel and two tall masts, a description that fitted the anticipated collier. The commander of *Buresk*—Kapitänleutnant d.R. Klöpper—had been told to make as little smoke as possible, so it was assumed aboard Emden that a fire that had been smouldering in the collier's bunkers was still alight.

Leutnant z.S. Albert von Guérard climbed the mast to confirm the sighting. No-one worried. At 09:12, von Guérard saw that the previously indistinct shape not only had two raked masts and four funnels but was also approaching very rapidly. Sirens were sounded to recall the landing party at 09:13, flag signals being run up the foremast in confirmation at 09:15. At 09:17, von Guérard shouted down to the bridge that the warship—a cruiser—was flying three White Ensigns and a 'large blue flag' subsequently identified as that of Australia. HMAS *Sydney* had only been using half-power to acknowledge Direction Island's wireless transmission; the Germans had been fooled completely.

Abandoning the landing party, which had been slow to respond to the recall signals, von Müller raised anchor and steamed out of harbour at 09:30. The story of the final battle has often been told with the emphasis on the German viewpoint. An Australian journalist, Bennet Copplestone, described the scene:

"The light cruiser 'Sydney', completed in 1913 for the Australian unit, is very fast and powerful. She is of 5,600 tons, built with the clipper bows and lines of a yacht, and when oil is sprayed upon her coal furnaces can steam at over twenty-five knots. She bears upon her deck eight six-inch guns of the latest pattern, one forward, one aft, and three on either beam, so that she can fire simultaneously from five guns upon either broadside. Her lyddite shells weigh one hundred pounds each . . . Speed and gun-power, with the simplicity of control given by guns all of one size, are the doctrines on which the New Navy has been built, and by virtue of which it holds the seas. The 'Sydney' was much more powerful than the 'Emden', whose ten guns were of 4·1 inches firing shells of thirty-eight pounds weight. The German raider had been out of dock in warm waters for at least three and a half months, her bottom was foul, and her speed so much reduced that in the action ... she never raised more than sixteen knots. In speed as in gun-power she was utterly outclassed.

"Before the foremast [of HMAS *Sydney*] stands the armoured conning tower ... designed for the captain's use; forward of the conning tower rises the two-storeyed bridge, the upper part of which is the station of the gunnery control officer; upon the mast, some fifty feet up, is fitted a spotting top for another officer. This distribution of executive control may look very pretty and scientific, but Glossop, who had tested it in practice, proposed to fight on a system of his own ... Glossop placed himself beside his Gunnery Lieutenant Rahilly upon the upper bridge with nothing between their bodies and the enemy's shot except a frail canvas screen. Accompanying them was a lieutenant in charge of certain instruments. At the back of the bridge—which measured some ten feet by eight—stood upon its pedestal the principal range-finder with a seat at the back for the operator. This concentration of control upon the exposed bridge had its risks, as will presently appear, but it made for simplicity and for the rapid working both of the ship and of her guns. Another lieutenant, Geoffrey Hampden, is in charge of the after control station, where also was fitted a range-finder ... the most unhappy person on board is the Second in Command—in this instance Lieutenant-Commander John F. Finlayson—who by the rules of the Service is condemned to safe and inglorious, though important duties in the lower conning tower.

"At 9.15 land is sighted some ten miles distant and five minutes later a three-funnelled cruiser, recognised at once as the 'Emden', is seen running out of port. Upon the 'Sydney' a bugle blows, and then for twenty minutes all is quiet orderly work at Action Quarters. To the 'Emden' the sudden appearance of 'Sydney' is a complete surprise. Her destruction party of three officers and forty men are [sic] still ashore and must be left behind if their ship is to be given any, the most slender, chance of escape. Captain von Müller recognises the 'Sydney' at once as a much faster and more heavily gunned ship than his own. His one chance is to rush at his unexpected opponent and utilise to the utmost the skill of his highly trained gunners and the speed with which they can work their quick-firing guns. If he can overwhelm the 'Sydney' with a torrent of shell before she can get seriously home upon him, he may disable her so that flight will still be possible. He can hope for nothing from torpedoes, for, though he has three left, his torpedo flat is out of action. In rapid and good gunnery, and in a quick bold offensive, may rest safety; there is no other chance. So out he comes, making straight for the 'Sydney' as hard as he can go and gives her as lively a fifteen minutes as the most greedy of fire-eaters could desire."

*Emden*'s gunners were well practised, and soon forced the Australian cruiser to withdraw out of range, but the most experienced gunlayers were ashore with the landing party. In addition, one of the primary reasons that von Müller attacked—though he had little alternative—was that the Australian cruiser had been tentatively identified as HMS *Newcastle*. This particular warship was older and weaker than *Sydney*; her two 6-inch guns (one forward and one aft) outranged the German 10·5cm patterns and fired a much heavier shell, but the German gun was superior to the 4-inch weapons that constituted the remainder of *Newcastle*'s armament.

Against *Newcastle*, von Müller believed that he had a good chance; only when the water-splashes from the first salvoes fired from *Sydney* revealed an entire battery of large-calibre guns did the German captain realise the strength of his opponent.

Testimony from some of the German survivors—e.g., Leutnant z.S. Franz Joseph, Prinz von Hohenzollern, or Torpedo-Maschinistenmaat Ernst Püschel—reveals not only that the torpedo flat was in full working order at the outset, but also that its crew was waiting to launch torpedoes until comparatively late in the action. Bennet Copplestone continued:

"When the two cruisers first see each other they are 20,000 yards distant, but as both are closing in, the range comes quickly down to 10,500 yards ... To the astonishment both of the Captain and the Gunnery Lieutenant of the 'Sydney', who are together looking out from the upper fore bridge, von Müller opens fire ... and gets within a hundred yards with his first salvo. It is wonderful shooting. His next is just over and with the third he begins to hit. At the long range the 'Emden's' shells fall steeply—at an angle of thirty degrees—rarely burst and never ricochet from the sea. They whine overhead in torrents, plop into the sea on all sides, and now and then smash on board. One reaches the upper fore bridge, passes within a foot of Lieutenant Rahilly's head, strikes the pedestal of the big range-finder, glances off without bursting, cuts the leg off the operator, who is sitting behind, and finishes its career overboard. If that shell had burst, Glossop and his Gunnery Lieutenant, together with their colleague at the rate-of-change instrument, must have been killed or seriously wounded ... Not one of them was six feet distant from where the shell struck in their midst. The range-finder is wrecked and its operator killed, but the others are untouched. A few minutes later two, possibly three, shells hit the after control, wound everyone inside, and [immediately] wipe that control off the effective list."

*Sydney* had been a most fortunate beneficiary of some inaccurate fuze-setting aboard *Emden*. The Australians had also begun to fire. The first salvo had been far too long, the second was ragged and the third straddled *Emden*. However, the simultaneous destruction of the bridge range-finder and the after control position aboard *Sydney* temporarily reduced the efficacy of her gunfire; though Rahilly managed to maintain careful spotting, hits became difficult to obtain. Temporarily discomfited by the accuracy of the German shooting—the Australian ship was hit at least ten times in the first fifteen minutes of the contest—and worried about the use of torpedoes, Glossop withdrew to more than 8,000 yards. This enabled him to make the best use of the range of his 6-inch guns and the striking power of their hundred-pound shells. Copplestone reported that—

"the 'Emden' was hit again and again during the long drawn-out two hours of her hopeless struggle. After twenty minutes the ... forward funnel went and she caught fire aft. Her steering gear was wrecked, and she became dependent upon the manipulation of her propellers, with the inevitable falling off in speed to about thirteen knots. During the early critical minutes of the action the 'Sydney' had the 'Emden' upon her port side, but all her casualties were caused on the starboard or disengaged side due to the steepness with which the German shells were falling.

"After the lapse of about three-quarters of an hour, the 'Emden' had lost two funnels and the foremast; she was badly on fire aft and amidships, so that at times nothing more than the top of the mainmast could be seen amid the clouds of steam and smoke. Her guns, now occasionally firing, gave out a short yellow flash by which they could be distinguished from the long dark red flames of the 'Sydney's' bursting lyddite. Once she disappeared so completely that the cry went up from the 'Sydney' that she had been sunk, but she appeared again, blazing, almost helpless. Glossop, who had been circling round to port, then drew in to a range of 5,500 yards . . . and determined to try a shot with a torpedo. It was a difficult shot as the torpedo gunner was obliged to set his gyroscope to a definite angle and then wait until the rapidly turning 'Emden' came upon his bearing. But in spite of the difficulties it was very good; the torpedo ran straight for its mark and then stopped short at the distance of 5,000 yards for which it had been set. The moment after the one [torpedo] had been fired, [Glossop] swung the ship round to starboard, opened out his range, and resumed the distressful game of gun-pounding. The 'Emden' also went away to starboard for about four miles and then von Müller, finding that his ship was badly pierced under the water as well as on fire, put about again and headed for North Keeling Island, where he ran aground.

"When he had settled with the collier 'Buresk', and taken off all those on board of her, Glossop returned to the wreck of the 'Emden' lying there helpless upon the North Keeling Island. The foremast and funnels were gone, the brave ship was a tangle of broken steel fore and aft, but the mainmast still stood and upon it floated the naval ensign of Germany. Until that flag had been struck the 'Sydney' could not send in a boat or deal with the crew as surrendered prisoners. For a quarter of an hour [Glossop] sent messages by International code and Morse flag signals, but the German ensign remained floating aloft. As von Müller would not surrender he must be compelled [to re-open fire], and compelled quickly and thoroughly. In order to make sure work the 'Sydney' approached to within 4,000 yards, trained four guns upon the 'Emden', and then when the aim was certain and steady smashed her from end to end. The destruction had been frightful, and it is probable that von Müller's obstinacy cost his crew greater casualties than the whole previous action. These last four shots did their work, the ensign came down, and a white flag of surrender went up. It was now late in the afternoon."

When Glossop requested a formal surrender, von Müller, lacking suitable facilities, ordered 'No signal book!' to be flashed back in morse. However, no-one on *Sydney* saw the reply and so shooting resumed. The precise number of shots fired is this period is in dispute, but was probably two salvoes: eight shells in all. Contrary to Bennet Copplestone's opinion, most of the damage had already been caused; the Germans estimated the additional casualties as about 25 dead and wounded. The base of the mainmast was red-hot, owing to the fire that had raged aft, and destruction of the ensign halliards prevented the imperial ensign being lowered.

Eventually, Matrose Arthur Werner scaled the mast to replace the ensign with a white flag and Glossop sent over Leutnant z.S. Fikentscher, in one of *Buresk*'s boats, to tell von Müller that *Sydney* would return to take off survivors after investigating Direction Island. Most of the Germans hoped that Hellmuth von Mücke and his landing party would offer a spirited resistance.

At 11:00 on 10 November, *Sydney* reappeared with a doctor and two assistants collected from Direction Island. The Australian cruiser's whaler, commanded by Lieutenant R.C. Garsia, was sent to negotiate with

**Below:** HMAS *Sydney*. By courtesy of the Trustees of the Imperial War Museum, negative no. Q21817.

**Below:** the shattered wreck of *Emden*, aground on North Keeling Island, looking forward from the after compass position to the bow. By courtesy of the Trustees of the Australian War Museum, Canberra, negative no. EN399.
**Below right:** standing beside the remnants of the transmitting equipment, the operator who made the distress calls from Direction Island poses for the camera. Author's collection.

von Müller, who had survived the carnage unscathed. Glossop's letter was extraordinary. Addressed to 'The Captain, H.I.G.M.S. "Emden"...', it read: "Sir, I have the honour to request that in the name of humanity you now surrender your ship to me. In order to show how much I appreciate your gallantry, I will recapitulate the position. (1) You are ashore, 3 funnels and 1 mast down and most guns disabled. (2) You cannot leave this island, and my ship is intact. In the event of your surrendering in which I venture to remind you is no disgrace but rather your misfortune I will endeavour to do all I can for your sick and wounded and take them to hospital. I have the honour to be, Sir, Your obedient Servant, [signed] John C.T. Glossop, Captain".

The German ship was utterly wrecked, blackened by fire aft. Shattered funnels sprawled across the deck amidships whilst the foremast lolled drunkenly over the port side, trailing the topmast and remnants of the rigging in the water. Fatalities eventually amounted to 134: seven officers, a Marine-Oberzahlmeister, four warrant officers, 25 petty officers, 92 men, a civilian cook, a barber and three Chinese washermen.

By 17:00, after a day of debilitating work in the blazing sun, the German cruiser had been cleared of the living. It was then realised that some of the Germans, including wounded men, had managed to get ashore. Garsia managed to get through the surf to the beach in darkness, but had been unable to locate the survivors. In the morning of 11 November, a rescue party of sailors from *Sydney* and uninjured members of *Emden*'s crew went ashore under Lieutenant Garsia and Leutnant z.S. Schall to find a few men—several of whom were very seriously wounded. The dead were hurriedly buried in the sand and the living returned to *Sydney*. Glossop then headed for Colombo in pursuit of the convoy he had left in the morning of 9 November.

Burying the German dead was left to crewmen of HMS *Cadmus*. In January 1915, the Admiralty ordered *Cadmus* back to North Keeling Island to salvage two safes and at a least one gun. On 9 February 1915, Admiral Jerram reported to London that $500-worth of Mexican dollars, two guns and their mountings, a searchlight and a torpedo had been taken from the wreck. At least one 10·5cm gun was displayed in Hyde Park, London, but was subsequently returned to Australia. One is now owned by the Australian War Memorial in Canberra, whilst another stands in a park in Sydney to commemorate not only the German dead but also the five sailors who died on the Australian cruiser.

The German landing party ashore on Direction Island had the last laugh. The men from *Sydney* found that von Mücke and his men had made off into the vastness of the Indian Ocean in the 97grt trading barquentine *Ayesha*. Eventually, even as their comrades were kicking their heels in a Maltese prison, most of von Mücke's men got back to Germany by way of the Red Sea and Constantinople. The story is related graphically in von Mücke's book *Ayesha*.

**Above:** the *Emden* landing party prepares to leave Direction Island in the 97grt barquentine *Ayesha*, seen in the background. By courtesy of the Trustees of the Imperial War Museum, negative no. Q22706.

# GREIF

23 January–29 February 1916; one victim (15,831grt).
A converted cargo ship, destroyed by the Royal Navy in a classic ship-to-ship engagement
before her cruise could begin in earnest.

◆◆◆

Type: Hilfskreuzer.
Builder: AG 'Neptun', Rostock (yard no. 340). Equipped by the Kaiserliche Werft, Kiel, 1915.
Owner: Deutsch-Australische Dampfschiffs-Gesellschaft, Hamburg (named *Guben*).
Launch date: 29 July 1914.
Commissioned: 23 January 1916.
Crew: 10 officers and 297 men.

**Dimensions**
Registered tonnage (grt): 4,962.
Full-load displacement: 9,900 tonnes.
Overall length: 131·7 metres.
Waterline length: 127·4 metres.
Beam: 16·5 metres.
Full-load draught: about 7·5 metres.

**Weapons**
Guns: four 15cm SK L/40 and one 10·5cm SK C/88 L/40.
Maximum range of main armament: 13,700 metres (15cm guns), 12,200 metres (10·5cm).
Lesser guns: machine-guns and small arms.
Torpedo tubes: two.
Munitions: 600 15cm shells, 200 10·5cm shells and twelve 50cm C/08 torpedoes.
Armour protection: none.

**Performance**
Powerplant: one vertical three-cylinder triple expansion steam engine, supplied by two boilers. One propeller shaft.
Boiler pressure: 13at (191psi).
Coal bunkerage: about 6,000 tonnes.
Speed, service maximum: 13 knots (3,000ihp).
Range: 35,000 nautical miles at 10 knots.

*Greif* was an interesting and most distinctive ship, built with two funnels—most unusual in a tramp—and a characteristically German break between the bridgework and the boat-deck and funnels. Launched only a few days before the First World War began, she was impressed into navy service at the beginning of 1916 and taken into Kiel dockyard for alteration. Not surprisingly, the second funnel was immediately removed. Two 15cm guns were fitted on the upper deck between the foremast and the bridge, one on each beam, and two more were mounted ahead of the mainmast abaft the bridge deck; the solitary 10·5cm gun was hidden in a house on the after deck.

In mid-February, shortly before the cruise was to begin, *Greif* was inspected in Kiel by Prinz Heinrich von Preussen, Admiral Bachmann (commander of the Marinestation der Ostsee) and a gaggle of celebrities. An indiscreet speech had even been made telling of the plan to sail down the Atlantic, around the Cape of Good Hope, and into the Indian Ocean to assist the forces under Paul von Lettow-Vorbeck that were struggling gamely in East Africa. Unfortunately for *Greif*, this only succeeded in drawing the attention of espionage rings to her imminent departure.

The vessel left Kiel for Hamburg on 25 February 1916, and then started out on 27 February up the North Sea—just as *Möwe* (q.v.) was running for home in the opposite direction. Weather was obligingly poor, grey mist being accompanied by flurries of snow, but was bad enough for the reconnoitring *U70* to lose contact with the raider. The U-Boat subsequently reported a sighting of a British submarine, which may have relayed the emergence of *Greif* to the Admiralty. Information had certainly reached

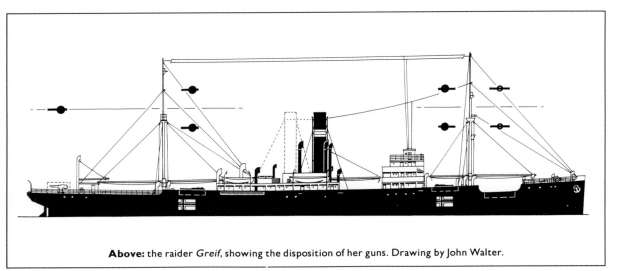

**Above:** the raider *Greif*, showing the disposition of her guns. Drawing by John Walter.

London that, at 20:20 on 28 February, a steamer was seen proceeding off Eckersund on the south-west coast of Norway at about ten knots.

The message reached Admiral Jellicoe at 23:38, whereupon the light cruisers *Inconstant* and *Cordelia*, screened by four destroyers, were ordered out of Rosyth, and *Calliope*, *Comus*, *Blanche* and three destroyers left Scapa Flow to reinforce the impressed merchantmen of the 10th Cruiser Squadron.

The armed merchant cruisers *Alcantara* (15,831grt) and *Andes* (15,620grt), commanded by the Royal Navy Captains Thomas Wardle and George Young respectively, were out on patrol together. Built by Harland & Wolff in 1913 and 1914, the sister-ships had served the Royal Mail Steam Packet Company in peace-time; both had been impressed for patrol duties in April 1915 and had been armed with eight 6-inch and two 6-pdr guns apiece. Their propelling machinery—two triple-expansion steam engines exhausting to a low pressure turbine on the central shaft—gave a service speed of about seventeen knots, which was more than sufficient to overhaul most tramp steamers.

*Alcantara* was due to leave southward to coal, but the instruction was countermanded at 08:05 on 29 February. At 08:45, lookouts aboard her reported smoke off the port beam in 61°45'N 0°58'E. At 08:55, *Andes* signalled that the suspicious vessel was in sight, steering north eastward at a speed that was optimistically estimated as fifteen knots. At 09:10, *Andes* added that the ship had changed course northward, was painted black, had two masts and a plain black funnel.

Being the closer, Wardle increased speed to bring *Alcantara* between *Andes* and the target. As he closed with *Greif*, two large Norwegian flags, RENA and TONSBERG could be seen on the steamer's side. 'This is the suspicious ship' signalled *Andes* as she turned away north-eastward. Approaching the raider from astern, *Alcantara* hoisted the signal MN ('Stop instantly') and fired two blank rounds as a warning.

The steamer obligingly hove-to off the starboard bow of the merchant cruiser, claiming to be bound for Rio de Janeiro and La Plata from Trondheim. At 09:40, however, just as preparations were being made to send over a boarding party, *Greif* cleared her poop gun for action and the very first shell fired from a range of about 800 yards smashed squarely into *Alcantara*'s bridge, wrecking the communications equipment and the engine-room telegraph. Hits from the German guns, all of which had been unmasked, soon wrecked boats and cut the steering gear; for nearly ten minutes, the British steamer wallowed out of control whilst *Greif* raked the bridge with machine-gun fire.

Once control of *Alcantara* was regained, Wardle piled on speed to get ahead of the slower German ship and prevent her running for the Norwegian coast. The first shell fired by the port after 6-inch gun of *Alcantara*

destroyed the 10·5cm poop gun on the raider, killing most of the gun-crew and setting fire to the ready-use ammunition. The sound of the first shots had also carried to *Andes*, then about five miles distant, whereupon Captain Young immediately turned to assist.

One of the first shells from *Andes*, fired at a range of about 6,500 yards, demolished the bridge of the raider, wrecking the steering gear and incapacitating the captain. *Alcantara* and *Greif* were slugging it out at close quarters, hitting each other repeatedly on the waterline, and were in an increasingly bad way. One British shell destroyed the forward 15cm gun on the port side of the raider, another penetrated the side to burst in the engine room, and a third set fire to the oil-fuel tanks between the bridge and the engine-room. It seems that a torpedo from *Greif* struck the British ship amidships in this period, but that the stokehold bunkers minimised the damage. At 10:02, *Greif* fired a second torpedo which passed under *Alcantara*'s stern as she turned.

By 10:15, however, under attack from the 6-inch guns of *Andes* as well as *Alcantara*, the German ship was ablaze amidships and ceased fire about 10:18. At 10:22, boats could be seen pulling away from her side. Fragments from *Alcantara*'s shells decapitated the German skipper as he was sliding down a rope over the port quarter of his ship.

> **Above right:** the Royal Mail Steam Packet Company's *Alcantara*, fatally damaged in the duel with *Greif* whilst serving as an armed merchant cruiser. By courtesy of Laurence Dunn.
>
> **Right:** an artist's impression of the duel between *Alcantara* and *Greif*.

*Alcantara*, meanwhile, had developed a list to port. Realising that she was doomed, Captain Wardle ordered the ship to be abandoned at 10:45. By 11:00 the Royal Mail liner had rolled over on to her beam ends and sank at 11:02 with the loss of 72 men. *Greif*, meanwhile, had been abandoned but was still afloat. The cruiser *Comus* and destroyer *Munster* arrived from the 4th Light Cruiser Squadron at about 11:15, whereupon Captain Alan Hotham of *Comus* ordered the destroyer to search for survivors whilst he finished off the raider with his two 6-inch guns. Listing increasingly to port, *Greif* sank by the stern at 13:01 in 61°45'N 1°10'E, still flying the German ensign.

*Andes* and *Munster* retrieved, in addition to Captain Wardle and the survivors of *Alcantara*, five German officers and 115 men.

Casualties aboard the German ship are recorded by Gröner, Jung and Maass (in the third volume of *Die deutschen Kriegsschiffe 1815–1945*, p. 152) as only 97 dead, but subtracting 120 from a theoretical complement of 307 predicts an actual death-roll of 187. This problem has yet to be satisfactorily resolved.

# KAISER WILHELM DER GROSSE

2–26 August 1914; three victims (10,685grt).
An old-but-fast passenger liner, once holder of the Blue Riband on the North Atlantic.
Destroyed after a short and comparatively unsuccessful raiding career.

Type: Hilfskreuzer, also known as *Hilfskreuzer D*.
Builder: AG 'Vulcan', Stettin-Bredow (yard no. 234). Equipped by the technical department of Norddeutscher Lloyd, Bremerhaven, 1914.
Owner: Norddeutscher Lloyd, Bremen.
Launch date: 4 March 1897.
Maiden voyage: November 1897.
Commissioned: 2 August 1914.
Crew: 24 officers and 560 men.

**Dimensions**
Registered tonnage (grt): 14,349.
Full-load displacement: 24,300 tonnes.
Overall length: 199·5 metres.
Waterline length: 191·2 metres (pp).
Beam: 20·1 metres.
Full-load draught: about 8·5 metres.

**Weapons**
Guns: six 10·5cm SK C/88 L/40.

Maximum range of main armament: 12,200 metres.
Lesser guns: two 3·7mm Hotchkiss revolver cannon, machine-guns and small arms.
Torpedo tubes: none.
Munitions: 400 10·5cm shells.
Armour protection: only on gun shields.

**Performance**
Powerplant: two vertical three-cylinder triple expansion steam engines, supplied by fourteen boilers. Two propeller shafts.
Boiler pressure: 12·5at (183psi).
Coal bunkerage: 4,550 tonnes.
Speed, trials: 22·5 knots (31,000ihp).
Speed, service maximum: 22 knots (28,000ihp).
Range: 5,000 nautical miles at 18 knots.

*Kaiser Wilhelm der Grosse* was amongst the most famous of all the pre-1914 German passenger liners. The first German ship to hold the Blue Riband (see Introduction),

**Below:** a longitudinal section of the Blue Riband holder *Kaiser Wilhelm der Grosse*, from the magazine *Engineering* for April 1898. By courtesy of the Trustees of the British Engineerium, Hove.

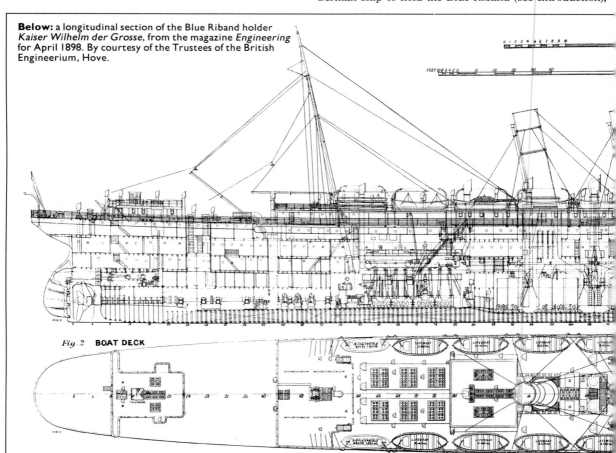

*Fig. 2* **BOAT DECK**

she was nonetheless past her prime mechanically by the beginning of the First World War. However, owing to her size, ability to mount guns and a speed of greater than twenty knots, *Kaiser Wilhelm der Grosse* was immediately converted into an armed merchant raider.

She was taken into Norddeutscher Lloyd docking facilities at the end of July 1914 to receive six 10·5cm guns, and to exchange her peacetime colours—black hull, white upperworks and yellow-buff funnels—for the sombre combination of black and dark grey. Two guns were placed on the forecastle ahead of the foremast, two lay ahead of the superstructure, and the remaining pair was mounted on the poop abaft the after deck house.

On 4 August 1914, commanded by Kapitän z.S. Reymann, *Kaiser Wilhelm der Grosse* left the Weser estuary, steamed hard up the North Sea, hugging the neutral Norwegian coast, then swung around the Shetland Islands in a broad arc and escaped out into the Atlantic Ocean. By 7 August Reymann was still little more than fifty nautical miles west north-west of Iceland when he unaccountably stopped and sank the 227grt *Tubal Cain* (Smith's Dock, North Shields, 1905), owned by Rushworth & Atkinson of Grimsby. The trawler was

regarded as too good a source of information to be allowed to escape.

The sea lanes around the Canaries (Islas Canarias), patrolled only by the obsolescent British cruisers *Highflyer* and *Vindictive*, were potentially lucrative. Many steamers called at Santa Cruz de Tenerife to coal and Reymann hoped to be able to take his pick of prizes.

On 15 August, running shorter and shorter of coal—which her furnaces consumed profligately—the raider seized the British steamer *Galician* (6,762grt), owned by the Union-Castle Mail Steam Ship Co. Ltd and bound for London from Cape Town under the command of Captain William Day.

A message transmitted from the steamship, asking if the coast was clear, was intercepted aboard the raider; Reymann ordered his wireless operator to reply that he would meet *Galician*, as there was greater safety in numbers. Accordingly, at 14:45, the two ships met in mid-ocean. Day was greeted with the message 'Stop immediately. Do not use wireless or I will sink you'.

The German boarding party went over to the prize, only to discover that *Galician* was carrying nearly 250 passengers. As many were women and children,

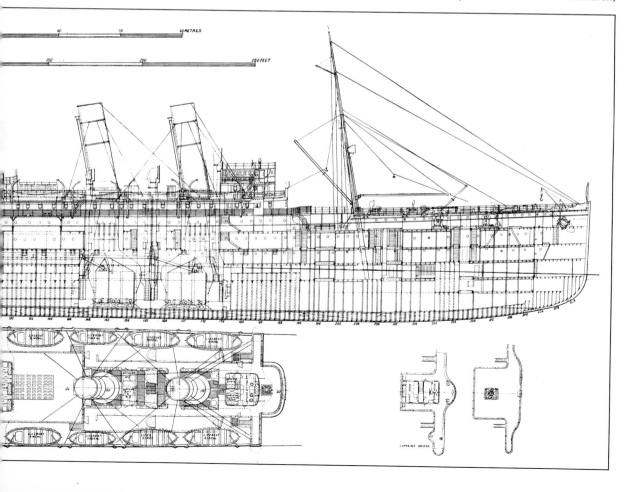

Reymann decided to release the steamship at 05:00 on 16 August. Two hours later, however, he encountered an interesting-looking four-masted freighter with a black hull and a large yellow-buff funnel. Owned by the New Zealand Shipping Co. Ltd, the 7,392grt *Kaipara* had been built by John Brown & Co. of Clydebank in 1903 and was returning to Britain with a cargo of meat loaded in New Zealand and Montevideo. Captain Henry Makepeace was heading for a coaling stop at Las Palmas when he had been halted 170 nautical miles south-west of Tenerife. The captive was promptly sunk by a combination of open sea cocks and, apparently, 53 precious 10·5cm shells.

Pleased with this success, Reymann steamed away south-westward. In late afternoon, the raider spotted a smoke trail. A very large steamship with a black hull, white upperworks and a plain yellow-buff funnel appeared, heading north-eastward on a converging course. Judging the newcomer to be British, the Germans were overjoyed and eagerly awaited the capture. The ship obligingly stopped to order. A boarding party was despatched, but there was great disappointment in store for the men of *Kaiser Wilhelm der Grosse*; the 15,044grt *Arlanza* of the Royal Mail Steam Packet Company, a 1911-vintage product of Harland & Wolff of Belfast, was carrying 335 women and nearly a hundred children. She, too, had to be sent on her way.

In the early evening of 16 August, the 3,066grt freighter *Nyanga* of the Elder Line Ltd, built on the Tyne in 1900, was accosted sailing homeward with a mixed cargo loaded in southern Africa. After taking what was necessary, Reymann sank the British tramp by the customary method of opened sea-cocks and explosive charges. He was now running dangerously low on coal and needed the help of the Etappe system. *Kaiser Wilhelm der Grosse* immediately headed for the Spanish African colony of Rio de Oro, where, in defiance of neutrality, a rendezvous had been arranged on 21 August with the steamships *Arucas* and *Duala*, the former having escaped from Tenerife and the latter from Las Palmas.

Both ships had been seconded to the Etappe Westafrika. Built by H. Nüske & Co. AG of Stettin in 1914, 2,056grt *Arucas* was owned by Oldenburgisch-Portugiesische Dampfschiffs-Rheederei; *Duala* of the Hamburg–Amerika Linie, launched from the West Hartlepool shipyard of William Gray & Co. Ltd in 1911, had a gross registered tonnage of 3,511.

The raider and her two colliers were soon joined by the 1900-vintage steamship *Magdeburg* (4,497grt), built for Deutsch-Australische Dampfschiffs-Gesellschaft by Flensburger Schiffbau-Gesellschaft, and then by the Hamburg–Amerika Linie *Bethania* (7,548grt), which had been launched from the Linthouse yard of Alex. Stephen & Sons in 1899. The transhipment of large quantities of coal, fresh water and food began.

> **Below:** *Kaiser Wilhelm der Grosse* was a distinctively lean and rakish ship. **Above right:** the cruiser *Highflyer*, pictured by E. Hopkins, 'Photographic Publisher' of Southsea, prior to 1914. Author's collection.

Local Spanish officials took a belated interest in the proceedings, but Reymann proffered a well-rehearsed story: his engines were in need of maintenance, he said, and the colliers had come to assist. Though *Kaiser Wilhelm der Grosse* was painted in peculiarly drab colours, her crewmen still wore the uniforms of Norddeutscher Lloyd and the visiting officials were initially fooled into accepting the story.

Coaling was still underway at a leisurely pace on 26 August, when lookouts at the masthead of the raider spotted a warship approaching. As the ship drew closer, she was seen to have three funnels and be flying the White Ensign. Panic ensured; Reymann ordered his guns cleared for action, the colliers were hastily sent packing, and steam was raised in an attempt to get under way. But it was all too late.

The obsolescent 5,560-ton British cruiser *Highflyer* had been completed by the Fairfield Engineering & Shipbuilding Company of Glasgow in December 1899. Though she had been reduced to a training ship by 1914, war had brought a new commission for patrol duties. *Highflyer*'s eleven 6-inch guns had a similar range to the 10·5cm patterns of *Kaiser Wilhelm der Grosse*, but fired a much more destructive shell.

Had the raider been underway, with a full head of steam, Reymann may have been able to out-run his adversary; *Highflyer* had never been speedy, having raised only 20·1 knots on full-power trials. However, the liner had been caught virtually immobile. The British captain invited Reymann to surrender, but was predictably refused. Both ships opened fire. The contest was one-sided. Though the German gunners hit the cruiser several times, *Kaiser Wilhelm der Grosse* was soon being pounded by 6-inch shells. After a brisk, but brief engagement she rolled onto her side at 16:20 and sank in shallow water off Durnford Point (23°34′N 16°02′W). The British believed that they had sunk her, whereas the Germans claimed to have scuttled. It was a fine point of difference. The most important result was that the raider had been eliminated.

Reymann, nine of his officers and 72 men reached the shore in the ship's boats, walked to the nearest Spanish post and surrendered. They were eventually taken to Las Palmas and interned aboard the German merchant ships in harbour. Almost 400 men were taken off by the collier *Bethania*, which had remained in the vicinity while the battle raged and then steamed westward for the USA; intercepted by HMS *Essex* in 30°20′N 75°50′W, she was subsequently sent into Kingston in Jamaica. *Arucas* and *Duala* made off at high speed before the action began, carrying the crews of *Kaipara* and *Nyanga*.

Casualties on both sides had apparently been minimal. *Highflyer* lost one man dead and six injured, losses on the raider being unknown. Some modern German sources have suggested that there was no loss of life aboard *Kaiser Wilhelm der Grosse* at all, but this is improbable in view of the pounding administered by *Highflyer* in the closing minutes of the action. Claims that casualties amounted to more than a hundred—based on the theoretical complement of 584 and survivors numbering nearer 480—have never been satisfactorily resolved.

# KARLSRUHE

I August–4 November 1914; sixteen mercantile victims (72,225grt).
A conventional light cruiser, destroyed by an internal explosion in November 1914 after
a highly successful, but largely unpublicised cruise.

●◆●

Type: Kleine Kreuzer (light cruiser).
Authorisation: as 'Ersatz Seeadler', 1910.
Builder: Krupp'sche Germaniawerft, Kiel.
Laid down: 1911.
Launch date: 11 November 1912.
Commissioned: 15 January 1914.
Crew: 18 officers and 355 men.
**Dimensions**
Design displacement: 4,900 tonnes.
Full-load displacement: 6,191 tonnes.
Overall length: 142·2 metres.
Waterline length: 139·0 metres.
Beam: 13·7 metres.
Full-load draught: 6·2 metres.
**Weapons**
Guns: twelve SK 10·5cm C/88 L/40.
Maximum range of main armament: 12,200 metres.
Lesser guns: none, excepting machine-guns and small arms
Torpedo tubes: one submerged on each beam.
Munitions: 1,750 10·5cm high-explosive shells, fifty 10·5cm
shrapnel shells; five 50cm C/08 torpedoes.
Armour protection: belt 18–60mm, deck 40–60mm, collision
bulkhead 40mm, conning tower 100mm, gun-shields 50mm.
**Performance**
Powerplant: two sets of Navy steam turbines, supplied from
fourteen boilers (twelve coal-fired, two oil). Two shafts.
Boiler pressure: 16at (235psi).
Coal bunkerage: 400 tonnes normal, 1,300 tonnes maximum.
Oil bunkerage: 70 tonnes normal, 200 tonnes maximum.
Speed, trials: 28·5 knots (37,885shp).
Speed, service maximum: 27·5 knots (25,000shp).
Range: 5,000 nautical miles at 12 knots, 900 miles at 25 knots.

The brand-new cruiser *Karlsruhe* was sent out from
Germany in the early summer of 1914 to replace *Dresden*,
meeting in Port-au-Prince in Haiti on 25 July. There,
the captains—Fregattenkapitäns Lüdecke and Köhler—
exchanged commands, the intention being for Lüdecke
and the crew of *Dresden* to return home. Erich Köhler
was to remain senior officer on the Ostamerikanische
Station, with responsibility for the gunboat in West
Africa and any merchant cruisers commissioned for
service in the southern Atlantic Ocean.

Köhler was born in Westfalen on 6 September 1873
and had entered the Kaiserliche Marine in April 1891.
Promoted to Leutnant z.S. in April 1896, he was posted to
SMS *Moltke*; an advance to Oberleutnant z.S. occurred a
year later, with the commencement of service aboard
*Sachsen*. A posting to the Admiralstab in March 1903,
with the rank of Kapitänleutnant, was followed by a spell
aboard the cruiser *Hamburg* in 1907–8. In October 1908,
Korvettenkapitän Köhler became the navigating officer
aboard the battleship *Deutschland* before returning to
the Admiralstab to serve the navy inspectorate. On 16

June 1913, he was appointed to command the incomplete
*Karlsruhe* with the rank of Fregattenkapitän.

A telegram from the Admiralstab in Berlin told Fritz
Lüdecke to return with *Dresden* by way of the Danish-
owned island of St Thomas, which doubled as a
Hamburg–Amerika Linie coaling station, and then Horta
in the Ilhas dos Açôres (Azores). He was expected back
in Wilhelmshaven on 12 August. Simultaneously, the
cruiser *Strassburg*, which had been on a courtesy visit to
Central America, was also ordered home.

*Karlsruhe* left Port-au-Prince on the afternoon of 26
July, bound for the Cuban port of Habana by way of the
Windward Passage. Arriving safely in Habana a few
minutes before noon on 28 July, Köhler was expecting to
leave for the eastern coast of Mexico to show the German
flag, then proceed southward to attend the opening of the
Panama Canal. He was also expected off the west coast of
North America in the autumn to provide German naval
presence at the San Francisco World Fair. Instead, on
reaching Habana, he was appraised of the latest news
from Europe. Little of it was good. A coded telegram
from Berlin, relayed by the Key West station, warned
that diplomatic relations between Austria-Hungary and
Serbia had been severed and that worse was bound to
follow. The Etappe Westindien and the consulates in New
Orleans, Tampico, St Thomas, Vera Cruz and Puerto
Mexico were immediately placed on alert.

Köhler left Habana at 10:00 on 30 July to cruise off the
Mexican coast until the clouded international situation
resolved. In the morning of 31 July, whilst off Cay Sal
Bank, he was warned of the likelihood of war with
Russia, France and Britain. On 1 August, Köhler received
a message from the naval attaché in Washington,
Fregattenkapitän Boy-Ed, informing him that the
steamship *Kronprinz Wilhelm* would shortly be leaving
harbour and would need to be armed at sea. Köhler used
the period of uncertainty to calibrate his guns, undertake
firing practice, and hone his inexperienced crew to full
efficiency.

The homeward voyage of *Dresden* had been cancelled,
and the cruiser was ordered southward into 'Cruiser War
Zone III' off the east coast of Brazil. On 2 August, news
came that Germany was at war with Russia and France.
The terms of the Entente Cordiale honour-bound Britain
to side with France; clearly, the British 4th Cruiser
Squadron commanded by Rear-Admiral Sir Christopher
Cradock K C V O C B would soon ally with the French ships
*Déscartes* and *Condé*. Köhler immediately set his course

for a point off the Bahamas, where he had been ordered to meet with a German passenger liner. On 4 August, the German authorities informed Köhler that Britain had declared war on Germany and that he was free to disrupt trade in the middle Atlantic.

One of Köhler's first acts was to secure supplies of coal. On 4 August, the German consul in St Thomas informed the headquarters of the Etappe Westindien in Habana that the 'German steamer *Spreewald* leaves 6 August with 4,000 tonnes of coal on board. Second German steamer *Patagonia* will sail 10 August with 4,000 tonnes coal. Despatch of another ship depends on receiving fresh supplies of coal from the United States of America. German steamer *Präsident* left on 3 August from San Juan de Puerto Rico for Habana'. The wheels of war had been set in motion.

The Royal Navy in the Western Atlantic was thinly stretched at the beginning of the First World War. Admiral Cradock had at his command four County class armoured cruisers—*Suffolk* (flagship), *Berwick*, *Essex* and *Lancaster*—plus the light cruiser *Bristol*. When war was declared, *Suffolk* was in harbour in Kingston, Jamaica, but left at 18:00 on 4 August to meet *Essex* off Nantucket, the latter already being in position to patrol

the sea lanes from Britain to New York. The goal was partly to look after the interests of the British merchant fleet, but also to intercept and destroy any of the German passenger liners should they attempt to break out of New York harbour.

HMS *Berwick* was left to patrol the channel between Florida and the Bahamas; *Bristol* was originally ordered northward from the West Indies, but the orders were soon countermanded. *Lancaster* was docked in Bermuda for minor repairs, leaving on 6 August to patrol the Cabot Strait.

One of Cradock's first priorities was to eliminate *Karlsruhe*, which, as he was well aware, was a fast and modern ship which could wreak terrible havoc along the shipping lanes if allowed to roam unfettered. Intercepted messages intended for the German warship had confirmed that Köhler was to be allowed a free hand; as he was highly unlikely to seek a direct confrontation with Cradock's cruisers—even *Bristol* could prove a match for the lightly-armed German ship—the only practicable option was to attack British maritime trade.

Cradock, aware that *Karlsruhe* had last been seen in Habana, despatched *Bristol* to search the Florida Channel. However, as the British cruiser swept back and

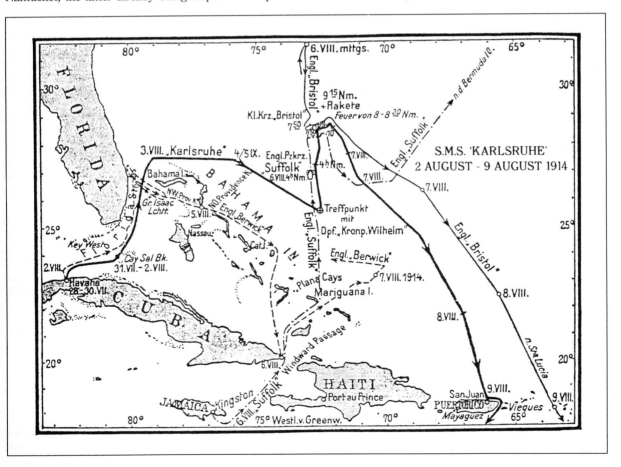

forth, the German ship skulked between Crooked Island and Mariguana Island. At Plana Kays, she was able to eavesdrop British wireless traffic. Köhler's orders required him to meet the liner on 6 August, to the north of Plana Kays. However, as he wirelessed instructions to Kapitän Grahn of *Kronprinz Wilhelm*, the transmissions were overheard off Great Isaac Light at the entrance to North West Providence Channel by a steamship of the United Fruit Company. News of the proximity of the German ships was immediately relayed to HMS *Berwick*. Abandoning the fruitless search of the Florida Channel, the British warship had sailed south-eastward into North East Providence Channel and was in the vicinity of Cat Island (24°20′N 75°30′W) by 6 August.

At 07:00 on 5 August, in mid-ocean, *Karlsruhe* had stopped the Italian steamer *Mondibello* of Società de Navigatori a Vapori 'Creole' of Messina. The neutral vessel was bound in ballast for Galveston, Texas, and had nothing to offer. At 03:00 on 6 August, Köhler finally made wireless contact with *Kronprinz Wilhelm* (q.v.). The imposing Norddeutscher Lloyd liner, dating from 1901, was to become a merchant cruiser.

At 07:00 on 6 August, with immaculate navigation, *Karlsruhe* met *Kronprinz Wilhelm* in 25°36′N 72°36′W, remote from the nearest landfall. The cruiser lashed alongside the liner, port side to port side, and the ships steered slowly south-eastward at a couple of knots. *Kronprinz Wilhelm* towered so far over *Karlsruhe* that lashing the vessels together presented a major problem, though fenders minimised the damage as the Atlantic swell ground the hulls together.

The cruiser handed over two 8·8cm guns with 290 rounds of ammunition, an 8mm Maxim machine-gun, 36 Mauser rifles (Gewehre 98), small-arms ammunition and bayonets, intending to receive coal and oil-fuel in return. Kapitänleutnant Paul Thierfelder, navigating officer of *Karlsruhe*, was appointed to command the liner whilst two reservists—Leutnants z.S. d.R. Eyring and Hentschel—came aboard the cruiser.

At 10:15, with the transfer of fuel and equipment well under way, lookouts announced the appearance of smoke south by west. The Germans had to assume that this signified the approach of a hostile warship, presumed to be HMS *Berwick*. Panic-stricken efforts to extricate the German ships ensued, whereupon *Karlsruhe* headed off north by west at 21 knots and *Kronprinz Wilhelm* followed a north north-east course at eighteen. The cruiser had only been able to take aboard fifty tonnes of coal, and had abandoned her launch in the confusion.

The newcomer was the armoured cruiser *Suffolk* of the 4th Cruiser Squadron, flying the flag of Rear-Admiral Cradock. The warship was bound for Nantucket out of Kingston, Jamaica, intending to meet *Essex* on station to protect the New York–Britain sea lanes. *Essex* had left Bermuda in the night of 2/3 August. The light cruiser *Bristol* was also steaming northward for St John's,

Newfoundland, and had reached 31°30′N 73°W. *Karlsruhe* had been caught between *Bristol* and *Suffolk*, respectively to the north and south of the rendezvous with *Kronprinz Wilhelm*. Springing the trap had owed something to luck, though this had been minimised by the choice of Windward Passage on the run north and also by the interception of wireless traffic between *Karlsruhe* and *Kronprinz Wilhelm* immediately prior to their meeting.

The sighting of the two German warships caused Cradock to transmit a message to *Bristol*, giving, amongst other things, an estimate of *Karlsruhe*'s course and speed. Captain Basil Fanshawe was ordered to intercept the German cruiser if he could. Cradock then instructed *Suffolk*'s helmsman to follow *Karlsruhe*, judging the cruiser to be a more dangerous adversary to let loose than a converted liner.

Though the 6-inch guns of the British cruiser presented a real threat to *Karlsruhe*, *Suffolk* was a much older ship. She had only been capable of 24·7 knots on her trials back in 1904, whereas the German ship was brand-new and could easily reach 26 knots. The outcome of the chase was predictable. Köhler simply increased speed to 22 knots—fast enough to outpace her pursuer, but not so fast that fuel would be consumed unnecessarily. By dusk, *Karlsruhe* had finally disappeared over the horizon.

At 19:50, however, *Bristol* appeared in the bright moonlight off the starboard bow of the German ship, much to Köhler's discomfiture. The contestants seemed evenly matched; the British vessel was older and a knot or two slower, but had two 6-inch guns that outranged the German 10·5cm patterns by a thousand yards. Eager for a fight, *Bristol* turned sharply to port to allow her starboard guns to bear and opened fire at a range of about 7,000 yards. *Karlsruhe* turned eastward to bring her port guns to bear and joined battle whilst simultaneously increasing speed to 26 knots on a south eastward course. No hits were gained by either ship, and firing had stopped by 20:30.

From the German viewpoint, the engagement had been very disappointing. Only about ten of the eighty 10·5cm shells that had been fired had reached *Bristol*, even though the range was comparatively short. Leutnant z.S. von dem Borne, the gunnery officer, estimated that some had fallen as much as 1,500 metres short of the target. The guns on the main deck amidships had performed particularly poorly; the brilliant flash of the guns had undoubtedly made range-taking difficult, but poor adjustment of the sights was also suspected to have played a part.

It was soon clear that the German vessel was easily outstripping her British rival. The problem lay in the quality of the American Pocahontas coal *Bristol* had taken aboard. As in the case of *Suffolk*, which was similarly loaded, speed fell away as furnaces clogged; eighteen knots was about all that the supposedly 26-knot

**Above:** SMS *Karlsruhe* running her full-power trials in 1914. From von dem Borne's *S.M.S. "Karlsruhe"*. **Below:** one of a series of postcards issued during the First World War by Bell's of Westcliff, Essex, this commemorates the duel between *Karlsruhe* and *Bristol*. Author's collection.

Inscribed on BRITAIN'S

ENGAGEMENTS

H.M.S. BRISTOL.

In the first action of the War with the KARLSRUHE, Augt 6, 1914. The Battle of the FALKLAND ISLES, Dec. 8, 1914.

H.M.S. BRISTOL.

ROLL OF FAME!

BELL'S, WESTCLIFF, ESSEX.

*Bristol* could muster. However, by the time *Karlsruhe* had lost the pursuer, her own coal stocks had been depleted by a worryingly large amount. Speed was cut back to eighteen knots at 23:00, to sixteen at 00:20 on 7 August, then to fourteen at daybreak once it became obvious that no British cruisers were in sight. Knowing that *Karlsruhe* could travel little more than a thousand nautical miles at full speed, Köhler eventually rang down twelve knots and headed for the Danish-administered island of St Thomas.

Fuel reserves were estimated as 112 tonnes of coal and 31 tonnes of fuel oil at noon on 8 August. As *Karlsruhe* consumed about 5·6 tonnes of coal per hour at ten knots, reaching harbour presented problems. Lookouts strained for a glimpse of an approaching threat; the German ship had so little coal that Köhler dared not ring up maximum speed to elude an aggressor. Neither did he wish to slug it out with a British County-class cruiser, which would surely annihilate him. At 06:00 on 9 August, *Karlsruhe* made the harbour of San Juan de Puerto Rico with no more than twenty tonnes of coal in her bunkers.

The US authorities in Puerto Rico informed Köhler that he was to adhere strictly to their neutrality. This allowed him to take on only the coal necessary to reach the next friendly harbour—fortunately, Saint Thomas—and could stay for no more than 24 hours. This was often

flouted by warships when they visited the waters of minor Powers (e.g., *Dresden* in Chile), but the Germans dared not antagonise American administrators for fear of the US Navy.

The insistence of the Puerto Rico authorities on a trip to St Thomas, though it had been his intended destination, troubled Erich Köhler greatly. It clearly limited his options; one high-profile visit to the Danish island would prevent him using it again for some time. Adding greatly to Erich Köhler's woes, German consul Wilhelm Hopp, who was also the local representative of the Hamburg–Amerika Linie, discovered that the coal that had been promised was contained in barges. It could not be transferred quickly enough to satisfy the neutrality requirements.

However, as the 3,537grt steamer *Odenwald* of the Hamburg–Amerika Linie was also lying in San Juan harbour, Köhler was able to take 550 tonnes of coal from her and nineteen naval reservists to swell his crew. He also discovered that the 3,016grt collier *Patagonia* was travelling from Mayaguez on the west coast of Puerto Rico. Instructions were telegraphed so that Kapitän Koldewey would head for St Thomas, coal there, and proceed to a rendezvous south-east of Barbados.

At 20:10 on 9 August, *Karlsruhe* left San Juan de Puerto Rico. Sighting Cabo San Juan at 21:15, Köhler

**Left:** taken from one of the German tenders, this picture shows the capture of the grey-hulled steamer *Bowes Castle*. By courtesy of Emden-Archiv Günter Huff.

**Right:** a dramatic view of *Karlsruhe*, one of the most successful but least known of the German raiding cruisers. Author's collection.

turned southward, passed through the channel and set a course across the Caribbean, bound for Curaçao in the Netherland Antilles. At 04:45 on the morning of 12 August, the German cruiser dropped anchor in St Anna's Bay with only 150 tonnes of coal and 29 tonnes of fuel-oil remaining.

Before much could be done, Commodore Coenen of the Royal Netherlands navy came aboard *Karlsruhe* with a friendly warning; no-one in Curaçao knew much about the precise political situation in Europe, so the governor had telegraphed for information. Meanwhile, the 1906-vintage 4,920-tonne battleship *Jacob van Heemskerck* and the obsolescent 3,464-tonne *Kortenaer* had cleared their guns for action and would open fire at *Karlsruhe* if necessary.

Köhler decided to take the risk and came alongside the coaling stage of the Austrian-owned Maduro & Söhne

at 08:30. Coaling was accomplished with such gusto that 1,200 tonnes had been taken aboard by mid-afternoon. The arrival of the 1,103grt German merchantman *Stadt Schleswig* of Reederei H.C. Horn, commanded by Kapitän Fritz Zimmermann, had been another unexpected bonus. The steamship had come from the coast of Mexico with coal destined for the local Hamburg–Amerika Linie stockpile. At 20:00, *Karlsruhe* steamed away northward, sending *Stadt Schleswig* to a rendezvous by São João island off the northern coast of Brazil.

Köhler then turned eastward along the coast of Venezuela, hoping to take a prize travelling between Curaçao and the Testigos islands. Lack of success soon persuaded the German skipper to move to the channel between Trinidad & Tobago and Grenada, but no British ships could be found. At 08:30 on 18 August, therefore, the cruiser met the steamer *Patagonia* off São João.

Lookouts aboard *Karlsruhe* spotted a tell-tale smoke plume at 16:00 on 18 August, and, after a short chase, a steamer with a grey hull and a black-topped red funnel hove-to. Registered in Liverpool, 4,650grt *Bowes Castle* had been stopped in 9°54′N 55°10′W. Owned by the Lancashire Shipping Co. Ltd and managed by James Chambers & Company, she had been completed in 1913 by Sir James Laing & Sons Ltd of Sunderland. Nitrates and silver ore were being hauled from Antofagasta to St Lucia for orders. A boarding party comprising Oberleutnant z.S. Wilhelm Schroeder, Leutnant z.S. d.R. Hentschel, a signalman, a wireless telegraphist and an assistant writer soon discovered not only that *Bowes Castle* had been in contact with HMS *Glasgow* in Montevideo harbour, where the steamer had coaled, but also that much of the cargo was American-owned.

Köhler nonetheless determined to sink her, and, after the 36-man crew had been transferred to *Patagonia*, sea-cocks were opened and scuttling charges were fired. *Bowes Castle* finally sank at 19:35.

*Karlsruhe* then turned south-eastward along the shipping lanes, coaling from *Patagonia* off Maraca island at the mouth of the Amazon on 21 August. By 23 August, the cruiser had 1,300 tonnes of coal aboard, 130 of which were bagged on deck. *Stadt Schleswig*, meanwhile, had left Curaçao on 14 August and hove-to off São João a day

before *Karlsruhe* and *Patagonia* arrived on 25 August. *Stadt Schleswig* was too small to be an effectual collier, so Kapitän Zimmermann was instructed to land the crew of *Bowes Castle* in San Luis de Maranhão after all his coal had been transferred to the cruiser and *Patagonia*. The steamship eventually made harbour on 2 September.

Köhler elected to concentrate on the shipping lanes off the north-eastern coast of Brazil, which provided a natural confluence of several trade routes—from the ports on the eastern seaboard of South America to New York and the Caribbean; or, alternatively, across the Atlantic to Tenerife, Las Palmas, southern Europe or north-west Africa. By roving continually across the lanes from east to west and then back again, *Karlsruhe* needed comparatively little luck to achieve success. After coaling from *Patagonia* on 30 August, Köhler summoned the Norddeutscher Lloyd steamers *Asuncion* and *Crefeld*.

At 10:30 on 31 August 1914, *Karlsruhe* finally met the new tenders. At 16:00, about fifty nautical miles west north-west of Atol de Rocas, Köhler chased and then stopped a black-hulled steamship with a tall black funnel. The 4,336grt *Strathroy* had been built by William Hamilton & Co. Ltd of Port Glasgow in 1909 for the Strathroy Steamship Co. Ltd and was managed by Burrell & Son of Glasgow. As her cargo was 6,000 tons of coal from Norfolk, Virginia, for Rio de Janeiro, she

was invaluable to *Karlsruhe*. Coal supplies were rarely plentiful, and Köhler was relying on capturing a collier or two to eke them out. As a heavy sea was running, Köhler decided not to risk a boarding party; instead, he gave *Strathroy*'s captain the clearest warning of what would happen if the prize did not sail to instructions signalled from the raider. The two ships immediately set a course for Atol de Rocas.

*Asuncion*, *Crefeld* and *Rio Negro* had been sent ahead to Rocas. Once there, Köhler examined his prize and her part-European, part-Chinese crew. Owing to her load, *Strathroy* was too useful merely to be sunk immediately. Transferring the Europeans to *Patagonia*, Erich Köhler appointed Kapitänleutnant d.R. Lubinus, the First Officer of *Crefeld*, to command of the new collier with effect from 1 September 1914. Lubinus was given Leutnant z.S. d.R. Gundlach and Maschinisten Büchmann, Second Officer and Third Engineer of *Asuncion* respectively, plus fourteen men from *Crefeld*, *Asuncion* and *Rio Negro* to ensure the Chinese took *Strathroy* in company with *Patagonia* to remote Lavendeira reef (5°S 36°W).

The British crewmen were finally landed in Tenerife on 22 October, nearly a month after their ship had been scuttled. *Strathroy* had served Köhler and the Kaiserliche Marine as 'Kohlendampfer I'.

*Patagonia*, after safely shepherding *Strathroy* to Lavendeira reef, reached Pernambuco on 6 September with mail for Germany. The steamer—leaking from the many plates sprung during coaling operations alongside *Karlsruhe*—then sailed for Bahia Blanca and a period in dry dock. She left Bahia for Montevideo in late November, loaded coal and provisions, but was apprehended by an Argentine warship early in December and returned to internment in Bahia.

With supplies of coal secured, *Karlsruhe* steered a north-eastward course, passing close to Fernando Noronha. Atol de Rocas lay to the west; several hundred miles north-eastward was São Pedro e São Paulo (St Paul's Rocks), a natural marker for trans-ocean traffic turning for the Cabo Verde islands. Shortly after dawn on 3 September, 250 nautical miles south-west of São Pedro e São Paulo, *Karlsruhe* captured the steamer *Maple Branch* (4,338grt) of the Nautilus Steam Shipping Co. Ltd. Registered in Sunderland, the tramp had been built in 1905 by Gourlay Brothers & Co. Ltd of Dundee. She was bound from England to Punta Arenas and Valparaiso, with a mixed cargo and a largely Chinese crew of 42 men.

Cattle aboard the captive were gleefully slaughtered to provide *Karlsruhe* and *Crefeld* with fresh meat. Sea cocks were opened and scuttling charges were fired at 17:00, but *Maple Branch* was reluctant to leave hurriedly. Oberleutnant z.S. von dem Borne requested permission to use the steamship as a target to teach his gun crews the use of time fuzes; finally, the ship sank at 18:45 in 1°59'S 32°47'W—or about 120 nautical miles north of Fernando Noronha.

*Maple Branch* provided the men of the cruiser with an asthmatic cockerel, which was named August, and several live pigs which were subsequently kept in a pen on the port side of the afterdeck. One of the pigs—christened Julius—became a firm favourite even though, said the German seamen, he had been born a British Colonial: a *Maple Branch* crewman had apparently won him in a market in Kingston, Jamaica. The pig competed for attention with the ship's dog, a terrier named Flocke which had been given to Köhler in Vera Cruz by the crew of *Dresden*.

By 5 September, supplies of coal were running low. Köhler simply headed for Lavendeira reef and *Strathroy*, 850 tonnes being transferred from the collier on 7–8 September. On 9 September, *Karlsruhe* left the reef without *Patagonia*, intent on meeting *Crefeld* on 11 September about 250 nautical miles north north-east of Fernando Noronha. There *Rio Negro* also joined the formation, steaming out of sight more than ten nautical miles to eastward.

The Germans had been told to communicate by signal flags and lamps to avoid the characteristically high-pitched Telefunken signature. Messages were intercepted in this period from the Nelson Steam Navigation Co. Ltd steamer *Highland Corrie*, but the British ship could not be found in the darkness.

The German convoy had led a charmed life. HMS *Bristol*, after visiting São João, passed within 25 nautical miles of Lavendeira reef in the early afternoon of 9 September on an easterly course for Cabo São Roque. The armoured cruiser *Cornwall* passed between the Atol de Rocas and Fernando Noronha on the same day, steaming southward, and the merchant cruiser *Macedonia* had cut through the German track at noon on 10 September, forty nautical miles off Cabo São Roque.

At about 03:30 on 14 September, lights of a steamer travelling south-westward were seen distantly. Dawn revealed the 5,159grt Nelson Steam Navigation Co. Ltd steamship *Highland Hope*, built by Russell & Co. of Port Glasgow in 1903 and bound for Buenos Aires to load meat. The ship had left Liverpool on 31 August, but had been stopped 190 nautical miles south-west of São Pedro e São Paulo.

The boarding party reported that *Highland Hope* had 1,600 tons of coal, plentiful provisions, and a Marconi wireless-telegraphy installation. Köhler worried that messages had been sent, identifying the position of the raider, and determined to sink the steamer as quickly as possible.

As the crew of the British steamship was being transferred to *Crefeld*, however, *Reina Victoria Eugenia* of Compañia Maritima SA, Barcelona, chanced by bound for Montevideo. A message flashed out from the newcomer's bridge: 'Who are you?'. 'Convoy of British ships', replied Köhler, and the Spaniard, apparently satisfied by the presence of a four-funnel cruiser, went on her way. The

**Top:** the steamer *Maple Branch* (4,338grt) of the Nautilus Steam Shipping Co. Ltd, sunk on 3 September. **Above:** the Spanish steamship *Regina Victoria-Eugenia*, released after examination. Photographs by courtesy of Laurence Dunn.

Germans subsequently detected wireless traffic between *Reina Victoria Eugenia* and the battleship *Canopus*, escorting a valuable tanker to Pernambuco. Fortunately for *Karlsruhe*, though the position of the 'convoy' had been given accurately, Captain Heathcoate Grant of *Canopus* held to his orders. The German ships and their captive were little more than ninety minutes hard steaming away.

*Highland Hope*, of no further use to Köhler, was scuttled at 11:45 and the Germans sped off westward. Next day brought *Sørfareren* (2,649grt), a full-rigger built by Oswald, Mordaunt & Co. of Southampton in 1888 and registered in the Norwegian port of Christiansand. The vessel was carrying German-owned chromium ore from New Caledonia to Goteborg. Captain Aanonsen sent over meat, fresh provisions, and Argentinian newspapers which most helpfully revealed the South American sailing schedules of the Royal Mail Steam Packet Company. Köhler was particularly keen to capture one of these large passenger liners.

The activity in the north-easterly trade routes was bound to arouse the attention of the Royal Navy, so Köhler decided to move on. The morning of 15 September found *Karlsruhe*, *Crefeld* and *Rio Negro* heading west, but the course was then changed to west south-west so that the sea lanes between South America, the West Indies and the USA could be threatened.

At noon on 17 September, in 3ºS 35º40′W, 145 miles north-west of Cabo São Roque, the British collier *Indrani* was taken. Managed by T.B. Royden for the Indra Line of Liverpool, built by Charles Connell & Co. Ltd of Glasgow in 1912, the 5,706grt ship was laden with 6,700 tons of

American Pocahontas coal bound for Rio de Janeiro from Norfolk, Virginia. She also had a new Marconi wireless unit. *Indrani* was too good a prize to be sunk so, following his customary pattern, Köhler ordered the European crewmen to transfer to *Crefeld* whilst the Chinese ratings were retained to serve under German officers. Command of the new collier—'Kohlendampfer II' (or 'K.D. II')—was given to the First Officer of *Rio Negro*, Jalaes, assisted by two technicians and four sailors under the command of Leutnant z.S. d.R. Hentschel.

*Crefeld* and *Rio Negro* were sent away to supply the armed merchant cruiser *Kronprinz Wilhelm* whilst *Karlsruhe* returned to Lavendeira reef to encounter *Strathroy*, 870 tonnes of coal being transferred before the cruiser left the anchorage at 05:00 on 19 September.

21 September 1914 proved to be a busy day off the Brazilian coast. First *Karlsruhe* took 3,804grt *Maria* of the Holland–Gulf Stoomvart Maatschappij of Rotterdam, which was unluckily carrying a load of British-owned wheat from Portland, Oregon, to Dublin and Belfast for orders. Built in 1898 on Wearside, by Priestman & Company, the steamer had left Punta Arenas on 1 September. The Dutch crewmen soon revealed that *Maria* had encountered the battleship *Canopus* in the night of 18/19 September, and also that the light cruiser *Glasgow* had been seen coaling in Rio de Janeiro.

Köhler then turned to pursue a second steamship, leaving his tenders to supervise the recall of the boarding party and the destruction of the Dutch vessel. At 14:45, *Karlsruhe* seized *Cornish City* of the Instow Steam Ship Co. Ltd. Built by Joseph L. Thompson & Sons Ltd of Sunderland in 1906 as *Charlton*, the 3,816grt steamer had been bought by Instow in 1912, renamed, and registered in Bideford. Now she was to be sunk 245 miles southwest by south of São Pedro e São Paulo: *Karlsruhe* had so much coal that Köhler could forego the 5,500-ton load bound from Barry Docks to the British-owned Brazilian Coal Company of Rio de Janeiro.

As *Cornish City* was being hastened to a watery grave at 19:45, *Karlsruhe*'s wireless operators picked up signals from *Amazon*, a 10,037grt steamer built in 1906 for the Royal Mail Steam Packet Company by Harland & Wolff Ltd of Belfast, which had left Pernambuco bound for Europe. Lights were seen at 21:30 and Köhler seriously considered intercepting the ship until he realised that he could not accommodate her passengers aboard his tenders. So *Amazon* was allowed to proceed, little knowing how close she had brushed with fate.

*Rio Iguassu* (3,817grt) of the London-American Maritime & Trading Co. Ltd was stopped at 06:40 on 22 September in 0°40′S 32°18′W, hauling 4,800 tons of coal from Newcastle upon Tyne to the Tramway, Power & Light Company of Rio de Janeiro. The crew was taken aboard *Asuncion*, as much of the coal as possible was was transferred, and the 1898-vintage Sunderland-built British steamship was sunk at 16:00 roughly twenty

nautical miles north-west of the point at which she had been taken.

The next ships to be accosted were disappointingly neutral. The Genova-registered Italian steamer *Ascaro*, sighted at 06:00 on 22 September, was carrying maize from Rosario to São Vicente in the Cabo Verde islands for orders; then came *Princessan Ingeborg*, owned by Axel Johnson & Co., registered in Stockholm, heading for Pernambuco with passengers and a cargo of piece goods.

By 25 September, *Karlsruhe* had sailed eastward to 1°10′S 33°30′W in the middle of the Atlantic Ocean. Here, well away from the sea lanes, attention could be paid to the welfare of the ship. The turbines were stripped for maintenance, first the port unit then starboard to ensure that way could always be maintained on one propeller in an emergency; minor plating damage was repaired where practicable; the most easily accessible rust was removed, and a coat of paint was applied to needy areas. Thus reconditioned, the cruiser set a course for Lavendeira reef on 27 September. The collier *Asuncion* was encountered on the following day, a hundred nautical miles north-west of Atol de Rocas. The remaining 1,100 tons of coal had finally been taken from *Strathroy* and the British tramp had been sunk in 0°42′N 44°30′W.

*Karlsruhe*, *Rio Negro* and *Indrani* arrived off Rocas in the afternoon of 29 September, though *Asuncion* and *Crefeld* had already left for the next rendezvous. At 17:00 on 1 October, the cruiser left the reef with 1,420 tonnes of coal aboard—so much, indeed, that it was piled a metre deep on deck, only the training arcs for the guns being left clear.

On 2 October, *Asuncion* brought news that *Cap Trafalgar* had been sunk off Trindade island, and that the ships of the Kreuzergeschwader were on their way across the Pacific. *Dresden* was off the west coast of South America, and *Leipzig* was in the Galapagos islands. More worrying was news that Atol de Rocas and Ilha da Trindade had been compromised, and that Bermuda was being watched. The papers also reported that Rear-Admiral Sir Christopher Cradock, flying his flag in the armoured cruiser *Good Hope*, was steaming south to intercept von Spee.

Like most Germans, Erich Köhler was certain that the Kreuzergeschwader would be too much of a handful for the ships available to Cradock—his flagship *Good Hope*, powerful but old; *Monmouth*, manned mainly by reservists recruited amongst Scottish fishermen; and *Glasgow*, sister-ship of *Bristol* and thus indirectly very familiar to those aboard *Karlsruhe*.

Accompanied by *Crefeld* and *Rio Negro*, *Karlsruhe* set off to cruise the shipping lanes north of Fernando Noronha, arriving at 08:30 on 3 October. The tenders were deployed the next morning to shepherd victims towards the cruiser.

At 15:00 on 5 October, *Crefeld* signalled that a steamship was in sight. *Farn* blundered into the trap in

0º46'S 30º50'W and was stopped by *Karlsruhe* at 17:00. Owned by the Fargrove Steam Navigation Co. Ltd of London and managed by Farrar, Groves & Co., the 4,393grt tramp had been launched from the Sunderland yard of William Doxford & Sons Ltd in 1910. Her cargo proved to be high-grade Welsh steam-coal and coke, 5,810 tons according to some reports and 7,000 to others,* bound for Montevideo from Barry. *Farn* became another of *Karlsruhe*'s tenders ('Kohlendampfer III'), under the supervision of Kapitänleutnant d.R. Lubinus, Leutnant z.S. d.R. Hentschel and the crew that had previously manned the discarded *Strathroy*.

No sooner had *Farn* been packed away to a new rendezvous with *Asuncion* than wireless signals from HMS *Cornwall* were intercepted at such great strength that Köhler precipitately withdrew eastward towards São Pedro e São Paulo. The British warship visited Fernando Noronha on 6 October, accompanied by the merchant cruiser *Macedonia*, then nosed northward to pass close to the spot where *Farn* had been taken two days previously. On 7 October, *Cornwall* steamed off to the West Indies, passing about seventy miles west south-west of *Karlsruhe*. *Bristol* had passed Cabo São Roque at midday on 6 October, steaming north-westerly and passing close enough for *Karlsruhe* to receive her wireless messages; on the same day, the merchant cruiser *Orama* approached Atol de Rocas from the south. The net seemed to be closing.

However, though Erich Köhler had moved farther eastward than the established shipping lanes, the British Admiralty had advised ships to be wary of the peace-time routes. Luck remained with the Germans when, at 15:00 on 6 October, a hundred nautical miles south by west of São Pedro e São Paulo, a steamship belonging to the

Miguel de Larrinaga Steamship Co. Ltd was spotted by *Rio Negro*. Köhler soon trapped 5,018grt Liverpool-registered *Niceto de Larrinaga* in 0º35'S 29º47'W, laden with eight thousand tons of oats, maize, cattle fodder and agricultural machinery being hauled from Buenos Aires to London. Completed in 1912 by Russell & Company of Port Glasgow, the steamship had a Marconi transmitter/receiver unit and had recently been in contact with the cruisers *Bristol* and *Glasgow*. She was scuttled at 19:00, after the 42-man crew had been taken off, but did not sink until 20:30.

At about 08:00 on 7 October 1914, the Liverpool-registered 3,384grt steamer *Lynrowan* was captured, travelling northward with 5,500 tons of maize, sugar, talc and hides—plus twelve motor cars—bound for Liverpool from Buenos Aires. The tramp had been completed by Craggs & Son of Middlesbrough in 1907, and was owned in 1914 by the Liver Shipping Co. Ltd. A mixed crew of Britons, Frenchmen, a Belgian, Russians and blacks was taken off and *Lynrowan* was used for gunnery practice. She sank at 15:00, ninety miles south south-west of São Pedro e São Paulo.

The Liverpool, Brazil & River Plate Steam Navigation Co. (Lamport & Holt Ltd) were the only shipowners to lose two vessels to *Karlsruhe*. The first was 1895-vintage 4,635grt *Cervantes*, a product of the Glasgow yard of D. & W. Henderson & Company, which was captured at 07:00 on 8 October merely ten miles from *Lynrowan*'s demise. *Cervantes* had left Rio de Janeiro on 1 October, with a 43-man crew and four passengers from Punta Arenas and Rio Grande do Sul. She had also been hauling 4,500 tons of cattle fodder, wool, sugar and hides for

* It is suspected that the higher figure includes bunkerage, and that the lower, therefore, is the 'paying cargo'. They are not necessarily incompatible.

**Below:** *José de Larrinaga*, an identical sister of *Niceto de Larrinaga*. By courtesy of Laurence Dunn.

Liverpool from the South American ports—but was sunk shortly after noon by explosives and a few 10·5cm shells.

At about 23:15 on 8 October, the Germans spotted the 4,408grt London-registered *Pruth*, belonging to the Mercantile Steam Ship Co. Ltd. Captained by Joseph Evans, the ship—a 1905-vintage product of the West Hartlepool yard of W. Gray & Co. Ltd—was stopped shortly after midnight in 0°26′S 29°45′W, laden with 3,800 tons of potassium nitrate and 2,300 tons of barley being hauled from Chile to São Vicente for orders. Transfer of her crew and provisions to *Crefeld*, together with meat from *Rio Negro*, began at 05:30. Finally, *Pruth* was sunk at about 10:00.

*Cadiz*, a neutral Spaniard bound from Valparaiso to Barcelona, was stopped for examination at 15:00 on 9 October; the Norwegian *Bergenhus*, carrying 4,100 tonnes of maize from Rosario to Las Palmas for orders, was similarly treated at 03:00 on the following morning.

With coal once again running short, Köhler turned *Karlsruhe* westward towards Lavendeira reef and a rendezvous with the captured collier *Farn*. Shortly before 15:00 on 11 October, *Karlsruhe* discovered *Farn* exchanging signals with the tramp steamer *Condor* (3,053grt) in 2°S 34°W, or 215 nautical miles north-east of

Cabo São Roque. Ship's papers revealed that *Condor* had been built in 1893 by J.L. Thompson & Co. Ltd of Sunderland and was owned by the New York & Pacific Steam Ship Company. Registered in London, the vessel was carrying four thousand tons of piece goods from New York, Philadelphia and Ferdinanda to the coasts of South America.

*Condor* had been warned of raider activity and was sailing more than a hundred miles eastward of the usual shipping lane as a precaution. Now, however, she lay hove-to with engine trouble; and a request for help from *Farn*, still flying the Red Ensign, was to seal her fate.

The boarding party reported that the cargo included dynamite, lubricating oil, conserves and condensed milk. The Germans decided to take off the oil, transhipping 148·5 tonnes—781 drums and about seven hundred cases—to *Karlsruhe* on 13 October. The intention was to mix the lubricant with petrol in the hope that the result could be used in the cruiser's oil-fired boilers. At 02:00 on 14 October, *Condor* was scuttled. Shortly after she had slid below the waves, two enormous sub-aqueous explosions showered *Rio Negro* with debris.

*Crefeld* was now crammed with prisoners taken from the ships that had been sunk. In his memoirs, based on a diary kept during the cruise, Oberleutnant z.S. Hubert Aust recorded the total on 8 October—prior to the taking of *Condor*—as 398: 223 'enemies of Germany' and 175 neutrals. There were 205 Britons, including two women, 107 Chinese and 22 Spaniards, whilst Belgium, Cuba, Denmark, Ecuador, Greece and Arabia each provided one man. As provisions were running short, Köhler determined to send his tender into a South American port, but instructed Kapitän Vierth to delay his arrival until the cruiser had moved well away from the area in which the captured crews had been released.

*Crefeld* departed at 16:00 on 13 October, heading north-eastward for Tenerife. Travelling with studied deliberation, the steamer eventually reached port on 22 October. The British prisoners were freed and mail destined for Berlin was sent on its way. Much to the annoyance of the British, who regarded *Crefeld* as an auxiliary warship, the Spanish authorities refused to intern the steamer; her presence in harbour, therefore, necessitated a blockade by Royal Navy cruisers.

The German merchantmen, even those supposedly interned in harbours around the Atlantic rim, provided an invaluable service in relaying messages to Köhler and his fellow raider captains during the early months of the First World War. A major offender was the steamship *Holger* of the Roland Linie, interned in Pernambuco, which used her short-range wireless installation to broadcast movements of merchant shipping and, particularly, the British warships. As Pernambuco was a focal point of the trade along the eastern seaboard of Brazil, the information was of inestimable value to the raiders. And though *Holger* could not transmit very far, *Asuncion* cruised off the Brazilian coast to pick up the messages undetected before relaying them to *Karlsruhe*.

Newspapers aboard captured merchantmen were another fertile source of information, particularly as they regularly published details of arrivals in and departures from the most important ports.

However, neutral powers—particularly those in South America—grew increasingly impatient of the violation of their trust, and gradually tightened the restrictions on the use of their ports by what were effectively German auxiliary warships. Once this happened on a grand scale, the activities of raiding cruisers such as *Karlsruhe* would be curtailed either by shortages of fuel or by better supervision of the remote possessions (such as Fernando Norohna) that were being used as improvised bases.

The existence of emergency coaling stations could not escape the notice of captive crewmen, so it would only be a matter of time until an investigation by a British warship coincided with the visit of a raider. Most of the British cruisers in the Atlantic were powerful enough to blast *Karlsruhe* into submission, provided that waters were restricted enough (or bunkers sufficiently empty) to prevent the German cruiser from exploiting her advantageous speed. The Germans had many narrow

escapes. Typical of these was the visit of the merchant cruiser *Edinburgh Castle* to Lavendeira reef on 25 October, and the examination of Atol de Rocas by the armoured cruiser *Defence* a day later.

Köhler left for Lavendeira reef shortly after midnight on 14/15 October, soon after sinking *Condor*. The transfer of coal from *Farn* began at 08:30 on 15 October and continued until, by next morning, 1,100 tonnes had been taken aboard *Karlsruhe*. The cruiser left at 17:00, passing the Argentine government transport *Chaco* the following afternoon, to meet *Rio Negro* and then *Asuncion* in 2°S 34°W by 18:00 on 17 October. In the morning of 18 October, *Karlsruhe* and *Rio Negro* departed to cruise about 130 nautical miles north of Fernando Noronha.

At 11:00 on 18 October, about two hundred miles south-west of São Pedro e São Paulo, Montevideo-bound *Glanton* (Captain George Arthur) provided Karlsruhe with another conquest. Registered in London on behalf of Steel, Young & Company, the 1894-vintage 3,021grt collier was hauling machinery and 3,800 tons of best Welsh coal loaded at Barry Dock for Wilson & Sons. However, as Köhler was in no pressing need of fuel, explosive charges were laid and the steamer was scuttled at 17:25 once the boarding party had removed the few things of interest.

Two neutrals, the Dutch mail steamer *Zaanland* and an unidentified Italian tramp, were simply left to proceed on 18 October by a tired German crew.

Wireless transmissions from the Nelson Steam Navigation Co. Ltd vessel *Highland Scot* were overheard on 21 October, thirty nautical miles south south-east of São Pedro e São Paulo, but the ship could not be found. On 22 October 1914, Karlsruhe stopped the Swedish steamer *Atland*, registered in Goteborg, but released her after a cursory search. However, the next day brought another prize in the shape of the 2,752grt *Hurstdale*, built by Blumer & Company of Sunderland in 1902 and owned by Lambert Brothers of Liverpool. Bristol-bound with 4,644 tons of maize from Rosario, the tramp was spotted at 16:15 and stopped at 17:00 only a few miles away from the watery grave of *Glanton*. As the newcomer carried nothing of special interest, the sea-cocks were opened once the twenty-man crew had been removed. *Hurstdale* dutifully sank at 21:00. Axel Johnson's *Annie Johnson*—a neutral—was then allowed to proceed unmolested.

On 25 October, Köhler set a westward course for São João island with *Farn*, despatching the tenders *Rio Negro*, *Asuncion* and *Indrani* with rendezvous instructions. The intention was to attack Barbados as a prelude to a reign of terror in the Caribbean.

At about 10:15 on 26 October, whilst running for São João island, lookouts aboard *Karlsruhe* spotted a large ship east south-east of the cruiser. The vessel was shadowed until 11:00, then stopped in 1°12'S 40°49'W. On 21 October, Captain Arthur Cadogan, the master of 10,328grt *Vandyck*, owned by the Liverpool, Brazil &

River Plate Steamship Company (Lamport & Holt Ltd), had been warned by Captain Basil Fanshawe of HMS *Bristol* that *Karlsruhe* remained at large. Nonetheless, Cadogan had still left Bahia on 23 October, bound for New York by way of Trinidad and Barbados, and was plying the regular shipping route from Cabo São Roque to Trinidad.

Built by Workman, Clark & Co. Ltd of Belfast in 1911, *Vandyck* was carrying 210 passengers, piece goods, a small quantity of gold bullion and a thousand tons of frozen meat. The steamer had tried to run, but fifteen knots were no match for Karlsruhe's 25 and *Vandyck* hove-to after a brief chase.

Köhler was well aware of the value of such a rich prize and was determined to sink *Vandyck* even though there were many women and children amongst the passengers. He wirelessed a message to *Asuncion*, *Rio Negro* and *Indrani*, arriving to meet them in 0°50'S 41°W at 04:30 on 27 October. Passengers were ordered to begin packing their belongings at 06:00, transhipment being complete by 19:00. The crews of *Hurtsdale* and *Glanton* were also transferred to *Asuncion* and the prison-tender was despatched in the evening of 27 October with instructions to land everyone in Para no earlier than 1 November, allowing the cruiser several days in which to disappear once again.

The landing was actually made on the morning of 2 November, after an agonisingly protracted and discomfiting voyage in the small Hamburg–Amerika steamship. Allegations were soon being made in the Anglo-American Press that the voyage on *Asuncion* was yet another example of Teutonic barbarity. The passengers were more philosophical; one American aboard *Vandyck* wrote to Köhler that he wished 'to thank [the German captain]...for the very courteous and generous treatment accorded to the passengers, officers and crew of the S.S. 'Van Dyck'.—No-one with reason could expect more under the circumstances'.

*Vandyck* was finally scuttled at 06:00 on 28 October, sinking within thirty minutes in 0°50'S 41°45'W, the last of Erich Köhler's victims. The London-registered steamship *Royal Sceptre* had been stopped during the previous day, but was found to be taking an American-owned cargo of coffee from Santos to New York. Wary of asking the German government to pay compensation if he sank the ship, Köhler let the steamer go her own way.

The raider coaled from *Farn* off São João island on 29–30 October, then left to meet *Rio Negro* and *Indrani* in 0°30'S 45°30'W on 31 October. A course was then set for Maraca, off the mouth of the Amazon, allowing *Karlsruhe* to drop anchor fifteen miles seaward of the island at 16:30 on 1 November. The crew of the cruiser badly needed

---

**Above right:** *Karlsruhe* towards the end of her cruise, a shadow of the pristine warship that had been sent out from Germany in the summer of 1914. From von dem Borne's *S.M.S. "Karlsruhe"*, courtesy of Emden-Archiv Günter Huff.
**Below:** the Lamport & Holt passenger liner *Vandyck*. By courtesy of Laurence Dunn.

rest but, before inactivity could be permitted, Köhler determined to terrorise the Barbadians in a surprise attack that—he hoped—would cause panic and disrupt communications.

On 1 November, *Karlsruhe* coaled from *Indrani* and then set a course for Barbados in company with *Rio Negro*. As evening fell on 4 November 1914 and *Karlsruhe* glided serenely northward, many of her crew relaxed on the forecastle to the soothing tones of the ship's band. Köhler and Oberleutnant z.S. Freiherr von Althaus, the officer of the watch, watched disinterestedly from the bridge; aft, the off-duty officers were gathering in the wardroom for supper. Suddenly, with devastating swiftness, flame speared the darkening sky and a tremendous explosion momentarily stunned observers on *Indrani* and *Rio Negro*.

When the smoke cleared, nothing remained of *Karlsruhe* forward of the forefunnel. The bow, bridge and foremast had been blown to fragments in 11°7'N 55°25'W, along with Köhler and 262 of his men. The after part of the warship, though listing sharply to port, floated long enough for 123 survivors to launch their boats. The stern portion eventually sank at 18:57. As the survivors pulled hard for the colliers, they knew their war-cruise was over. Barbados had been spared, and one of the Kaiser's Pirates was no more.

Command of the remaining men of the cruiser and the accompanying tenders passed on the death of Fregattenkapitän Köhler to Kapitänleutnant Studt.

*Farn* had been detached, eventually entering the harbour of San Juan de Puerto Rico on 12 January 1915 after aimlessly steaming in pursuit of new instructions from a force that no longer existed. Studt decided to scuttle *Indrani* and return to Germany in *Rio Negro*,

accepting the risks of running the British blockade. The homeward journey involved a great northward loop around the British Isles, but the passage was assisted by the withdrawal in November 1914 of old British cruisers from patrol duties. Their replacement with lightly armed (but undoubtedly more seaworthy) merchant cruisers not only took time to perfect but also coincided with the advent of *Rio Negro*. Helped by strong gales, which hid her from the gaze of hostile patrols, the collier reached Ålesund on 29 November.

By the first week in December, the men had all returned to Germany. So well had the secret of the loss of the cruiser been kept that a signal had been despatched to Köhler on 27 November from the wireless-telegraphy station in Nauen. Ironically, it had given the Kaiser's permission for *Karlsruhe* to return to Germany. Even the German Admiralty had realised that the utility of the raiding cruiser was receding fast. Once the Kreuzergeschwader had been destroyed off the Falklands, only *Dresden* remained at liberty.

The loss of *Karlsruhe* has been ascribed to many differing causes, most notably an explosion in the forward boiler room arising from an attempt to use the lubricating oil taken from *Condor* as fuel. However, this in itself seems unlikely to have caused the destruction witnessed by observers in *Rio Negro* and *Indrani*. A boiler explosion, if indeed it occurred, may have touched off the magazine or the spare torpedo warheads; alternatively, the loss may simply have been due to spontaneous ignition of sweating cordite—by no means unknown prior to 1918.*

* Among the major warships lost to this cause have been the French battleships *Iéna* (1907) and *Liberté* (1911), in addition to the British battleship *Bulwark* (1914), the armoured cruiser *Natal* (1915) and the dreadnought *Vanguard* (1917).

# KÖNIGSBERG

1 August 1914–11 July 1915; one mercantile victim and one warship victim
(6,601grt and 2,135td). A conventional light cruiser, destroyed on 11 July in the delta of the
Rufiji river in East Africa.

◆◆◆

Type: Kleine Kreuzer.
Authorisation: as 'Ersatz Meteor', 1903.
Builder: Kaiserliche Werft, Kiel (yard no. 31). Extensively rebuilt in the Kiel dockyard in 1911–13.
Laid down: 1905.
Launch date: 12 December 1905.
Commissioned: 6 April 1907.
Crew: 14 officers and 308 men.

**Dimensions**
Design displacement: 3,390 tonnes.
Full-load displacement: 3,814 tonnes.
Overall length: 115·3 metres.
Waterline length: 114·8 metres.
Beam: 13·2 metres.
Full-load draught: about 5·3 metres.

**Weapons**
Guns: ten SK 10·5cm C/88 L/40.
Maximum range of main armament: 12,200 metres.
Lesser guns: originally ten 3·7cm automatic cannon.
Torpedo tubes: one submerged on each beam.
Munitions: 1,470 10·5cm high-explosive shells, thirty 10·5cm shrapnel shells; five 45cm C/03 torpedoes.
Armour protection: deck 20–30mm, conning tower 100mm, gun-shields 50mm.

**Performance**
Powerplant: two three-cylinder triple expansion steam engines, supplied by eleven boilers. Two propeller shafts.
Boiler pressure: 15·5at (228psi).
Coal bunkerage: 400 tonnes normal, 820 tonnes maximum.
Speed, trials: 24·1 knots (13,918ihp).

Speed, service maximum: 23 knots (13,200ihp).
Range: 3,750 nautical miles at 12 knots.

The early career of *Königsberg* had been passed on comparatively uneventful home service, the highlight being the escort of the Imperial yacht *Hohenzollern* during the visit of the Kaiser to Britain in the autumn of 1906. The cruiser was then brand-new and had not even been commissioned into the Kaiserliche Marine.

The warship was a conventional design, with three widely spaced upright funnels of identical circular section. There were two 10·5cm guns on the fore-deck and two on the after deck, both protected by enveloping blast shields, whilst the customary three additional guns appeared on the main deck along each beam. The fore and aft supplementary guns were in embrasures, with dropping segmental shields, whilst the midships gun was mounted in an open-top sponson. *Königsberg* was very similar to the preceding Bremen class—particularly the ships such as *Danzig* and *Leipzig*, with vertical funnels.

**Below:** resplendent in yellow-buff and white, the cruiser *Königsberg* is seen off Kiel in August 1907. From a postcard by Gebr. Lempe, Kiel ('1907. No. 75'). Author's collection.

**Above:** a tinted postcard of the cruiser *Hyacinth*, published prior to 1914 by Valentine's from a photograph by Crockett. Author's collection.

However, the bridgework was more extensive than in earlier cruisers and the fore funnel was set noticeably farther back from a fore mast placed centrally in the bridge structure. Unlike *Danzig*, *Königsberg* had a small deck house abaft the main mast instead of one through which the mast passed.

In 1911, when only four years old, *Königsberg* was recalled to Kiel dockyard for an extensive refit in preparation for overseas service. Among the most obvious changes was the replacement of the ornate decoration on the stem with a simple shield on each side of the bow ahead of the anchor.

On Monday 6 July 1914, under the command of Fregattenkapitän Max Looff, *Königsberg* arrived off Dar-es-Salaam to take pride of place on the East African Station. Soon, Looff was taking his ship to show the Imperial German flag in the harbours of German East Africa. If Emden was the 'Swan of the East' in Tsingtau, then *Königsberg* was 'Manowari na Bomba Tatu' (the 'warship with three funnels') in Deutsch-Ostafrika.

As the situation in Europe worsened, Looff was sent orders by way of the Nauen wireless telegraphy station telling him that, in the event of war, he should leave port and cruise whilst awaiting definitive instructions. It was not clear which of Germany's potential opponents would become hostile.

Looff's immediate problem was provided by the Cape Squadron of the Royal Navy, commanded by Rear-Admiral Herbert King-Hall. Flying his flag in HMS *Hyacinth*, King-Hall and his ships arrived off Dar-es-Salaam in the evening of 31 July to block the exit of *Königsberg* should hostilities commence. But the German ship had already left.

Max Looff had been told by the captain of the Deutsch–Ostafrika passenger steamship *Tabora* that the British squadron had set course for Dar-es-Salaam. *Königsberg* had already raised steam and was ready to sail at a moment's notice, having arranged a rendezvous with the tender *Somali* to re-fuel. At 16:30 on 31 July, therefore, the German warship headed out into the Indian Ocean. At about 17:55, however, the masthead-lookout reported to Looff that he could see the topmasts of the British warships on the horizon.

As the German cruiser maintained twelve knots, King-Hall deployed his three ships around her: *Pegasus* ahead, *Hyacinth* astern and *Astraea* off the port beam. The intention was clearly to shadow *Königsberg* in case war should be declared. Looff inspected his unwelcome neighbours. *Hyacinth*, the flagship, had been completed by the London & Glasgow Shipbuilding Company in September 1900. Though slightly shorter than SMS *Königsberg*—350ft between perpendiculars compared with 376ft on the waterline—she was heavier, displacing 5,560 tons.

The eleven 6-inch guns may have been old, but *Hyacinth* packed a punch that had to be treated with respect. However, though high freeboard would enable speed to be maintained in high seas, she had only managed 19·4 knots on her trials in 1900 and would be unable to catch *Königsberg* in a chase; the German ship could still raise 23 knots when required.

Much less imposing was the 4,360-ton *Astraea*, completed by the royal dockyard in Devonport in November 1895. Though ships of her class had gained a reputation for their good sea-keeping qualitites, the armament of two old 6-inch, eight 4·7-inch and ten 6-pdr QF guns did not worry Looff. He knew that his effectual 10·5cm guns outranged *Astraea* by at least 2,000 metres.

The Third Class Cruiser *Pegasus*, displacing only 2,135 tons, was the weakest member of the Royal Navy squadron. Armament comprised eight 4-inch and eight 3-pdr QF guns, plus two 18-inch torpedo tubes; as service speed had been rated as only 18·5 knots when new, 1899-vintage *Pegasus* could neither run sufficiently quickly nor hit hard enough to present a great threat.

Yet Max Looff was well aware of the dangers he faced. The three British ships may have been inferior individually, but would have a great advantage in numbers in the event of a fight. Quietly, the German skipper ordered chief engineer Gustav Schilling to raise steam for a high speed dash without arousing suspicion. Fortuitously, a sudden squall then hid the ships from each other; when the squall had cleared, the German cruiser had reversed her course by turning hard to starboard and was making off at 22 knots. *Hyacinth* had been passed within half a mile, starboard to starboard, but had seen nothing. When the squall cleared as suddenly as it had begun, the British ships were well out of range astern of *Königsberg*.

Looff maintained speed for some time, confident that the slower British ships would lose contact, and then turned southward before slowing to twelve knots. In the morning of 1 August, the German captain turned northward for Aden. As Aden was one of the principal British coaling stations, many steamships stopped there to replenish their bunkers after a homeward trip across the Indian Ocean—or, alternatively, to take on coal after the outbound voyage through the Suez Canal. Looff was sure that he would find a prize or two in such an important area.

In the late evening of 5 August, Fregattenkapitän Looff learned from a wireless message that Germany was at war with Britain, France and Russia. His mission at last became clear: the destruction of British merchant shipping, and the distraction of as many Royal Navy ships as possible into an otherwise unimportant war-zone off the East African coast. At last he had been freed to raid the shipping lanes, and was ideally placed off Cape Guardafui to act decisively.

He immediately broadcast messages asking all German merchant ships in the vicinity to contact the cruiser for instructions or head directly to Dar-es-Salaam.

He was particularly keen to raise Kapitän Kühlken of *Reichenfels* (DDG 'Hansa'), carrying six thousand tons of coal. Unfortunately, though it was not known at the time, the collier had been interned in Colombo.

Smoke seen off the starboard bow in the Gulf of Aden, at 11:10 on Thursday 6 August, resolved into the Norddeutscher Lloyd steamer *Zieten* (Käpitan von Senden) bound for Dar-es-Salaam with men of III. Seebataillon. The marines had been travelling homeward on leave from Tsingtau, but would now reinforce the East African garrison.

No sooner had the German steamer stopped than another ship appeared on the horizon. She had a black hull, a large funnel, and the general description of a British tramp. The suspicion was redoubled when the ship altered course when challenged and piled on steam. Irritated, Looff ordered a chase. *Königsberg* was soon racing along at twenty knots and easily overhauled the eleven-knot quarry. Once the range had closed to a few thousand metres, Looff ordered Leutnant z.S. Richard Wenig, the gunnery officer, to open fire. A single 10·5cm shell was immediately fired across the fleeing steamer's bow in the time-honoured fashion. The mystery ship hove-to at 15:00 and ran a flag up to her mast head.

The crew of the cruiser watched in astonishment as a black, white and red flag fluttered in the breeze. It was a German mercantile ensign.

Kapitän Paul Diedrichsen had been taking *Goldenfels* of DDG 'Hansa', laden with copra, to Hamburg by way of the Suez Canal and had mistaken *Königsberg* for one of the many British three-funnelled protected cruisers. His 7,438grt ship had been built by Swan, Hunter & Wigham Richardson of Newcastle upon Tyne in 1911, which explained her British looks. Looff was keen to tranship any fuel that Diedrichsen could spare, until the skipper of the merchantman explained that the quality of the Indian coal was very poor. It worked satisfactorily in his ship, he said, but would undoubtedly clog the hearths and fire-tubes of the more sophisticated machinery in the warship. However, Diedrichsen also ventured the opinion that the Khuriya Muriya islands off the south east coast of Arabia would provide a safe anchorage.

A brightly-lit ship was spotted at 21:00 on 6 August, but identified herself as a Nippon Yusen passenger liner. Japan was still neutral. The Germans were exasperated; the escape from the British Cape Squadron and the high-speed chase of *Goldenfels* had consumed fuel at a prodigious rate. Supplies were declining alarmingly. When another ship was spotted in the evening of 6 August, Looff and his engineers worried whether she could be stopped quickly enough.

As the cruiser closed, the ship was seen to have a black hull and a buff funnel with a black top above a white band. Though the forecastle and poop were unusually long, the newcomer had the look of a British ship rather than another German.

Fortunately, the captain of the steamer hove-to on request and the boarding party went over. The officers of the Ellerman Line *City of Winchester* (6,601grt) were aghast, having made the same mistake as the captain of *Goldenfels*, as they were expecting to greet fellow countrymen. Delivered from the Hull yard of Earle's Ship Building Company only a short time before war had been declared, the British ship was on the homeward leg of her maiden voyage with a cargo of Persian carpets, gold and silver bullion, and a large consignment of Calcutta tea valued at £250,000. As the steamer's bunkers held a substantial quantity of coal, Looff decided to send the prize to a safe anchorage.

*Königsberg* arrived off Ra's Burum at 16:00 on 7 August 1914 to find that *Zieten* was already riding at anchor. Soon the gathering was swelled by the arrival of the Hamburg–Amerika Linie steamship *Ostmark*, which was homeward bound from Karachi. The steamers could transfer provisions to the cruiser, but had no coal to spare. In the evening of 7 August, therefore, *Ostmark* departed for Massawa.

On 10 August, the remaining ships set course for Sowda Island and a rendezvous with *Goldenfels*. The merchantman handed over a small quantity of coal, just sufficient to ensure that *Königsberg* could reach Hallaniya island to meet *Zieten* and *City of Winchester*. Four hundred tons of coal, provisions and fresh water were subsequently transferred to the raider from the British prize. In the morning of 12 August, *City of Winchester* was finally taken out to sea and scuttled by the normal method of opened sea-cocks and explosive charges, two 10·5cm shells being fired into the waterline to accelerate the process. *Goldenfels* then left for Padang.

Unfortunately for Looff, *City of Winchester*'s coal also proved to be low-grade Indian, taken on board in Bombay. This was suitable for the simple furnaces and boilers of a slow-speed merchantman, but clogged the more sophisticated hearths of a high-speed cruiser. It also gave off copious clouds of smoke. However, as the cruiser had also made contact with the steamship *Somali*, one of a pair of potential colliers allocated to the East African Etappe, the supplies of poor coal would soon be superfluous.

Completed by Blohm & Voss in December 1889, as *Osiris* for DDG 'Kosmos', the 2,638grt single-screw steamship had been sold to the Deutsch-Ostafrika Linie in 1901. She had had the distinction of being chartered for the colonising 'Wissmann Flotille' in 1890 and was well known along the East African coast. Though not particularly large—being recorded by the builders as 97·53m long by 12·19m in the beam—she could carry several thousand tonnes of coal and maintain ten knots.

*Königsberg* had six hundred tonnes of Indian coal to last until the meeting with *Somali*, which had been arranged for mid-August. However, this would not guarantee Looff security if he was forced to out-run a pursuer or engaged in lengthy chases of prizes.

The loss of *City of Winchester* had caused panic on the London tea market and drawn the attention of the Admiralty to the vulnerability of the routes through the Red Sea. Instructions were sent to merchant ships to avoid the area in which the capture had occurred; simultaneously, naval reinforcements were sent to assist in the search for *Königsberg*. As late as 5 September, convoys were being prevented from passing from the Red Sea out across the Indian Ocean unless at least two escorts of cruiser size could be provided.

During the night of 12/13 August, Looff had a lucky escape. Approaching a pre-arranged rendezvous with *Somali*, he was met instead by an unidentified cruiser of the Royal Navy's East India Squadron. The British warship opened fire, but the poor visibility hindered shooting and *Königsberg* escaped unscathed.

A new rendezvous was arranged for 19 August off Socotra island, whereupon the information was wirelessed immediately to the collier. When Max Looff

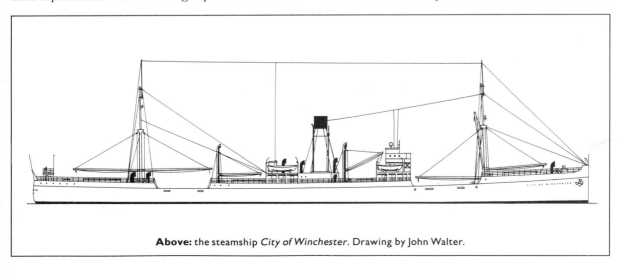

**Above:** the steamship *City of Winchester*. Drawing by John Walter.

finally reached the anchorage, *Königsberg*'s bunkers were virtually empty and drinking water had been rationed owing to restrictions on the use of the coal-fired water-distillation unit. The collier was nowhere to be seen. After sending out armed boats on a fruitless search for fresh water, the Germans were becoming increasingly desperate when *Somali* finally hove into view on 21 August. The propects of food, water and good-quality steam coal suddenly seemed much better.

With his ship's bunkers restored to capacity and additional coal bagged on deck, the German skipper headed southward on 23 August to threaten the sea lanes around Madagascar. He was keen to prey on the large merchantmen of the French Messageries Maritimes shipping line but, after sailing brazenly into Majunga in north-west Madagascar on 30 August, Looff discovered that the ships had been diverted to the strongly defended harbour of Diégo-Suarez and were no longer risking a passage of the Moçambique channel.

Soon, coal supplies began to dwindle again. *Somali* was summoned to Aldabra island, north-west of Madagascar, but the swell was so great that coaling had to be stopped after only a few hundred tonnes had been taken from the collier on 1 September.

*Königsberg* was now showing signs of strain. In addition to the wear and tear of coaling at sea, which buckled plates or sprang rivets, a boiler had failed after the high-speed escape from the Cape Squadron of the Royal Navy at the end of July. Several boiler tubes had been blanked off, but the poor-grade Indian coal aggravated the problems. Looff reluctantly accepted that his cruiser was in need of attention. The most obvious facilities were at Dar-es-Salaam, but wireless traffic had ceased suddenly on 8 August—owing to the destruction of the transmitter during a Royal Navy bombardment— and there was no way of knowing whether the town was still under German control.

Cautiously, after consulting his charts, Max Looff set a course for the mouth of the Rufiji river whilst continuously transmitting misleading messages from a ship heading for a mythical rendezvous off the Horn of Africa. These signals were sufficient in themselves to cause panic, ensuring the unproductive despatch of several British warships to reconnoitre.

The mouth of the Rufiji formed a broad delta, connected with the sea by several major outlets. The distance from the Kikunja to the Kiassi channels, the most northerly and southerly respectively, was more than twenty miles. The Kikunja, Ssimba Uranga and Kiomboni passages were barely navigable at high water by ships of comparatively low draft. If *Königsberg* could pass unnoticed through the shallows and over the sandbanks, the Rufiji seemed to be an ideal place for protracted repairs to be undertaken in secret.

By mid September, the cruiser had not only been joined by the collier *Somali* but had effected sufficient repairs to be operational again. On 19 September 1914, the Germans intercepted a wireless message that a two funnelled warship had anchored in Zanzibar harbour.

Looff was unaware that Admiral King-Hall and *Hyacinth* had been ordered back to patrol the Cape of Good Hope by an Admiralty worried that von Spee and the Kreuzergeschwader would try to cross the southern Atlantic. Neither did he know that *Astraea* had been sent to South West Africa for convoy-protection duties. But the German captain was well aware that *Königsberg* was more than a match for any of the three British ships that had been on the East Africa Station and was quite prepared to join battle with them individually.

The one remaining ship, unhappily for the British, was the weakest of the trio; HMS *Pegasus* also had severe boiler troubles, arising from the use of local Natal coal instead of the much harder (and greatly preferred) Welsh steam variety. On 19 September, Lieutenant-Commander Ingles, commanding *Pegasus*, decided that his ship could no longer wait for attention and put into Zanzibar harbour. As the gun crews remained at action stations, the fires were dropped and boilers were stripped down for cleaning.

King-Hall had ordered that enough steam should be maintained at all times so that one engine could be run in an emergency, but Ingles, basing his decision on the absence of recent information concerning *Königsberg*, decided that repairs would be accomplished more rapidly if all the boilers were cleaned at once. He also knew that the approaches to Zanzibar were patrolled by the armed steamer *Khalifa* and an armed tender named *Helmuth*, formerly belonging to the Deutsch-Ostafrika Linie, which had been seized from the Germans on 4 August 1914.

Fregattenkapitän Looff set a course north-west by north, encountering *Helmuth* to port at about 04:23. Sub-Lieutenant Clement Charlesworth of the Royal Naval Reserve, commanding the tender, spotted *Königsberg* heading for the harbour but assumed that the cruiser was simply a merchantman unaware that the channel had been barred. As *Helmuth* approached briskly with a warning, *Königsberg* ran up the imperial ensign and opened fire; wisely, Charlesworth hauled away from danger before near misses and a hit or two encouraged him to order abandon ship.

As Chumbe island and its lighthouse appeared to starboard, Looff came around and headed north by east at 04:30. At 04:45 he turned again to starboard, setting a north-easterly course between the Panga and Mtwana sandbanks. At 05:10, the cruiser hoisted her mast-head battle flags, turned north-westward and then, at 05:21, came back east by north to bring the five guns of the port side to bear on the British cruiser lying motionless a few hundred yards from the shore. Wenig opened fire at less than 7,000 metres. The first salvo fell short, the second was a straddle and the third hit home. As the range gradually came down to 5,000 metres, the German 10·5cm

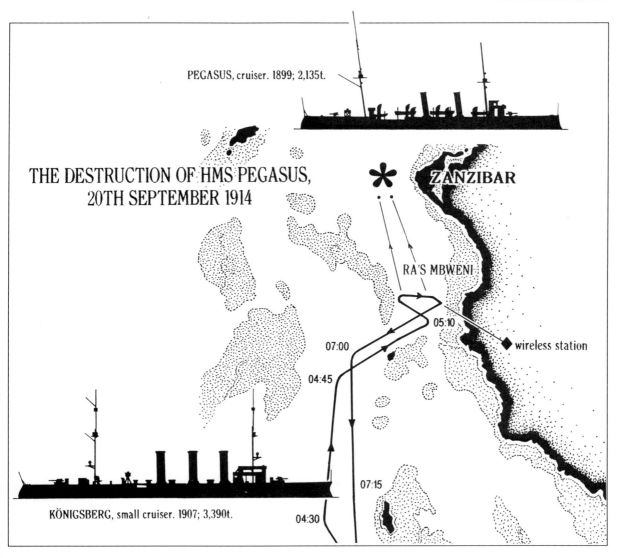

PEGASUS, cruiser. 1899; 2,135t.

THE DESTRUCTION OF HMS PEGASUS,
20TH SEPTEMBER 1914

ZANZIBAR

RA'S MBWENI

05:10

wireless station

07:00

04:45

07:15

04:30

KÖNIGSBERG, small cruiser. 1907; 3,390t.

guns reduced the decks of *Pegasus* to a shambles of twisted metal.

A few British guns mounted an ineffectual reply, but the destruction of the fire-control apparatus and the deaths of the First and gunnery officers in the opening moments hindered a concentrated reply. Fire stopped briefly when Looff considered a report that a sailor on the after deck was waving a white flag, but the lull was short-lived. The smoke of battle cleared long enough to reveal the White Ensign still flying at the mast head, so Richard Wenig was instructed to resume firing.

The battering stopped at about 05:37, by which time *Pegasus* had been hit at least sixty times. *Königsberg* disengaged, having sunk a steam lighter to westward with a few rounds from the starboard after guns, and proceeded to shell the wireless-telegraphy station at Ra's Mbweni. By 05:50, after expending about 350 shells, Looff turned his ship south-west by south and steamed back

out through the sandbanks. Turning south by east at about 07:00, the German cruiser sped off for her hiding place in the Rufiji delta, passing Chumbe island at 07:15.

When the smoke had cleared, the British took stock. *Pegasus* was wrecked, little more than a smoking shell containing 33 dead and 59 seriously injured. Twelve of the dead had been serving the forward port 4-inch gun, which had been blown bodily off its mount by a direct hit and the explosion of ready-use ammunition. The wireless station had been severely damaged, the masts had been felled and more than forty native soldiers had been killed. However, by concentrating his energies on *Pegasus*, Looff had spared not only a collier chartered by the Admiralty but also the town of Zanzibar itself.

*Helmuth*, which was not badly damaged, had been retrieved by her crew; repairs to the main steam pipe were effected and the tug got under way again. An attempt was made to beach *Pegasus* but, under tow from

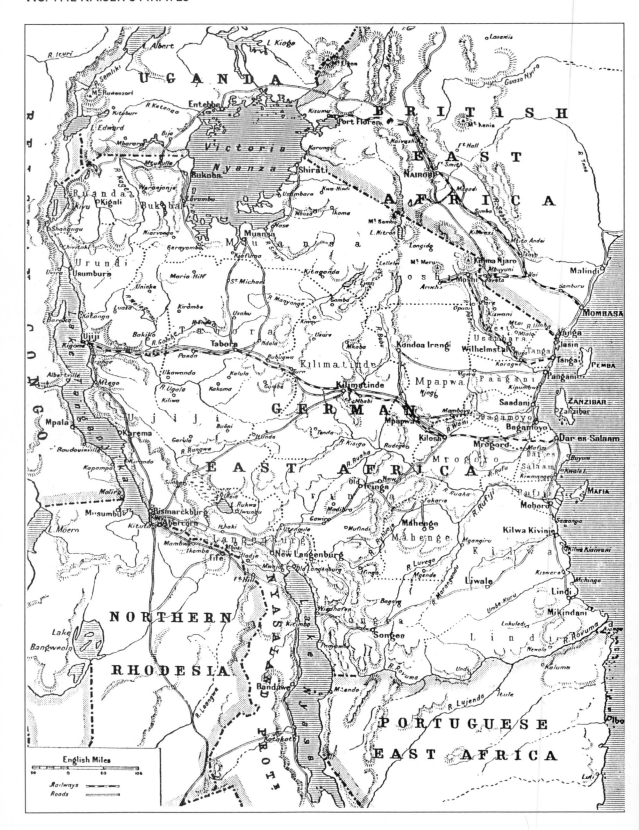

*Helmuth*, the hulk turned slowly over and sank at 14:00 in shallow water.

The destruction of *Pegasus* proved to be a last victory for Max Looff. The undamaged cable station in Zanzibar immediately relayed the sad story of the action to London. The Admiralty, suitably chastened, reacted quickly. On 21 September, Captain Sidney Drury-Lowe, commanding the light cruiser *Chatham*, was ordered to the East African Station from the Red Sea. Completed most appropriately by HM Dockyard, Chatham, in December 1912, the cruiser measured 458ft between perpendiculars and displaced 5,400 tons at normal draught. Armament comprised eight 6-inch BL Mk XII L/45 low-velocity guns and four 3-pdrs, plus two 21-inch torpedo tubes. Quadruple propellers were driven by Parsons turbines, maximum service speed being rated at 25·5 knots.

Sister-ships of the Weymouth Class, *Dartmouth* and *Weymouth* were ordered to join Drury-Lowe from the Indian Ocean and the Mediterranean respectively, at the risk of reducing the pressure on *Emden*. Both cruisers had been completed in October 1911—*Dartmouth* by Vickers Ltd in Barrow and *Weymouth* by Sir W.G. Armstrong, Whitworth & Co. Ltd in Elswick. Displacing 5,250 tons at normal draught and 453ft long between perpendiculars, they each carried eight 6-inch BL Mk XI L/50 high-velocity guns, four 3-pdrs and two 21-inch torpedo tubes. Parsons turbines driving four shafts gave them a service speed of 25 knots.

Each of these powerful ships could be expected to give *Königsberg* a hiding. The problem was that the British did not know where the German cruiser had gone. This forced Drury-Lowe to divide the East African coast into three sectors: Portuguese East Africa was to be patrolled by *Dartmouth*, *Weymouth* was to take the Moçambique channel, and *Chatham* was to cruise off the German East African colonies.

The situation was not helped by a vast number of contradictory 'sightings' of the German cruiser, all of which had to be investigated. None provided clues. *Königsberg* could easily be reported off Portuguese East Africa and coaling in Jeddah simultaneously. It was also obvious that an improvised German coast-watching system was keeping track of the British ships with flags and fires. Drury-Lowe suspected that this was for the benefit of *Königsberg* and that, therefore, the cruiser was still in Deutsch Ostafrika. Accordingly, he decided to recall *Dartmouth* and *Weymouth* so that the squadron could once again operate in concert.

Before orders could be issued, the Royal Navy had good fortune. On 9 October, whilst patrolling off Madagascar, *Dartmouth* intercepted the German tender *Adjutant* heading for the port of Lindi in the southern part of Deutsch Ostafrika. Drury-Lowe suspected the tender of going to the assistance of the Deutsch-Ostafrika Linie steamship *Präsident*, and that, therefore,

the steamer would also be found in Lindi harbour. *Chatham* arrived off Lindi on 19 October to find the vessel at anchor. Suspecting that the Red Cross on her side was a ruse, Drury-Lowe sent in a boarding party. When nothing remotely connected with a hospital ship was found aboard *Präsident*, the British captain, oblivious to protests, ordered the engines of the German ship to be destroyed.

The most useful information, however, was supplied by documents revealing that *Präsident* had been off-loading coal and supplies to the steam lighter *Hedwig* and the coastal steamship *Rowuma* for transmission to Ssalale, four miles up the Rufiji. Armed with German charts, which showed the area in far greater detail than did their Admiralty equivalents, Drury-Lowe set course for the river delta. *Chatham* dropped anchor on 29 October and lookouts went up to the mast head with the most powerful binoculars aboard.

The charts indicated that the deepest of the delta channels would be impassable even at high water. However, Drury-Lowe was aware that *Königsberg* drew several feet less than *Chatham*. Even though the British cruiser could not pass over the sand bars, it seemed possible that the German ship could have done so on a favourable tide.

A shore party was sent to gather information, returning with natives who confirmed that the 'Manowari na Bomba Tatu' was indeed skulking in the delta. The British officers were still considering their moves when a lookout reported that he had located a mast, cunningly camouflaged with palm fronds. No sooner had an officer been sent up to confirm the sighting than the distinctive topmasts of a warship were also spotted. *Königsberg* and *Somali* had been found. Retaining full-height masts to improve wireless communications was a costly error.

The German cruiser had re-entered the Rufiji delta on 20 September after sinking *Pegasus* in Zanzibar. The refuge was reasonably safe from seaward assault whilst the enveloping mangrove swamp, in spite of its pestilential mosquitoes and all-pervading humidity, made ideal camouflage. Max Looff was too canny to simply commit himself to a tropical prison, believing instead that laying-up in the Rufiji presented the best chance of returning to Germany. *Königsberg*'s boiler problems had been exacerbated during the flight from Zanzibar and major repairs were needed.

Deprived of suitable dockyard facilities, Looff and his engineers decided to send the most seriously damaged boiler overland. Organisation of the incredible feat was entrusted to Kapitänleutnant d.R. Werner Schönfeld, who had retired from the Kaiserliche Marine in 1910 to become a planter in East Africa. Schönfeld spoke Swahili and had enough local knowledge, Looff hoped, to turn a plan that seemed impossible into reality. Soon the indefatigable Schönfeld had organised construction of two large sledges on neighbouring plantations, and then produced a force of nearly a thousand men to lift the dismantled boiler from the ship. Soon the boiler had been despatched on a long, slow journey to Dar-es-Salaam. Three weeks later, it reached a foundry.

Efforts were made to keep *Königsberg* mobile enough to change her location in the delta in an emergency, but, with an entire engine stripped for maintenance and a boiler away for repair, the cruiser was unseaworthy. To assist local defence and discourage any penetration into the Rufiji by scouting forces, Looff created a defence force ('Abteilung Delta') reinforced by local Askaris and German sailors brought down from Dar-es-Salaam. Secondary guns commanded the major channels, and miles of field-telephone cable were run from the cruiser to outlying observatories. Looff hoped that this would enable the fall of shot to be spotted effectually if *Königsberg* needed to fire her 10·5cm guns in anger, alleviating lack of mobility.

The boiler returned in the last week of October; by the end of the month, the engines had been reassembled and ran smoothly. The irony was that HMS *Chatham* had anchored off the mouth of the Rufiji only a day earlier. When the German observation post on Komo island was taken by a British landing party on 30 October, prospects of a homeward voyage suddenly looked less attractive.

Outside the Rufiji delta-mouth, Drury-Lowe traced and retraced his patrols impatiently. His cruisers could not penetrate the delta itself, as even the deepest channel was passable only on the highest of spring tides. These would not arrive for several months. Testing the mettle of Abteilung Delta with small craft soon proved that the Germans were well ensconced, and even a bombardment of the Ssimba-Uranga channel by the British cruisers failed to discomfit the defenders.

On 3 November 1914, guided by a picket boat taking soundings, *Dartmouth* managed to move in through the shoals and reefs to about 3,500 yards offshore. *Chatham* and *Weymouth* also managed to stand in as far as possible, and began to fire in the direction of *Königsberg*. However, even with their 6-inch guns at maximum elevation—giving a range of about 14,500 yards—Drury-Lowe's ships were unable to hit *Königsberg*. When shells fell close enough for shrapnel to clatter off his cruiser's deck and hull, Looff merely moved a few hundred yards upriver. The only success came when a salvo from *Chatham* turned *Somali* into a blazing wreck. The collier was scuttled four days afterward.

Unable to call on sufficient men to mount an assault on Abteilung Delta, Drury-Lowe decided on desperate measures. On 7 November, therefore, a flotilla of small

ships attempted to run the gauntlet, screening the cable-ship *Duplex* towing a picket boat armed with torpedoes. The attack was abandoned when the picket boat was hit by a 3·7cm shell and loosed a torpedo aimlessly into the mangrove swamp.

On 10 November, the Admiralty told Captain Drury-Lowe that the raider was to be destroyed at all costs. Drury-Lowe had enough problems of his own. Thick mud in the estuary soon clogged his ships' condensers, and the problems took two days to clear. If Looff made a run for freedom whilst one of the patrolling British cruisers was under repair, incapable of raising full steam, the odds would tilt in German favour. The British captain elected to block the Ssuninga arm of the Ssimba-Uranga channel with *Newbridge*, a 3,737grt turret-deck steamship—built by Doxford in 1906—which had been purchased by the Admiralty from the Temperley Steam Shipping Co. Ltd of London. The collier was filled with dynamite and crushed rock in an attempt to alter the odds in British favour by reducing the options open to Looff.

At 05:25 on 10 November, manned by fourteen volunteers led by Commander Raymond Fitzmaurice, *Newbridge* was escorted slowly into the channel under a barrage provided by the cruisers' 6-inch guns. However, dense vegetation minimised the effects of gunfire and Abteilung Delta gave a ferocious reception. Amazingly, the collier reached the intended mooring without

problem, swung athwart the channel and dropped anchors at bow and stern. The charges were fired at 05:50 to block the Ssuninga for the remainder of the campaign. *Königsberg* was immediately moved upstream into the Ssimba-Uranga channel, where she remained until 17 November. Looff then moved back downstream to the divergence of the Ssimba-Uranga and Ssuninga channels and waited there until 18 December.

Drury-Lowe was still concerned that Looff would escape from one of the other channels if a fortunate combination of high water and a moonless night was presented. He was also worried that loss of any one of his cruisers would make the task of interception more difficult.

In the middle of November 1914, worried by the threat offered by the Kreuzergeschwader to British interests in southern Africa in the wake of the battle of Coronel, the Admiralty ordered *Dartmouth* and *Weymouth* south to reinforce Admiral King-Hall. Only *Chatham* remained on station.

The situation aboard *Königsberg* was little better. Max Looff realised that his escape depended on a peculiar combination of tide and moonlight, and that the slightest error could leave his ship stranded on a sand-bar at the mercy of British 6-inch guns. He was well aware of the fate of *Emden*, which was broadly comparable to *Königsberg*, under the guns of HMAS *Sydney*—a near facsimile of *Chatham*.

In a most perceptive moment, Sidney Drury-Lowe decided that the answer lay in aerial observation. A single-engine Curtiss hydroplane owned by an intrepid aviator named Cutler was traced in Durban and shipped aboard *Kinfauns Castle*. Cutler was given a temporary commission in the Royal Naval Reserve.

The Curtiss flying boat, soon christened 'Cuckoo', arrived on 16 November; beginning on 22 November, Cutler made three flights over the delta before the plane was wrecked in a crash. On the third flight, however, *Königsberg* had been spotted in the upper reaches of the blocked Ssuninga channel. Drury-Lowe was delighted, and ordered another aeroplane to be impressed. On 3 December, *Kinfauns Castle* arrived with a replacement that was sturdy enough to carry Cutler and an observer. On 10 December, however, the new scout was wrecked after an emergency landing in the mouth of the Kikunja channel. The soaked, but seemingly indestructible Cutler was taken prisoner by Abteilung Delta and marched off for an interview with Fregattenkapitän Looff.

On 19 December, *Königsberg* raised anchor off Kikale and moved to a creek off the Bumba arm of Mssala channel. Here the cruiser was to remain until 13 April 1915, berthed behind the Batja peninsula.

The first year of war ended in a stalemate. Drury-Lowe was unable to reach *Königsberg*, out of range of even his 6-inch guns and stoutly defended by the men of Abteilung Delta, whilst Looff was unwilling to risk breaking out on his opponents' terms. Even Christmas 1914 had brought little cheer to Germans penned in the sweltering Rufiji; half the crew was manning guns ashore, whilst a large proportion of the remainder had dysentery or malaria.

Quinine was in short supply and, perhaps worst of all, the wireless had intercepted a message telling Drury-Lowe of the destruction of the Kreuzergeschwader at the Battle of the Falkland Islands.

The Germans held an impromptu, but cheerless football match on a patch of cleared ground near their ship; and the British contented themselves by sending a few ribald wireless messages into the swamp. On New Year's Day 1915, Drury-Lowe wirelessed in German 'We wish you a Happy New Year and hope to see you soon'. Looff replied in English, 'Thanks. Same to you. If you want to see me, I am always at home'. A vestige of humour remained on both sides.

In early January, six companies of Indian and African troops, supported by a bombardment, wrested Mafia island—off the mouth of the Rufiji—from two NCOs and twenty Askaris commanded by Leutnant Schiller of the Schutztrupp Deutsch Ostafrika. Shortly afterwards, Abteilung Delta had a success of its own when a shell cut the steam-pipe of the ex-German tender *Adjutant* and the vessel drifted ashore to be captured, along with Lieutenant-Commander Price and 22 men. The British had fitted the tender with three 4·7-inch QF and two ·303 machine-guns, which were useful reinforcements for the positions along the channel mouths, but *Adjutant* was eventually destroyed by the guns of *Hyacinth* and *Pioneer* on 6 July.

On 20 February, *Kinfauns Castle* arrived with two new Sopwith 'Folder' floatplanes and eighteen men of the Royal Naval Air Service under the command of Flight Lieutenant John Tull. Though both of the previous aircraft had been lost, Drury-Lowe and the Admiralty had decided that the adventure was worth perpetuating.

One Sopwith stalled in mid-air on its second flight, though Tull somehow survived the ensuing crash. The

**Below:** the cruiser *Dartmouth* leaves the Vickers shipyard in Barrow in Furness for her acceptance trials, October 1911. Author's collection.

remaining plane overheated so frequently that it rarely left the sea on take-off. The problems were traced to a flaw in the design of the engine, which had never been intended for use in the tropics; once again, the promise of aerial reconnaissance was tantalisingly unfulfilled.

Disappointed by lack of progress, and conscious that a fleet of British ships was being paralysed by a single cruiser holed up in an inaccessible swamp, the Admiralty ordered Admiral Herbert King-Hall back to take charge of operations. Arriving off the Rufiji on 7 March 1915, flying his flag in the battleship *Goliath*, King-Hall determined to take the initiative.

He hired the hunter Pieter Pretorius not only to find *Königsberg* but also to determine whether or not the cruiser's guns were operative; if the torpedoes had been removed to Abteilung Delta outposts; and which of the major channels could prove navigable. The way in which the hunter, his wireless operator and six Africans painstakingly supplied the answers, often working under the noses of the Germans in the guise of fishermen, is entertainingly described in Pretorius's autobiography *Jungle Man*.

Aboard the German cruiser, conditions had grown much worse. Ever-increasing numbers of crewmen were succumbing to disease, whilst the ship and her engines were deteriorating under a layer of mould.

Better news came in March, when Looff was told that a supply ship had been despatched from Germany. To run the British blockade, 'Sperrbrecher A' was disguised as a Danish merchantmen named *Kronborg*. Preparations were made with maniacal thoroughness; the papers and equipment were all Danish, and the crew was recruited from Danish-speaking areas of Schleswig-Holstein. Oberleutnant z.S. d.R. Carl Christiansen was appointed to the new command.

Christiansen had served in the German mercantile marine prior to 1914, spoke Danish fluently, and had extensive knowledge of the Baltic. After serving aboard the light cruiser *Lübeck*, he had been posted to the staff of Admiral Behring aboard the armoured cruiser *Friedrich Carl*. Surviving the loss of this ship on a Russian mine, Christiansen had then been selected to take a blockade-runner southward into the Atlantic to assist the Kreuzergeschwader. With the destruction of Von Spee's command at the Battle of the Falkland Islands, the plan had miscarried. Now it was to be revived.

The 3,587grt steamer *Rubens* had been completed in 1906 by William Gray & Co. of West Hartlepool for the Bolton Steam Shipping Co. Ltd of London. She had been seized in Hamburg when the First World War began and was ideally suited to the clandestine mission. *Rubens* had the nondescript lines of a classic British-built tramp steamer and was unlikely to attract undue suspicion from British North Sea patrols.

At 13:00 on 18 February 1915, initially in Danish disguise, *Rubens* left Wilhelmshaven with a most impressive cargo. In addition to 2,000 tonnes of coal, a thousand tonnes of distilled water and fifty tonnes of machine-oil and assorted parts for *Königsberg*, she carried two 6cm Bootskanone in Ladungslafette, four 8mm Maxim machine-guns and 1,500 1898-pattern Mauser infantry rifles. There were 3,000 rounds for the 3·7cm cannon taken from the scuttled gunboat *Möwe*, 3,000 6cm shells, 500 shells for the 8·8cm guns carried by *Königsberg* to arm auxiliary cruisers, a thousand 10·5cm-calibre shells, 4·5 million 8mm cartridges, and a tonne of explosive trinitroanysol. Uniforms, shoes, tents, field telephones, wireless transmitters and provisions would be welcome in the beleaguered African colony.

A gale in the North Sea assisted Christiansen and his men to evade British patrols. Changing her disguise to masquerade as a British India Line steamship, steering well south of the established sea lanes to avoid detection by Royal Navy patrols, *Rubens* rounded the Cape of Good Hope on 22 March. On the night of 3/4 April, 150 nautical miles south-east of the French-administered Îles de Comores and still largely ignorant of the situation in East Africa, Christiansen sent a message asking *Königsberg* for directions to a safe port. Though he did not realise the significance of his mistake at the time, the lengthy transmission would ultimately prove fatal.

Early in the morning of 10 April, after narrowly avoiding a British merchant cruiser only a few hours earlier, *Rubens* dropped anchor off Aldabra island and discarded her disguise.

The conversations between Christiansen and Looff had been monitored by French warships cruising off Madagascar and were relayed immediately to Admiral King-Hall. Though the code was impenetrable, the high-pitched signal could only have come from a Telefunken transmitter and its strength suggested that the source was comparatively close. As 13 August dawned, therefore, *Kinfauns Castle* arrived to inspect Aldabra; Christiansen had left only on the previous afternoon.

King-Hall fretted impatiently. *Goliath* had been sent to the Dardanelles on 25 March and *Chatham* was refitting in Bombay. The imminence of the highest spring tides forced him to leave *Weymouth* to guard the Rufiji, and thus only the ageing *Hyacinth* could be spared to seek the German supply ship. But what if the signal proved to come from a modern German cruiser? The old British warship would have very little chance.

On 13 April, *Königsberg* moved back to Kikale on the Kikunja channel. The British ships concentrated on the Rufiji delta. Would Looff gamble on a dash to meet his supply ship? Only the erstwhile cable ship *Duplex* had been left to patrol the approaches to the port of Tanga, and would be able to do little to prevent an armed adversary making port. The desperate situation needed a desperate remedy, so King-Hall elected to take the risk and set *Hyacinth* for Tanga. His guess was inspired.

At 05:30 Christiansen spotted Ulenga lighthouse, which marked the beginning of the approach channel to Tanga harbour. Simultaneously, lookouts aboard *Hyacinth* spotted the approach of *Rubens*. The British cruiser was soon surging ahead at eighteen knots. Christiansen, realising the peril of his position, ordered full steam ahead even though there was little point in running; *Hyacinth* was rapidly overhauling the merchantman and it was only a matter of time before she came within range.

However, just before King-Hall could order fire to begin, a connecting rod snapped in the starboard engine and *Hyacinth* rapidly began to lose way. It soon became clear that the port engine could only maintain about ten knots by itself and that *Rubens* had been handed a chance to escape. Desperate to hide the information from Christiansen, King-Hall ordered his gunners to fire.

The first salvoes dropped astern of the German freighter, but Christiansen, knowing nothing of the predicament of his opponent, turned toward the apparent safety of nearby Manza bay instead of taking the six-mile gamble to Tanga. *Rubens* anchored at 06:30, secure in the knowledge that *Hyacinth* would not risk crossing the Manza sand bar. As the supply ship was still within range, however, King-Hall simply swung his ship broadside and opened fire.

Salvoes soon bracketed *Rubens*; one shell carried away a large portion of the funnel, whilst two more holed the waterline. Christiansen gave the order to scuttle the ship; sea-cocks were opened, decks were doused with petrol, and, in an instant, *Rubens* was a blazing inferno.

The attention of the British guns was turned on the lifeboats that were striking frantically for safety, not so much to injure the occupants as to prevent them getting ashore; King-Hall was desperate to capture some men to gain information about their mission. However, the Germans took the risk and scampered up the beach into the mangrove swamps. When his landing party was repelled by a field company of the Schutztrupp Deutsch Ostafrika, King-Hall withdrew southward confident in the knowledge that *Rubens* would never leave Manza Bay. The severity of the fire and several audible below-deck explosions suggested that there would be no ammunition for the guns that were said to be aboard.

Eventually, the Germans salvaged much of the cargo, particularly equipment that had been stored beneath the waterline when the ship caught fire. The German forces in eastern Africa received virtually all the rifles that had been despatched, together with a surprising amount of ammunition. As far as Max Looff and *Königsberg* were concerned, however, the British had achieved their goal; the precious coal had been destroyed.

On 25 April 1915, Flight Lieutenant Tull and his observer took off in one of three antiquated floatplanes supplied to replace the troublesome Sopwiths. In the face of spirited opposition from Abteilung Delta—not to mention 10·5cm shells fired at maximum elevation from two of the cruiser's main guns modified by the removal of the upper part of the gun-shield—Tull managed to return with new information. He had even managed to take some photographs with a box camera. *Königsberg* had emerged from her camouflaged lair and was resplendent in a fresh coat of light grey paint instead of the previous swamp green. Smoke issued from her funnel. Was Looff about to make a dash along the Kikunju channel?

Reconnaissance flights were hastily arranged, but nothing happened and it was assumed that the German cruiser had merely been testing her engines and boilers after an overhaul. Life on the Rufiji returned to its customary torpor.

As Royal Navy vessels came and went, *Chatham* was ordered to the Dardanelles in mid-May; once again, Admiral King-Hall had been left with only one cruiser— *Weymouth*—capable of destroying *Königsberg* in a ship-to-ship confrontation. As any blockading ship had to visit Zanzibar or Mombasa periodically for maintenance, there would be times, King-Hall supposed, when Looff and his men could attempt a break-out virtually unopposed.

Locked in the Rufiji delta, however, the Germans had problems of their own. The cruiser had been repainted simply to keep the remaining crewmen occupied. Looff and his engineering staff knew that protracted inactivity in a muddy swamp had done irreparable damage to *Königsberg*'s engines. Four officers and 111 men been detached to fight for the Schutztrupp on 1 May and it was doubtful whether the skeleton crew could fight the ship successfully in battle. Just as King-Hall had no way of knowing his opponent's situation, so Looff, unaware that only *Hyacinth* and *Weymouth* remained to confront him, fretted that a battle fleet waited just over the horizon. Berlin had simply abandoned the cruiser to her fate.

The situation changed dramatically at 19:00 on 3 June, when an odd-looking flotilla dropped anchor off Mafia Island. HM Ships *Severn* (Captain Eric Fullerton) and *Mersey* (Commander Robert Wilson), formerly *Solimoes* and *Madeira*, were two of three shallow-draught river monitors which had been ordered from Vickers Ltd in 1912 by the Brazilian government. All three ships had been completed by February 1914, but the purchasers defaulted and the monitors had been laid up in Barrow. With a nominal tonnage of 1,260 and a length of 226ft 9in, they had twin triple-expansion steam engines and were capable of 9·5 knots.

Purchased by the Admiralty when the First World War began, the monitors had successfully bombarded the Flanders coast and were seen as the ideal means of destroying *Königsberg* without risking expensive and sophisticated cruisers.

By the Spring of 1915, excepting for *Humber* (formerly *Javary*), they carried two 6-inch BL Mk VIII guns mounted singly forward and aft. Two 4·7-inch howitzers were mounted on the boat deck, whilst five

3-pdr QF guns and several ·303 machine-guns were provided for short-range defence.

All three monitors had left Devonport on 14 March under the escort of the HMS *Trent*, an 1899-vintage Royal Mail steamer which had been impressed as a mother ship. Each monitor was towed by two large ocean-going tugs—*Sarah Jolliffe* and *Southampton* being in charge of *Severn*, with *T.A. Jolliffe* and *Revenger* towing *Mersey*. After a torrid journey across the Bay of Biscay and around Spain, the convoy entered the Mediterranean through the Pillars of Hercules, reached Malta and anchored in the Grand Harbour, Valletta, on 28 March. *Humber* and her tugs left for the Dardanelles whilst *Severn*, *Mersey*, their four tugs, *Trent* and the collier *Kendal Castle* proceeded to Port Said, through the Suez Canal and down the Red Sea.

Reaching Aden on 15 May in heat so intense that two crewmen died of heat-stroke, the procession passed Cape Guardafui on 20 April. Mafia island was finally reached by way of Mombasa, Pemba and Zanzibar. The low freeboard and shallow draught of the monitors were not suited to an ocean journey and there had been many anxious moments.

When they reached the Rufiji, *Severn* and *Mersey* were leaking copiously through sprung seams and buckled plates. Work began immediately to restore the integrity of the monitors' hulls. Armour plating was added to protect the wheelhouse, on the deck covering the machinery, and around the magazines; shields were fashioned for the otherwise unprotected 3-pdr guns that would be needed to discourage the attentions of Abteilung Delta. By the end of June, work on the ships had been completed and firing trials commenced, aided by spotting from the air. The four large tugs, meanwhile, had been armed to serve as patrol boats.

Two Caudron C.III amphibians and a solitary Henry Farman F-27 biplane had arrived from Britain to use a makeshift aerodrome constructed on Mafia island. The idea of correcting fall of shot by airborne wireless telegraphy was novel, but practice soon showed its efficacy. At altitudes of up to four thousand feet, aircraft would be comparatively immune to ground fire. On 2 July, an attempt was made to attack *Königsberg* from the air, one small bomb landing on the bow without causing much damage. As the aeroplanes were far more valuable for reconnoitring, the direct attack was not repeated.

Herbert King-Hall briefed the pilots of the spotter aeroplanes and the commanders of every ship in his Rufiji squadron in the afternoon of 5 July 1915. The assault was planned for the following dawn, when *Mersey* and *Severn* were to cross the sand-bar at the entrance to the northerly Kikunja channel.

**Below:** portly Fregattenkapitän Max Looff (centre right, hand raised) instructs the officers and men of *Königsberg* being detached with the landing party to join the forces of Paul von Lettow-Vorbeck. Author's collection.

**Below:** *Königsberg* among the swamps of the Rufiji delta. From an artist's impression published in *The War Illustrated* on 28 November 1914.
Author's collection.
**Below right:** her deck awash and one funnel down, SMS *Königsberg* has found her final resting place.
Author's collection.

At 04:15 on 6 July, the flotilla duly weighed anchor. At 05:20, five minutes before a spotter aeroplane armed with six bombs took off, the monitors passed Ssimba Uranga Head and arrived at the mouth of the Kikunja. No sooner had they crossed the sand-bar, however, than they were spotted by Abteilung Delta; all hell broke loose around the ships as the battery of one 6cm gun, a 3·7cm gun, an 8mm machine-gun and fifty rifles opened fire.

At 05:45, King-Hall hoisted his pennant and *Weymouth*, *Hyacinth*, *Pyramus*, *Pioneer* and their escorts headed for the delta to bombard the shore defences. *Weymouth*, *Pyramus* and the four armed trawlers pounded the mouth of the Kikunja channel, whilst *Hyacinth* and *Pioneer* engaged the defenders of Ssimba Uranga. Not surprisingly, the accuracy of the defensive fire deteriorated perceptibly under the hail of shells. By 06:15, the monitors had run the gauntlet without sustaining serious damage. Within a few minutes, Tull had appeared overhead.

*Severn* dropped anchor behind Gengeni island at 06:23, followed by *Mersey*, but not until 06:58 were the British monitors ready to fire.

The artillery duel was fascinating, pitting the four 6-inch guns of the monitors, spotted from the air, against five of the 10·5cm guns of *Königsberg* spotted by observation from tree-top positions near the British ships. The first laurels went to Leutnant z.S. Richard Wenig and his gunners, who bracketed *Severn* as early as 06:50 and scored a direct hit on the forward 6-inch gun of *Mersey* at 07:40. Tull reported that the Germans were shooting with great precision, whereas the monitors were firing so wildly that he could not spot for them effectually. A second hit, virtually on the waterline, persuaded Commander Wilson that the German gunners had his

range. As he moved to a new anchorage upstream, several shells landed directly on the spot *Mersey* had vacated only a few minutes previously.

At about 07:55, a shell fired by *Severn* pierced the fore-deck breakwater of *Königsberg* to burst on the shield of the forward starboard 10·5cm gun, killing two men. A second hit wrecked the starboard wing of the bridge, destroying the fire-control instruments and wounding Looff, navigating officer Hinrichs and the helmsman. A third hit destroyed the officers' galley, killing the Boatswain. A fourth exploded on the main deck amidships, doing little damage but severely injuring gunnery officer Wenig in the legs.

The British warships were still threatened by the outstanding gunnery of their opponent; Fullerton was the next beneficiary of good fortune, moving *Severn* just as a salvo of shells landed squarely on his former position. Temporarily deprived of spotting assistance, as Tull had returned to Mafia island to refuel, the fire of the monitors grew increasingly ragged. However, lookouts on *Severn* had spotted a nearby tree-top observation post and destroyed it with a few well aimed 3-pdr shells. Deprived of the vital fall-of-shot information, *Königsberg*'s fire also lost direction. For much of the period between 12:30 and 14:40, therefore, the delta was quiet.

The reappearance of Tull caused confusion. Two British spotter planes were now working at once, and the instructions to the monitors became hopelessly confused. Ultimately, at 15:35, *Severn* and *Mersey* headed back out to sea on the ebb tide. Abteilung Delta predictably hammered them at the channel mouth, but both ships returned to rejoin King-Hall off Koma island. *Severn* was unscathed, but *Mersey* had lost her forward 6-inch gun and had two punctures on the waterline. Emergency

repairs were begun. The damaged gun and its mounting were removed from *Mersey* and the resulting hole in the deck was plated over; seams and bulkheads that had sprung in both ships were reinforced or shored up; and a tactical conference was convened.

The two ships had fired 635 6-inch shells, but had obtained only four hits on *Königsberg*. *Mersey* had lost one of her main guns; four men had been killed, and two of the four most seriously injured subsequently succumbed to their wounds. More creditably, the two spotter aircraft had remained in the air for a total of thirteen hours and had covered about 1,100 miles without incident. King-Hall was sufficiently encouraged to try again, but the plan was changed to separate the monitors by a half-mile. The hamstrung *Mersey* was to anchor farther from the island in an attempt to divide the fire of *Königsberg* or, alternatively, ensure that *Severn* could fire at will.

At 11:45 on the morning of 11 July 1915, after chafing for the flood tide, the flotilla braved the fire of Abteilung Delta under the protection afforded by *Weymouth* and *Pyramus* in the Kikunju channel and *Hyacinth* and *Pioneer* in Ssimba Uranga. Owing to her comparatively shallow draft, *Pyramus* was able to steam more than three miles up the Kikunju to assist the monitors.

Looff and his men had improved communications with the spotting station on Pemba hill and at 12:10, according to the British account, the Germans opened fire on *Severn*. At 12:30, the monitors began to return fire under the watchful eye of Flight Lieutenant Tull. One shot from the fourth British salvo fortuitously cut the telephone lines between *Königsberg* and Pemba hill, whereupon German fire became increasingly wayward.

The British had finally become accustomed to aerial spotting. One shell of the eighth salvo from *Severn* hit the deck forward of *Königsberg*'s bridge at 12:42, knocking out the forward starboard 10·5cm gun for the second time. A second shell burst immediately behind the conning tower, splinters entering through the vision ports to wound Looff and the men inside. German gunfire was then directed from the after control position, but was confined to the three aftermost 10·5cm guns on the starboard side. Casualties grew amongst the gun crews and ammunition-supply parties.

The centre funnel fell at 12:52 and a serious fire had begun aft. Only a single German gun remained firing. At 12:53, a tremendous explosion was heard and a pall of smoke marked the position of the stricken warship. Fire had ignited ready-use ammunition stored around the aftermost guns, forcing the Germans to flood the after magazine. Fregattenkapitän Looff had been hit in the stomach by a shrapnel fragment and eventually gave command to Kapitänleutnant Georg Koch.

The engine of Tull's Henry Farman, meanwhile, had been hit by one of the last shots from *Königsberg* and the aeroplane was losing height rapidly in the direction of

*Mersey*. Tull attempted to ditch, but the wheels of the undercarriage caught the water and the crippled biplane somersaulted to destruction. Tull and his observer, Sub-Lieutenant Arnold, shaken and bruised but otherwise unharmed, were rescued by the crew of the monitor.

Now that their gunners had the range, *Severn* and *Mersey* methodically fired salvo after salvo. Between 13:00 and 14:20, the former had fired 84 shells and the latter 28. At 14:20, however, the observer of the spotter aircraft wirelessed that the target had been destroyed. The once-proud 'Manowari na Bomba Tatu', pride of the Ostafrikanische Station, was a smoking wreck. At 13:30, unknown to Fullerton, Max Looff had ordered that the breech-blocks of the guns be thrown overboard. The magazines were flooded and, at 13:40, the order was given to abandon ship.

Command passed to Kapitänleutnant Koch, who remained aboard with a few men to supervise the scuttling operations. Finally, shortly after 14:00, two torpedo warheads were fired to sink the wreck to the upper deck in the shallow water. At 17:45, the imperial ensign and Looff's command pennant were hauled down from the mast and presented to the injured skipper. Three cheers were given for the Kaiser.

Their job done, the British monitors retreated past the demoralised remnants of Abteilung Delta to rejoin their colleagues. The raider had finally been destroyed without incurring additional casualties on the British side. The ferocity of the action had not been reflected in German losses. Of the 220 men aboard *Königsberg*, nineteen had been killed, 21 were seriously injured and 24 had minor wounds. Many of the wounded men were transferred to the hospital in Neustieten; most of the dead were buried in a makeshift cemetery alongside the wreck of the ship, and the three men killed in the attack of 6 July. A few of the injured died in hospital, apparently raising the overall death toll to about thirty.* A few months later, the dead were reinterred in the Friedhof in Neustieten, where a cairn displaying a commemorative plaque recorded the date of the final battle and the names of the fallen.

The story had an ironic twist. Persuaded by the irrepressible Schönfeld that the 10·5cm guns could be salvaged, Looff subsequently sent down divers to retrieve the breech-blocks. The guns were unshipped and sent overland to Dar-es-Salaam, where they were mounted on special improvised field carriages and assisted materially in the defence of the German colony in East Africa until the end of hostilities.

---

* According to Gröner, Jung and Maass, *Die deutschen Kriegsschiffe 1815–1945*, vol. I, p. 133, the toll was a mere nineteen. The anomalies between these figures and those given elsewhere—e.g., Charles Miller in *Battle for the Bundu* suggests from a visit to the cemetery that they were appreciably higher—has yet to be resolved. It has been suggested that the total of about thirty includes men killed whilst fighting for Abteilung Delta, but the case is not yet conclusively proven.

# KRONPRINZ WILHELM

6 August 1914–26 April 1915; fourteen mercantile victims (51,346grt).
Once a popular and successful passenger liner on the North Atlantic routes. Interned in
Newport News after a lengthy cruise.

◆◆◆

Type: Hilfskreuzer, also known as *Hilfskreuzer C.*
Builder: AG 'Vulcan', Stettin-Bredow (yard no. 249). Equipped at sea by *Karlsruhe*, August 1914.
Owner: Norddeutscher Lloyd, Bremen.
Launch date: 30 March 1901.
Maiden voyage: September 1901.
Commissioned: 6 August 1914.
Crew: 20 officers and 483 men.
**Dimensions**
Registered tonnage (grt): 14,908.
Full-load displacement: 24,900 tonnes.
Overall length: 202·2 metres.
Waterline length: 194·2 metres.
Beam: 20·2 metres.
Full-load draught: about 8·8 metres.
**Weapons**
Guns: two 8·8cm SK L/35 (see text below).
Maximum range of main armament: 12,200 metres.
Lesser guns: two old British 12cm guns (but no ammunition), one 8mm Maxim machine-gun and 36 rifles (Gewehre 98).
Munitions: 290 8·8cm shells.
Armour protection: only on gun shields.
**Performance**
Powerplant: two vertical six-cylinder quadruple expansion engines, supplied by sixteen boilers. Two propeller shafts.

Boiler pressure: 14·5at (213psi).
Coal bunkerage: 4,420 tonnes.
Speed, trials: 23·3 knots (36,000ihp).
Speed, service maximum: 22·5 knots (30,000ihp) when new.
Range: 4,800 nautical miles at 18 knots.

On 2 August 1914, as the forces of Russia and Germany went to war, the German naval attaché in New York, Fregattenkapitän Boy-Ed, delivered sealed orders to Kapitän Grahn of the Norddeutscher Lloyd liner *Kronprinz Wilhelm*. These advised Grahn to coal immediately, take on provisions, and leave New York harbour as soon as possible to meet a cruiser of the Kaiserliche Marine in mid-ocean. At 20:10 on 3 August, *Kronprinz Wilhelm* left harbour and headed southward at speed. Stokers worked feverishly to push the great liner up to twenty knots, whilst the crew disguised her pristine white uppers and mustard-yellow funnels with a coat of black paint. As Grahn ran south, he received a wireless message from *Karlsruhe* fixing the meeting for 6 August in 25º40′N 72º37′W. The cruiser had readied a pair of 8·8cm guns, together with a machine-gun, rifles and a

**Below:** in many parts of the world, particularly where port facilities were minimal, strenuous tasks such as loading or coaling were undertaken by manual labour. Author's collection.

large quantity of ammunition.* At 07:00 on 6 August, more than 150 nautical miles away from the nearest landfall, *Karlsruhe* met *Kronprinz Wilhelm*.

The two ships lashed together as best they could, owing to the great disparity in size and height. The two guns were hoisted aboard the liner in return for coal and fresh provisions. Time was of the essence, as both skippers were well aware of the proximity of British warships; if a cruiser caught *Karlsruhe* and *Kronprinz Wilhelm* lashed together and immobile, the consequences were unimaginable.

Impressment of the Norddeutscher Lloyd steamship into the imperial navy was accompanied by a change in command. Though Grahn was an experienced mariner, he had no training for war; consequently, command of the merchant cruiser was passed to Kapitänleutnant Paul Thierfelder, *Karlsruhe*'s navigator. Grahn was to be his deputy, and Kapitänleutnant der Seewehr-Infanterie Frese became the navigating officer. Fifteen technical personnel, sailors and stokers came over from the cruiser; in return, Grahn gave *Karlsruhe* Leutnants z.S. d.R. Eyding and Hentschel.

At 10:15, lookouts spotted smoke to the south. This could only mean that a British cruiser was approaching, wrongly presumed to be *Berwick*. Excepting the motor launch belonging to *Karlsruhe*, which was abandoned, boats were hoisted in; officers and men rushed to their new stations; hawsers were cast off and the ships surged away in differing directions. *Karlsruhe* sped off north by west, whilst the liner set a course north north-east.

The pursuit of *Karlsruhe* by *Suffolk* allowed *Kronprinz Wilhelm* to escape unscathed. Had the British cruiser pursued the liner the results would have been entirely predictable; instead, *Kronprinz Wilhelm* was given time to mount her new guns, protect vital areas with matting, turn the first-class dining saloon into a makeshift coal store, and strip out the smoking room for use as a first-aid station. The voyage eastward from the Bahamas to the Ilhas dos Açôres (Azores) was, however, uneventful.

By 17 August, the merchant cruiser was in sight of the islands and called for the collier that had been expected. Not until the following day did the 3,913grt steamer *Walhalla* of the Westafrikanische Etappe appear, the two ships meeting in 35ºN 25ºW. Owned by Rhederei AG 'Ocean' (H.H. Schmidt, Hamburg), the 1907 Doxford-built collier had left Las Palmas on 2 August with a full load of coal and provisions.

The absence of hostile warships and a lengthy period of calm weather allowed *Kronprinz Wilhelm* and *Walhalla* three days in which to transfer about 2,500 tonnes of coal, work being completed on 21 August. Hawsers were then released, the collier steaming back to Las Palmas

to refuel whilst the merchant cruiser set a south south-westerly course for the trade routes.

On 27 August, lookouts sighted a schooner which dutifully halted when ordered to do so by megaphone. Unfortunately, she proved to be the neutral Danish *Elizabeth* and was allowed to proceed unmolested. Shortly afterward, *Kronprinz Wilhelm* stopped a Russian barque named *Pittan*; though Germany and Russia were at war, Thierfelder did not consider his prize worthy of sinking. The small vessel was also allowed to go, her crew silently offering prayers for such a narrow escape. Still the fates denied the German merchant cruiser a prize worthy of the name.

On 3 September, two hundred nautical miles eastward of Cabo São Roque, *Kronprinz Wilhelm* met the 4,663grt collier *Asuncion* of the Brazilian Etappe, launched from the Hamburg shipyard of Blohm & Voss in 1895 for the Hamburg-Südamerikanische Dampfschifffahrts-Gesellschaft. Finally, on 4 September 1914, the 2,846grt steamship *Indian Prince* of the Prince Line Ltd blundered into Thierfelder's path. Completed by J. Readhead & Sons Ltd of South Shields in 1910, the Newcastle upon Tyne-registered ship had left Bahia on 2 September under the command of Captain Gray.

Once the passengers and crew had been taken off the doomed ship, and the scuttling charges were laid, Thierfelder ordered *Indian Prince* to be steered south south-east whilst *Kronprinz Wilhelm* followed astern to ensure that all went according to plan. Finally, at 09:00 on 9 September, the British merchantmen was sunk about two hundred miles north west of Ilha da Trindade.

The 4,275grt 1905-vintage steamship *Ebernburg*, built for DDG 'Hansa' of Bremen by Flensburger Schiffbau-Gesellschaft, appeared on 11 September to replenish the merchant cruiser's store of provisions. Soon afterward, the 5,703grt Hamburg–Amerika Linie merchantmen *Pontos* also arrived, four days out from La Plata and Montevideo. The British-built collier, a product of Priestman & Co. of Sunderland in 1900, was followed by the 3,557grt collier *Prussia*, also belonging to the Hamburg–Amerika Linie. Built by the Flensburger Schiffbau-Gesellschaft in 1912, *Prussia* had originally been serving *Dresden*, but had been sent into Rio de Janeiro with the crew of the sunken British tramp steamer *Hyades*. After replenishing her cargo of coal, *Prussia* had left Rio on 5 September.

Ilha da Trindade seemed an ideal coaling station: uninhabited, sufficiently far from the usual trade lanes for activity to pass unnoticed, yet close enough to South America to allow the German colliers easy access to ports in Brazil. The chances of a Royal Navy cruiser calling at this isolated outpost were remote; at this time only HMS *Glasgow* was on the South American station.

As he coaled from *Pontos* and *Prussia*, however, Thierfelder learned by wireless that the merchant cruiser *Cap Trafalgar* (q.v.) had been caught whilst coaling off

---

* The calibre of these has often been given as 10·5cm, implying that *Karlsruhe* transferred two guns from her main armament. However, the 8·8cm weapons were being carried separately, specifically to arm merchant cruisers.

**Above:** fast and powerful, the battle-cruiser *Von der Tann* would have been a great asset to the Kreuzergeschwader. From a postcard published prior to 1914 by M.L. Carstens, Hamburg (no. 3037). Author's collection.

his intended destination by the British merchant cruiser *Carmania*. The German ship had been sunk in the subsequent gunnery duel. *Kronprinz Wilhelm* was then less that 150 nautical miles away from Trindade, but continued to coal. The operation was protracted, lasting until 19 September.

On 17 September, Thierfelder despatched the captive crew of *Indian Prince* in *Ebernburg* and *Prussia*, the former reaching Santos on 24 September and the latter entering Rio de Janeiro a day later. The crew promptly gave as much assistance as they could to the British representatives, but *Kronprinz Wilhelm* had steamed away into the south Atlantic.

The raider remained inactive off Trindade until the end of September. On 7 October, however, a smoke cloud resolved into a large black-hulled steamship with a predominantly black funnel. As the vessel drew nearer, the funnel was seen to have a distinctive white cross on a red band: the Houlder Line Ltd of London. The manner of the capture was extraordinary. Disdaining the customary approach and a warning shot across the bows, Thierfelder brought *Kronprinz Wilhelm* alongside his intended victim, smashing boats and deck fittings on both ships, then sent a boarding party over the side as though inspired by the buccaneers of the seventeenth century! The 8,529grt steamship had been taken more than three hundred miles east of Montevideo. She proved to be *La Correntina*, completed in 1912 by Irvine's Ship Building & Dry Dock Co. Ltd of West Hartlepool. Captain

Murrison and his ship were homeward bound from La Plata with a cargo of meat

The Germans took off the passengers, crew and enough meat to last for months. They also removed two 4·7-inch guns that could have given *Kronprinz Wilhelm* an unpleasant surprise had the ship been provided with anything to fire; Thierfelder discovered the gun crews aboard *La Correntina*, but also that the ammunition was awaiting collection in Liverpool. The freighter was finally scuttled on 16 October.

The 8,226grt Norddeutscher Lloyd steamship *Sierra Cordoba*—completed by AG 'Vulcan' of Stettin in 1912—arrived on 20 October laden with coal, fresh vegetables, clothing and other essential supplies. On 22 October, in flat calm, the ships were lashed together and transfers began: coal and provisions to the raider, and the prisoners from *La Correntina* to the tender. In company with *Sierra Cordoba*, Thierfelder then steered toward the Brazilian coast to menace the sea lanes leading up to the northern Atlantic and the Caribbean from Cape Horn.

On 28 October, in 34ºS 52ºW, *Kronprinz Wilhelm* encountered a four-masted barque. As the vessel was grey, with a line of false gun ports along the upper deck, Thierfelder correctly suspected that she was French. Built by Russell & Co. of Greenock in 1882, the 2,183grt *Union* of Ant. Dom. Bordes et fils was heading for La Plata under Capitaine Riou with 3,100 tons of Welsh steam coal. Instead of sinking the Bordeaux-registered barque immediately, Thierfelder elected to remove as much coal from her as he could. As the weather was bad and the seas were running too high to risk coming alongside, Thierfelder took *Union* in tow. Finally, by 20 November, two thousand tonnes had been transferred.

However, before the remaining fuel could be removed, the sailing ship capsized alongside the raider. In similar circumstances, Thierichens of *Prinz Eitel Friedrich* had cut away the masts and rigging of a prize to reduce the danger; Thierfelder, however, had not shown the same perception. The crew of *Union* was transferred to *Sierra Cordoba*, whereupon the tender headed off to land the prisoners in Montevideo.

On 21 November, forewarned by transmissions from the Pernambuco wireless-telegraphy station, Thierfelder and his men stopped the Nantes-registered French barque *Anne de Bretagne* (2,063grt) of Société Nouvelle d'Armement, bound for Melbourne by way of Cape Horn with a cargo of European timber. The 1901-vintage sailing ship held little to interest the Germans, and so an attempt was made to scuttle her by opening the sea cocks and exploding the customary demolition charges. Owing to the bouyant timber cargo, the barque showed little sign of sinking. Thierfelder then rammed her, damaging

*Kronprinz Wilhelm*'s bow and fore-foot, and was then forced to expend more than twenty of his precious 8·8cm shells before the French ship slipped slowly beneath the waves in 27°S 32°W.

Lack of success persuaded Thierfelder that it was time to move position, and a course was set for the sea lanes between Cabo São Roque and the Cabo Verde islands. On 4 December the 3,814grt collier *Bellevue* of the Bellevue Steam Shipping Co. Ltd, outward bound from Glasgow, plodded into view and was captured in 3°S 29°9'W—450 nautical miles north-east of Pernambuco. Built by Charles Connell & Co. Ltd of Glasgow in 1895, the tramp was hauling about 5,400 tons of coal destined for Montevideo in the charge of Captain James Robertson.

Before the boarding party could finish inspecting *Bellevue*, another steamer was spotted and the Germans set off in pursuit. A brisk chase ensued before *Kronprinz Wilhelm* overhauled the freighter, which surrendered to a megaphoned command and the hoisting of the German ensign. The boarding party discovered that 4,803grt *Mont Agel* of Société Générale de Transportation Maritime à Vapeur, completed in 1911 by Ateliers et Chantiers de France of Dunkerque and registered in

**Below:** the Nelson Steam Navigation Company steamer *Highland Laddie* was a sister of the ill-fated *Highland Brae*. By courtesy of Laurence Dunn.

Marseilles, was travelling in ballast. She was soon sunk by opening the sea-cocks and firing explosive charges.

Curiously, Thierfelder again applied the finishing touches to a sinking by ramming. His penchant for such tactics has often been questioned, but it is important to remember that *Kronprinz Wilhelm* had been armed at sea by *Karlsruhe* and had very limited supplies of explosives. The supply of shells for the 8·8cm guns was also minimal. Thierfelder needed to conserve ammunition in case he had to fight, which also explained why he was so keen to retrieve the 4·7-inch guns from *La Correntina* when most of the raider captains would simply have destroyed them. The British guns were more powerful than the two German weapons *Kronprinz Wilhelm* already mounted, and there was a far greater chance of capturing supplies of British ammunition from a prize than finding German 8·8cm shells on the high seas.

Seduced by the lure of *Bellevue*, Thierfelder elected to transfer from the collier to *Kronprinz Wilhelm* as much of value as he could. Though the most valuable commodity was coal, the liquor, cigars, chocolate, food and water were all greatly appreciated aboard the raider.

Not until 20 December, therefore, was *Kronprinz Wilhelm* ready to scuttle *Bellevue* and return to the fray. Thierfelder had been joined by the 5,463grt steamship *Otavi* of the Hamburg–Amerika line, a product of Russell & Company of Port Glasgow in 1904, which had left Pernambuco on 4 December on the pretext of completing her pre-war voyage. There had been rumours that *Otavi* was to coal the German battle-cruiser *Von der Tann*, allegedly to be ordered southward from Germany to escort Von Spee and the Kreuzergeschwader homeward after they had rounded Cape Horn.

The destruction of the German ships during the Battle of the Falkland Islands on 8 December had left *Von der Tann* and *Otavi* without a mission, so the tender was ordered to join *Kronprinz Wilhelm* on 12 December. She was dismissed on 21 December and eventually landed the prisoners in Las Palmas on 4 January 1915.

By Christmas, Thierfelder had managed to fill *Kronprinz Wilhelm* with sufficient coal to extend his cruise for some time; during the preceding four months, however, he had accomplished very little. The German government had finally learned of the loss of *Karlsruhe*, so a message was sent to Thierfelder giving permission to enter a neutral port, if he wished to do so, and submit to internment. The skipper was not inclined to quit so readily.

On 28 December, eastward of the line drawn from Fernando Noronha to São Pedro e São Paulo (St Paul's Rocks), he seized the 3,486grt Liverpool-registered tramp *Hemisphere* of the Hemisphere Steam Ship Co. Ltd, completed by Bartram & Sons of Sunderland in 1897. Hauling coal from Hull to Buenos Aires, under the eye of Captain Robert Jones, the prize was taken in 4°20′S 29°25′W. She was moved eastward out of the sea lanes before transfer of cargo began on 30 December; on 7 January 1915, *Hemisphere* was finally scuttled.

*Kronprinz Wilhelm* had been met on 6 January in 1°N 20°W by the 5,556grt Roland Linie steamship *Holger*, which had been launched from the Tyneside yard of Swan, Hunter & Wigham Richardson in 1906. *Holger* had been anchored in Pernambuco harbour as a clandestine relay for wireless messages. Eventually, on 4 January, without bothering to obtain clearance, the steamer had sailed under cover of darkness and eluded the patrols.

British protestations about the underhand tactics employed by German merchant shipping interned in Brazilian ports could no longer be ignored. The escape of *Holger* cost the Captain of the Port and the commanding officer of the Brazilian guard-ship their jobs, neutrality was enforced to the point of removing components from transmitter/receivers aboard German ships, and the wireless telegraphy station on Fernando Noronha— which had served the raiders as a useful beacon—was closed for the duration of hostilities. The Germans soon improvised transmissions from the ships, often using hidden equipment, but the tide of opinion in southern America had turned; no longer would large scale violations of neutrality be tolerated.

Stores were sent over to the raider, whilst the crew of *Hemisphere* was transferred to *Holger* and the skipper of the tender gave Thierfelder the latest news. The ships then steamed off north-westward to menace the Las Palmas–Buenos Aires sea lanes in the knowledge that merchantmen had been warned to keep to the east of the normal routes. At 00:30 on 10 January, in 5°48′N 25°58′W, *Kronprinz Wilhelm* captured the 4,419grt *Potaro* of the Royal Mail Steam Packet Company. Outward bound from Liverpool in ballast, the vessel—black hulled with white uppers and a plain buff funnel—was heading for Buenos Aires and the promise of a cargo. Thierfelder decided that the 1904-vintage Harland & Wolff product could serve as a scout, so she was hastily repainted grey and fitted with a Telefunken transmitter/receiver.

On 14 January, after steaming southward, lookouts aboard the raider spotted a grey-hulled steamship with distinctive pale green upperworks. The red funnel had a black top and three narrow bands of equal width— white/black/white—though the most obvious feature was the superstructure amidships: comparatively short, but three decks high, it gave the vessel an ungainly top-heavy appearance.

*Highland Brae* had been completed in 1910 for the Nelson Steam Navigation Co. Ltd by Cammell Laird of Birkenhead, and had been bound from the Thames to Buenos Aires with a cargo that included refrigerated meat. Now the 7,364grt steamship lay stopped about 230 nautical miles north-east of São Pedro e São Paulo.

The Germans were still deciding the fate of *Highland Brae* when a small three-mast schooner was sighted. After a short chase, Thierfelder and his men stopped

*Wilfred M* (251grt), on a passage to Bahia from Halifax, Nova Scotia, with a cargo of dried fish. Ship's papers revealed the schooner had been completed five years previously by Smith & Rhuland in Lunenburg, Nova Scotia, but also that she was registered in Bridgetown in Barbados on behalf of The Ship 'Wilfred M' Co. Ltd. After transferring the crew, *Kronprinz Wilhelm* attempted to sink the schooner by running her down, cutting the hull in two before steaming to rejoin *Holger* and *Potaro* in mid-Atlantic.

The wreck of *Wilfrid M* remained afloat. On 18 January, the battleship *Canopus* had been alerted to the presence of a German ship by a British merchantman which had intercepted signals from a Telefunken-type transmitter in 1°N 24°27′W. Whilst patrolling the zone from which the signals had come, the crew of the battleship detected a strong smell of rotting fish and then—on 21 January—found the fore-part of the wrecked schooner in 2°40′N 25°50′W. Another attempt was made to sink the hulk by ramming; eventually, the remnants of the Barbadian schooner were seen off Belsamos Island and drifted ashore on Grenada on 28 April 1915.

The four-ship convoy then sailed leisurely southward, gradually unloading *Highland Brae* until, on 30 January 1915, a hundred miles south-east of Ilha da Trindade, the British steamer was scuttled. Thierfelder had a change of heart and also sank the erstwhile scout *Potaro*.

Accompanied only by *Holger*, *Kronprinz Wilhelm* headed back for the sailing-ship routes. On 3 February, in 26°30′S 27°W, Thierfelder overhauled the 2,280grt four masted barque *Semantha*, which proved to have been built in 1888 by Hamilton & Company of Port Glasgow but had subsequently been sold to Akties. 'Semantha' of Lyngnør and flew the neutral Norwegian flag. However, as the cargo of wheat was bound for Rio de Janeiro from Britain, *Semantha* was promptly scuttled once Captain Halvorsen and his crew were put aboard *Holger*.

The tender left on 12 February for Buenos Aires, arriving five days later—after passing unnoticed within sight of the British cruiser *Carnarvon*, flying the flag of Admiral Stoddart.

The German merchantman was rightly regarded as an auxiliary warship and granted no more than the customary 24-hour stay in Argentine waters. However, as her engines were in need of attention and her bottom was foul, the Germans decided on internment. This unexpected decision was eventually conveyed to the Admiralty early in March, whereupon the merchant cruiser *Celtic* was ordered back to the Falklands from her patrol off the Rio de la Plata.

On 22 February, Thierfelder stopped the 4,583grt steamship *Chasehill* in 6°15′S 26°10′W. The steamer had been built by Doxford & Company of Sunderland in 1891 and was owned by the Essex Chase Steam Ship Co. Ltd of London. Her cargo of 2,860 tons of British coal, bound for La Plata, brought relief for Thierfelder;

however, no sooner had the transfer of provisions begun on 23 February than another steamer was spotted and *Kronprinz Wilhelm* surged off in pursuit.

The 6,600grt *Guadeloupe* of Compagnie Générale Transatlantique, completed in 1906 by Chantiers de l'Atlantique of Saint Nazaire and registered in Le Havre, was soon brought back to *Chasehill* by a prize crew. Amongst the most useful of the goods aboard the French ship was grey cloth, which provided the crew of the raider with new uniforms. *Guadeloupe* was scuttled on 9 March, but *Chasehill* was retained until all her coal had been transferred. The captured crews, plus the passengers of *Guadeloupe*—including women and children—were loaded aboard *Chasehill* and the battered steamer was sent in Pernambuco, docking on 12 March.

On 10 March 1915, the British merchant cruiser *Macedonia* passed through the area in which *Chasehill* and *Guadeloupe* had been captured, but Thierfelder's luck held. On 24 March, *Kronprinz Wilhelm* stopped the coffee-laden 3,207grt British steamship *Tamar* about five hundred nautical miles east north-east of Pernambuco. Built by Craig, Taylor & Co. of Stockton on Tees, registered in Middlesbrough and owned by the Royal Mail Steam Packet Company, *Tamar* was promptly sunk by gunfire.

On 27 March, 460 nautical miles north-east by east of Pernambuco, Thierfelder overhauled the 3,824grt tramp *Coleby*, homeward bound with five thousand tons of wheat from South America. Completed in 1907 by Ropner & Son of Stockton on Tees, for R. Ropner & Company, the distinctive trunk-deck steamship was sunk by scuttling charges and gunfire.

The British authorities remained convinced that *Kronprinz Wilhelm* was still operating in the southern Atlantic, but the last of her many disappearances had been problematical. Few of the sailing ships carried wireless transmitters and so the taking of *Wilfrid M*, to name but one, was not immediately apparent. The only hope seemed to lie in keeping a careful watch on German merchant ships interned in supposedly neutral ports in the hope that, when the raider's fuel began to run low, an attempt would be made to replenish her bunkers.

Interest centred on the 4,312grt Hamburg–Amerika Linie collier *Macedonia*, completed by Swan, Hunter & Wigham Richardson of Newcastle upon Tyne in 1900, which had left New Orleans shortly before hostilities began and had been interned by the Spanish authorities in Las Palmas on 17 October.

Though the Spanish had removed a cylinder cover to prevent *Macedonia* leaving harbour without their knowledge, a replacement part had been obtained by the local Etappe. On 4 March, a coded message had ordered the freighter to meet *Kronprinz Wilhelm*. At 01:30 on 15 March, *Macedonia* slipped out of harbour under the cover of darkness, eluded the guard-ship without trouble, and escaped into the night.

Unfortunately, to maintain cordial relations with Spain, the Royal Navy had withdrawn its patrols so far from the Canary islands that the escape of *Macedonia* was not only difficult to prevent but also virtually impossible to follow. Only by decoding the messages transmitted from Nauen wireless-telegraphy station was the rendezvous deduced as just north of the equator in 32–35°W. The light cruiser *Gloucester*, commanded by Captain W.A. Howard Kelly MVO, was hastily despatched to search the area.

On 28 March, *Gloucester* spotted a steamship in the designated area, steering south-eastward. Almost immediately, however, the ship swung around and headed off to northward at full speed. *Gloucester* gave chase at twenty knots, rapidly overhauling the quarry. Kelly hoisted 'Stop immediately. What Ship?' The steamer replied by hoisting the Dutch mercantile flag. The name HENDRICK could be discerned on the stern. However, the boarding party discovered that she was actually *Macedonia*.

Papers found aboard the collier revealed that she was to wait in the vicinity of 3°N 37°W between 9 and 23 April. Captain Kelly immediately transmitted the details to Admiral Stoddart, flying his flag in the cruiser *Sydney*, who had been patrolling off the Arquipélago dos Abrolhos in company with the merchant cruiser *Edinburgh Castle*.

An escape from San Juan de Puerto Rico by the German steamship *Odenwald*, on the night of 22/23 March, though thwarted by the authorities, confirmed the Admiralty's view that attempts would be made to coal a raider in the vicinity—though whether it would be *Karlsruhe* or *Kronprinz Wilhelm* was still not known.

*Kronprinz Wilhelm* had become a ghost of her once glorious self. Her sides were streaked with rust and battered by coaling; plates had sprung; seams had come apart; and the bow bore the marks of ramming. Aware that many of his crewmen had the first signs of scurvy, Thierfelder weighed the odds against his survival as a raider. If *Kronprinz Wilhelm* remained at sea, she must surely fall victim to one of the patrolling British cruisers, as her quadruple-expansion steam engines—in their day, the epitome of the machinist's art—could no longer summon much more than twenty knots. The best course seemed to be to lay-up in a suitably neutral harbour. Favoured for this purpose was Newport News in Virginia, where *Prinz Eitel Friedrich* had appeared at the beginning of April.

The presence of a British cruiser squadron eagerly anticipating an exit by *Prinz Eitel Friedrich* forced Thierfelder to proceed with great caution. Early in the morning of 11 April, however, he crept past the solitary picket, HMS *Suffolk*, to enter Newport News harbour.

The German skipper brazenly asked the US authorities for three weeks in which to effect repairs, apparently intending to continue raiding. However, though *Kronprinz Wilhelm* was eventually allowed into dry-dock on 19 April, the port authorities would permit nothing but scraping the foul bottom. The damage to the bows and side plating were regarded as fortunes of war, and could not be repaired in a neutral port. On 26 April, realising the futility of continued resistance, Thierfelder submitted to internment. His ship was impressed into US service on 7 April 1917, as the troopship *Von Steuben*, and was scrapped by the Boston Iron & Steel Metal Company in 1923.

**Below:** a pre-1914 picture of the light cruiser *Glasgow*, veteran of the battles of Coronel and the Falkland Islands, and a sister-ship of *Gloucester*. By courtesy of Ray Burt.

# LEIPZIG

1 August–8 December 1914; four victims (15,279grt).
A conventional light cruiser, sunk by the Royal Navy during the
Battle of the Falkland Islands.

Type: Kleine Kreuzer.
Authorisation: as 'N', 1903.
Builder: AG 'Weser', Bremen (yard no. 143).
Laid down: 1904.
Launch date: 21 March 1905.
Commissioned: 20 April 1906.
Crew: 14 officers and 287 men.

**Dimensions**
Design displacement: 3,278 tonnes.
Full-load displacement: 3,816 tonnes.
Overall length: 111·1 metres.
Waterline length: 110·6 metres.
Beam: 13·3 metres.
Full-load draught: about 5·6 metres.

**Weapons**
Guns: ten SK 10·5cm C/88 L/40.
Maximum range of main armament: 12,200 metres.
Lesser guns: ten 3·7cm automatic cannon.
Torpedo tubes: one submerged on each beam.
Munitions: 1,470 10·5cm high-explosive shells, thirty 10·5cm
shrapnel shells; five 45cm C/03 torpedoes.
Armour protection: deck 20–35mm, conning tower 100mm,
gun-shields 50mm.

**Performance**
Powerplant: two three-cylinder triple expansion steam
engines, supplied by ten boilers. Two propeller shafts.
Boiler pressure: 15at (221psi).
Coal bunkerage: 400 tonnes normal, 860 tonnes maximum.
Speed, trials: 22·1 knots (11,116ihp).
Speed, service maximum: 22 knots (10,000ihp).
Range: said to have been 4,690 nautical miles at 12 knots.

This member of the 'Town' class of cruisers had three
funnels and ten 10·5cm guns in the classical layout: two
on the fore-deck, two on the after-deck immediately abaft
the mainmast, and three on each side of the main deck.

*Leipzig* was one of the ships of the German Far
East Squadron, the Kreuzergeschwader. In the first week
of June 1914, having waited for her annual draft of
replacement crewmen—nearly half her complement—
she sailed from Tsingtau, bound first for Yokohama and
thence to protect German interests on the western coast
of Mexico.

Yokohama harbour was reached on 10 June, allowing
Fregattenkapitän Johannes Haun to cast a practised eye
over the fleet assembled in the Yokosuka navy base
before being appraised by the German naval attaché of
the latest plans to capture Kiautschou if war was to
be declared between Japan and Germany. *Leipzig* left
Yokohama in mid June, entering Honolulu harbour in the
Hawaiian Islands on 27 June.

Haun left Honolulu in the morning of 28 June, heading
eastward across the Pacific to reach Matzalán on 7
July. *Leipzig* had arrived to replace *Nürnberg*, which

was travelling north from Panama before heading off
westward for Tsingtau and a refit. Fregattenkapitän von
Schönberg of *Nürnberg* had chartered the British collier
*Citriana* (Captain Minister) through the offices of the
German consulate in San Francisco, though the American
Pocahontas coal offered very poor quality. Von Schönberg
offered to take one of Haun's officers northward to San
Francisco to arrange a suitable supply of coal for *Leipzig*,
either by telegraphing instructions to Berlin or obtaining
supplies locally.

On 8 July 1914, von Schönberg departed northward
accompanied by *Citriana*, whose coal supplies had
finally been exhausted. *Leipzig*, meanwhile, had set a
course for Guaymas. There General Tellez, loyal to the
Huerta regime, was besieged by the forces of the rebel
Pancho Villa. Tellez had been threatening the German
community in Guaymas with direst retribution unless it
donated money to buy ammunition. However, word of the
situation had reached the government in Berlin and
Johannes Haun had been instructed to show the Mexican
general the error of his ways—if necessary, by shelling
him into submission. However, no sooner had *Leipzig*
arrived than Tellez decided on a strategic withdrawal
seaward in a flotilla of ships sent by Huerta. When the
Carranzist rebels arrived, property belonging to foreign
nationals was being guarded by American, British and
German sailors.

On 23 July 1914, as the clouds of war gathered, *Leipzig*
was ordered to Matzalán on the eastern coast of the
Gulf of California. Here Haun encountered a fleet of
foreign ships: the US cruisers *Albany* and *California*, the
British sloop *Algerine* and the Japanese cruiser *Idzumo*.
The German captain soon learned that the international
situation had deteriorated greatly, and worried that the
British would prevent the return of *Citriana* with much-
needed fuel.

On 2 August, owing to the German declaration of
war on Russia, Fregattenkapitän Haun left Matzalán for
San Francisco to organise supplies of coal through the
Etappe system. *Algerine* followed in the early morning
of 3 August, steaming to join the cruiser *Rainbow* in
Esquimault in case war between Germany and Britain
encouraged *Leipzig* to attack.

The German cruiser coaled in Bahia Magdalena, on
the western coast of southern Baja California, leaving on
5 August. By the time *Leipzig* arrived off the Farallon
Islands at the entrance to the Golden Gate on 14 August,
the ship had been stripped for action; many of the

home comforts—panelling, comfortable chairs and wall hangings—had either been thrown overboard or fed into the furnaces.

Haun cruised around for a few days, intent on avoiding the powerful Japanese armoured cruiser *Idzumo* or the old British cruiser *Rainbow*, which intercepted wireless messages suggested was in the area. The Germans had a particular fright when two shapes had materialised in fog, but they had proved to be two US Navy warships returning to the base at San Diego.

Haun was met by the German vice-consul, who had come out to find him in a motor boat crammed with journalists. The representative announced that the two thousand tons of coal intended for the cruiser had been confiscated as war material, and that the US government showed signs of applying strict rules of neutrality. He also proffered information that *Idzumo* had requested docking facilities on 18 August; Haun would be wise to avoid a confrontation.

*Leipzig* eventually entered San Francisco Harbor on the night of 15/16 August, intending to coal the next day. Less than half the agreed amount had been loaded when the colliers suddenly decided that they needed payment in cash, and stopped work. The impasse was solved by an American admiral, who decided that Haun could have 500 tons of coal in San Francisco and 500 more in Honolulu. At 20:00 on 16 August, therefore, the cruiser was ready to depart. Guided by a pilot who was apparently the worse for drink, *Leipzig* collided with a British barquentine, severely damaging the sailing ship and loosening a 10·5cm gun in its mount.

By 23 August, *Leipzig* was waiting patiently in Bahia Ballinas, Baja California, for the collier *Matzalan* from San Francisco and orders to be relayed by wireless telegraphy.

The 1,815grt steamship *Matzalan* had been built by Laxevaags Maskin- og Jernskibsværft of Bergen in 1903 and had sailed under the Norwegian flag until sold to Friedrich Jebsen of Hamburg in 1914, initially registering in Mexico. When hostilities commenced, the vessel was impressed into the San Francisco Etappe to serve as a collier. *Matzalan* arrived in Bahia Ballinas on 26 August, but the presence aboard of a Mexican official ensured that the coal could only be unloaded at Guaymas—the destination stated on the bills of lading.

Coaling operation had become complicated, as a second collier, *Marie*, had been directed into Matzalán. Finally, Haun decided to take *Leipzig* into Guaymas on 8 September and coal from German-owned wharfside stocks as quickly as possible. Then he would sail, to be joined at sea by *Marie*. Owned by M. Jebsen of Apenrade, the 1,866grt 1905-vintage collier was a product of Howaldtswerke AG of Kiel and had been impressed by the San Francisco Etappe.

**Below:** SMS *Leipzig*, from a tinted postcard (no. 51215) published by Stengel & Co. GmbH of Dresden prior to 1914. Author's collection.

On 11 September, Haun took his first prize eighty miles south-west of Cabo Corrientes. The victim was the 6,542grt British tanker *Elsinore*, bound in ballast for Central America after delivering her cargo to San Francisco. Owned by the Bear Creek Oil & Shipping Co. Ltd (managed by C.T. Bowring & Company), the Liverpool-registered steamship had been completed by Swan, Hunter & Wigham Richardson of Newcastle upon Tyne in 1913. Captain Roberts had attempted to run when challenged, but stopped after a shot had been fired across his ship's bow. A boarding party under Leutnant z.S. Jöhnke reported that there was little aboard of use to the cruiser, so the crew was taken off and the tanker sunk by gunfire at 17:30.

*Leipzig* and *Marie* then set a course for the Islas Galápagos, several hundred miles to the west of the Ecuadorean coast, where Haun had learned that another collier would await him. The cruiser eventually reached Freshwater Bay on Isla Isabela (Indefatigable Island) on 18 September to find *Amasis* of Etappe Peru waiting with provisions and three thousand tonnes of good quality coal. The 7,224grt tender had been completed by Flensburger Schiffbau-Gesellschaft in 1914 for DDG 'Kosmos' of Hamburg.

Haun went ashore to release the prisoners into the charge of the local government representative, sending *Leipzig* to meet *Marie* in Bahia Tagus on the western side of Isla Santa Cruz (Albemarle Island). The tanker crew was put ashore and eventually landed at Guayaquil, Ecuador, in the middle of October.

On 22 September *Leipzig*, *Amasis* and *Marie* headed for the Golfo de Guayaquil, where, on 25 September, Haun took the Liverpool-registered tramp *Bankfields* (3,763grt) of the Bank Shipping Company, bound from Peru for Panama with five thousand tons of sugar cane. A product of the Pickersgill yard in Sunderland, *Bankfields* had been completed in 1905. She was sunk after her crew, chicken and pigs had been taken off, the men being landed at Callao by *Marie* a week later.

On 27 September, *Leipzig* anchored off Isla Lobos de Tierra to finish coaling. Unfortunately for Haun, the skipper of an American four-masted schooner and a local Peruvian government official came aboard the cruiser to ask the Germans to do them no harm. Johannes Haun gave his word willingly—he was, after all, in neutral waters—but the damage had been done. The message that *Leipzig* and her two colliers were off the coast of Peru was common knowledge along the western seaboard of South America within two days.

In October, *Leipzig* rejoined the Kreuzergeschwader off Easter Island, coaled at Más Afuera on 26 October, and took an active (if inconsequential) part in the Battle of Coronel. *Leipzig* had opened fire at HMS *Glasgow* seven minutes after the first shots of the action had been fired, hitting the British cruiser at least once, but then lost touch with her adversary in the darkness.

The victorious Kreuzergeschwader set a course for Bahia Valparaiso, arriving on 3 November. On the day after the battle, however, *Leipzig* had stopped the 3,120grt four-masted French barque *Valentine*, ninety days out of Port Talbot and Iquique-bound with a cargo of Welsh steam coal. Captained by François Guillou, the barque had been completed in 1901 by Chantiers de Normandie of Grand Quevilly for Ant. Dom. Bordes et fils and was registered in Dunkerque. She was immediately towed by *Prinz Eitel Friedrich* to Más Afuera, where Admiral von Spee and his ships arrived on 5 November to prepare for a voyage around Cape Horn.

The French crew refused to co-operate with the Germans and was transferred to *Prinz Eitel Friedrich*; the barque was rigged down and transfer of coal began. Only about 1,200 tonnes had been shifted when a fire in the saloon seriously damaged *Valentine* aft and forced the Germans to scuttle the next day. The French crewmen were eventually landed in Valparaiso by *Sacramento*, a 1900-vintage product of a British shipyard—the Palmer Shipbuilding Company of Newcastle upon Tyne—but owned in 1914 by the 'Northern & Southern Steamship Company' of San Francisco. This was a ruse employed by the San Francisco Etappe to allow the vessel to coal in American ports unhindered, as she had been bought by the Hamburg–Amerika Linie.

On 9 November, *Leipzig* and *Dresden* were sent into Valparaiso to convey messages to Berlin and allow their crewmen time ashore. The warships rejoined the Kreuzergeschwader on 18 November. On 21 November the ships reached the Golfo de Penas, where coaling was undertaken in Bahia San Quentin until 26 November, when the run for Cape Horn began. The weather was truly awful, tossing even the heavier armoured cruisers like corks. Life aboard *Leipzig* and her near-sisters was a nightmare.

On 2 December, as the squadron passed into the Atlantic Ocean, *Leipzig* encountered Captain James Eagles and his 1,844grt four-master *Drummuir*. The barque had been built in Liverpool in 1882 by W.H. Potter & Son but, by 1914, was owned by The Ship 'Drummuir' Co. Ltd and registered under the British flag in Victoria, British Columbia. Apparently managed by James Rolph of San Francisco, *Drummuir* had been bound for San Francisco from Swansea with a cargo of coal.

Haun towed his prize about seventy nautical miles north north-east of Cape Horn to the north side of Picton Island, so that her coal could be transferred to *Baden* and *Santa Isabel*. The barque was sunk by explosive charges on 6 December in 55o30′S 65oW.

On 8 December, *Leipzig* and the other members of the Kreuzergeschwader (excepting *Dresden*) were overwhelmed and sunk during the Battle of the Falkland Islands. The battle is described in greater detail in the chapter devoted to *Dresden*. When it became clear that the battle-cruisers *Invincible* and *Indefatigable* had closed

**Above:** the armoured cruiser *Cornwall* engages *Leipzig*, from a watercolour by Lieutenant-Commander H.T. Bennett RN. From *The Battle of the Falkland Islands* (1919) by Commander Henry Spencer-Cooper MVO, RN.

to a range where the German light cruisers were threatened, von Spee had elected to occupy the British warships long enough to allow his smaller units time to make their escape. Consequently, led by *Dresden* to starboard, with *Nürnberg* to port and *Leipzig* lagging behind in the centre, the cruisers worked up to 22 knots in a desperate attempt to elude *Cornwall*, *Kent* and *Glasgow*.

However, *Glasgow* rapidly overhauled *Leipzig* and *Nürnberg*, engaging them at 15:02 with her forward 6-inch gun to force the German commanders to take evasive action which would slow their progress. The British ship engaged *Leipzig* at 15:45 and again at 16:06, without results. At 16:09, *Leipzig* scored a hit that killed one man aboard *Glasgow* and wounded four others.

At 16:25, Captain John Luce of *Glasgow* took the momentous decision to let *Dresden* escape, ensuring instead that the other German ships would be caught by the two County-class cruisers that were working up to greater speeds than had been achieved—brand new and lightly loaded—on their original measured-mile trials.

At 16:15, *Kent* and *Cornwall* opened fire on *Leipzig* at a range of 10,900 yards, but no hits were seen and *Kent* hauled off in pursuit of *Nürnberg* at 16:30. This left *Leipzig* to fire at *Cornwall*, but the opening salvoes went over the British ship. The next few fell short before the range was found. Just as *Leipzig* threatened her powerful rival, however, a 6-inch shell brought down the fore-topmast at 16:22, killing the gunnery officer and disrupting fire control. At 16:56, when the range had reduced to about eight thousand metres, *Leipzig* scored her first hits and forced Captain Walter Ellerton to turn

*Cornwall* away to starboard. *Glasgow* then joined in the fight off *Cornwall*'s port quarter.

The gunnery of the German cruiser settled into an effectual pattern, forcing *Cornwall* to haul out of range and temporarily cease fire. At about 17:32, *Leipzig* hit her tormentor nine times in rapid succession at 9,500 metres; once again, Ellerton withdrew out of range even though the lightweight 10·5cm shells had done little damage. When *Cornwall* closed again at 18:15, a change to explosive lyddite ammunition had been ordered. This wrought such havoc aboard *Leipzig* that the fire of the German gunners soon slackened.

By 18:51, the German cruiser was on fire forward but still registering an occasional hit on *Cornwall*. At 19:05, firing stopped completely as the 10·5cm ammunition had been exhausted. The top of the fore funnel and the whole of the middle funnel had been shot away, the foremast had gone, the bridge was a shambles, and the ship glowed dully from the many fires that had started below decks. At 19:10, *Cornwall* ceased fire in the hope that Haun would strike his colours, but re-opened fire at 19:13 in the absence of a response from the German cruiser. At 19:43, an internal explosion rocked *Leipzig* and her mainmast fell; finally, at 20:12, two green lights were sent up to signal distress.

Searchlights revealed that the German cruiser had heeled to port, almost onto her beam ends. The stern and forecastle were aflame, the masts had gone and only a small piece of one funnel remained. The ship eventually foundered at 21:22. *Cornwall*'s boats rescued six officers and nine men, but Haun was not among them. Fatalities aboard the British ship amounted to one canary.

# MÖWE

1 November 1915–22 March 1917; 38 victims (165,340grt, plus one
of unknown tonnage). A converted cargo ship, which, uniquely, survived two major and
three lesser raiding cruises.

Type: Hilfskreuzer.
Builder: J.C. Tecklenborg AG, Geestemünde (yard no. 258).
Equipped by the Kaiserliche Werft, Wilhelmshaven, 1915.
Owner: F. Laeisz, Hamburg (named *Pungo*).
Launch date: 9 May 1914.
Commissioned: 1 November 1915 (as H D 10).
Crew: 16 officers and 219 men.

**Dimensions**
Registered tonnage (grt): 4,788.
Full-load displacement: 9,800 tonnes.
Overall length: 124·5 metres.
Waterline length: 117·8 metres.
Beam: 14·4 metres.
Full-load draught: about 6·8 metres.

**Weapons**
Guns: four 15cm SK L/45 and one 10·5cm SK C/88 L/40.
Maximum range of main armament: 13,700 metres (15cm),
12,200 metres (10·5cm).
Lesser guns: small-arms only.
Torpedo tubes: two.
Munitions: 600 15cm shells, 200 10·5cm shells, 500 mines and
twelve 50cm C/08 torpedoes.
Armour protection: none.

**Performance**
Powerplant: one vertical three-cylinder triple expansion steam
engine, supplied by five boilers. One propeller shaft.
Boiler pressure: 13.5at (198psi).
Coal bunkerage: 3,440 tonnes.
Speed, service maximum: 14 knots (3,200ihp).
Range: about 8,700 nautical miles at 12 knots.

The transformation of *Möwe* into a raider—she had
already been commissioned into the navy as a tender—
represented a significant change in policy. Previous
attempts relied on light cruisers, or fast passenger ships
armed with a few guns, to disrupt trade sufficiently in the
sea lanes to embarrass the British economy.

Unfortunately, the warships consumed too much fuel
to be effectual and needed constant support from a fleet
of colliers. Though *Emden* and *Karlsruhe* had been
successful enough, the effects of their ravages had been
short lived. The two cruisers had been eliminated within
a week of each other, whilst the destruction of *Leipzig* and
*Nürnberg* a month later, during the Battle of the Falkland
Islands, reduced the availablity of suitable warships still
further. Once *Dresden* had been hunted down and
*Königsberg* had finally been eliminated in 1915, the
Kaiserliche Marine had no light cruisers in the Atlantic or
Pacific oceans.

Attempts to use fast passenger liners had had a
similar lack of long-term success. Some had been sunk;
the remainder had all been interned by the summer of
1915. Admiral von Pohl had declared in this period that
unrestricted submarine warfare would commence, but

the inventory of serviceable U-Boats stood at a mere 23.
Clearly, another means of disrupting British trade was
needed until supplies of submarines had been assured.

The answer was found in a paper written in October
1915 by a junior officer, Leutnant z.S. Theodor Wolff,
which advocated the use of more modest steamers—
anonymous freighters, which, loaded with extra coal,
would have the requisite range. As long as they were fast
enough to overhaul the average British tramp, and were
prepared to achieve results more by deception than force,
they would be successful. German merchant ships of
this type were comparatively plentiful, so they could be
considered as expendable.

Admiral von Pohl, persuaded to give the merchant-
raider concept another try, approved the selection
of 36-year-old Korvettenkapitän Nikolaus Graf und
Burggraf zu Dohna-Schlodien to command a suitable
ship. An urbane, serious-minded, even-tempered and
chivalrous man, formerly navigating officer aboard the
dreadnought *Posen*, Dohna-Schlodien had enjoyed a
lengthy if comparatively undistinguished career in the
Kaiserliche Marine. His family had friends at Court, it
was true, but his appointment to a command owed more
to his own level-headedness. Karl von Müller of *Emden*
had provided a role-model for the ideal raider skipper;
Dohna-Schlodien, though much more approachable than
von Müller, came from a similar mould.

The original scenario apparently called for a short
cruise to lay mines off the Pentland Firth, Lough Swilly
and Bantry Bay—the precise details being left to the
captain's discretion—after which a southward course
would be set for the Bay of Biscay to threaten the
Gironde estuary. Prizes could be taken whenever
appropriate, but Dohna-Schlodien argued for a more
active role and requested permission to act as a
commerce raider once the mines had been sown. The
arguments were attractive enough to convince the navy
high command of their merits. However, disintegration of
the Etappe system meant that the perpetual supplies of
coal enjoyed by the raiders of 1914 were no longer
available. Graf zu Dohna-Schlodien and his crew would
be on their own, therefore, and their ship would have to
carry as much coal as possible.

*Pungo*, a typical refrigerated freighter, had been
completed for the Laeisz shipping line only a few months
before the First World War began. She was intended
to carry bananas from Togo or the other German
colonies in Africa, and was somewhat faster than the

general run of single-funnelled single-screw tramps. Her nondescript appearance suited the navy's purposes admirably. Bulwarks were added between the bridge and forecastle to hide guns and torpedo tubes; sufficient material was carried to erect a false funnel, extend the superstructure, or alter the shape of the stern. Paint was to be used to change the colour of the funnel or upperworks, and the telescoping topmasts could be adjusted at will. Seen from a distance, the effects were most convincing; a few simple alterations could change the entire character of the ship.

The experience of *Emden*, *Karlsruhe* and others had shown that the 10·5cm L/40 gun, though accurate and dependable, did not have enough power to sink a merchant ship without expending several rounds. It was even less useful against a rival warship. Consequently, *Pungo*, by now renamed *Möwe*, was given 15cm guns taken from disarmed battleships of the Zähringen class.

Two guns were mounted under the forecastle, their embrasures concealed by folding plates, with a second pair abaft the break in the forecastle alongside the forward cargo hatch. Abaft the foremast, one on each side, were two single torpedo tubes. Two more tubes were placed aft, virtually alongside the mainmast, and the single 10·5cm gun was mounted on the poop disguised as hand-steering gear. Thus the one-time banana boat could out-gun many genuine warships.

## The first cruise

*Möwe* left Kiel in December 1915 to lay mines off the Orkneys before embarking on a raiding career.

Sailing close to the Norwegian coast, helped by foul weather, Dohna-Schlodien evaded British patrols without difficulty. On New Year's Day, 1916, *Möwe* laid her mines east of Cape Wrath; the beams of Sule Skerry and Cape Wrath lighthouses, visible for many miles, had helped to fix position. By 23:30, in spite of winds gusting to gale force, more than 250 mines had been laid in eleven separate lines to threaten the western approaches to Pentland Firth. The raider then steamed away, her crew relieved to be rid of much of the deadly cargo.

The field claimed its first victim at 07:00 on 6 January, when the old battleship *King Edward VII* hit a mine in 58°43′N 4°4′W and eventually foundered in heavy seas. A Norwegian merchantman sank next day. The presence of mines eventually forced the authorities to send warships by a route that skirted considerably northward of the Orkneys. As the area could only be partially swept, major ships avoided it for the remainder of the war. The desired disruption had indeed been caused.

*Möwe* had swung in a wide arc to the west of Ireland after laying the mines off Scotland, but then came back eastward to sew the remainder off La Rochelle. Though the presence of mines was detected as early as 10 January, the Spanish steamship *Bayo*, bound for La Pallice from Huelva, sank forty miles west of La Rochelle on 13 January. The loss was followed by that of *Belgica*, a Spaniard bound for Bordeaux from Port Glasgow.

Korvettenkapitän Dohna-Schlodien was anxious to begin his raiding exploits as soon as possible, to add to the disruption he was sure would be caused by his mines. He had, however, decided to abide by a few basic rules. Ships with two funnels were to be ignored; they were generally passenger liners, often creating more problems than they solved, and would often prove to be faster than his converted banana boat. He would also avoid ships with funnels painted in pale colours, unless they were obviously British. Light-coloured funnels more often than not signified neutral vessels. The most desirable victim would be single funnelled, comparatively slow, and have either a plain black funnel or one with simple markings. Ships of this type were invariably British owned.

At 10:00 on 11 January, 150 nautical miles west of Cape Finisterre, smoke was sighted off the starboard bow. *Möwe* immediately raised speed in pursuit, disguised as a vessel of the Ellerman Line, but did not begin to gain on the intended victim until 16:00. A second plume of smoke was then sighted to port. As this was nearer than the vessel he had been chasing, the German captain reduced speed, turned towards the newcomer and ran up a signal requesting her name.

Deceived by the nondescript appearance of *Möwe*, the 3,146grt steamer *Farringford* of the Harrogate Steam Ship Co. Ltd, homeward bound with a cargo of copper ore, obligingly gave her identity. At that, the Germans ran up the battle ensign and fired a single blank round across the bows of the British ship. Approaching to within fifty metres, Dohna-Schlodien signalled the crew of the steamer—completed by J.L. Thompson & Sons of Sunderland in 1906—to abandon ship immediately. Captain Frederick Foley and his men hastily complied with the instruction, in spite of the heavy swell, and were safely gathered aboard the raider. *Farringford* was rapidly sunk with a few well-aimed shells, which testified to the efficacy of the 15cm gun.

The ship that *Möwe* had originally been pursuing had escaped into the squally rain. Unwittingly, but most unwisely, Captain Barton of the Cambridge Steam Ship Co. Ltd tramp *Corbridge* (3,687grt) held to his original course until the raider eventually caught up. The Germans fired a blank, but the steamer replied by making smoke and piling on as much speed as she could.

Irritated, Dohna-Schlodien also increased speed. It was soon obvious that *Möwe* was about two knots faster than *Corbridge*, which had been completed by R. Thompson & Sons Ltd of Sunderland in 1910 and was handicapped by a load of four thousand tons of steam coal bound from Cardiff to Brazil. When the range had shortened sufficiently, a live shell was fired across the British ship's bows. Finally, realising the risk he ran, Barton hove-to.

The boarding party—a couple of junior officers, four armed seamen, two technicians and a signalman—reported the discovery of good-quality Welsh coal to Dohna-Schlodien, who decided to send *Corbridge* to a suitable rendezvous rather than destroy her on the spot.

Elated by their successes, the Germans headed south, to westward of the well-patronised shipping lanes from Cape Finisterre to the Islas Canarias (Canaries). On 13 January, about two hundred nautical miles west of Lisboa, *Möwe* approached a black-painted steamship of moderate size. The 3,627grt *Dromonby*, owned by R. Ropner & Co. and registered in West Hartlepool, tried to run before being brought to a halt by the customary shot across the bows. The boarding party discovered that the 1900-vintage steamship was laden with coal destined for the Royal Navy cruiser squadron off South America. With great satisfaction, Dohna-Schlodien ordered the scuttling of the collier. Scuttling charges were laid, the boarding party was taken off, and *Dromonby* was consigned to a watery grave.

No sooner had the excitement subsided than another smoke plume was reported. At 15:30, only a few miles from the demise of *Dromonby*, the raider stopped *Author*, owned by the Charente Steam Ship Co. Ltd (T. & J. Harrison) of Liverpool. Launched from the Glasgow yard of Charles Connell & Company in 1905, the 3,496grt three-island tramp fitted Dohna-Schlodien's requirements: she had a black hull, plain white uppers and a black funnel with a narrow red band on a broader white one. She had left London on 8 January, bound for Beira, Durban and Delagoa Bay with a mixed cargo. Her master, Captain James Arthur, had seen the approach of

**Above:** *Appam* (7,781grt). By courtesy of Laurence Dunn.

*Möwe*, but the German ship was flying the Red Ensign at her jack-staff and was no cause for undue concern.

Only when the raider came alongside, ran the imperial ensign up to the mast head, and trained her guns on *Author* did the truth become inescapable. 'Stop immediately. Abandon ship' read the message hoisted on *Möwe*. Three boatloads of armed Germans rowed over to the Harrison steamer, taking off the 58-man crew and as many provisions as they could carry. Simultaneously, the scuttling party opened the sea cocks, laid their explosive charges and set the time fuzes. *Author* sank at 17:50.

At 17:25, another ship chanced by. Following the well-rehearsed procedure, *Möwe* stopped 3,608grt *Trader* of the London Traders Shipping Co. Ltd, completed in 1906 by Craggs of Middlesbrough and bound for Liverpool with West Indian sugar cane. By 17:40, the vessel had been sunk by a combination of opened sea cocks and explosive charges.

That evening, Nikolaus Graf zu Dohna-Schlodien reflected on the luck that had brought him three prizes in a single day, in an area of just a few square miles. He also pondered on the fate of his 150 prisoners, the Europeans being packed into the mine-room forward with Lascars and Chinese in the aftermost hold.

At 07:00 on 15 January *Möwe* stopped the 3,055grt British steamer *Ariadne*, laden with grain, which was speedily despatched by gunfire and a torpedo about 140 miles east by north of Madeira. The vessel had been completed in 1904 by W. Gray & Co. Ltd of West Hartlepool for the Ariadne Steam Shipping Company of London. Then came a large liner, steaming northward towards the raider. Dohna-Schlodien ordered the helmsman to take *Möwe* across the steamship's bows so that her name could be read; Lloyd's Register would then provide additional details.

Liverpool-registered *Appam* (7,781grt)—completed by Harland & Wolff of Belfast in 1913—belonged to the British & American Steam Navigation Company, managed by Elder, Dempster & Co. Ltd.

In common with many of the British ships, *Appam* declined to stop when ordered to do so, transmitted distress messages frantically, and was brought to halt 135 miles east of Madeira only by a shot across the bows. Dohna-Schlodien soon noticed that the steamship had a single 4-inch* gun at the stern, but subsequently learned that the captain had sensibly withheld fire to protect his passengers' lives from the inevitable German reply.

The Germans took great care to jam the many signals from *Appam*'s wireless telegraph, well aware that the Royal Navy was patrolling the area in force. Rear-Admiral Sir Archibald Moore, Flag Officer of the area covering Madeira and the Canary islands, could call on the armoured cruisers *King Alfred* and *Essex*, plus the armed merchant cruisers *Carmania* and *Ophir*. In addition, *Highflyer* was cruising off the Cabo Verde islands in company with the merchant cruiser *Marmora*.

* Sometimes listed as either a 12pdr (3in) or 4·7in pattern. The calibre given here is believed to be correct.

Dohna-Schlodien had taken a calculated gamble in stopping *Appam*, which met very few of his basic requirements. Noting lofty masts, wireless antennae and the absence of the customary Red Ensign, the Germans suspected that the steamship could be a well-armed merchant cruiser.

The liner was soon discovered to be carrying more than 150 passengers, including the Governor of Sierra Leone and the Administrator of Nigeria. There were also German nationals being sent into internment in England from Togoland and Kamerun. The manifest showed that the cargo contained, amongst many other things, rubber and gold bullion valued at £50,000. But the greatest advantage of *Appam* was that she provided an ideal means of ridding Dohna-Schlodien of two hundred prisoners. Accordingly, command of the liner was given to Leutnant z.S. d.R. Hans Berg, a 39-year-old native of Schleswig-Holstein, and an armed prize crew was sent aboard to ensure that trouble was kept to a minimum.

On 16 January, 120 miles south by west of Madeira, *Möwe* and *Appam* encountered a dark-coloured ship of substantial size. As night had fallen, *Möwe* asked for identification by signal lamp. The steamer flashed back: 'Tell us your name first'. Without hesitation, Dohna-Schlodien ordered the name 'Author' to be transmitted, as he had sunk the ship only a few days earlier and suspected that this would not yet be widely known. In the darkness, *Möwe* and *Author* fitted the same broad description well enough to dupe the inquirer even if details of *Author* were sought from Lloyd's Register.

Satisfied, the mystery ship identified herself as *Clan Mactavish*. Once again, she fitted the desired criteria: a plain black hull, and a black funnel with two red bands separated by a narrow circlet of black. Launched from the Newcastle upon Tyne shipyard of Sir W.G. Armstrong, Whitworth & Co. Ltd in December 1912, for The Clan Line Steamers Ltd, the 5,816grt freighter had been bound for London from Wellington.

*Möwe* immediately trained her 15cm guns in the direction of *Clan Mactavish*, flashing the order to stop immediately. The British ship indicated that she had stopped, but the wireless operators aboard *Möwe* were convinced that she was transmitting calls for help. Dohna-Schlodien ordered his gunners to fire at *Clan Mactavish*'s bridge, the intervening distance being no more than three hundred yards. Suddenly, the steamer, armed with a 6-pdr gun at the stern, fired back.

The action was short and furious. After only five minutes, *Clan Mactavish* signalled that she had stopped altogether and Dohna-Schlodien instantly gave the order to cease fire. The navigating bridge and superstructure of the British tramp had been badly damaged, whilst eighteen men had been killed and five wounded. Most of the casualties had occurred when a shell burst amongst Lascar crewmen racing to abandon ship. Though *Clan Mactavish* was carrying a cargo of considerable value, including leather and wool, the destruction of her engines by a German shell had left Dohna-Schlodien with little option but to sink the steamship before British warships appeared in response to her wireless messages. *Clan Mactavish* was promptly scuttled in 30°40′N 17°10′W.

Captain William Oliver informed Dohna-Schlodien that his orders had been to get his ship to England and that, as he had been provided with a gun, he considered it his duty to resist. The German captain shook hands with his adversary, admitting that he would have wished to act similarly had the roles been reversed, and then confined the Scotsman and his gunners in *Möwe* for the remainder of the voyage. They were subsequently interned in Germany.

*Möwe* had had a very lucky escape. Unknown to Dohna-Schlodien, a short and partially incoherent

**Below:** *Clan Mactavish* (5,816grt), which gallantly attempted to fight the raider and suffered the unfortunate consequences. Photograph by courtesy of Laurence Dunn.

**Above:** Leutnant z.S. Hans Berg (inset) and the prize-crew of *Appam*, from a postcard by Paul Hoffmann & Co. of Berlin-Schönberg (no. 1411). Author's collection.

distress signal transmitted by *Clan Mactavish* had been received by wireless-telegraphy ratings aboard the British cruiser *Essex*, but had not been passed to the supervising officer. This remarkable oversight allowed the raider to escape unhindered.

The Germans continued to steam south-westward. On 17 January, Dohna-Schlodien ordered Hans Berg to take *Appam* into a neutral American port—far enough away to delay freeing the captives for several days and ensure that *Möwe* could disappear. All but 54 of the Britons held in the raider were transferred, the exceptions being Captain Oliver, a handful of military and naval personnel, the gunners of *Clan Mactavish* and those of *Appam*. A hundred Lascars were also held on the raider to man ships retained as colliers.

Berg finally put *Appam* into Newport News on 16 February. At last, the Admiralty was made aware of the existence of another raider; but Dohna-Schlodien had moved to another sea lane. *Möwe* had continued to travel south-westerly into the trade routes between Pernambuco and the Cabo Verde islands. At Ilha Maraca, off the mouth of the Amazon, the captured collier *Corbridge* waited with supplies of fuel.

On 20 January, still only some 700 miles west by south of São Vicente in the Cabo Verde islands, *Möwe* captured the 1,473grt three-masted barque *Edinburgh*, belonging to J. Stewart & Company of Glasgow and bound for Liverpool from La Plata. The old sailing ship—completed by Charles Connell & Company in 1885—had little to offer, so she was sunk by explosive charges after the crew had been taken off. In his memoirs, Graf Nikolaus zu Dohna-Schlodien regretted the sinking; the barque, he said, had been 'beautiful even in death'.

The raider found *Corbridge* on 27 January and then spent three days coaling. Once *Möwe*'s bunkers had been filled, the captured British steamship was towed out to sea and scuttled. Dohna-Schlodien immediately headed back out to the trade routes, but days passed without action. German crewmen amused themselves by constantly repainting their ship in differing colours.

The raiders then had a stroke of good fortune. *Möwe* was spotted by HMS *Glasgow*, which turned to give chase. The cruiser was fast and well armed, and Dohna-Schlodien knew he would have little chance in a fight. However, just as *Glasgow* came within range, a tropical rainstorm descended. When it had cleared, neither ship could see the other. As *Glasgow* searched, she encountered a steamer. Though the vessel had three masts instead of the two carried by *Möwe*, it was known that the raiders were not averse to camouflage. *Glasgow* was obliged to stop the ship to check her papers, allowing Dohna-Schlodien and his merry men to escape.

On 4 February, the 4,322grt steamer *Luxembourg* was stopped. The boarding party reported that the vessel was owned by Compagnie Nationale Belge de Transportation Maritime (Armement Adolf Deppe) and was registered in

Antwerp. She had been completed in 1908 by Flensburger Schiffbau-Gesellschaft and was hauling 5,900 tons of good-quality steam coal to Buenos Aires and, ultimately, a British owned Argentine railway. As he had just coaled from *Corbridge*, Dohna-Schlodien reluctantly ordered the Belgian ship to be sunk.

On 6 February, about 310 miles north-east by north of Pernambuco, *Flamenco* (4,629grt) of the Pacific Steam Navigation Company failed to stop after the customary shot had been fired across her bows, heaving-to only after being hit by a live shell that killed a sailor. The tramp had been built by Sir James Laing & Sons of Sunderland in 1906.

*Flamenco* contained nothing of interest, so sea-cocks were opened, explosive charges were laid and the vessel was sunk. A neutral passenger brought over from the doomed ship told the German captain that HMS *Glasgow* had stopped *Flamenco* late the previous afternoon to warn her skipper of raider activities. The warship would still be in the vicinity; in addition, before stopping, the steamer had sent out wireless messages requesting assistance. Some of the German officers dismissed the story, but British crewmen claimed to have taken photographs and the films were immediately developed aboard the raider. The story was true.

It was clear that *Möwe* could not remain in an area in which she was being sought by *Glasgow*, *Amethyst*, *Edinburgh Castle*, *Macedonia* and *Orama*. Dohna-Schlodien turned around and steamed north eastward; by 8 February, *Möwe* was about five hundred nautical miles north north-east of Pernambuco. As he had passed the Norwegian steamship *Estrella* on route, the German skipper ordered a change of camouflage.

Later that evening, the British collier *Westburn* (3,300grt), owned by James Westoll of Sunderland, was seized on a voyage from Cardiff to Buenos Aires. Completed in the Wearside yard of Short Brothers in 1893, the steamship was old, slow and of no great value. As *Möwe* had sufficient coal for the immediate future, Dohna-Schlodien decided to transfer all his prisoners, excepting the master and second officer of *Westburn*, before releasing the ship under the supervision of Unteroffizier Badewitz and eight German seamen. Badewitz eventually put into Santa Cruz de Tenerife at about 15:00 on 22 February, released his captives, then left harbour the following day to avoid internment. However, as *Westburn* set a course to rejoin *Möwe*, lookouts noticed that a large warship flying the White Ensign was waiting outside Spanish territorial waters. The armoured cruiser HMS *Sutlej* was clearly intent on a confrontation, so Badewitz promptly scuttled his charge.

At 05:00 on 9 February, roughly eighty miles north east of the capture of *Westburn*, the raider stopped the 3,335grt steamship *Horace*. Built in 1895 by D. & W. Henderson & Co. Ltd of Glasgow, the London-registered ship flew the colours of the Liverpool, Brazil & River Plate Steam Navigation Co. Ltd, better known by the name of the managers Lamport & Holt. Black hulled, *Horace* had a large mid-blue funnel with a broad white band separating the body colour from the black top. A distinctive small diameter donkey-boiler exhaust was attached to the back of the funnel.

The boarding party soon reported that the cargo contained piece goods and copper ore, but nothing of especial interest, so *Horace* was sunk by the trusted combination of open sea-cocks and explosive charges.

Dohna-Schlodien then had another lucky escape when his ship passed perilously close to HMS *Highflyer*—the cruiser that had been credited with sinking *Kaiser Wilhelm der Grosse* more than a year earlier. It was clear that the Royal Navy had regained much of the command of the southern Atlantic that had been temporarily lost in 1914 to raiders such as *Karlsruhe*, and also that the methods of patrol had been so thoroughly overhauled that they had become much more effectual.

Dohna-Schlodien decided that to linger was to invite destruction, and that losing his ship for meagre additional gains could not be justified. He decided to return to Germany. However, the outward voyage had been undertaken in the depths of winter, long dark nights and foul weather having assisted *Möwe* to elude the British patrols off the Orkney Islands. This advantage would reduce with each extra day spent in the tropics.

On 8 February, Dohna-Schlodien set a northward course to cut across the many trade routes from Europe to North America. Wireless messages were passed back to Berlin, keeping the German admiralty informed of progress; in return, the skipper learned that his ship had been awarded fifty Iron Crosses to be distributed amongst the crewmen.

Not until 23 February did *Möwe* take another prize. The 3,109grt steamship *Maroni* of Compagnie Générale Transatlantique was stopped north-west of Cape Finisterre, bound for New York out of Bordeaux with a mixed cargo. Registered in Le Havre, the vessel had been completed in the early 1900s by Chantiers et Ateliers de Provence of Port de Bouc. After taking off her crew, the Germans sank *Maroni* with explosive charges and, apparently, a few well-aimed shells.

Setting a course that took his ship well away from the British Isles, and, he hoped, British patrols, Dohna-Schlodien was six hundred nautical miles west of Fastnet when he took *Saxon Prince* at 06:00 on 25 February. Owned by the Prince Line Ltd of Newcastle upon Tyne, the steamship had a black hull, white upperworks, and a black funnel on which a red band bore the Prince of Wales' feathers in white metal.

Completed in 1899 by Short Brothers of Sunderland, *Saxon Prince* had a gross registered tonnage of 3,471; commanded by Captain William Jameson, she was bound from Norfolk in Virginia for London with a mixed cargo that included guncotton.

**Above:** the French steamship *Maroni*. Photograph by courtesy of Laurence Dunn.

When the German boarding party examined the prize, they found that though an attempt had been made to destroy the steamer's papers, many recent newspapers were untouched. These were taken back to *Möwe* to be carefully scrutinised, particularly for the movements of shipping in general and British warships in particular. The information was so new that Dohna-Schlodien learned that *Appam* had safely docked in Newport News in Virginia, USA, and that *Möwe* had allegedly been sunk off Bermuda by the British armoured cruiser *Drake*!

As their steamship entered northern latitudes, inching ever closer to Britain, the German crewmen became increasingly anxious. Lookouts saw smoke on every horizon, and danger riding on each wave; nerves tautened in the expectation that Royal Navy warships lurked behind every shadow to blast *Möwe* into a thousand fragments. The arrival of snow and icy fog on 28 February, driven by strong winds, was taken by the superstitious as a good omen. When the raider began to head south for the coast of Norway—potentially the most dangerous part of the homeward voyage, clouds providentially hid the moon.

By the beginning of March, *Möwe* was almost home. The Kaiserliche Marine sent out an escort of awesome strength from Wilhelmshaven; nature supplied a fog bank. Steamship and escort met on 4 March 1916 off the island of Amrum. Later that day, Dohna-Schlodien and his men sailed triumphantly into port, flying from the mast head the house-flags of ships *Möwe* had taken. The gallant Korvettenkapitän was a national hero; not only had he deprived the Allies of fourteen ships, but he had managed to return unscathed. Excepting aboard *Clan Mactavish* and *Flamenco*, no lives had been lost. The

cruise had been marked by behaviour as chivalrous and correct as could be expected in any war that had run for such a long time.

Once again, the Royal Navy had been unable to stop a single commerce-raider operating successfully along the trade routes. Many of the fears that had been allayed by the destruction of *Emden* in November 1914 had been revived at a stroke. The most important suggestions made in Britain to counter raiders of *Möwe* type included the introduction of the convoy system and the use of decoys or 'Q-Ships' to lure a solitary raider into duelling with an auxiliary warship of similar offensive power.

Though the convoy system was delayed while the considerable organisational problems were overcome, the Admiralty did equip ten suitable colliers as decoys. Three were ordered to operate off the south-eastern coast of the USA, two in the area of the Cabo Verde islands, three to accompany the 9th Cruiser Squadron, and the remaining two to traverse the Pacific Ocean. The ships were given a selection of spurious papers and sufficient material to change appearance periodically.

They were intended to act much as the German tenders had done, supporting Royal Navy cruisers in efforts to hunt raiders down. Alternatively, the raider would capture the collier, stop to coal, and be surprised by the British cruiser. The problem was that the raiders were so few that the odds against the ten British ships being in the right place at the right time were very long.

Owing to her effectual armament, *Möwe* was rechristened *Vineta* on 12 June 1916 and despatched on the first of three raiding cruises undertaken in the Skagerrak, Kattegat and Baltic, accounting for one ship—apparently Russian—of 3,226grt. On 24 August, however, the name *Möwe* was re-adopted in preparation for another foray into the Atlantic Ocean.

## The second cruise

Little was done until the autumn of 1916, when several raiders were despatched simultaneously. *Möwe* was to undertake an unprecedented second cruise. Nikolaus Graf zu Dohna-Schlodien, by now promoted to Fregattenkapitän, had been awarded the Iron Cross, first class, and the coveted Pour le Mérite or 'Blue Max'—the highest decoration the Kaiser could bestow. The entire crew of Möwe had also been awarded the Iron Cross, second class. A medallion had even been struck to honour the first cruise, showing a seagull ('Möwe' in German) with a fish in its mouth soaring over a chain guarded by two comatose sea lions representing the Royal Navy.

By November, the raider had been refitted. Subtle changes had been made to her appearance, altering the basic ship's character appreciably. The funnel was shorter and broader; the masts, previously slightly raked, had become vertical; two large combination ventilators/derrick posts had been removed from the break ahead of the poop, and gunwhales had been added to hide the torpedo tubes. Whereas the ship had previously been a typical German three-island tramp with a raised forecastle, she now had the lines of a flush-decker with a raised forecastle.

On 22 November 1916, *Möwe* steamed out of Wilhelmshaven. *Wolf* followed on 29 November, and the auxiliary-engined sailing ship *Seeadler* emerged on 21 December. The raiders' threat to British maritime trade routes had been resumed.

Dohna-Schlodien steered northward along the Norwegian coast then, favoured by bad weather, cut across westward to the north of the Shetland Islands. The weather was sufficiently foul to encourage the German captain to turn quicker than on his first course, when *Möwe* had been steered almost into Arctic latitudes. The gamble was repaid by a saving of several days; by 26 November, he was well clear of the British blockade and out into the North Atlantic. The weather deteriorated until it was so bad that *Möwe* could do little more than keep station with her head into the wind. By the end of the month, the gales had moderated to allow the raider to set a course southward a few hundred nautical miles off the west coast of Ireland.

On 2 December, more than six hundred miles west of Fastnet, a large black-hulled steamship was stopped. Her funnel colours—black top, white band, mid-blue body—betrayed the owners of the handsome 8,618grt *Voltaire* as the Liverpool, Brazil & River Plate Steam Navigation Co. Ltd, managed by Lamport & Holt Ltd. She had been completed in 1907 by D. & W. Henderson & Co. Ltd of Glasgow, and was bound for New York in ballast. Once the 95-man crew had been taken off, *Möwe* sank *Voltaire* with explosive charges.

The next ship to be stopped—at about 07:00 on 4 December—was a refrigerated freighter. Inspection revealed *Samland* (9,748grt) of Société Anonyme de Navigation Belge–Américaine, registered in Antwerp and loaded with nearly nine thousand tons of meat to relieve the suffering of the people of Belgium. As the voyage had the full blessing of the German government, Dohna-Schlodien had no option but to release the American-built steamship immediately. On 5 December, an ostensibly neutral Norwegian steamer was found to be carrying machine parts and a large quantity of steel tube destined for Britain. Suspecting the tubes to be unfinished gun

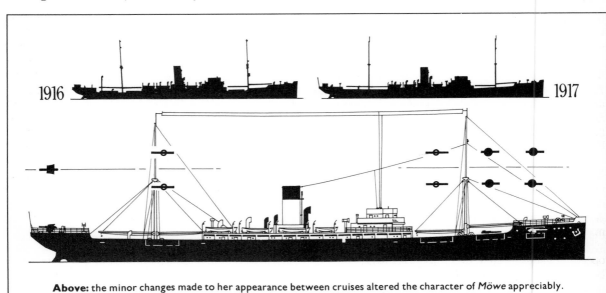

**Above**: the minor changes made to her appearance between cruises altered the character of *Möwe* appreciably.
Drawings by John Walter.

**Above:** the Lamport & Holt steamer *Voltaire*. Photograph by courtesy of Laurence Dunn.

barrels, Dohna-Schlodien ordered the ship to be sunk in the practised manner.

On 6 December, *Möwe* overhauled a large freighter. Captain Sargent of the Canadian Pacific Steamship Company, master of *Mount Temple* (9,792grt) initially refused to stop as instructed, but submitted to shelling that cost three lives. Ship's papers revealed that *Mount Temple* had been built by Armstrong, Whitworth & Co. Ltd of Newcastle upon Tyne in 1901 and was bound for Brest with horses, wheat and general cargo. As none of these were of much use to *Möwe*, *Mount Temple* was sunk by a combination of open sea cocks and explosive charges 620 nautical miles west of Fastnet.

Almost immediately, a 152grt three-masted barque blundered into the raider's path and was sunk; *Duchess of Cornwall* had been bound for Gibraltar with a cargo of salted meat. She had been built by Nash of Burgeo, Newfoundland, about 1900 and was owned by Robert Moulton Ltd of St John's. On 8 December, by then about 700 miles east of Cape Race, Newfoundland, *Möwe* seized and then sank 3,852grt *King George* of the Glasgow King Shipping Co. Ltd, laden with a cargo that included six hundred tons of gunpowder. The tramp had been built by R. Craggs & Sons Ltd of Middlesbrough in 1896.

Early next day, 4,234grt *Cambrian Range* of the Neptune Steam Navigation Co. Ltd was stopped ninety miles nearer the Canadian shore and scuttled with her cargo of wheat. The ship had been built on the Clyde by A. Rodger & Company of Port Glasgow and was managed by Furness, Withy & Co. Ltd.

On 9 December, however, the German wireless operators intercepted a message from the land station in Bermuda warning that a raider had been spotted at 07:00 on 7 December. The Belgian relief ship had passed details of the meeting with *Möwe* to the authorities. However,

though instinct told Dohna-Schlodien to move away from the sea lanes, he knew that he was in the area most likely to be favoured by ships carrying munitions and war materials from North America to Britain. He elected to stay in the vicinity for a few days.

His reasoning soon paid off. On 10 December, the 10,077grt *Georgic*, completed in 1895 by Harland & Wolff Ltd of Belfast, was sighted 590 miles east south-east of Cape Race. A valuable cargo was suggested by the size of the ship and a large gun mounted at the stern. *Georgic* initially declined to halt, whereupon *Möwe* opened fire to prevent the British gunners doing so. One man was killed aboard the Oceanic Steam Navigation Company (White Star Line) vessel before she eventually hove-to.

An inspection revealed a cargo including horses, wheat and oil. The sea cocks were opened and explosive charges laid, but Dohna-Schlodien worried whether even these measures would enable *Georgic* to sink as quickly as he wanted and finished the steamer off with a torpedo.

The morning of 11 December brought the 4,652grt British steamer *Yarrowdale*, completed in 1912 by W. Dobson & Co. of Newcastle upon Tyne for the Mackill Steam Ship Co. Ltd of Glasgow. The valuable cargo included a hundred motor vehicles and several thousand tons of steel. As she also had appreciable stocks of coal, Dohna-Schlodien decided to send *Yarrowdale* home to Germany. If the steamer failed to elude the British blockade, he reasoned, the only sacrifice would be the prize crew. He could also rid himself of the accumulation of prisoners without the tell-tale risk of sending them into a convenient neutral port.

Command of the British prize was entrusted to Unteroffizier Badewitz, who had achieved a measure of success with the captured collier *Westburn* during the earlier cruise. Badewitz had been interned in Spain, but

escaped and returned to Germany in time to sign on with *Möwe* for a second time.

*Möwe* and *Yarrowdale* steamed off south-eastward. On 12 December, 520 miles westward of Flores, the raider captured the 4,992grt *Saint Theodore*, owned by the British & Foreign Steam Ship Co. Ltd of Liverpool. Built by William Hamilton & Company of Glasgow in 1913, the single-funnel three-island tramp was loaded with seven thousand tons of American coal. This chance encounter allowed Dohna-Schlodien to dismiss Badewitz and *Yarrowdale* the next day, whilst *Saint Theodore* was sent off to a pre-arranged rendezvous under the command of Fähnrich z.S. Köhler.

Realising that the capture of two ships in such close proximity was bound to arouse the interest of the Royal Navy, Dohna-Schlodien immediately headed south until—about five hundred miles south-west of Flores—he reached the shipping lane that ran from Central America to Britain by way of St Thomas and the Ilhas dos Açôres. He did not have to wait for his next victim.

On 18 December, a three-island merchantman with a black hull, white upperworks, and a predominantly black funnel hove into sight. As she came closer, the funnel was

Three of the ships accosted by von Dohna-Schlodien.
**Top left:** the Belgian relief-ship *Samland* (9,748grt), which was allowed to proceed unmolested.
**Centre left:** the unlucky White Star steamship *Celtic* (10,077grt).
**Bottom left:** *French Prince* (4,766grt), which was sunk.
Photographs by courtesy of Laurence Dunn.

seen to have a thin red band on a broader white one, and the Red Ensign was identified at her jackstaff. The newcomer was stopped after the customary brief chase and a shot across the bows. The boarding party reported her to be *Dramatist*, owned by the Charente Steam Ship Co. Ltd of Liverpool (T. & J. Harrison) and bound for home from St Lucia with a cargo that included fruit and explosives. Built by Charles Connell & Co. Ltd of Glasgow, the vessel entered service in January 1914, had a gross registered tonnage of 5,415, was 410ft between perpendiculars, and could make about twelve knots.

Dohna-Schlodien took enough fruit from *Dramatist* to satisfy the needs of the German crew, whereupon the steamship was scuttled by the usual combination of explosive charges and open sea-cocks.

On 23 December 1916, *Möwe* met *Saint Theodore* as planned. Supplies were passed over to the captured ship, a wireless and two old 5·2cm L/55 guns were fitted, and the vessel was commissioned as the raider *Geier* (Appendix 1, q.v.) under the command of Kapitänleutnant Wolf. On 28 December, Dohna-Schlodien despatched *Geier* to disrupt British trade. However, as the steamer was comparatively slow (her trials speed had been 12·6

knots) Wolf was advised to restrict his operations to the pursuit of sailing vessels.

Christmas Day 1916 brought an unhappy present for the crew of the French four-masted barque *Nantes* (2,679grt) of Société Nouvelle d'Armement, a 1900-vintage product of Ateliers et Chantiers de Normandie in Grand Quevilly. Registered in the town whose name she bore, the barque was stopped by *Möwe* with a cargo of 3,300 tons of saltpetre bound under the direction of Capitaine Schaeffer for London from Valparaiso. As saltpetre was a vital component of gunpowder, Dohna-Schlodien was more than satisfied with his capture. *Nantes* was promptly sunk in the customary fashion.

News came over the wireless on 31 December 1916 that the captured collier *Yarrowdale* (subsequently equipped as the raider *Leopard*, see Appendix 1) had arrived safely in Wilhelmshaven. The men aboard *Möwe* hoped that this boded well for the new year. On 2 January 1917, the 3,103grt four-masted barque *Asnières* was seized whilst Bordeaux-bound—under Éduard Hogrel—with four thousand tons of North American wheat. Owned by Société Anonyme des Longues Couriers Français and registered in Le Havre, the barque had been built in 1902 by Forges et Chantiers de la Méditerranée.

Shortly after *Asnières* had been consigned to the depths of the Atlantic Ocean, *Möwe* halted the 3,798grt steamship *Hudson Maru* of Tatsuma Kisen Goishi Kaisha. Instead of sinking the prize, which had been built by the Sunderland Ship Building Co. Ltd in 1900, Dohna-Schlodien put a prize crew aboard with the intention of using *Hudson Maru* to land prisoners when the time was judged to be right.

The 4,310grt British steamer *Radnorshire* of the Royal Mail Steam Packet Company, completed by Bartram & Sons of Sunderland in 1913, blundered into the raider's path on 7 January and was taken 110 miles east of Pernambuco. Her cargo, principally coffee beans from Santos, was plundered before the ship was sunk by explosive charges.

On 9 January, north-eastward of the demise of *Radnorshire*, Graf zu Dohna-Schlodien and his men stopped the 2,890grt British collier *Minieh*.

The Germans did not initially realise the risk they were taking; formerly owned by the Khedivial Mail Steam Shipping & Graving Dock Co. Ltd of London, battered old 1876-vintage *Minieh* was one of the ten ships that had been entrusted by the Admiralty with the task of decoying raiders. When the men of the boarding party reached the British ship, they learned that she had coaled the light cruiser *Amethyst* only two days previously.

Dohna-Schlodien assumed that the collier had called up the cruiser, and thus that he should leave immediately. *Amethyst* was by no means the most powerful of his opponents, but was much faster and would undoubtedly handle the raider roughly in any encounter. So, after sinking the collier by explosive charges and a shell or

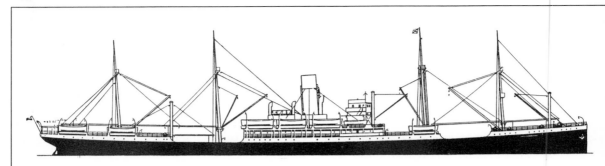

**Above:** *Brecknockshire*, drawn from builder's plans by Laurence Dunn for his book *Ships of the Past, Belfast Built*.

two, *Möwe* headed for mid-Atlantic at full speed.

On 10 January, the raider fell in with the British tramp *Netherby Hall*, belonging to the Ellerman Lines Ltd of Liverpool, which was captured and then sunk about three hundred miles from Pernambuco. The 4,461grt tramp had been built by Swan, Hunter & Wigham Richardson of Newcastle upon Tyne in 1905.

Dohna-Schlodien was then forced to send his ever-growing band of prisoners—more than 250 men—back into Pernambuco in *Hudson Maru*. On 17 January, the raider met with *Geier* (the former *Saint Theodore*) to coal and exchange information. Kapitänleutnant Wolf had little to report, as he had managed to capture only a single small three-masted schooner. Owned by J.C. Crosbie of Liverpool, Nova Scotia, 215grt *Jean* had been built on the Canadian Atlantic seaboard in 1905 and was commanded by Captain Edward Burke. She had been taken east of São Pedro e São Paulo (St Paul's Rocks).

Coaling proved problematical, owing to the heavy Atlantic swell, and was quickly abandoned after *Geier* had torn several of *Möwe*'s side plates.

On 22 January 1917, the ships set off in opposing directions. Dohna-Schlodien elected to try his luck along the trading route leading to the Cape of Good Hope; however, by the first week in February, in the absence of prizes, he had turned back towards South America and a rendezvous with *Geier* off Ilha da Trindade. The collier had had another unsuccessful cruise, accounting for only a second solitary sailing ship. As her stocks of coal were low, Dohna-Schlodien sank *Geier* on 14 February.

Choosing an area roughly five hundred miles east by north of Cabo Frio, which was thought to be free of Royal Navy cruisers, Dohna-Schlodien tried his luck again.

Within a day of sinking *Geier*, the raider had taken *Brecknockshire*—a 8,422grt steamer built by Harland & Wolff Ltd of Belfast for the Royal Mail Steam Packet Company, on her maiden voyage with a cargo of seven thousand tons of coal. The captive provided some comparatively recent newspapers and was then sunk. Next came *French Prince*, ordered to stop on 16 February when about 490 miles east north-east of Cabo Frio with a cargo of corned beef, wheat and provisions from La Plata

for Le Havre. Registered in Newcastle upon Tyne, the 4,766grt vessel had been completed by Sir James Laing & Sons Ltd of Sunderland in 1901 and acquired by the Prince Line Ltd in 1912. She sailed as *Bulgarian Prince* until 1915, but Bulgaria had then joined the war on the German side and the steamer had been renamed. As most superstitious sailors knew, a change of name soon brought ill fortune...

*French Prince* was sunk by opening the sea-cocks and exploding scuttling charges: a fate that also befell 2,652grt *Eddie* on 16 February. Captained by Robert Bradley for Thomas Turnbull & Son Shipping Co. Ltd, the ship was registered in Whitby. She had been launched there in 1895. Just as *Möwe* set off in pursuit of a third steamer, the merchant cruiser *Edinburgh Castle* appeared and Dohna-Schlodien ran for his life. The 13,300grt British ship, built for the Union-Castle Mail Steamship Co. Ltd in 1910, had twin screws and could raise seventeen knots. Fortunately for the slower German raider, a rain-squall facilitated escape.

*Möwe* set an eastward course to elude *Edinburgh Castle*, then headed northward for several days whilst machinery was repaired—in particular, a boiler forced too much during the chase. Dohna-Schlodien, realising that his ship would benefit from a sojourn in a shipyard, decided to return once again to Germany. As he would cut across northerly trade routes, a few more prizes could be expected on the homeward journey.

The first was the 2,926grt steamship *Katherine*, stopped on 23 February 1917 whilst homeward bound from Rosario with 4,500 tons of Argentine wheat. Distinguished by a blue funnel with a red top above a broad white band, the tramp had been sold by the Seaton Shipping Co. Ltd to Chr. Salvesen & Company of Leith in 1914. Though Salvesen had Norwegian ties, the ship flew the British flag and was registered in West Hartlepool—where she had been launched from the Furness, Withy & Company shipyard in 1904. *Katherine* was sunk 200 miles north-east of São Pedro e São Paulo.

The last week of February was spent overhauling *Möwe*'s engine and boilers, in case full power was needed to elude the British patrols on the final run down the

North Sea. On 4 March the raider met and stopped the 3,061grt British steamship *Rhodanthe* of the London Marine Steam Ship Co. Ltd, bound under Captain William Maclean to load Cuban sugar. Completed in 1902 by W. Gray & Company of West Hartlepool, the prize held little to interest the Germans and was sunk 330 miles north north-west of the Cabo Verde islands.

The morning of 5 March brought a Norwegian sailing ship, but Dohna-Schlodien released her after sending over the inspection party. Prizes were now at a premium; not until 10 March did *Möwe* find another victim, destroying 4,491grt *Esmeraldas*—a sister of *Flamenco*, which the Germans had taken on the first cruise. Built for the Pacific Steam Navigation Company by Sir James Laing & Sons of Sunderland in 1906, the Liverpool-registered tramp was bound for Baltimore to fetch horses for the British Army.

Shortly after *Esmeraldas* had been scuttled, *Möwe* encountered a large steamship with a yellow-buff funnel. Bound for New York out of London, in ballast, 9,575grt *Otaki* had been completed for the New Zealand Shipping Co. Ltd by William Denny & Bros. of Dumbarton in 1908. She was the first ship—apart from the destroyer *Velox*— to have an exhaust-steam turbine, which drove a central shaft between two conventional triple-expansion engines. Service speed of fourteen knots, however, was much the same as that of *Möwe*.

As the raider approached, the captain of *Otaki*, Archibald Bissett-Smith, elected to run in the hope that this would give his single 4-inch stern gun* a chance to engage. The British ship also turned deliberately into a head sea to frustrate the aim of the German gunlayers as spray broke over the bows of *Möwe*.

The action opened at a range of about 3,000 yards. *Otaki*'s Royal Navy gunners soon hit the German ship, one shell penetrating under the bridge to explode above the boiler room, with sufficient force to kill five of Dohna-Schlodien's crew and wound ten others. Another started a bunker-fire, and a third burst close enough for the raider to ship water forward through shrapnel holes. Once the four 15cm guns on *Möwe* had got the range, however, *Otaki* was hit repeatedly.

By the time the range had been reduced to little more than a mile, the German gunners had registered thirty hits. Eventually, on fire and listing to starboard, *Otaki* rolled farther over and sank by the stern. Most of her crew were rescued from the water, but six brave souls were lost—including Captain Bissett-Smith, who went down with his ship after ensuring that the boats had got the wounded away safely. Graf zu Dohna-Schlodien, relieved to have despatched a doughty opponent, regarded the duel 'as gallant as naval history can relate'; the Admiralty, equally impressed, recommended Archibald Bissett-Smith for a posthumous Victoria Cross, facilitating the award by commissioning him (also posthumously) in the Royal Naval Reserve.

* This gun is sometimes given—apparently wrongly—as a 12-pdr, which would equate to a calibre of 3in.

---

**Below:** the sinking of *Otaki*, from a painting commissioned by the New Zealand Shipping Co. Ltd. By courtesy of Laurence Dunn.

Inspection parties had soon reported to Dohna-Schlodien that the damage was not serious enough to impair the performance of *Möwe*, though the fire that started in a bunker smouldered for five days before it was finally extinguished. The holes in the waterline were plugged as effectually as possible and the bridge was patched up. The homeward journey continued.

On 13 March, *Möwe* encountered *Demeterton* about 730 nautical miles east of Cape Race. Owned jointly by the Carlton and Camboy steamship companies, and registered in Newcastle upon Tyne, the 6,048grt freighter had been completed early in 1914 by Ropner & Sons Ltd of Stockton on Tees. Noticing that *Demeterton* had a gun at the stern, Dohna-Schlodien ordered his gunners to open fire as soon as the German ensign had been run up to the mast head. The British ship stopped immediately and prepared to receive the boarding party. Scuttling charges were laid, but the cargo of timber made *Demeterton* a difficult ship to sink. The task was eased by firing a few 15cm shells into the waterline.

The afternoon of 14 March revealed *Governor*, another of the ships owned by the Charente Steam Ship Co. Ltd of Liverpool and, ironically, a sister of *Dramatist*—taken by the raider only three months previously. The merchantman had a gross registered tonnage of 5,524, measured about 410ft between perpendiculars, and had been completed in October 1915 by D. & W. Henderson & Co. Ltd of Glasgow. Encountered 930 miles west of Fastnet, *Governor* was aware of her sister-ship's fate and Captain Packe elected to try his luck with the stern gun.

Dohna-Schlodien was not to be caught a second time and, by adroitly manoeuvring *Möwe* out of the arc of fire, quickly blasted the Harrison ship into submission. Four men were killed in the action, the British skipper having a lucky escape when a shell from the raider blew an officer standing alongside him to pieces. By the time the smoke had cleared, much of *Governor*'s navigating bridge had been blown away and her decks were a shambles. After the crew had been taken off and the sea-cocks had been opened, the luckless steamer was hastened to her demise with a torpedo amidships.

The raider was now crowded with more than eight hundred men. Supplies ran short. By 18 March, however, *Möwe* had reached northerly latitudes in the vicinity of Iceland, then turned to run past the Shetland Islands and down the Norwegian coast. On 22 March, Dohna-Schlodien and his men sailed triumphantly into Kiel.

The German admiralty decided that the career of *Möwe* as an auxiliary warship was at an end. The rapidly increasing success of submarine warfare against Allied maritime trade had been underscored by the sinking of 103 ships in March 1917, followed by 155 in April. This success was achieved at far less cost than the meagre returns of the raiders. Submarines were far easier to build in quantity, and required smaller crews. The day of the Kaiser's Pirates was rapidly drawing to a close.

There was no doubt that Dohna-Schlodien and his men had undertaken their tasks with exemplary skill and determination. They had survived two lengthy cruises—an unprecedented raiding feat in itself—but only at the cost of mental strain. This was especially noticeable towards the end of the second voyage, when several Germans had been killed when a hopelessly out-gunned British steamer offered unexpectedly spirited resistance. The casualties merely emphasised the vulnerability of converted cargo ships to hostile fire.

However, Nikolaus Graf zu Dohna-Schlodien had also acted most honourably and had tried to adhere as best he could to the Cruiser Rules. Consequently, though he had deprived the Allies of about forty ships, casualties had amounted only to five dead aboard *Möwe* and less than thirty on her victims. Though the general tenor of war had changed out of all recognition since the legendary cruise of *Emden* in 1914, when the chivalrous Karl von Müller had been respected almost as greatly by his prisoners as his own crew, Dohna-Schlodien deserves to be held in similar esteem.

*Möwe* subsequently served in the Baltic as an auxiliary minelayer, masquerading as *Sperrbrecher 10*, the British *Sutton Hall* or the French *Théodore Monté*. Her post-war career was equally fascinating. Ceded to Britain in May 1920 she was refitted to become *Greenbrier* for Elders & Fyffes Co. Ltd of London.

The ship was sold in 1933 to Deutsche Seeverkehrs AG 'Midgard' (Union Handels- u. Schifffahrts AG) of Nordenham, christened *Oldenburg*, given a distinctive white funnel with a blue snake between two pairs of narrow blue bands, and was eventually sunk by an Allied air attack off Vadheim in the Søgnefjord on 7 April 1945 (61°12'N 5°50'E). The wreck was raised in 1953.

# NÜRNBERG

1 August–8 December 1914; no victims.
A conventional light cruiser sunk by the Royal Navy during
the Battle of the Falkland Islands.

Type: Kleine Kreuzer.
Authorisation: as 'Ersatz Blitz', 1904.
Builder: Kaiserliche Werft, Kiel (yard no. 32).
Laid down: 1906.
Launch date: 28 August 1906.
Commissioned: 10 April 1908.
Crew: 14 officers and 308 men.

## Dimensions

Design displacement: 3,469 tonnes.
Full-load displacement: 3,902 tonnes.
Overall length: 117·4 metres.
Waterline length: 116·8 metres.
Beam: 13·3 metres.
Full-load draught: about 5·3 metres.

## Weapons

Guns: ten SK 10·5cm C/88 L/40.
Maximum range of main armament: 12,200 metres.
Lesser guns: eight 5·2cm SL L/55.
Torpedo tubes: one submerged on each beam.
Munitions: 1,470 10·5cm high-explosive shells, thirty 10·5cm
shrapnel shells; five 45cm C/03 torpedoes.
Armour protection: deck 20–30mm, conning tower 100mm,
gun-shields 50mm.

## Performance

Powerplant: two three-cylinder triple expansion steam
engines, supplied by eleven boilers. Two propeller shafts.
Boiler pressure: 16at (235psi).
Coal bunkerage: 400 tonnes normal, 880 tonnes maximum.
Speed, trials: 23·4 knots (13,154ihp).
Speed, service maximum: 23 knots (13,200ihp).
Range: 4,120 nautical miles at 12 knots.

*Nürnberg* was a typical three-funnelled German Kleine Kreuzer, distinguished from the otherwise similar *Königsberg* (q.v.) by a characteristic gap between the second and third funnels and—originally at least—by a secondary armament of 5·2cm guns instead of 3·7cm machine-cannon.

In the summer of 1914, under the command of the experienced Fregattenkapitän Karl von Schönberg, *Nürnberg* was patrolling off the west coast of Mexico to protect Geman interests from the depredations of Mexican revolutionaries. News of the assassination of Erzherzog Franz Ferdinand in Sarajevo reached von Schönberg on 29 June. He immediately despatched an appropriate message to Graf von Spee, bound in his flagship *Scharnhorst* for a rendezvous with sister-ship *Gneisenau* in the Marianas.

*Nürnberg* was due to return to Tsingtau for attention to her boilers and machinery, *Leipzig* (q.v.) being despatched to replace her off the Mexican coast. The two cruisers met off Matzalán on 7 July, von Schönberg reappearing from a short voyage to Panama ready to coal prior to crossing the Pacific. He had chartered the ageing British collier *Citriana*, but the quality of the fuel was not what he had hoped it to be. However, as the status of stockpiles arranged by the Etappe system on the Mexican mainland was questionable, the poor-quality

**Below:** a broadside view of the cruiser *Nürnberg*, showing the gap between the second and third funnels. From a postcard ('No. 105. R3.') published by Gebr. Lempe, Kiel, 1915. Author's collection.

Pocahontas coal would have to suffice in an emergency. The political situation was so confused that neither von Schönberg or Fregattenkapitän Haun of *Leipzig* had been able to gauge the progress of tension in Europe.

After discussions between the German captains had been completed, both cruisers took on coal from *Citriana*. On 8 July, *Nürnberg* left for San Francisco and then set a course for Honolulu. Arriving in the middle of June, von Schönberg immediately went to collect messages from von Spee, which had been transmitted by way of Hackfeld & Co. There he learned that he had been promoted to Kapitän z.S., but also that *Nürnberg* was to coal immediately—all leave being cancelled—and sail as soon as possible for Ponape to rejoin the Kreuzergeschwader.

By 4 August, Germany was at war with France, Russia and Britain, and command of the seas had acquired the utmost importance. Vizeadmiral von Spee had mustered his squadron off Ponape, waiting only on the arrival of *Emden* from Tsingtau and *Nürnberg* from Honolulu to be at full strength. Von Schönberg arrived on 6 August to discover that he was to prepare his ship for war immediately and be ready to sail again that evening. Von Müller and *Emden*, however, were some distance away; von Spee decided to order his missing cruiser to Pagan and meet her there in the second week of August.

On 12 August, *Emden* steamed into the Pagan anchorage to join *Scharnhorst*, *Gneisenau*, *Nürnberg* and a selection of supply ships. By 19 August, the Kreuzergeschwader had moved to Eniwetok Atoll in the Marshall Islands (then German territory) and coaling began once again. At 06:00 on 22 August, anxious to gain information and despatch coded signals, von Spee sent *Nürnberg* back to Honolulu. The British had already destroyed the vital German wireless station on Yap and communications with the consulate in San Francisco—through which messages were relayed to Berlin—were becoming increasingly difficult.

Von Schönberg and his ship reached Pearl Harbor, Honolulu, at dusk on Tuesday 1 September. Requests for coaling were complicated by the hostile attitude of the commander of the port, a US Navy admiral, and by the state of war that existed between Germany and the coalition of Britain, France and Russia. Belligerent warships could not re-enter a neutral port in which they had previously coaled unless three months had elapsed. However, as no state of war had existed when *Nürnberg* had previously visited Honolulu in June, von Schönberg was eventually allowed to take on 750 tons of good quality coal.

As work was undertaken feverishly, *Nürnberg* welcomed on board sixty naval reservists recruited from Germans living in Hawaii together with crewmen of the interned Norddeutscher Lloyd passenger steamship *Pommern*. Von Schönberg and his ship left Pearl Harbor at dawn on 2 September, successfully eluded the Japanese

battle-cruiser *Kongo*, and set a course for Christmas Island in the Line archipelago.

Von Schönberg arrived off Christmas Island on 6 September to rejoin von Spee and the ships of the Kreuzergeschwader, excepting the detached *Leipzig* and *Emden*. The captain of *Nürnberg* immediately reported to the admiral aboard *Scharnhorst*, taking with him news that had been gleaned in Honolulu. He also reported the interception of wireless-telegraphy signals transmitted from the British relay station on Fanning Island, several hundred kilometres west north-west of Christmas Island. Von Spee was well aware of the nuisance caused to the Germans by the destruction of the Yap transmitter and determined to exact revenge. Accompanied by the tender *Titania*, which carried specialist cutting equipment, *Nürnberg* was despatched in the evening of 6 September.

The approach of a warship on the morning of 8 September was seen on Fanning Island, but little attention was taken. British, American and Japanese ships had all called occasionally, including a few three-funnel cruisers. Nobody recognised the most distinctive gap between the second and third funnels of the newcomer, and few people could raise enthusiasm when the warship hove-to in Whaler Anchorage and lowered a boat. The German landing party came ashore to face a small committee of welcome. One of *Nürnberg*'s four 8mm Maxim machine-guns was man-handled over the gunwhale and, in an instant, had been mounted on its tripod at the edge of the surf; sailors sprang ashore and levelled rifles at the astonished crowd. The officer in charge, drawing his Parabellum pistol, demanded surrender and the Britons raised their hands in bewildered compliance.

A search revealed that the captives were unarmed, so the Germans herded them up the beach towards the wireless station. The mast was felled, then cut to pieces; the transmitter was smashed with rifle butts; the accumulators that powered the electrical cable apparatus were smashed; and, finally, buildings were destroyed with explosive charges. A squad of sailors was sent to cut the trans-Pacific cable connecting Australia and Canada where it emerged from the surf. Satisfied that their work had been done, the Germans then returned to their ship whilst *Nürnberg* stood off the beach and *Titania* cut the submarine cable in three places. Warship and tender then steamed off on a false course to westward, waiting until they were over the horizon before turning for Christmas Island and Admiral von Spee.

The two ships reappeared at Christmas Island in the evening of 9 September, to find that von Spee had given *Nürnberg* the task of escorting the supply ships to the Marquesas Islands whilst he attacked British Samoa and then, he hoped, the French-administered Isles de la Société (Society Islands).

From the Marquesas, *Scharnhorst*, *Gneisenau*, *Nürnberg* and the supply ships set a course for Easter

**Above:** a photograph of *Nürnberg*, allegedly taken immediately after the Battle of Coronel. The four masts of the tender *Baden* are visible aft of the funnels, whilst *Scharnhorst* or *Gneisenau* may be discerned in the background. By courtesy of the Trustees of the Imperial War Museum, negative no. Q80704.

Island, where they arrived on 12 October to meet *Leipzig* and *Dresden*; von Spee remained at Easter Island for seven days, flouting the neutrality of the Chilean dependency with impunity. *Nürnberg* and the collier *Baden* collided whilst coaling, damaging the cruiser's port propeller. Consequently, von Schönberg ran his ship into shallow water and, by selectively flooding compartments, heeled her over until the propeller could be reached at low tide. The remainder of the squadron used the enforced inactivity to coal, transfer provisions, go ashore or rest.

On 18 October, the Kreuzergeschwader set sail for the Juan Fernández islands off the coast of Chile, arriving at Más Afuera on 26 October. Simultaneously, the Rear-Admiral Sir Christopher Cradock was assembling his Royal Navy squadron only a few hundred nautical miles to the north. Cradock sent the light cruiser *Glasgow* into Coronel harbour on 29 October and, as the warship ran southward off Valparaiso, her wireless operators intercepted high-pitched squeals characteristic of German Telefunken transmitters. At least one element of the Kreuzergeschwader—later identified as *Leipzig*—had been found.

*Glasgow* remained off Coronel for two days, searching for clues whilst awaiting replies to the coded messages despatched to London on Cradock's behalf. In the early morning of 31 October, the merchant cruiser *Otranto* recognised the call sign of *Leipzig* off the Chilean coast near Coronel. The scene was set for a decisive action.

*Nürnberg* played little part in the opening phases of the Battle of Coronel, a brief description of which will be found in the chapter devoted to *Dresden*. Von Schönberg and his ship had been detached from the Kreuzergeschwader and sent into Valparaiso in company

with *Dresden*. Now both cruisers were hastening southward to rejoin von Spee, but *Dresden*, the faster by several knots was making much better headway. *Nürnberg*, badly in need of an overhaul, was lagging so far behind that it seemed to von Schönberg that he would play very little part in the action. Eventually, *Nürnberg* encountered *Dresden* and *Leipzig*. Von Schönberg learned that the battle had been decisive, but was virtually over. The small cruisers were to search for *Glasgow*, which was believed to be escaping.

At about 20:30, lookouts on *Nürnberg* spotted a dark shape off the port bow. As the range closed, the shape resolved into a warship, listing, badly hit, but apparently still under way. Von Schönberg ordered a challenge to be issued, 'What ship?' being signalled by lamp three times without reply. Knowing little of the battle, the German captain could not afford to open fire in case the stricken warship was one of the Kreuzergeschwader. Finally, he risked a searchlight. As the shaft of light probed the darkness, it revealed that the ship was listing so badly to port that her guns were nearly touching the water. Then the Germans saw that the White Ensign still fluttered at the jack-staff. It was the hulk of *Monmouth*, her fires all but extinguished, gamely battling to stay afloat.

Von Schönberg ordered a course to be steered around the cripple, knowing that the ravaged British cruiser could not bring her 6-inch guns to bear. The port 10·5cm guns were then ordered to open fire as *Nürnberg* swept past her enemy. *Monmouth* made no reply, but, thanks to a superhuman effort, was slowly getting up speed. Von Schönberg, suspecting that Captain Brandt was aiming to beach on the Chilean shore, cruised back and forth, blasting his opponent from close range on each pass. More than forty shells were fired; most hit home. Then

*Monmouth* suddenly swung her bow towards *Nürnberg* and gathered speed in a last attempt to ram her tormentor.

Alarmed, von Schönberg stood off, still firing as fast as he could at the wreck. Finally, after nearly eighty shells had been fired, the British cruiser rolled slowly over to port onto her beam ends and then capsized at 21:28. Lookouts on *Nürnberg* could see survivors on the upturned hull and in the numbingly cold water, but could do little to help. The ship's boats had been filled with water as a precaution and could not be lowered until they had been emptied. Von Schönberg had no intention of waiting; lookouts reported smoke in the vicinity—*Glasgow*, perhaps?—and his orders were to report to von Spee as soon as possible. *Nürnberg* steamed away from the scene at high speed. There was nothing anyone could do for the men of *Monmouth*, mostly reservists and volunteers drawn from the ranks of the Scottish fishermen. None survived the battle to tell the tale from the British viewpoint.

The victorious Kreuzergeschwader set a course for Valparaiso, the two big armoured cruisers and *Nürnberg* dropping anchor in the bay on 3 November. The success was acclaimed by the sizeable German population of the city, where von Spee and his men were suitably feted before returning to Más Afuera to prepare for a voyage around Cape Horn. On 21 November, *Nürnberg* and the other members of the squadron, accompanied by supply ships, reached the Golfo de Penas. There they coaled in Bahia San Quentin until 26 November, when the journey around Cape Horn began in dreadful weather.

Enthusiastically supported by Kapitän z.S. von Fielitz of *Scharnhorst* and Kapitan z.S. von Schönberg of *Nürnberg*—but not, apparently, by Kapitan z.S. Maerker of *Gneisenau* nor Fregattenkapitäns Haun and Lüdecke of *Leipzig* and *Dresden*—von Spee had decided to attack the Falkland Islands as a prelude to the long voyage homeward up the Atlantic. The plan made sense, but had unseen flaws. The first was that a Royal Navy squadron of tremendous power, commanded by Vice-Admiral Sir Frederick Doveton Sturdee and led by two powerful battle-cruisers, had been despatched to hunt von Spee down; secondly, by coaling too leisurely from the captured sailing-ship *Drummuir*, the German admiral had delayed his arrival off the Falklands by more than 24 hours. This was to be the difference between fighting the battle from a position of advancing strength or one of retreating weakness.

The course of the battle on 8 December 1914 is described in the chapter devoted to *Dresden*. Once *Invincible* and *Indefatigable* had closed sufficiently to threaten the safety of *Dresden, Leipzig* and *Nürnberg*, von Spee ordered them to escape if they could. Led by *Dresden* to starboard, with *Nürnberg* to port and *Leipzig* lagging behind in the centre, the cruisers piled on speed to elude *Cornwall, Kent* and *Glasgow*.

However, the speedy *Glasgow* soon overhauled *Leipzig* and *Nürnberg*, forcing an engagement at 15:02 even though only one 6-inch gun could be brought to bear. This clever tactic eventually forced von Schönberg and Haun to take evasive action, reducing their lead over *Kent* and *Cornwall*. At 16:25, Captain Luce of *Glasgow* elected to let *Dresden* escape in the expectation that the remaining German ships would be caught by the County-class cruisers careering along in their wake.

The two British armoured cruisers opened fire on *Leipzig* at a range of 10,900 yards at 16:15, before *Kent* hauled off in pursuit of *Nürnberg* at 16:30 in accordance with a signal from Captain Walter Ellerton of *Cornwall*. On paper, *Nürnberg* had a chance of escaping, as she supposedly had a service speed of 23·5 knots; though the British cruiser had touched 23·7 knots on the measured mile, she was eleven years old and seemed unlikely to be able to duplicate a performance obtained in full-power trials with a light load. Unfortunately for von Schönberg, *Nürnberg* was in a poor condition mechanically. Not only were the boilers in a bad way, but her engines were in need of a thorough overhaul and the propeller that had been repaired on Easter Island vibrated badly at high speed. Her maximum speed was no more than 22–22·5 knots, even though the seas were calm.

On *Kent*, Captain Allen had decided to risk everything in the chase and thus bring *Nürnberg* into action before the misty conditions deteriorated too greatly. He was also well aware than *Kent* was lightly laden with coal—refuelling had been interrupted—and had a clean bottom. Gleefully, his stokers fed the furnaces like demons and, slowly, speed crept up to an unbelievable 25 knots.

By 17:00, *Nürnberg* had opened fire with her after 10·5cm guns at a range of about 11,000 metres, but the first few salvoes were long. *Kent* replied at 17:09 from her forward 6-inch guns at a range of about 11,000 yards, the opening shots falling short.

The German guns did not have sufficient power to threaten the British cruiser, whose 100lb 6-inch shells were potentially far more deadly. One of *Kent*'s shells then burst below the waterline in the after steering flat, killing all but one of the occupants; another hit the after deck; and a third struck amidships at 17:35, by which time the range had shortened to 7,800 yards. Two of the hard-pressed boilers burst in this period, though whether this arose from structural weakness or shellfire is moot.

Wheezing smoke and steam, her speed reduced to no more than eighteen knots, *Nürnberg* could do little but come around through 90º at 17:45 to confront her aggressor. Allen ordered *Kent* to turn to port so that the cruisers were on slightly converging courses, allowing him to bring his full starboard broadside to bear on *Nürnberg*'s port side. The range fell from 6,000 yards at 17:47 to no more than 3,000 yards by 17:58.

Allen ordered a change to lyddite shells at about 17:55, which soon turned the decks of *Nürnberg* into a charnel house. The main topmast had fallen by 18:00 and fires had broken out. The fore top-gallant mast of *Kent* was cut through in this period by a 10·5cm shell, but remained held in suspension by its stays.

By 18:05, *Nürnberg* was a smoking wreck. The fore-topmast had gone and, according to one of the British observers, 'her foretop and foremost funnel were so riddled that they appeared to be covered with men'. Speed had slackened perceptibly and only two of the five port 10·5cm guns remained in action. *Kent* had also been struck many times, but the lighter German shells had done comparatively little damage. However, the upper decks of the British warship were chaotic and a German shell, passing through the wireless room, had wrecked the transmitter.

The worst hit had been on A3 (midship) casemate on the main deck, where shell fragments had killed one man and injured nine others. Fire in the casemate had passed down the ammunition hoist, igniting a propellant charge, but disaster had been averted when Sergeant Charles Mayes of the Royal Marines coolly closed the hoist-scuttle and ordered the flooding of the compartment.

At 18:10, von Schönberg ordered a turn to port in an attempt to bring his undamaged starboard guns to bear. As *Kent* crossed the bow of the German ship, however, two 6-inch shell hits reduced *Nürnberg*'s forecastle to a shambles and wrecked the forward 10·5cm guns. The British cruiser then came about until the two warships were travelling on roughly parallel courses 4,750–5,000 yards apart, with the port broadside of *Kent* duelling with the remaining starboard guns of *Nürnberg*. By

18:25, the German ship, battered out of all recognition, had almost lost way. Only an occasional gun still fired. By 18:36, *Nürnberg* was out of ammunition. However, though on fire forward and listing to starboard, she still flew the imperial ensign.

Captain Allen stood off awaiting the colours to be struck, but nothing happened. *Kent* renewed fire for a few minutes with as many guns as could be brought to bear, but there was no reply; at 18:57, von Schönberg finally ordered the ensign to be hauled down.

The surviving members of the crew were mustered on deck to give three cheers for the Kaiser, then given permission to abandon ship. An attempt was made to launch a boat containing the wounded, but it foundered shortly afterward in the increasingly heavy seas. The crew of *Kent* managed to patch up two damaged boats by 19:25, launching the first one just as *Nürnberg* shuddered and heeled over to starboard at 19:37. As the cruiser capsized, a group of men could be seen on the after deck waving the imperial ensign in a last gesture of defiance.

Perhaps as many as two hundred of the German crewmen had survived the hammering *Kent* had given *Nürnberg*, but delays in launching rescue boats cost most of them their lives. Though the search for survivors continued until 21:00, only twelve men were taken out of the water alive; five subsequently died aboard *Kent* from the effects of wounds or exposure. Casualties aboard *Kent* totalled five dead, three fatally injured and eight wounded; the death toll aboard *Nürnberg*—allowing for the presence of additional reservists—has been reliably estimated at about 350.

'Der letzte Mann' ('The Last Man').

Painted by the renowned German marine artist Hans Böhrdt, this famous—but vastly overrated—picture commemorates the waving of the ensign aboard *Nürnberg* shortly before the cruiser sank. In reality, an ensign was far larger than just one man!

Author's collection.

# WARSHIPS ON COLONIAL STATIONS

Disposition at the commencement of hostilities. Service speeds are those quoted by B. Freidag in the 1914 edition of *Führer durch Heer und Flotte*. Many of the ships returned better figures on trial. Lengths are waterline; tonnages are standard draught displacements.

## FAR EAST STATION

**Scharnhorst** (large cruiser; Kapitän z.S. Felix Schultz). Blohm & Voss AG, Hamburg, yard no. 175; commissioned on 24 October 1907. 11,616t, 143·8 × 21·6m; eight 21cm, six 15cm and eighteen 8·8cm guns, some 8mm machine-guns and four 45cm torpedo-tubes. Triple-expansion steam engines, three shafts; 22·5 knots. Crew: 764.

**Gneisenau** (Scharnhorst-class large cruiser; Kapitän z.S. Maerker). AG 'Weser', Bremen, yard no. 144; commissioned on 6 March 1908. Otherwise as *Scharnhorst*.

**Leipzig** (Bremen-class small cruiser; Fregattenkapitän Johannes Haun). AG 'Weser', Bremen, yard no. 143; commissioned on 20 April 1906. 3,278t, 110·6 × 13·2m; ten 10·5cm and two 45cm torpedo-tubes. Triple-expansion steam engines, two shafts; 22 knots. Crew: 297.

**Nürnberg** (small cruiser; Fregattenkapitän Karl von Schönberg). Kaiserliche Werft, Kiel; commissioned on 10 April 1908. 3,469t, 116·8 × 13·3m; ten 10·5cm L/40 guns, eight 5·2cm L/55 guns, two 45cm torpedo-tubes. Triple-expansion steam engines, two shafts; 23 knots. Crew: 322.

**Emden** (Dresden-class small cruiser; Fregattenkapitän Karl von Müller). Kaiserliche Werft, Danzig; commissioned on 10 July 1909. 3,664t, 117·9 × 13·5m; ten 10·5cm L/40 guns, ten 5·2cm L/55 guns, two 45cm torpedo tubes. Triple-expansion steam engines, two shafts; 24 knots. Crew 361.

**Iltis** (Iltis-class gunboat; Korvettenkapitän Fritz Sachsse). F. Schichau AG, Danzig, yard no. 630; commissioned on 1 December 1898. 894 tonnes, 63·9 × 9·1m (wl); four 8·8cm L/30 guns, ten 3·7cm revolver cannon. Triple-expansion engines, two shafts; 13·5 knots. Crew: 126.

**Jaguar** (Iltis-class gunboat; Korvettenkapitän Lüring). F. Schichau AG, Danzig, yard no. 631; commissioned on 4 April 1899. Otherwise as *Iltis*.

**Tiger** (Iltis-class gunboat; Korvettenkapitän von Bodecker). Kaiserliche Werft, Danzig; commissioned on 3 April 1900. 894t, 63·9 × 9·1m; two 10·5cm L/40 guns, six 3·7cm revolver cannon. Triple-expansion steam engines, two shafts; 13·5 knots. Crew: 126.

**Luchs** (Iltis-class gunboat; Korvettenkapitän Thierichens). Kaiserliche Werft, Danzig; commissioned on 15 May 1900. Otherwise as *Tiger*.

**Tsingtau** (river gunboat; Kapitänleutnant von Möller). F. Schichau AG, Elbing, yard no. 710; commissioned on 3 February 1904. 223t, 48 × 8m; one 8·8cm SK L/30, one 5cm SK L/40 and several 8mm Maxim machine-guns. Triple-expansion steam engines, two shafts; 13 knots. Crew: 47.

**Vaterland** (river gunboat; Oberleutnant z.S. Dressler). F. Schichau AG, Elbing, yard no. 711; commissioned on 28 May 1904. Otherwise as *Tsingtau*, above.

**Otter** (river gunboat; Kapitänleutnant Seuffert). J.C. Tecklenborg AG, Geestemünde, yard no. 232; commissioned on 1 April 1910. 266t, 53 × 8·65m; two 5·2cm SK L/55 and three 8mm machine-guns. Triple-expansion steam engines, two shafts; 14 knots.

**S90** (torpedo-boat, officially known as 'T90' by August 1914; Kapitänleutnant Brunner). F. Schichau AG, Elbing, yard no. 644; commissioned on 24 October 1899. 310t, 61 × 7m; three 5·2cm guns, three 45cm torpedo-tubes. Triple-expansion steam engines, two shafts; 26 knots. Crew: 56.

## AUSTRALIAN STATION

**Cormoran** (colonial gunboat; Korvettenkapitän Adalbert Zuckschwerdt). Kaiserliche Werft, Danzig; commissioned on 25 July 1893 and refitted extensively in 1907–8. 1,612t, 79·6 × 10·6m; eight 10·5cm L/35 guns, several 3·7cm revolver cannon, two 45cm torpedo tubes. Triple-expansion engines, two shafts; 15 knots. Crew: 162.

**Geier** (colonial gunboat; Korvettenkapitän Carl Grasshoff). Kaiserliche Werft, Wilhelmshaven; commissioned on 24 October 1895. Otherwise generally as *Cormoran*.

**Planet** (survey ship; Korvettenkapitän Oswald Collmann). AG 'Weser', Bremen, yard no. 150; commissioned on 16 November 1905. 658t, 49 × 9·8m; three 3·7cm revolver cannon, two 8mm machine-guns. Triple-expansion steam engines driving two shafts; 9·5 knots. Crew: 104.

## EAST AFRICAN STATION

**Königsberg** (small cruiser; Fregattenkapitän Max Looff). Kaiserliche Werft, Kiel, yard no. 31; commissioned on 6 April 1907, but extensively rebuilt in 1911–13. 3,390t, 114·8 × 13·2m; ten 10·5cm SK L/40, ten 3·7cm semi-automatic cannon, two 45cm torpedo tubes. Triple-expansion steam engines, two shafts; 23 knots. Crew: 322.

**Möwe** (survey ship; Korvettenkapitän Zimmer). Kaiserliche Werft, Wilhelmshaven, yard no. 29; commissioned on 12 March 1907. 653t, 49 × 9·8m; three 3·7cm revolver cannon, two 8mm machine-guns. Triple-expansion steam engines, two shafts; 9·5 knots. Crew: 102.

## EAST AND WEST AMERICAN STATION

**Karlsruhe** (small cruiser; Fregattenkapitän Fritz Lüdecke). Friedr. Krupp'sche Germaniawerft, Kiel, yard no. 181; commissioned on 15 January 1914. 4,900t, 139 × 13·7m; twelve 10·5cm SK L/40, two 50cm torpedo-tubes. Steam turbines driving two shafts; 27·25 knots. Crew: 373.

## WEST AFRICAN STATION

**Panther** (Iltis-class gunboat; Korvettenkapitän Förtsch). Kaiserliche Werft, Danzig; commissioned on 15 March 1902. 894t, 64·1 × 9·7m; two 10·5cm L/40 guns, six 3·7cm revolver cannon. Triple-expansion steam engines driving two shafts; 13·5 knots. Crew: 130.

**Eber** (Iltis-class gunboat; Kapitänleutnant Wirth). AG 'Vulcan', Stettin, yard no. 257; commissioned on 15 September 1903. Otherwise as *Panther*.

**Below:** SMS *Scharnhorst*, flagship of the Kreuzergeschwader.

# PRINZ EITEL FRIEDRICH

5 August 1914–8 April 1915; eleven victims (33,424grt).
A converted passenger/cargo ship, interned in Newport News after a protracted
but only moderately successful cruise.

◆◆◆

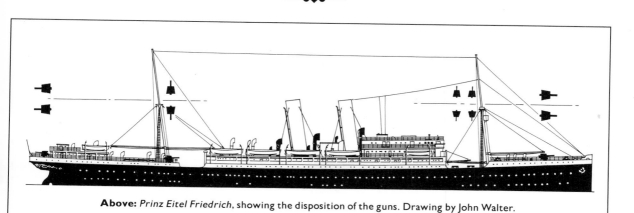

**Above:** *Prinz Eitel Friedrich*, showing the disposition of the guns. Drawing by John Walter.

Type: Hilfskreuzer.
Builder: AG 'Vulcan', Stettin-Bredow (yard no. 254). Equipped
by the Gouvernements Werft, Tsingtau, 1914.
Owner: Norddeutscher Lloyd, Bremen.
Launch date: 8 June 1904.
Commissioned: 5 August 1914.
Crew: 25 officers and 377 men.

**Dimensions**

Registered tonnage (grt): 8,797.
Full-load displacement: 16,000 tonnes.
Overall length: 154·6 metres.
Waterline length: 149·1 metres.
Beam: 17·0 metres.
Full-load draught: about 8·5 metres.

**Weapons**

Guns: four 10·5cm SK C/88 L/35 and six 8·8cm SK L/40.
Maximum range of main armament: 9,800 metres (10·5cm).
Lesser guns: twelve 3·7cm machine cannon and small-arms.
Munitions: not known.
Armour protection: confined to the gun shields.

**Performance**

Powerplant: two vertical four-cylinder quadruple expansion
steam engines, supplied by four boilers. Two propeller shafts.
Boiler pressure: 15·5at (227psi).
Coal bunkerage: 6,000 tonnes.
Speed, trials: about 17 knots.
Speed, service maximum: 15 knots (7,000ihp).
Range: 10,000 nautical miles at 14 knots.

The outbreak of the First World War predictably
threatened the German colony of Kiautschou and its port,
Tsingtau. It was an open secret that the Japanese were
keen to eject the Germans from their toehold on the
Chinese mainland and would strike immediately war was
declared. Tsingtau could not be defended for long against
the might of the Japanese army, supported by the most
powerful navy in the Far East. Consequently, the
Germans could only send away the Kreuzergeschwader

to cruise the Pacific Ocean; little was to be gained by
defending the indefensible.

The Norddeutscher Lloyd steamship *Prinz Eitel
Friedrich* was equipped as an auxiliary cruiser to counter
the British ships of the same class active in the Far
East—principally three Canadian Pacific Empresses and
the P&O *Himalaya*—or, alternatively, embarking on a
career as a raider.

The elegant two-funnelled *Prinz Eitel Friedrich* was
not especially large, but was deemed fast enough to
be useful. She was recalled to the navy dockyard at
Tsingtau to be fitted with the guns of *Luchs* and *Tiger*,
gunboats that were of little fighting value in the event of
a full-scale war.

By the standards of some of other German raiders, the
armed merchant cruiser was well equipped. Two 10·5cm
guns were placed port-and-starboard on the forecastle,
midway between the stem and the break, with the other
two on the poop aft of the deck house. Four of the 8·8cm
guns were placed in the well ahead of the bridge, two to
port and two to starboard; the remaining pair of 8·8cm
guns lay at the front of the poop alongside the mainmast.
There were also no fewer than twelve 3·7cm cannon.

A crew was mustered from the gunboats *Luchs* and
*Tiger*, and the river gunboats *Vaterland* and *Otter*.
On 6 August, *Prinz Eitel Friedrich*, commanded by
Korvettenkapitän Thierichens of *Luchs*, left Tsingtau to
escort a convoy of supply ships aiming to meet the
Kreuzergeschwader at Pagan Island on 12 August.
Accompanying von Spee and the cruisers as far as the
Marshall Islands, the *Prinz Eitel Friedrich*—together with
the jinxed *Cormoran* (see Appendix 1)—was detached to
wage war along the sea lanes in the southern Pacific.

Fortunately, the steamship had been able to fill her bunkers shortly before the German colonial empire capitulated and was able to avoid immediate internment owing to lack of fuel.

Realising that little was to be gained by staying in the area to which he had been ordered, Thierichens set out eastward to rejoin the Kreuzergeschwader. On 27 October 1914, *Prinz Eitel Friedrich* rejoined Admiral von Spee at Más Afuera in the Juan Fernández islands. Von Spee detached the ship to collect information, arrange coaling facilities and send signals home from Valparaiso.

On 31 October, *Prinz Eitel Friedrich* chased the 5,732grt steamship *Colusa*—completed in 1913 by W. Hamilton & Co. Ltd of Port Glasgow, owned by the New York & Pacific Steam Ship Co. Ltd of London, but managed by Grace Brothers of San Francisco. Thierichens was preventing from capturing his first prize by the intervention of a Chilean warship. The captain explained forcefully that the raider had entered Chilean waters and would be attacked if she did not withdraw.

The liner entered Valparaiso on 1 November, but stayed for only four hours owing to the presence of British warships. The battle of Coronel was fought that evening. On 4 November, *Prinz Eitel Friedrich* returned to Valparaiso secure in the knowledge that the Royal Navy's influence had waned with the loss of Admiral Cradock and his squadron. On 8 November, the steamship rejoined von Spee at Más Afuera and was ordered to remain off the Chilean coast until early December to persuade British naval intelligence that the Kreuzergeschwader— eventually intent on raiding the Falkland islands—had not yet rounded Cape Horn. *Prinz Eitel Friedrich* could then begin her commerce raiding exploits in earnest.

The raider took her first prize on 5 December, seventy miles south of Valparaiso, when the 5,067grt steamship *Charcas*—also owned by the New York & Pacific Steam Ship Co. Ltd—was overhauled with a cargo of Chilean nitrates. A boarding party was sent over, whereafter explosive charges were laid and the 1906-vintage product of the Armstrong, Whitworth shipyard was scuttled. The crew was put ashore a day later near Valparaiso.

On 10 December, wireless operators aboard the German raider intercepted a message, sent to Port Stanley from Montevideo, which suggested that von Spee and the Kreuzergeschwader had met an ominous fate. This was confirmed on 12 December by a message sent in clear from the newspaper *Daily Mail*, asking the Bishop of the Falkland Islands for details of the sinking of *Scharnhorst*, *Gneisenau* and *Leipzig*. Clearly, any attempt made by *Prinz Eitel Friedrich* to round the Horn and run northward up the Atlantic would be thwarted by British warships. Virtually any of these would be able to reduce the steamer to a wreck, however well armed an auxiliary warship she may have been; Thierichens also knew that his ship did not have the speed to outrun merchant cruisers such as *Carmania* or *Otranto*.

The German skipper decided to retrace his steps to Easter Island, then proceed westward across the Pacific relying on uninhabited islands and a prize or two to support his raiding role. On 11 December, three hundred miles from the west coast of South America in 44°50′S 81°40′W, *Prinz Eitel Friedrich* captured the French three-masted barque *Jean* (2,207grt, Capitaine Griffon), fortuitously laden with 3,500 tons of Welsh coal being hauled from Barry to Antofagasta. The sailing ship had been completed by Ateliers et Chantiers de la Loire of Saint Nazaire in 1902, and was owned by Société Anonyme des Armateurs Nantais. Deciding that coaling in mid-ocean was too risky, Thierichens took the French barque in tow and resumed his course for Easter Island.

On 12 December, nearly nine hundred miles south west of Valparaiso, *Prinz Eitel Friedrich* came across the 1,784grt three-masted barque *Kildalton*, commanded by Captain Charles Dagwell, owned by the Kildalton Barque Company and registered in Glasgow. The ship had been built in the Troon yard of the Ailsa Shipbuilding Co. Ltd in 1903. Bound out of Liverpool for Callao by way of Cape Horn, she contained nothing to interest the raider and was scuttled once the crew had been put aboard *Jean*.

On 23 December 1914, *Prinz Eitel Friedrich*, having cast-off *Jean* with a prize crew aboard, steamed into Cook's Bay harbour on Easter Island. The Germans attempted to purchase cattle from the British manager of the local ranch, but refused to give any details of the war in general or their role in particular. The islanders were upset by the unfriendly behaviour of Thierichen's men and, in particular, by the erection of a wireless station atop Rano Aroi. This was regarded as an affront to Chilean neutrality.

On Boxing Day, the steamship left the harbour to return with *Jean*, whose coal was transferred once the two vessels had been secured together. To prevent the barque capsizing in the swell, her masts and yards were shot away. On 31 December, still lashed together, *Prinz Eitel Friedrich* and *Jean* left Cook's Bay and sailed outside the three-mile limit. There the barque was cut loose, with only her mizzen still standing, and was shelled until she sank. The German liner then returned to land the crews of *Kildalton* and *Jean* in the knowledge that it would be many months before news of their plight filtered back to civilisation. Not until February 1915 did a Swedish trading ship call at the island to take off all the Britons and about half of the Frenchmen, though they had previously all refused to embark in the British barque *Skerries* in case, having given their parole, they encountered *Prinz Eitel Friedrich* again.

The raider left Easter Island for the last time on 6 January. Thierichens had elected to make the risky passage round Cape Horn, hoping for bad weather to hide his ship from Royal Navy patrols, and then run northward up the Atlantic. An attempt would then be made to break the British blockade and steam down the

**Above:** *Prinz Eitel Friedrich* off Port Said. Photograph by courtesy of Laurence Dunn.

North Sea back to Germany. The passage around the tip of South America went so far southward that, according to C. Ernest Fayle in *Seaborne Trade* (London, 1920), *Prinz Eitel Friedrich* reached 61°S and passed through the Shackleton Sea in order to evade British warships.

After swinging back northward, in mid-Atlantic, Thierichens chanced on 26 January upon *Isabel Browne* in 33°S 28°30′W, considerably more than a thousand nautical miles off the coast of Uruguay. The three-masted barque had been built by Russell & Co. of Port Glasgow in 1885, but had passed by 1914 into the ownership of Aug. Troberg of Mariehamm and was flying the Russian mercantile ensign. The barque was sunk once Captain Lindqvist and his crew had been taken off.

On 27 January, Thierichens seized the French barque *Pierre Loti* and the American-registered *William P. Frye*. Capitaine Allée was taking the 2,196grt *Pierre Loti*, owned by Société Nouvelle d'Armement, home to Nantes; Captain Nickerson was apparently taking his ship-rigged four-master (3,375grt) to San Francisco. The two ships had been completed in 1901, *Pierre Loti* by Chantiers Nantais de Construction Maritime of Nantes and *William P. Frye* in the yards of A. Sewall & Company of Bath in Maine. The French vessel was sunk immediately.

*William P. Frye* was carrying wheat from Seattle to Queenstown in Ireland—a cargo which could be regarded as assisting the British war effort and legitimately destroyed. But the fabric of the ship was a different matter. Thierichens ordered the crew of *Prinz Eitel Friedrich* to begin dumping wheat overboard, but the task proved to be far more difficult than he had thought. Eventually, worried in case an unfriendly warship should appear, he took off the crew of *William P. Frye* and sunk the sailing-ship by gunfire. When news of the loss reached the USA, the government of the day was appalled; Germany eventually had to pay a considerable sum in compensation.

On 29 January, Thierichens seized *Jacobsen* (2,195grt), a three-masted barque owned by Société Anonyme les Voiliers Dunkerques. Completed in 1901 by Ateliers et Chantiers 'Loire' of Nantes, the barque was being guided by Capitaine Cavelan.

In early February, wireless operators aboard the raider intercepted a message intended for *Kronprinz Wilhelm* (q.v.), giving her captain leave to head for a Spanish or North American port once her cruise had been completed. Thierichens regarded this as a safer course of action than running the British blockade, and cruised purposelessly around for several days. On 12 February, however, *Prinz Eitel Friedrich* came across *Invercoe*, homeward bound with wheat from Portland in Oregon. Ship's papers revealed that the three-masted 1,421grt barque, owned by G. Milne & Co. and registered in Aberdeen, had been completed by A. McMillan & Co. of Dumbarton in 1892. She was sunk in 26°31′S 26°15′W, about nine hundred miles east by south of Cabo Frio.

The raider was now running short of coal, having exhausted most of the supplies taken from the barque *Jean* over the Christmas period in 1914. Realising that his chances of capturing a collier would be greater on the steamship routes than in the lanes frequented by sailing ships, Thierichens sailed northward until he was east of Ilha Fernando Noronha. On the morning of 18 February, four hundred miles east of Pernambuco, *Prinz Eitel Friedrich* accosted the 3,605grt British steamship *Mary Ada Short*, owned by James Westoll, built in 1896 by Short Brothers of Sunderland and bound from Rosario to St Vincent with a cargo of maize.

An examination by a boarding party revealed that the steamer contained little to interest the raider, so she was sunk by explosive charges and gunfire at 11:00. Next morning, the British armed merchant cruiser *Otranto* passed the very same spot, homeward bound with the survivors of the German ships sunk at the battle of the Falkland Islands.

On 19 February, *Prinz Eitel Friedrich* sank the 1907-vintage 6,629grt French steamer *Floride* of Compagnie Générale Transatlantique in 2°28'S 31°10'W, north east of Fernando Noronha. On 20 February, having turned for São Pedro e São Paulo (St Paul's Rocks), the raider took 3,630grt *Willerby* of R. Ropner & Company of Stockton on Tees. Completed by Ropner & Sons in 1912, the steamship had been La Plata-bound in ballast prior to being sunk 490 miles north-east of Pernambuco.

The last supplies of captured coal had been used, and the ever-growing gaggle of prisoners meant that provisions were running low on board *Prinz Eitel Friedrich*. Thierichens elected to run for the port of Newport News, nearly three thousand miles away on the eastern seaboard of the USA. In the night of 21/22 February, the raider passed unseen by, but perilously close to the British merchant cruiser *Edinburgh Castle* steaming south-westward for South America. On 11 March 1915, *Prinz Eitel Friedrich* finally reached harbour.

The absence of a screen of patrolling British warships was explained simply by the fact that the Royal Navy still believed that the raider was operating in the Pacific. By keeping all his prisoners aboard, Thierichens had duped everyone.

The American authorities, soon discovering that the liner was heavily armed, declared her to be an auxiliary warship and allowed her skipper only until 14 March to dock for essential repairs. It was widely believed that *Prinz Eitel Friedrich* would go back to sea in an attempt to resume her raiding career. Time passed. On 5 April, the ship was seen taking in stores. British intelligence could not fail to notice and had arranged for the armoured cruisers *Cumberland* (1904, 9,800 tons) and *Niobe* (1898, 11,000 tons) to be waiting in neutral waters off Chesapeake Bay. The German ship took a pilot aboard on 6 April and seemed ready to sail; on 8 April, however, the raider was handed over to the American authorities with a request for internment. Thierichens had wisely decided that he did not have the speed to escape from the British cruisers nor the gun-power to slug it out with their thirty 6-inch guns. Another of the Kaiser's Pirates had been forced into early retirement.

The ship was seized by the American authorities on 7 April 1917, serving as the trooper *De Kalb*. Sold in 1921 to the United American Lines, Inc., and renamed *Mount Clay*, she was laid up in 1924 and finally went to the breakers in 1935.

# SEEADLER

2 December 1916–2 August 1917; fourteen victims (28,140grt).
The only sailing-ship to be used as a raider, until wrecked in the Pacific Ocean. Renowned more
for the story of her exploits than real success.

Type: Hilfskreuzer.
Builder: R. Duncan & Company, Port Glasgow (yard no. 237).
Equipped by J.C. Tecklenborg, Geestemünde, 1916.
Owner: River Plate Shipping Company, New York (named *Pass of Balmaha*).
Launch date: 9 August 1888.
Commissioned: 2 December 1916.
Crew: 7 officers and 57 men.

**Dimensions**
Registered tonnage (grt): 1,571.
Full-load displacement: 4,500 tonnes.
Overall length: 83·5 metres.
Waterline length: 74·3 metres.
Beam: 11·8 metres.
Full-load draught: about 5·5 metres.

**Weapons**
Guns: two 8·8cm SK L/40.
Maximum range of main armament: 9,800 metres?.
Lesser guns: machine-guns and small-arms only.
Munitions: 400 8·8cm shells.
Armour protection: none.

**Performance**
Powerplant: one Carels Frères diesel driving a single propeller.
Oil bunkerage: 2,100 tonnes.
Speed, service maximum: 14–16 knots under sail in optimum winds, 9 knots on auxiliary engine alone (900shp).
Range: 40,000 nautical miles at 9 knots, but could be extended greatly by the use of the sails.

*Kapitänleutnant Graf Luckner,*
*Führer des Hilfskreuzers "Seeadler."*

The success of the surface raiders active immediately after the outbreak of the First World War depended greatly on the efficacy of the Etappe system and the constant attention of colliers. Once the Royal Navy had neutralised most of the raiders, and destroyed the Kreuzergeschwader at the Battle of the Falkland Islands, this support was removed. Thus the idea of disrupting British seaborne trade by surface ships lay dormant until the end of 1915.

A change of emphasis to economical ships with large bunker capacity revitalised raiding, exemplified by the success of *Möwe* on her first cruise. The most extreme method of freeing a raider from dependence on coaling was to use a sailing ship. The idea has been credited to several people, but was apparently due to Leutnant z.S. d.R. Alfred Kling.

Kling was a popular adventurer, having explored the Arctic with the pre-war Filchener Expedition. At first, his suggestion was met largely with scepticism; gradually, however, objections were overcome. The fitting of an economical auxiliary diesel engine would enable the ship to avoid becalming and, initially at least, no one would suspect a full-rigged ship of being a raider. This would undoubtedly facilitate breaking the Royal Navy blockade

on the outbound voyage, though homecoming would obviously be more problematical.

Another major problem was that few German naval officers had experience under canvas. Success would clearly hinge entirely on finding the right man. The right man proved to be Korvettenkapitän Graf Felix von Luckner. Born on 9 June 1881, he was a robust character whom, in pre-1914 days, had sailed at Cowes aboard the Krupp yacht *Germania*. But he had had an extraordinary adolescence, having run away to sea in 1893 to serve as 'Phelax Luedige', cabin boy aboard a Russian full rigger named *Niobe*. After serving on the American four-masted schooner *Golden Shore*, von Luckner joined the British four-master *Pinmore* in 1902 before returning to Hamburg. He then had spells in the German ship *Cæsarea*, the Canadian schooner *Flying Fish* and the steamer *Lisbon*. He claimed to have joined the Salvation Army in Australia; to have hunted kangaroos; to have been a prize fighter; and to have joined the Mexican army to guard the presidential palace of Porfirio Diaz.

By 1908, Felix von Luckner had passed his mate's examinations and joined the Hamburg-Südamerikanische steamer *Petropolis*. He intended to serve for the requisite nine months, then volunteer for a year in the imperial navy, from which, if successful, he would receive a commission. In 1910, Leutnant z.S. d.R. Felix Graf von Luckner returned to the Hamburg-Südamerikanische Dampfschifffahrts-Gesellschaft and served until he was called up for active service in February 1912.

Owing to his extraordinary background and a penchant for lurid story-telling, von Luckner soon became a favourite of Kaiser Wilhelm II. Eventually, after telling how he had once been rebuffed by the officers of the gunboat *Panther*, he found himself posted to that very ship. There he remained until the outbreak of the First World War.

Von Luckner was present at the Battle of Heligoland Bight, and in the raids on Yarmouth and the Yorkshire coast. At Jutland, he served as a turret commander aboard the dreadnought *Kronprinz*. Shortly afterward, the German admiralty was persuaded to send out a

sailing-ship raider. In spite of objections from officers who thought their seniority more deserving of the command, Felix von Luckner was the ideal candidate to captain such a vessel.

Selecting a suitable ship was not especially difficult. *Pass of Balmaha* had been built on the Clyde in 1888, but was sold to the River Plate Shipping Company of New York in the early years of the twentieth century. In June 1915 she had left New York under the command of a bluff New Englander named Scott, loaded with a cargo of cotton for Arkhangelsk, but was stopped by a British patrol north west of Cape Wrath and sent into a Scottish port for examination. Before safety could be gained, *Pass of Balmaha* was seized by Kapitänleutnant Graefe of *U36*. A prize crew of a single German Fähnrich z.S. (midshipman) was put aboard and a course set for Cuxhaven complete with the British boarding party hiding in the hold.

Now the bald-headed British full-rigger—from 16 July 1916 temporarily renamed *Walter*, befitting a schoolship*—was to be converted into a raider. Two 8·8cm guns were hidden behind hinged gunwhales at the break immediately behind the forecastle, one to port and

* In this era—though now no longer common— 'Walter' meant 'leader' or 'teacher' in German.

---

**Below:** the full-rigger *Seeadler*, seen here at San Francisco in her pre-war guise of *Pass of Balmaha*. Author's collection.

the other to starboard, whilst large quantities of small arms and ammunition were put aboard. A powerful wireless transmitter was installed, the hold was converted into a prison for four hundred men (with rows of bunks made from canvas and steel pipes) and special quarters aft were prepared for the captains of captured ships. Most ingeniously, the after saloon was mounted on a hydraulic lift. At the touch of a button concealed behind the barometer in the chart room, the floor of the saloon could be lowered into the deck. The intention was to capture unwanted visitors if the circumstances demanded it.

Finding a suitable auxiliary engine presented problems. The compression-ignition diesel (then known simply as an oil engine) was a comparatively new product; the first patents had been granted in 1893, but an effectual engine had not been made until 1897. Though many firms had negotiated licences, development of engines powerful enough to propel large ships had been protracted. The first coastal tanker had only been launched in the Netherlands in 1910, though an ocean-going cargo ship—the highly successful Danish *Selandia*—followed in November 1911.

The four-stroke engines made in København by Burmeister & Wain, when carefully maintained, had proved particularly reliable and economical. But other manufacturers had problems. Though Krupp introduced a 1,250hp two-stroke engine in Germany in 1912, a Junkers engine had been tried unsuccessfully aboard *Primus*, launched from the AG 'Weser' shipyard for the Hamburg–Amerika Linie in March 1912.

Blohm & Voss spent much time developing a 'double acting' two-stroke engine for the 4,499grt *Secundus*, launched in January 1913, but eventually admitted defeat and reverted to a conventional MAN diesel.

When the time came to find a suitable engine for *Seeadler*, therefore, high-power diesel engines were in short supply. Acquiring a Burmeister & Wain engine was impossible, as too many questions would be asked; German manufacturers were concentrating on urgent war-work. The answer was eventually found in occupied Belgium, where a 900bhp four-cylinder two-stroke unit was provided by Usines Carels Frères SA of Ghent.

As *Seeadler* was to masquerade as a Norwegian full rigger, the preparations were extremely thorough. In von Luckner's words, *Seeadler*—

"was painted the same colour as *Maleta*, [we] arranged her deck the same, and decorated the cabins with the same ornaments. In my captain's cabin, I hung pictures of the King and Queen of Norway and also of their jovial relative, [the late] King Edward VII of England. The barometer, thermometer and chronometer were all of Norwegian make. I had a Norwegian library and a Norwegian phonograph and records. We had enough provisions from Norwegian firms to last us through the blockade..."

Requisite papers were forged, and von Luckner claimed to have stolen the log-book of the real *Maleta* in København harbour. To complement the disguise, von Luckner selected Norwegian-speaking German sailors whose physical characteristics matched those of the real sailors aboard the real *Maleta*. The thoroughness with which the raiders intended to prepare the ship knew no bounds. Von Luckner remembered that—

"the British always inspected the fo'c'sle, to see that everything looked right there. I immediately got together a lot of photographs to pass as those of the Norwegian sailors' parents, brothers and sisters, uncles and aunts, sweethearts, wives and mothers-in-law... We even sent a man to Norway for the pictures in order to have the names of Norwegian photographers stamped on them".

Sailing orders were forged to suggest that the ship was bound for Melbourne. Leutnant z.S. d.R. Kling was the instigator of the sailing-ship raider concept; Leutnant z.S. d.R. Preiss had once been a shipmate of von Luckner's; and the Mate, Leutnant z.S. d.R. Leudemann, had served in Laiesz sailing ships prior to 1914. More than twenty Norwegian speakers bunked above deck—the same complement as *Maleta*—whilst the German-speaking majority was initially confined in hiding below.

The crew soon mastered their parts, even the seaman who had to play the key role of Captain's Wife. However, just as preparations were being made to sail, von Luckner was ordered to wait until the mercantile submarine *Deutschland* returned to port in Germany from a voyage to the USA; the Royal Navy was known to have doubled patrols in an effort to intercept the submarine, and would be sure to catch the sailing-ship raider. *Deutschland* did not appear for more than twenty days; by the time the spurious *Maleta* was allowed to leave Hamburg, the real ship had left Denmark. All the careful preparations had been in vain.

After a search of Lloyd's Register to find another Norwegian vessel matching the particulars of *Seeadler* and *Maleta*, von Luckner selected *Carmoe*.* No-one knew where this particular ship could be found, but the risk seemed worth taking. Just before *Seeadler* set out on her cruise, however, an up-to-date Norwegian newspaper acquired to give the voyage greater authenticity revealed that the real *Carmoe* had only recently been examined by British patrols. The plan had miscarried again.

Von Luckner finally decided to name the ship *Hero*.† The false papers and the stolen log-book were deliberately damaged by water in the hope that they would still be good enough to fool the British examiners.

On 21 December 1916, *Seeadler* left the estuary of the river Weser, intent on running up the coast of Norway, around the northern tip of Scotland and out into the Atlantic along the normal trade routes. By 23 December, the ship was running before a roaring gale. This was a

---

* According to Lowell Thomas, *The Sea Devil. The Story of Count Felix von Luckner, the German War Raider* (Heinemann, London, 1928).
† Some of von Luckner's memoirs claim that *Irma* was selected in honour of his fiancée, but this change seems to have been made for effect at the expense of historical accuracy.

blessing in disguise, as it lent credence to the 'storm damage' explanation of the soaked papers.

By Christmas Day, 1916, von Luckner had reached a point 180 nautical miles south-west of Iceland when he was stopped by the 15,000grt British merchant cruiser *Avenger*, which could easily blow *Seeadler* out of the water. A boarding party was sent over, but the raider's disguise held. In spite of a delay whilst the inspectors relayed information offered by Leudemann about the presence of 'the *Moewe* and the auxiliary cruiser, *Seeadler*', von Luckner and his men had duped the British. Even though the inspection had been thorough, the skill with which the 'Norwegian' ship had been prepared had triumphed. *Seeadler* had been handed the best Christmas present imaginable.

The raider's deck guns had been covered with canvas painted to resemble pig-pens, and strewn with sailors' clothing as if spread out to dry. Machine-guns were mounted out of sight on the poop, and fifty men armed with rifles could hide behind the gunwhales to open fire if required. The Norwegian camouflage was discarded, the deck cargo of timber was thrown overboard, and the ship was smartened until her appearance befitted a German warship.

On 9 January 1917, an elegant single-funnelled steamship with a black hull and a clipper bow was spotted 120 miles south by west of the Ilhas dos Açôres. The Germans decided that she looked British, though neither flag nor name were visible. *Seeadler* hoisted a request for chronometer time, common enough in days when sailing ships, in particular, were out of sight of land for long periods. Captain Chewn, bound for Buenos Aires from Cardiff with a cargo of steam coal, changed course to windward of the raider and slowed. His 3,268grt ship *Gladys Royle*, launched on Wearside by Short Brothers in 1894, was owned by James Westoll and registered in Sunderland.

The German ensign was run up to the mast head and Leutnant z.S. Kircheiss, who combined the roles of navigator and gunnery officer, ordered the false bulwark that hid the starboard 8·8cm gun to be dropped. The first shot flew across *Gladys Royle*'s bows. Much to the surprise of the Germans, the steamer ran up her Red Ensign and then dipped it. A second shot screamed over her bow, then a third over the funnel.

Finally, the steamer hove-to and lowered a boat. Captain Chewn climbed aboard the raider, mystified; firing a mortar to mark time was an age-old method, so he had raised his flag to act as his 'mortar shot'. The second German shot was assumed to have been aimed at a hostile submarine, whereupon *Gladys Royle* began zig-zagging.

Only when the third round had passed close to the funnel did the Britons notice that the German ensign fluttered from *Seeadler*'s masthead. After Leutnant z.S. d.R. Preiss and the boarding party had taken what they wanted, scuttling charges were fired and *Gladys Royle* sunk slowly by the stern.

At noon on 10 January 1917, an anonymous black hulled steamship—no flag, no visible name—crossed the path of *Seeadler*. Requests for information went unheeded, so von Luckner deliberately steered across the newcomer's bows in the hope that the rule that steam gave way to sail would be honoured. But the steamer simply ploughed onward, forcing the raider to haul away.

Up went the German ensign, and a shell flew over the steamship's bow. Captain George Bannister of 3,095grt *Lundy Island*, owned by the Williams Steam Navigation Co. Ltd of West Hartlepool, decided to run even though a second shot passed perilously close to his funnel. His charge had been built by W. Gray & Co. Ltd in the last years of the nineteenth century, but could still evade a mere sailing ship by steaming into the wind—or so Bannister hoped. Von Luckner gave the order to open fire in earnest. One shell passed through the funnel, two slammed into the hull, and another burst on deck. Finally, the steamer hove-to and the boats were lowered. Von Luckner signalled the British skipper to come aboard *Seeadler*, without result, so the Germans sent over a boat to investigate.

When Captain Bannister was eventually brought back to the raider, the reasons for the attempted escape and eccentric behaviour became clear. *Lundy Island* was bound for France with sugar from Madagascar. Bannister deemed the cargo important enough to risk outrunning the sailing ship, but his mixed-race crew had panicked when the first shells struck and rushed for the boats. The captain took the wheel himself, but the next hit cut the rudder chain and *Lundy Island* could only wallow helplessly. The crew then took all the boats and abandoned ship, leaving the captain behind.

Von Luckner learned that Captain Bannister had been captured by Nikolaus zu Dohna-Schlodien during the first cruise of *Moewe*, and, having given a worthless parole, had not been anxious to be taken for a second time. *Lundy Island* was subsequently sunk by gunfire.

Continuing on his voyage southward down the Atlantic, von Luckner arrived mid-way between Brazil and the coast of West Africa. On 21 January, after cruising the trade routes for some days, *Seeadler* captured the 2,199grt three-masted barque *Charles Gounod* of Société Nouvelle d'Armement, bound for Bordeaux with a cargo of corn. Registered in Nantes, the barque had been completed in the Saint Nazaire yard of Ateliers et Chantiers de la Loire in 1900. Scuttling charges were fired and the French ship sank gracefully by the bow, the Tricouleur at the mainmast-head fluttering defiance to the end.

The French ship's log revealed that contact had been made with other sailing ships and often noted the routes they were taking. On 24 January, acting on information gleaned from *Charles Gounod*, 150 miles north-east of

**Above:** the three-masted barque *Charles Gounod*. Author's collection.

São Pedro e São Paulo (St Paul's Rocks), von Luckner encountered the 364grt three-masted auxiliary schooner *Perce*. The small vessel ignored signals and, at first, was thought to be a neutral American. Just as von Luckner and Leudemann had resolved to let *Perce* go, the Red Ensign was run up the mast. Two shots across the bow forced the Canadian vessel to a stop. A German boarding party discovered that she was bound for her home port of Halifax, Nova Scotia, with a cargo of gaberdine, wood and salted fish. The crewmen of the schooner were taken off—including the newly married captain and his bride—and *Perce* was sunk by gunfire.

On 3 February 1917, lookouts aboard the raider spotted a large four-masted barque. As *Seeadler* closed, the crew could see that the ship was painted grey and had false gun-ports along her hull. She was clearly French, most probably belonging to Ant. Dom. Bordes et fils. The 3,071grt barque *Antonin*, launched by Ateliers et Chantiers de la France of Dunkerque in 1902, had been encountered in 7°N 36′W whilst homeward bound from Chile with a cargo of saltpetre. Von Luckner came up behind the French ship. The diesel engines had failed, but *Seeadler* had proved to be fast under canvas and the Germans decided to race the French for sport.

As a squally wind rose, Capitaine Lecoq, fearful of the cost of a ruined suit of sails to his owners, reduced canvas; von Luckner, answerable to no-one but himself, kept pressing on. The Frenchman was

seen taking a photograph for posterity as the raider overhauled him. When the range had dropped far enough, *Seeadler* machine-gunned the sails and rigging of *Antonin*. Simultaneously, the French skipper spotted the German naval ensign fluttering at the masthead; for him, all was lost. The barque hove-to, the crew was brought across to *Seeadler* and scuttling charges were laid. Soon, the victim had disappeared beneath the waves.

On 9 February, in 5°N 31°W, von Luckner and his men captured the scruffy 1,811grt sailing ship *Buenos Ayres* and her equally dishevelled captain, Antonio Barbieri. Owned by Lachianca of Napoli, the vessel had been built on the Clyde by Russell & Co. of Greenock in 1891. The cargo again proved to be Chilean saltpetre.

The morning of 19 February revealed another elegant sailing ship. *Seeadler* started after the four-masted barque, which piled on canvas to race and started to pull away. Fortunately for the Germans, the diesel engine was working well enough to add its effort to the sails. Gradually, *Seeadler* began to gain on her rival. Eventually, 540 miles north-west of São Pedro e São Paulo, von Luckner ordered the unknown—but familiar looking—ship to state her name. Soon the signal flags fluttered in reply: *Pinmore* (2,431grt), Captain James Mullen, laden with grain.

There was a special poignancy about the capture and impending destruction of this particular ship, built by J. Reid & Company of Port Glasgow in 1882, registered in Greenock, and owned in 1917 by Tridonia Ltd; in 1902, von Luckner had survived a terrible passage from San Francisco around Cape Horn to Liverpool, and his assumed name—'Phelax Luedige'—was still cut into her stern rail.

Von Luckner could not resist taking *Pinmore* into Rio de Janeiro to collect supplies, bandaging his hand to avoid having to duplicate the real Captain Mullen's signature on customs documents.* However, as the British ship was of no further use, scuttling charges were eventually fired and the old barque sank lazily by the bow. Many of the German crewmen, unaware of the whole story, wondered why their captain shut himself in his cabin as the vessel was consigned to a watery grave.

A four-masted Danish barque named *Viking*—built by Burmeister & Wain in 1907 for Det Forenede Dampskibs A/S of København—was stopped on 25 February, but released after an inspection found nothing untoward with her cargo.

A hazy shape was spotted by Leutnant z.S. d.R. Preiss through the morning mists of 26 February. Von Luckner unhesitatingly swung *Seeadler* onto an intercepting course and, within fifteen minutes, drew close to the 1,953grt three-masted barque *British Yeoman*. The crew of the vessel waved enthusiastic to the prisoners of many races who lined the raider's decks, so von Luckner,

judging the nationality of the barque by her name as no merchant flags were visible, ordered 'A Long Way to Tipperary' to be played on the phonograph as loudly as possible. Built by Oswald, Mordaunt & Company of Southampton in 1880, *British Yeoman* had indeed once sailed under the British flag and had been registered prior to 1916 in Victoria, British Columbia. However, she had been sold to her one-time managers, Eschen & Minor of San Francisco, and should have been sailing under the Stars and Stripes.†

Captain Armstrong shouted for news of the war, whereupon von Luckner replied that he had so much to tell that the information would be sent over in signals. As the crew of *British Yeoman* watched expectantly, *Seeadler* hoisted three signal flags: white with a blue edging top and bottom, and a central red band; yellow with a black circle; and blue with yellow edging top and bottom—C I D. 'Stop immediately or I will fire.'

The German ensign rattled up to the masthead and the guns were unmasked. There was consternation aboard the barque; sailors ran to the boats as she hove to. When the panic had died down, a boarding party from

* This is one of many incidents related in only some of von Luckner's memoirs (for example, it is absent from Lowell Thomas's 1928 *The Sea Devil*). It seems far-fetched in the extreme, as Mullen would have been well-known ashore.
† Oddly, though suggested by Lloyd's Register, this is not mentioned in any of the contemporaneous memoirs—some of which still list her as Canadian.

---

**Below:** the Danish four-masted barque *Viking*, stopped by von Luckner but released. Photograph by courtesy of Laurence Dunn.

*Seeadler* discovered a cargo which included live chicken and pigs. The livestock was transferred to the raider before scuttling charges were fired and *British Yeoman* sank 230 miles north-west of São Pedro e São Paulo.

In the evening of 26 February, a light was seen astern. Gradually, a large four-masted barque came up behind *Seeadler* as Felix von Luckner kept his ship moving steadily—but not too quickly—ahead. Dawn revealed the magnificent French *La Rochefoucauld* (2,200grt) of Société Nouvelle d'Armement, a product in 1899 of Ateliers et Chantiers 'Loire' of Nantes. Von Luckner signalled 'Stop. We have important news' and the barque obediently slowed. The 8·8cm guns were uncovered and the German ensign ran up to the mast-head.

Realising the futility of any resistance, Capitaine Malbert came aboard *Seeadler*, mortified; even when he had seen the raider's guns, he had still assumed his captor to be a British submarine tender. The boarding party reported that crewmen aboard *La Rochefoucauld* were saying that the barque had been searched only recently by a British cruiser. Re-examination of the log showed that Malbert had removed a page in the hope that the cruiser would catch the raider unaware, but his plan had been exposed and his ship was sunk on 27 February.

The evening of 5 March passed fine and clear as *Seeadler* cruised beneath the Southern Cross. As von Luckner scanned the horizon, he saw, silhouetted against the moonlight, a large four-masted barque. *Seeadler* approached the newcomer on the shadow side, unseen, before deciding that the vessel was probably British. Von Luckner sent 'Stop immediately. German cruiser' by signal lamp to panic the intended victim into believing that she faced a warship.

Soon a splashing of oars could be heard, and a voice hailed the raider in oath-spiced French. Jovial Capitaine Charrier, commanding the 2,206grt *Dupleix* of Société Anonyme des Armateurs Nantais, came aboard believing that a joke was being played by fellow-countrymen at his expense. The Germans prolonged his innocence before showing him into von Luckner's cabin—decorated with pictures of Kaiser Wilhelm, Hindenburg and Ludendorff, topped off with a large German flag. The Frenchman was inconsolable. He told how two other skippers had warned him not leave Valparaiso until instructions had been received from his owners. He had decided to sail on the fair wind and take the risk. He even ventured the names of the other French ships: *Antonin* and *La Rochefoucauld*.

Soon *Dupleix*, completed in 1900 by Ateliers et Chantiers de la Loire of Saint Nazaire, would join them on the ocean floor.

On 11 March, 220 miles east north-east of São Pedro e São Paulo, *Seeadler* spotted a black hulled steamship. As von Luckner approached, he ordered the signal sent to request chronometer time. This the steamer ignored, so the Germans used a smoke generator and a large quantity of magnesium powder to simulate a serious fire. Distress flares were launched, whereupon the 1911-vintage 3,609grt *Horngarth* of the Horngarth Steam Ship Co. Ltd of Cardiff immediately turned to assist. Von Luckner could see the wireless aerial and a large gun mounted on the poop. If the steamship elected to open fire, she was capable of dealing *Seeadler* a mortal blow.

Von Luckner elected to make the first moves. As *Horngarth* approached, the 'fire' was brought under control and seaman Schmidt, in the role of Captain's Wife, appeared on deck as a distraction. Within a moment, everything had changed. The guns had been unmasked, Schmidt became a German sailor, the imperial ensign was run up, and riflemen appeared above the deck rail to pick off anyone who moved towards the gun. A single 8·8cm shell knocked out the wireless installation aboard the British ship, and a 'noise cannon', made out of a length of large-diameter pipe loaded with blasting powder, was ignited with tremendous effect.

But still Captain Ivor Stainthorp of *Horngarth* refused to capitulate, instead ordering his gun crew to its post. The Germans could see the crew telling-off from the throng on deck to move towards the poop. Riflemen aboard *Seeadler* prepared to fire. Simultaneously, three men sent aloft with megaphones bellowed 'torpedoes clear', and the martial attitude aboard the steamer collapsed like a pricked balloon; white flags and white handkerchiefs fluttered on the breeze as *Horngarth* hove-to.

The boarding party on this occasion comprised men specially selected for their impressive physique, to discourage additional resistance. However, the incredulous British crew was taken off without incident and *Horngarth*—having surrendered several musical instruments and a grand piano—was sunk by the customary combination of open sea-cocks and explosives.

21 March brought the four-masted French barque *Cambronne* (1,863grt) of Ant. Dom. Bordes et fils, which surrendered to the German ensign in 20°10'S 25°50'W. Built by Laporte & Cie of Rouen in 1897, the barque was roomy and so well provisioned that von Luckner decided to rid *Seeadler* of nearly three hundred prisoners.

The method usually employed by the raider captains was to capture a steamship, transfer the prisoners, and place the vessel under the command of a German prize crew which would proceed as slowly as possible into a suitably neutral port. Using *Cambronne* to release the prisoners presented peculiar problems. Von Luckner could not afford to release sufficient crewmen to ensure that the prize sailed as he wanted; if he freed the barque without supervision, there were far too many men experienced under canvas to do anything but head for the nearest port under full sail. This would not buy sufficient time to ensure that *Seeadler* made an effectual escape.

The problem was eventually solved by removing *Cambronne*'s topgallant masts, destroying the spare spars and throwing the relevant sails overboard to ensure that she could not make Rio de Janeiro in less than ten days. Enough provisions to last a month were put aboard, and the barque was released eastward of Ilha da Trindade under the command of Captain Mullen of *Pinmore*. Mullen insisted on hauling down the Tricouleur in favour of the Union Flag, which did not please the French crew.

The raider set a course southward, pausing to lay a large cross of iron off the Falkland Islands to mark the graves of Admiral Graf von Spee—a friend of the von Luckner family—and the men that had been lost with him in December 1914. *Seeadler* then beat round Cape Horn on 18 April in a hurricane, emerging safely to run northward into the Pacific Ocean along the Chilean coast.

The passage had not been easy. Intercepted wireless messages revealed the presence of the Royal Navy and, though *Seeadler* had been taken so far south that icebergs had been encountered, von Luckner had still to run for his very life from a large armed merchant cruiser. The Germans believed their pursuer to have been *Otranto*, but had providentially escaped into a squall before the British ship could close within gun-range. The raider also passed within a few hundred miles of the cruiser *Lancaster* patrolling off the Chilean coast.

To confuse the British, von Luckner ordered lifeboats and lifejackets taken from sunken ships to be thrown overboard, ensuring that they were all prominently marked with the raider's name. He also broadcast spurious SOS messages from merchant ships allegedly being attacked by German submarines, deliberately finishing each transmission before completion.

Early in May, a message was received aboard the raider from an unknown source. '*Seeadler* gone down with all flags flying', it read, 'Commander and part of crew taken prisoners and on their way to Montevideo'. The British, it seemed, were playing a game of their own in an attempt to restore confidence in maritime trade.

Sailing by way of Más á Tierra (Robinson Crusoe Island) in the Juan Fernández group, *Seeadler* turned westward. By early June, the raider was to the east of Christmas Island and had learned that the United States of America had declared war on Germany. On 14 June, therefore, the 529grt four-masted schooner *A.B. Johnson* was captured and set ablaze in 1°N 150°W. Built by J. Lindstrom of Aberdeen, Washington, in 1900, the schooner had belonged to Wilson, Brothers & Company of San Francisco.

Owned by the Pacific Freighters Company of San Francisco, the 673grt four-mast schooner *R.C. Slade*—also built by Lindstrom in 1900—was destroyed on 15 June in 2°N 150°W, to be followed on 8 July by the essentially similar 731grt *Manila* (9°N 150°W). This Pacific Freighters Company schooner had been completed in 1899 by Simpson of North Bend, Oregon. *Seeadler* gained as prisoners 45 men, one woman and an opossum.

**Above:** the old Sea Devil—Felix, Graf von Luckner, pictured in the 1930s by Langhammer of Cassel. From a postcard published by 'Ross' B.-V.-G. of Berlin. Author's collection.

After cruising the Doldrums for several weeks without result, von Luckner put into Île Mopélie ('Mopelia Island') one of the Sous le Vent group in the Tahiti archipelago of the Îles de Société. The foul bottom of *Seeadler* needed to be cleaned of weed and barnacles whilst the crew would benefit from a rest.

The end came on 2 August 1917. At about 09:30, according to von Luckner's colourful account, he had—

"noticed a strange bulge on the eastern rim of the sea . . . At first we thought it was a mirage. But it kept growing larger. It came toward us. Then we recognized it—a tidal wave such as is caused by a submarine earthquake and volcanic disturbances. The danger was only too clear. We lay between the island and the wave.

"We dared not raise sail, for then the wind would drive us on the reef. So our only hope of getting clear of the island was our motor. The huge swell of the tidal wave was rushing toward us with breakneck speed.

"The motor didn't stir. The mechanics were working

frantically. They pumped compressed air into the engine. We waited in vain for the sound of ignition . . . By this time the tidal wave was only a few hundred yards away. We were lost."

The impact flung *Seeadler* onto the coral reef, said von Luckner. Masts and rigging had collapsed like matchwood, but the iron hull was sturdy. When the waters of the wave had ebbed, the raider was marooned in 16°53'S 153°55'W. A total wreck, the once proud ship had been dismasted and her hull had been pierced by coral jags.

American prisoners subsequently claimed the truth to have been more prosaic. They stated that most of the German crew—including von Luckner—had been picnicking on the island when *Seeadler* had simply dragged her anchor and run onto the reef to break her back, implying that von Luckner had deliberately coloured his account to cover negligence. Some modern authors have noted, in addition, that records on Tahiti made no mention of any tidal waves in August 1917.

The truth may lie somewhere between the two conflicting accounts; the tidal wave need not have been the 'wall of water' claimed by von Luckner in his memoirs, but could still have been a surge with sufficient power to ground the ship. Whatever the story, however, the survival unscathed of all the prisoners and crew suggests that the end was not one of Wagnerian proportions.

On 23 August, von Luckner and five of his men left in one of *Seeadler*'s 10-metre motor lifeboats, rigged as a sloop and named *Kronprinzessin Cecilie* in an ironic reference to the Atlantic liner of the same name. The goal was to sail by way of the Cook Islands (and if necessary Fiji) to capture a suitable sailing ship, return to Île Mopélie to retrieve the weaponry salvaged from the hulk of *Seeadler*, then continue the raiding cruise.

Masquerading as Dutch-American adventurers bent on crossing the Pacific Ocean for a wager, von Luckner and his men reached Atiu Island in the Cook group on 26 August. No ships were to be seen, so the Germans elected to continue to Aitutaki where, despite posing as Norwegians, their identity was discovered. Von Luckner mustered sufficient presence of mind to effect an escape.

An approach to Rarotonga in the Cook Islands was abandoned when the shape of a large auxiliary cruiser could be seen, riding at anchor without lights. The abandoned steamer had actually run aground on an offshore reef, but this was not obvious to the Germans.

A course was set for the Fijian Islands, accepting the risks of travelling far across the open sea in a tiny boat laden down to the gunwhales. The voyage was nearly von Luckner's last. Lashed by tropical rainstorms, burned by the sun, running short of food and water, ill with scurvy: the Germans eventually made a landfall on Niué, midway between the Cook and Fijian islands. Moving thence to Katafanga in the Tonga group, the little boat eventually reached Wakaya Island—off the Fijian

island of Viti Levu—and another flirtation with a jagged coral reef.

Von Luckner and his men eventually booked passage aboard a trading schooner, laden with a cargo of cloth, silk, preserved vegetables and fresh meat. The vessel even had an auxiliary engine. Before plans to seize the schooner could be executed, however, the steamship *Amra* arrived with armed policemen. Von Luckner refused to let his men fight, though, confronted by only a handful of poorly armed natives, they could undoubtedly have carried the day. Past experience indicated that fighting out of uniform was likely to end in hanging as franc-tireurs or spies. On 21 September 1917, Felix von Luckner and his companions were finally taken prisoner.

On the morning of 23 August, the crewmen and American prisoners remaining on Île Mopélie under the command of Leutnant z.S. d.R. Kling sighted the French barquentine *Lutece*. The French skipper had been snared by sight of the wreck of *Seeadler* and the promise of one-third of the salvage value. His reward was a boat-load of armed German sailors and the loss of his ship. Kling immediately sailed eastward, leaving the American prisoners to fend for themselves.

On 26 August, the 9,750-ton Japanese armoured cruiser *Idzumo* (Sir W.G. Armstrong, Whitworth & Co., 1900), delayed by misinformation proffered by von Luckner, appeared off Mopélie. All the Japanese admiral found were some very relieved Americans.

Kling headed his new ship for Easter Island, intending to refit her for a voyage round the Horn. The vessel, which had once been German-owned, had regained her original name *Fortuna*. On 4 October, however, *Fortuna* hit an uncharted rock and foundered off Easter Island. The crewmen succeeded in getting ashore without loss, but were rounded up by the Chilean authorities and interned on the mainland for the duration of the war.

Von Luckner and his men escaped from captivity in New Zealand on 13 December 1917 in *Pearl*, a motor-boat owned by the commandant of Motuihi detention camp. The boat was 'armed' with a dummy machine-gun, intended for a Christmas theatrical production, which enabled the escapees to capture the coastal trading schooner *Moa*. Unfortunately, the attack was witnessed and immediately reported to the authorities.

*Moa* reached Curtis Island in the Kermadec group on 21 December 1917 to raid provisions stored for shipwrecked mariners, but smoke rising from behind the island testified to the presence of a steamship. Von Luckner ordered the skipper of *Moa* to set full sail but, before any advantage could be gained, the schooner was approached by the armed patrol ship *Iris*—a New Zealand government cable layer in peacetime. The game was up, and von Luckner and his men were speedily ushered back to captivity.

Felix von Luckner eventually got back to Germany in 1919, the last of his crewmen returning in January 1920.

# WOLF

16 May 1916–19 February 1918; thirteen victims (33,335grt, plus one of unknown tonnage).
A converted cargo ship, renowned for undertaking the longest of all raiding cruises and the use
of a seaplane for reconnaissance.

———◆◆◆———

**Type:** Hilfskreuzer.
**Builder:** Flensburger Schiffbau-Gesellschaft (yard no. 331).
Equipped by the Kaiserliche Werft, Wilhelmshaven, in 1916.
**Owner:** Deutsche Dampfschifffahrts-Gesellschaft 'Hansa',
Bremen (named *Wachtfels*).
**Launch date:** 8 March 1913.
**Commissioned:** 16 May 1916.
**Crew:** 16 officers and 331 men.

**Dimensions**
Registered tonnage (grt): 5,809.
Full-load displacement: 11,200 tonnes.
Overall length: 135·0 metres.
Waterline length: 128·0 metres.
Beam: 17·1 metres.
Full-load draught: about 7·8 metres.

**Weapons**
Guns: six 15cm SK L/40 and one 10·5cm SK L/40 (see text).
Maximum range of main armament: about 13,700 metres
(15cm) or 12,200 metres (10·5cm).
Lesser guns: three 5·2cm SK L/55 to arm Hilfsschiffe (see *Iltis*),
and small-arms.
Torpedo tubes: four.
Munitions: 1,200 15cm shells, about 200 10·5cm shells, 465
mines and sixteen 50cm C/08 torpedoes.
Armour protection: none.

**Performance**
Powerplant: one vertical three-cylinder triple expansion steam
engine, supplied by three boilers. One propeller shaft.
Boiler pressure: 13at (191psi).
Coal bunkerage: 6,300 tonnes.
Speed, service maximum: 10·5 knots (2,800ihp).
Range: 32,000 nautical miles at 8 knots.

This raider was slower than even *Möwe* but had a
prodigious service range. Coal consumption at eight
knots was a mere 35 tonnes a day; as the capacity of the
bunkers and holds was 6,000 tonnes, the ship could
theoretically sail for months without refuelling.

*Wolf* had been built shortly before the outbreak of
the First World War for Deutsche Dampfschifffahrts-
Gesellschaft 'Hansa' of Bremen and had sailed under the
name *Wachtfels*. She was a typical three-island freighter
with a lengthy bridge deck amidships, but lacked
the break in the superstructure that characterised the
products of many German yards. *Wachtfels* entered
Wilhelmshaven dockyard in 1916 and emerged with two
15cm guns abaft the forecastle alongside the No. 1 hold;
two 15cm guns abaft the superstructure, alongside No. 3
hold; and a single 10·5cm gun on the poop. Single
torpedo-tubes were added alongside No. 2 hold.

Excepting for the gun on the poop, all the weaponry
was concealed behind hinged bulkheads. A searchlight
was fitted to a collapsible gantry on the boat deck behind
the funnel, ahead of a smaller unit, mounted on rails, that
could be moved from beam to beam. The range-finder
was also on the boat deck. Telescoping top masts allowed
the appearance of the ship to be altered, and a powerful
wireless transmitter/receiver was fitted.

*Wachtfels* emerged from refurbishment as *Wolf*, with
a black hull, black funnel and dark grey uppers—though
large quantities of paint were carried to effect disguise
during cruises. She was tried briefly as a submarine
depot ship in the summer of 1916, under the name *Jupiter*,
but was recommissioned as a raider on 29 November.

Before the first ocean cruise began, two extra 15cm
guns were added in embrasures beneath the forecastle
(cf., *Möwe*) and additional torpedo tubes were added aft
alongside No. 4 hold. The guns had all been taken from
the casemates of disarmed battleships of the Zähringen
class and, therefore, lacked protective shields. With a
range of 13,700 metres, they were more than powerful
enough for use against merchant shipping; indeed, they
provided a threat against British cruisers as they
outranged many elderly 6-inch guns.

Perhaps most interestingly of all, *Wolf* was to carry
a Friedrichshafen FF.33e seaplane to improve scouting

*Wolf*. Drawing by John Walter.

**Above:** one of the forward starboard 15cm guns aboard *Wolf*, taken from a disarmed Zähringen-class battleship. Though the guns were old, they packed a hefty punch. Courtesy of the Bayerisches Hauptstaatsarchiv IV, Staudinger Sammlung.

capabilities. The German admiralty realised that the new raider would be too slow to overhaul a fast cargo ship, and could not outrun a warship. The seaplane would provide early warning of danger and divert merchant ships into the raider's path.

Command of the raiding freighter was given to Korvettenkapitän Karl August Nerger, a regular officer whose previous ship had been the light cruiser *Stettin*. Nerger was not in the same mould as the urbane von Dohna-Schlodien; he spoke no English and was known to be something of an Anglophobe. But he was courageous, dogged and resourceful, and his crew had been carefully chosen. The first lieutenant, Kapitänleutnant d.R. Schmehl, spoke English well and had once been awarded a Royal Humane Society medal for an act of bravery aboard a burning British explosives ship in Calcutta. One of the prize officers, Kapitänleutnant Rose, had even been a member of Richmond Lawn Tennis Club prior to 1914.

Two experienced seaplane pilots, Leutnant z.S. d.R. Matthäus Stein and Oberflugmeister Paul Fabeck, arrived on 9 November in company with Flugzeug-Obermaschinistenmaat Remy. Two days later, the pilots were sent to collect a brand-new FF.33e from the manufacturer's Warnemünde factory.

On 16 November the seaplane landed alongside *Wolf*, which had steamed out of Kiel to preserve the element of secrecy. Much to the surprise of Stein, Fabeck and Remy, the raider's crew immediately began to dismantle the FF.33e. It was stowed on deck under a tarpaulin but, unfortunately, on 17 November, the wings were crushed by the blast of the guns during firing practice. Repairs were effected that night at a local airfield, the wings being returned to the ship before dawn. As the delicate structures could no longer be kept safely on deck, the wings were stowed in No. 4 hold and the fuselage was hidden in a specially built deck-house on the poop.

Nerger was instructed to lay mines, then cruise the Indian and Pacific Oceans—giving the shipping lanes a wide berth on the outward voyage. On 24 November, *Wolf* started out from Kiel but soon returned with a fire in a coal bunker. Nerger tried again on the last day of the month, but was foiled by fog until evening.

*Wolf* headed out into the North Sea, travelling at a maximum speed of merely ten knots. Fortunately, the weather was bad and Nerger managed to elude Royal Navy patrols. By 2 December 1916, he was clear of the British blockade and lay off Rockall.

By 17 January 1917 *Wolf* had reached the southern tip of Africa, where the lights of a distant convoy escorted by an armoured cruiser caused her to turn farther south for safety. Mines were laid off the Cape of Good Hope, then off Bombay and Colombo by the middle of February. These soon caused the loss of the British steamships *Worcestershire* (7,175grt) and *Perseus* (6,728grt), on 17 and 21 February respectively. By this time, Nerger had steamed off southward until he had positioned *Wolf* to intercept ships plying the sea lanes linking southern Africa with Bombay, or Aden with the Sunda Straits.

On 26 November, Nerger decided to assemble the Friedrichshafen seaplane. The components were taken out of their hiding places, but the heat and humidity encountered in the tropics had warped the wings. Remy attempted to use his tools to re-align them, but was defeated by the rolling of the ship; adjustments were then undertaken by eye and prayer. The task was complicated by the size of the FF.33e, which had a wing span of 16·75 metres. By late afternoon, work on the the seaplane had been completed. As evening fell, Matthäus Stein was ordered to start the engine. To everyone's relief the 150hp six cylinder Benz Bz.III burst into life immediately.

At 06:25 on 27 February 1917, the 5,528grt British steamship *Turritella* was spotted, and, after a short chase, stopped by a shot across the bows at 08:00 in 8°40′N 63°15′E. The captive was particularly interesting, as she had been completed in 1906 by Flensburger Schiffbau-Gesellschaft. Christened *Gutenfels* and owned by Deutsche Dampfschifffahrts-Gesellschaft 'Hansa' of Bremen—one-time owners of *Wolf*—*Gutenfels* had been interned in Port Said in August 1914, then impressed into British service as *Polavon*. She had been converted into the oil tanker *Turritella* in 1916 and was managed for the Royal Navy (as 'Oiler No. 147') by the Anglo-Saxon Petroleum Co. Ltd of London.

The captive ship was manned by a prize crew, given 25 mines and a 5·2cm gun, and told to sail for Aden. When the British captain boasted that the cruise of *Wolf* would be short, as HMS *Newcastle* was in the area, Nerger decided to send the seaplane aloft to keep watch. At 14:30, the FF.33e was swung over the side and christened *Wölfchen* (wolfcub) by smashing a bottle of

champagne on the propeller. Stein balanced on one of the floats to prime the engine whilst Fabeck swung the magneto crank. The engine sprang to life, whereupon the seaplane taxied away from the ship amid loud cheers.

The FF.33e was not especially fast, being capable of only 119km/hr (74·5mph), and took nearly thirty minutes to climb to 1,500 metres. Yet Stein and Fabeck were given such a breathtaking view of their surroundings that they were overcome with elation and offered three cheers to the Friedrichshafen company into the slipstream. Fabeck then made an elegant landing and taxied back to the ship at the head of a flotilla of ever-hopeful sharks. *Wölfchen* was hoisted back aboard *Wolf* and the pilots reported that the British cruiser was nowhere to be seen.

The flight was repeated the next morning. Two ships were spotted, but were well outside the area that *Wolf* could command. By the afternoon, both merchantmen had disappeared from sight. The disappointed pilots requested permission to bomb ships in an attempt to stop them, but, initially at least, Nerger refused.

Nerger then set a south-westerly course and headed for Australasia. On 1 March, lookouts aboard *Wolf* spotted a steamship on the horizon and *Wölfchen* was lowered overboard to prevent blast damage should the raider open fire. This did not satisfy Stein and Fabeck, who promptly took off. As the raider fired a shot to stop the 4,152grt British steamship *Jumna* in 8°9′N 62°E, the seaplane came swooping down and circled ready to bomb the steamer if necessary. *Jumna* obligingly hove-to, though elation about the capture was tempered by a

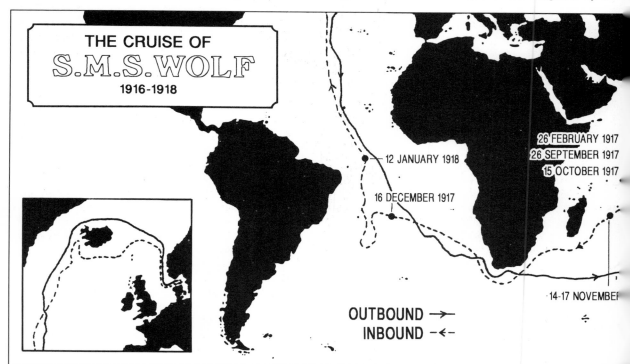

THE CRUISE OF
S.M.S. WOLF
1916-1918

12 JANUARY 1918

16 DECEMBER 1917

26 FEBRUARY 1917
26 SEPTEMBER 1917
15 OCTOBER 1917

14-17 NOVEMBER

OUTBOUND →
INBOUND ←

serious accident aboard the raider; the port after gun had been fired before it had been trained outboard, killing five German seamen and injuring more than twenty others.

*Jumna* had been completed by Bartram & Sons of Sunderland in 1902, and was owned by the Mercantile Steam Ship Co. Ltd of London. She was shepherded along until the most valuable of the stores had been removed, but met her end on 4 March.

*Iltis*, formerly *Turritella*, eventually laid her mines on the night of 4/5 March 1917. During the afternoon of 5 March, however, the sloop HMS *Odin* approached her. As the warship carried six 4-inch guns, *Iltis* was scuttled at 16:50 to prevent her reverting to British hands. The point at which she sank—west south-west of Aden—was given as 12°30′N 43°48′E in *Odin*'s log, but is now accepted to have been 12°26′N 44°12′E. Unfortunately for Nerger, Chinese crewmen gave detailed descriptions of *Wolf* to British interrogators. It was time to leave.

Nerger decided to put the seaplane over the side before approaching any potential victim, as the presence of the FF.33e on deck would not only attract attention but also compromise the disguise of *Wolf* as a humble merchantman. Stein and Fabeck were less happy about the arrangement, doggedly arguing that they should play a more active role. The seaplane had an endurance of 5–6 hours and could be put to better use than a mere reconnaissance tool.

At 09:30 on 11 March, about 680 miles east of the Seychelles, smoke was sighted on the horizon. Stein and Fabeck were immediately sent to investigate, returning to

26 AUGUST 1917

23 MAY-11 JUNE 1917

16/17 JUNE 1917

27 JULY 1917

10-12 JULY 1917

MARCH 1917

25-27 APRIL 1917

report that the ship was a merchantman. The FF.33e was hoisted back aboard and *Wolf* set off in pursuit. The seaplane was lowered over the side again at 12:30, bobbing around for several hours before *Wolf* signalled that she was within striking distance. The pilots started the engine and took off toward the distant raider. As *Wolf* fired a warning shot across the bows of the Shakespear Shipping Co. Ltd steamer *Wordsworth* (3,509grt), Stein and Fabeck swept low across the decks ready to bomb if necessary. However, the steamship, completed in 1915 by W. Gray & Co. Ltd of West Hartlepool, obligingly stopped in 4°30′S 67°E with a cargo of rice.

The vastness of the Indian Ocean allowed Nerger to proceed at a leisurely pace, taking only a few tons of rice from the new prize before sinking her on 18 March by the well-tried combination of open sea-cocks and explosives.

The seaplane, which had made fourteen flights in the Indian Ocean, was dismantled on 16 March and stored in No. 4 hold. Stein, Fabeck, Remy and the crew of the raider had kept the FF.33e in surprisingly good flying order, though minor damage to struts, snapped rigging wires and ripped fabric had been regular occurrences. Fortunately, repairs had all been straightforward and the engine had shown itself to be a model of reliability.

On 31 March, *Wolf* overhauled the three-masted barque *Dee* (1,169grt), bound for Perth in Western Australia. Built by Russell & Company of Port Glasgow in 1885, the barque was owned by Le Nouveau Chantier Ltd and registered in St Louis, Mauritius. Captain John Rugg hoisted the Red Ensign, signalling 'Report me all well'. In response, *Wolf* hoisted 'German cruiser. Stop immediately'. The barque was sunk 410 miles west by south of Cape Leeuwin, an isolated success in an isolated area. Nerger then sailed south of Australia without encountering the grain-ships he had hoped to destroy.

*Wölfchen* was reassembled on 23 May, making four flights in an unsuccessful search of prizes. On 27 May, *Wolf* had reached Sunday (or Rabaul) Island, the most northerly of the Kermadec Group, some six hundred miles north north-east of New Zealand. After anchoring his ship for maintenance, Nerger anxiously ordered the seaplane into the air on 2 June; a plume of smoke had been spotted on the horizon, followed by two masts and a wireless aerial. As a boiler had been dismantled for repair, *Wolf* could make no more than six knots.

Nerger needed to know whether the newcomer was an auxiliary warship, and had to prevent a merchantman escaping. He also ordered Stein and Fabeck to stop the ship if they could. This was what the pilots had been eagerly awaiting.

*Wölfchen* took off at 15:30 and climbed to a thousand metres above and behind the target, a black-hulled steamship with buff upperworks and a single black-topped red funnel. Stein opened the throttle and skimmed down the length of the ship at an altitude of sixty metres whilst Fabeck heaved weighted canvas message bags over the side. The surprise aboard *Wairuna* of the Union Steamship Company of New Zealand Ltd was complete. Some of the crew had never seen an aeroplane.

One bag was taken to the bridge. Curiously, Captain Hammand opened it. To his astonishment the message read 'Order, stear [sic] south to German cruiser. Do not use wireless. If not obeying orders you will be shelled by bombs'. To reinforce the message, when *Wairuna* slowed but did not stop, Fabeck dropped a bomb into the sea only thirty metres from her bow.

Any thoughts Hammand may have entertained about running disappeared when *Wolf* weighed anchor and headed out from Sunday Island. At 16:05, the boarding party arrived to take possession of the 3,947grt 1904-vintage steamship—built on Tyneside by Armstrong, Whitworth & Co. Ltd—which was loaded with cheese, meat, milk and 1,200 tons of coal: 'more precious to us than our daily bread' opined Nerger as he presented a captured New Zealand flag to his pilots.

*Wairuna* was brought back to Sunday Island and anchored to leeward, the intention being to transfer provisions to *Wolf*. Excepting the skipper, the officers and much of the crew were immediately transferred to the raider. Transhipment continued until 7 June, the anchorage occasionally being moved as prevailing winds fluctuated. Parties were sent ashore through the heavy surf to collect fresh water and fruit. On 5 June, unnoticed, the chief officer and second engineer of *Turritella* had escaped over the side of the raider, apparently intending to swim ashore. They were never seen again.

The seaplane was severely damaged by sparks from the funnel on 5 June, and then in a gale five days later. Fifty-knot winds tore off the ailerons, forcing the resourceful crew of the raider to build new parts from cigar boxes and tea chests.

At 18:00 on 16 June, *Wolf* and *Wairuna* got under way, the latter being prepared for scuttling. However, no sooner had Nerger hauled out from Sunday Island than *Wölfchen* sighted a small four-masted schooner. The weighted message bags either fell to leeward or bounced off the sails into the water, so Stein dropped a bomb off the schooner's bow from an altitude of 75 metres and Fabeck, after executing a skilful landing, taxied *Wölfchen* alongside. Stein then climbed out on the rear decking of the fuselage, brandishing a Parabellum pistol, and persuaded the astonished Captain Orville Fredericks to steer his ship towards *Wolf*. The seaplane took off and circled overhead to ensure that the instructions were followed to the letter.

The schooner proved to be 567grt *Winslow*, built in 1899 by Hall Brothers of Port Blakely, Washington. Owned by G.E. Billings of San Francisco, she had been bound for Samoa out of Sydney with a few hundred tons of coal, firebricks and petrol. This came as no surprise, as the German wireless operators had intercepted wireless messages between Apia and Sydney initially offering the information that *Winslow* was ready for orders and then confirming that the schooner had left harbour.

At 07:45 on 17 June, *Wairuna* was scuttled by a combination of opened sea cocks, explosive charges and sixteen 15cm shells fired into the waterline to hasten her demise. The FF.33e was dismantled again and returned to No. 4 hold.

*Nerger* remained at sea, intending to use *Winslow* as a decoy, but nothing untoward happened. On 20 March, therefore, the schooner was taken back to Sunday Island to be stripped of her provisions. Two days later, the vessel was towed back out to sea and four scuttling charges were fired. In a pointless attempt to bring down the masts and spars, nearly forty 15cm shells were expended. *Wolf* finally steamed off in the early evening, leaving the hulk of *Winslow* still burning.

Mines were laid off New Zealand during the night of 25/26 June, to foul the passage between Three Kings Island and the North Island mainland. The raider then made off southward toward Cook Strait, where fifty more mines were sown on the evening of 26/27 June. On 3 July, seventeen of an intended total of 25 more mines were laid by Gabo Island, a few miles south-west of Cape Howe on the eastern coast of Australia. The procedure had been interrupted by the unexpected appearance of a convoy escorted by a warship tentatively identified as HMS *Encounter*, forcing the raider to run for safety. The first victim of the minefield was *Cumberland* (9,471grt) which sank on 6 July south-west of Gabo Island.

*Wolf* then steamed north-eastward, out past Lord Howe Island and into the Pacific Ocean. By 9 July, Nerger had reached 26°42′S 166°40′E, capturing the American sailing ship *Beluga*\* with a cargo of case oil. Supplies of benzine were to be taken aboard the raider; the petrol would be useful to turn *Beluga* into a conflagration. No sooner had the prize crew gone aboard than smoke was sighted on the horizon and Nerger, ever cautious, steamed off. At 06:30 on 10 July, *Wölfchen* was sent aloft to ensure that nothing could prevent *Wolf* returning to reclaim her victim. On 11 July, *Beluga* was sunk by gunfire.

On 12 July, while readying for take off, the seaplane was struck by a wave that damaged the starboard float. The pilots noticed the problem only when they were airborne. At the end of their search mission, Fabeck landed *Wölfchen* with such a deft touch that the seaplane had almost come to a halt when the struts supporting the starboard float collapsed. As the FF.33e began to sink, Stein and Fabeck climbed onto the tail to await rescue. First-class seamanship then allowed *Wolf* to retrieve the seaplane before it could founder.

The lower wing was shattered, the starboard float had been torn away, the propeller had splintered, and the engine had suffered total immersion in seawater. Yet the value of *Wölfchen* was so great that Nerger ordered his

\* As no mention of this vessel could be found in Lloyd's registers, it is assumed that she was comparatively small—possibly even less than 100grt.

**Above:** the seaplane *Wölfchen* pictured aboard the raider, freshly painted after the return to Kiel.
Photograph by courtesy of the Bayerisches Hauptstaatsarchiv IV, Staudinger Sammlung.

crew to rebuild the seaplane as quickly as possible. Ubiquitous cigar boxes and tea chests provided ribs for the wings, whilst seasoned wood planks were shaped into struts for the wings and floats. The engine was stripped down, cleaned, greased, and reassembled so successfully that it ran better than it had done when new. On 27 July, to the relief of everyone aboard, *Wölfchen* made a successful trial flight.

13 July had brought the four masted barque *Encore* (651grt), built in 1897 by A.M. Simpson of North Bend, Oregon, for the Simpson Lumber Company and registered in San Francisco. Captain Palmgren was bound for Sydney from the Colombia river with a cargo of wood. The barque was taken to the east of the Îles Loyauté ('Loyalty islands') in 21°S 169°E. Knowing that wood-carrying ships were notoriously difficult to sink, Nerger ordered oil to be poured over *Encore*'s decks before she was set ablaze. *Wolf* was then steered north west, bypassing Fiji and the Solomon Islands until the raider was close to what had been Kaiser Wilhelm Land (German New Guinea) until captured by Australian forces. The seaplane was sent up daily from 25 July to 6 August whilst the raider waited to pounce on her lure.

On 28 July 1917, wireless operators aboard *Wolf* reported a message, sent in clear, that read 'Burns Philp Rabaul. Donaldson left Sydney on the 27th via Newcastle Brisbane with 340 tons piece goods, 500 tons Westport coal for Rabaul and 236 tons piece goods for Madang. [signed] Burns'.

Nerger knew that Burns, Philp & Co. Ltd were shipowners, and that a British governor had been appointed in the former German colonial town of Rabaul in the Bismarck archipelago. A ship would shortly be coming the way of the raider. At 20:00 on 29 July, a message was received that the steamship *Matunga* had arrived at Brisbane and would be off Cape Moreton on the following Monday. On 5 August, another message was heard; Donaldson would arrive in Rabaul at 07:00 the next morning.

At 19:45 on 5 August, *Wölfchen* finally sighted the 1,618grt *Matunga*, completed by Napier & Miller Ltd of Glasgow in 1900. One of the most distinctive features of Burns, Philp & Company ships was the black funnel, which had a two-row black and white chequerboard band with a white edge. Lookouts straining into the gathering gloom on the raider were relieved to see a white Very Light arc across the sky far to the south, followed by a red and another white. *Wölfchen* had found the quarry, returning to make an immaculate landing without the assistance of marker flares.

The steamer could be seen on the horizon from 22:00. *Wolf* turned to follow, lowering the seaplane overboard in the early hours of the morning. At 07:00, the raider and her aerial scout forced *Matunga* to stop. The boarding party went over. When Kapitänleutnant Rose reached the bridge, the British skipper appeared. Rose nonchalantly asked Donaldson about the five hundred tons of Westport coal and the steamer captain was suitably dumbstruck.

The German officer soon discovered that the ship was carrying not only the acting governor of the captured territory to Rabaul, but also a large quantity of bicycles and the entire liquor supply for the colony for a month.

The administrator and some of the bicycles were immediately transferred to *Wolf*, whereupon the raider and her prize headed north-west by west to anchor on 14 August in an isolated harbour on Waigeo Island. *Wölfchen* had been sent to survey the anchorage and ensure that no hostile ships were in the area.

Here Nerger ordered the erection of a temporary wireless station, preventing the undetected approach of an enemy whilst the transhipment of supplies from *Matunga* was organised. The raider's engine and boilers were stripped for cleaning, and divers were sent down to scrape the ship's bottom. Fouling had increased so greatly during the lengthy cruise in warm waters that at least a knot had been subtracted from *Wolf*'s already meagre top speed.

Finally, on 26 August, the ships put to sea again. Charges were fired to scuttle *Matunga* about twelve miles off the New Guinea coast and the raider resumed her voyage westward, passing the Celebes on 29 August to enter the Java Sea a day later. After sailing unchallenged within hailing distance of a British cruiser, Nerger laid the last of his mines—more than a hundred of them—off Singapore on the night of 2/3 September. Doubling back into the Java Sea and out into the Indian Ocean through the Lombok Straits, *Wolf* turned for home.

On 26 September, Nerger ordered *Wölfchen* to be reassembled. The airframe was still sound, but the fabric covering was in very poor repair. Stein and Fabeck risked a take-off, returning an hour later to report the sighting of a large merchantman in One-and-a-Half Degree Channel, separating the atolls of Haddumahti and Huvadu (Suvadiva) in the Maldives. The FF.33e was refuelled, several small bombs were taken aboard, and Stein and Fabeck were cast adrift in customary fashion.

However, as *Wolf* closed, smoke billowed from the single funnel of *Hitachi Maru* (6,557grt) of Nippon Yusen KK. Captain Tominaga was clearly intent on ignoring the German ensign hoisted on the mainmast and the signal 'Stop immediately. Do not use your wireless' that fluttered above the raider's bridge. Emergency signals were being broadcast frantically, so two rounds were fired across the bows of the Japanese vessel. Transmissions continued. As a gun was being cleared at the stern of *Hitachi Maru*, Nerger ordered his gunners to open fire in earnest whilst the German wireless operators tried to jam the Japanese signals. In the blink of an eye, four salvoes of 15cm shells had slammed into their target; fourteen of the steamer's crew had been killed and six were injured. To add to the confusion, Stein and Fabeck dropped three bombs into the sea alongside the badly damaged steamer as she finally hove-to. The last bomb allegedly blew two crewmen overboard.

Meanwhile, the engine of the seaplane had begun to knock so badly that the pilots made an emergency landing, only to discover that all but four of the bolts holding the propeller had sheared through. The scout was towed back to *Wolf* and the damage—ascribed to buffeting caused by shellfire—was speedily repaired.

The boarding party found that *Hitachi Maru* was carrying copper, silk and provisions, and that there were several women aboard. The passengers and most of the Japanese crewmen were transferred to the raider, the steamer was put under the command of a prize crew, and the two ships moved westward in company. Some weeks later, Captain Tominaga, haunted by the surrender of his ship, vanished overboard and was lost.

On 27 September, *Wolf* and *Hitachi Maru* hove-to off Dewadu island in the southernmost or Huvadu atolls of the Maldives. The ships were lashed together and the transfer of supplies commenced. The Germans were particularly keen to see if bales of silk could replace the damaged fabric on *Wölfchen*'s wings. The seaplane was still being sent into the air as a scout, but performance was suffering as the wings became increasingly ragged.

On 3 October, *Wolf* steamed away to search for a suitable collier. On the morning of 6 October, the seaplane reappeared ahead of *Wolf* to tell *Hitachi Maru* to raise steam ready to leave the anchorage. The two ships then set course for Coco Island, to the west of Cargados Carajos group, six hundred miles east of Madagascar. Nerger was confident of eluding the Japanese cruiser *Tsushima*, known to be searching for the missing freighter, while he removed the last of the things he needed. Finally, on 6 November, *Hitachi Maru* was scuttled in deep water and *Wolf* steamed off alone.

The seaplane was repaired with linen taken from *Matunga* and lacquer from *Hitachi Maru*, but the combination was ineffectual. By 15 October, *Wölfchen*, deemed no longer airworthy, was dismantled again. At about 06:30 on 10 November, *Wolf* spotted a steamship running with lights blazing and immediately stopped the Spanish *Igotz Mendi*. Ship's papers revealed that the vessel was owned by Compañia Navigación Sota y Aznar and registered in Bilbao, where she had been completed in 1916 by Euskalduna de Construción Maritima SA. A search revealed that the supposedly neutral ship had left Lourenço Marques on 4 November with 5,500 tons of coal bound for the Royal Navy dockyard in Colombo. Thus the collier was seized and taken under the supervision of a prize crew to Coco Island. *Wolf* and *Igotz Mendi* were lashed together to facilitate the transfer of coal and, by 17 November, a thousand tonnes had been transhipped—no mean feat in the prevailing swell. Both ships were then painted grey.

Entirely renewed with a covering of raw silk, the FF.33e was reassembled on 14 November 1917. The first two reconnaissance flights were unremarkable, small tears in the silk being repaired easily enough; on the third

**Above:** *Wolf* at sea. Author's collection.

flight, however, the covering began to disintegrate in a squall. Huge holes in the fabric were visible from the decks of *Wolf*; Stein and Fabeck seemed in grave danger. Somehow Fabeck, who had proved to be an excellent pilot, brought the seaplane down safely close to the raider. Damage to the fabric was so bad that *Wölfchen* was taken apart and replaced in No. 4 hold.

Tests undertaken aboard *Wolf* with fabric taken from *Hitachi Maru* showed that heavy silk known as Atlas Cloth made an excellent covering when treated with a combination of deck paint and lacquer. The skin of the seaplane was renewed for a second time and the FF.33E subsequently flew without difficulty.

Early in December, Nerger seized the three-masted barque *John H. Kirby* (1,395grt), completed in Britain in 1879 by the Whitehaven Ship Building Co. Ltd but owned by W.B. Gillican of New Orleans by 1917. The vessel had been bound for Port Natal from New York under Captain Joseph Swensson, but was scuttled once the crew had been taken off. On 5 December, *Wolf* rejoined *Igotz Mendi*. The two ships rounded the Cape of Good Hope together and set a course across the south Atlantic towards Ilha la Trindade. On the way, *Wolf* sank *Maréchal Davout* (2,192grt) of Société Nouvelle d'Armement. Completed in 1898 by Ateliers et Chantiers 'Loire' of Nantes, the three-masted barque had been bound for Dakar from Melbourne with a cargo of Australian wheat.

The FF.33e was assembled again on 16 December for a flight over Trindade to ensure that no hostile warships were in the area. After three more brief missions, without result, *Wölfchen* was stowed on deck until dismantled and returned to No. 4 hold on 12 January 1918.

Periodic interceptions of wireless transmissions, including some from hostile warships, sent shivers down the spines of Nerger and his men. One received on 19 December indicated the proximity of Royal Navy cruisers, so *Wolf* and *Igotz Mendi* immediately steamed southward away from Trindade. By Christmas Day 1917, the ships were seven hundred miles east of Montevideo. Coaling was attempted, but the raider was damaged by the buffeting from the collier and sprang several plates. Only a few tonnes of coal could be transferred before the operation was abandoned.

By 30 December, the ships were sailing northward up the Atlantic. On 4 January 1918, *Wolf* stopped and then sank the Norwegian four-masted barque *Størebror* (2,050grt), sailing in ballast from Beira to Montevideo and La Plata. Owned by A/S 'Excelsior' of Christiansand, the vessel had been built in 1891 by A. Stephen & Sons of Glasgow for the County Shipping Company of London—which provided a poor excuse for her destruction, even by the Anglophobic Nerger.

By this time, *Igotz Mendi* was carrying some married prisoners and many neutral passengers. Nerger showed little of the inclination of some of his predecessors to send captives into the nearest neutral port on humanitarian grounds, believing that this would compromise *Wolf*'s security. Instead, he was determined to send the Spanish ship back to Germany.

In the last week of January, lookouts spotted two very large grey-painted ships crossing the path of the raider some miles ahead. No signals were exchanged, as Nerger believed the ships to be carrying men of the US Army to Europe and suspected that there would be a heavily armed escort in the vicinity. The Spanish chief officer aboard *Igotz Mendi* took the opportunity to pitch the scuttling charges left aboard his ship over the side, which so infuriated the commander of the German prize crew that he promptly sentenced the Spaniard to three years in a German prison.

By early February, *Wolf* and her prize had reached the northern limits of their voyage and were ready to run down the coast of Norway as soon as conditions proved favourable. *Igotz Mendi* sailed to the north-west of Iceland on 7 February, but was turned back at the Arctic Circle by pack ice. This delayed progress until the Norwegian coast was spotted on 21 February. Her southward voyage was thereafter slow but steady, then north-east into the Skaggerak and down the Kattegat to Kiel. At 15:20 on 24 February, in thick fog, *Igotz Mendi* ran aground on the Danish coast. By 20:15, the fog had cleared sufficiently for a Danish gunboat to come alongside. The game was up at last.

The Danes landed the passengers in the lifeboats, allowing them to return on 28 February to recover their baggage. *Igotz Mendi* was still stuck fast.

*Wolf* had a happier experience, braving ice and fog to reach Germany on 19 February 1918 after 452 days away. Nerger estimated that his ship had covered 64,000 miles or roughly two and a half times the circumference of the globe. His achievement had been worthy of the acclamation given by the people of Kiel, who thronged the seaside promenade in their thousands to welcome the return of a ship that had long since been given up as lost. Stein and Fabeck insisted on flying the reassembled *Wölfchen*—freshly painted with her name, Cross Patée insignia and navy number '841'—to Kiel naval air station, showing that the seaplane was still airworthy after a fifteen month cruise.

The achievement of Nerger and his men was remarkable. They had proved that, properly handled, a raider of comparatively limited offensive power and unusually low speed could survive unscathed for long periods if supported by a seaplane to provide early warning of potential threats. But *Wolf* had returned at an unhappy time for Germany. The lessons of her cruise were no longer relevant, as the Kaiserliche Marine had fallen prey to months of inactivity; revolution, not celebration, was in the air.

*Wolf* was eventually ceded to France, arriving in Brest in April 1919. After an extensive refit, the vessel was bought by Compagnie Messageries Maritimes of Paris and served from 1921 as *Antinous*. The once famous raider was eventually scrapped in Italy in 1931.

**Below:** prisoners aboard *Wolf* disembark into captivity after the return of the raider to Kiel in February 1918. Note *Wölfchen* on No. 4 hold and the aftermost 15cm port gun covered with a tarpaulin. Photograph by courtesy of the Bayerisches Hauptstaatsarchiv IV, Staudinger Sammlung.

# APPENDICES

A concise directory of the less significant merchant raiders,
and information about the ships which were either sunk by the raiders or used
for their own purposes.

# 1: LESSER RAIDERS

Note: unless stated otherwise, no victims
were taken during the raiding cruises.

## BERLIN

Hilfskreuzer, also known as *Hilfskreuzer C.*
Builder: AG 'Weser', Bremen (yard no. 164).
Equipped by the Kaiserliche Werft,
Wilhelmshaven, 1914.
Owner: Norddeutscher Lloyd, Bremen.
Launch date: 7 November 1908.
Maiden voyage: May 1909.
Commissioned: 18 September 1914.
Crew: not known (about 310?).
**Dimensions**
Registered tonnage (grt): 17,324.
Design displacement: 23,700 tonnes.
Full-load displacement: 26,000 tonnes.
Overall length: 186·8 metres.
Waterline length: 182·7 metres.
Beam: 21·2 metres.
Full-load draught: about 8·8 metres.
**Weapons**
Guns: six 10·5cm SK C/88 L/40.
Maximum range of main guns: 12,200 metres.
Lesser guns: four 3·7mm cannon and
small-arms.
Munitions: 200 mines.
Armour protection: only on gun shields.
**Performance**
Powerplant: two vertical four-cylinder
quadruple expansion steam engines, supplied
by seven boilers. Two propeller shafts.
Boiler pressure: 15·5at (227psi).
Coal bunkerage: 4000 tonnes.
Speed, maximum: 19·0 knots (16,000ihp).
Speed, service: 17·5 knots (14,000ihp).
Range: 4,000 nautical miles at 10 knots.
**Career** The pre-war passenger ship was
commissioned to act primarily as a minelayer,
but her captain—Korvettenkapitän
Pfundheller—was given leave to raid merchant
shipping once the mines had been laid. Two of
the guns were mounted on the forecastle
ahead of the forward cargo hold, side by side;
two were fitted port and starboard abaft the
foremast; and the third pair was mounted in
the break between the superstructure and
after deck-house alongside the after hold.

The first sortie from Bremerhaven was
made at 23:00 on 21 September 1914, but the
moonlight was so bright that Pfundheller
decided to return to port at 08:00 on 22
September after travelling a mere eighty
nautical miles.

A second sortie began on 16 October. On
19 October *Berlin* passed between the Faeroes
and Iceland, steamed westward to 56°N 20°W
and then set a course eastward for the north
coast of Ireland. By 22 October, she was off
the Aran islands. As the coastal lighthouses
had been extinguished, Pfundheller decided
not to risk approaching the Clyde
estuary—his designated target—and instead

laid his mines off Tory Island. There they
accounted for the steamer *Manchester
Commerce* and the battleship *Audacious*, on
26 and 28 October respectively, and were not
cleared until the autumn of 1917.

By 1 November *Berlin* was in position off
the Norwegian coast to threaten the sea lanes
between Britain and northern Russia.
Pfundheller was too nervous of being seen to
be an effectual raider-captain, cruising around
for more than two weeks without achieving
anything. At 09:00 on 17 November, almost
out of coal, he put into Trondheim harbour.
**Fate** Owing to the presence of guns, the
Norwegian authorities regarded *Berlin* as an
auxiliary warship, granting Pfundheller a stay
in port of merely 24 hours. On 18 November,
the German ship submitted to internment.
*Berlin* returned to Bremerhaven in June 1919,
but was ceded to Britain in December. After
an extensive refit she became *Arabic* of the
White Star Line and was eventually sent for
scrapping in Italy in December 1931.

## CORMORAN

Hilfskreuzer, formerly *Ryazan.*
Builder: Friedr. Schichau AG, Elbing (yard no.
831). Equipped by the Gouvernments-Werft,
Tsingtau, 1914.
Owner: Russian Volunteer Fleet Association.
Launch date: March 1909.
Completion date: 30 November 1909
Commissioned: 7 August 1914.
Crew: 18–22 officers and 334 men.
**Dimensions**
Registered tonnage (grt): 3,522 as built.
Design displacement: 5,200 tonnes.
Full-load displacement: 7,250 tonnes.
Overall length: 104·0 metres.
Length (bp): 101·8 metres.
Beam: 13·7 metres.
Full-load draught: about 5·8 metres.
**Weapons**
Guns: eight 10·5cm SK C/88 L/40.
Maximum range of main guns: 12,200 metres.
Lesser guns: small-arms only.
Munitions: 1,200 10·5cm shells.
Armour protection: only on gun shields.
**Performance**
Powerplant: one vertical three-cylinder triple
expansion steam engine, supplied by four
boilers. One propeller shaft.
Boiler pressure: 14·5at (211psi).
Coal bunkerage: 2,500 tonnes.
Speed, trials: 16·42 knots (4,882ihp).*
Speed, service maximum: 14 knots (4,000ihp).
Range: 13,500 nautical miles at 14 knots.
* Note: figure for *Orel.*
**Career** This Russian steamship, one of five
sisters built in 1908–9, was captured by *Emden*
(q.v.) on 4 August 1914 in 35°05′N 129°29′W,
the first prize to be gained by the Kaiserliche
Marine in the First World War. She was
converted into a merchant cruiser and
unsuccessfully roved the Pacific Ocean in
search of victims. The guns were mounted in

pairs alongside the holds, before and abaft the
masts. The ship was apparently painted
mid-grey overall, though she originally had a
black hull separated from red boot-topping by
a thin white line. The funnels were once buff,
but, by 1914, had acquired black tops.
**Fate** Running short of coal, *Ryazan* was
interned in Guam on 14 December 1914.
Once war had been declared on Germany, the
US authorities attempted to seize the ship.
After a short struggle, the crew managed to
scuttle at 08:09 on 7 April 1917 in 13°24′N
144°38′E; seven Germans were killed.

## GEIER

Hilfsschiff, later Hilfskreuzer.
Builder: W. Hamilton & Co. Ltd, Glasgow
(yard no. 288). Equipped by *Möwe*, 1916.
Owner: British & Foreign Steam Ship Co. Ltd,
Liverpool (named *Saint Theodore*).
Launch date: 22 April 1913.
Commissioned: 14 December 1916 (as
'Hilfsschiff'), 28 December 1916
('Hilfskreuzer').
Crew: 2 officers and 46 men.
**Dimensions**
Registered tonnage (grt): 4,992.
Full-load displacement: 9,700 tonnes.
Overall length: 127·2 metres.
Waterline length: 123·5 metres.
Beam: 15·9 metres.
Full-load draught: about 6·4 metres.
**Weapons**
Guns: two 5·2cm SK L/55.
Maximum range of main guns: 7,500 metres?
Lesser guns: small-arms only.
Munitions: 300 5·2cm shells.
Armour protection: none.
**Performance**
Powerplant: one vertical three-cylinder triple
expansion steam engine, supplied by two
boilers. One propeller shaft.
Boiler pressure: 12·5at (185psi).
Coal bunkerage: 7,360 tonnes.
Speed, service: 11·5 knots (1,600ihp).
Range: 30,000 nautical miles at 8 knots.
**Career** This cargo ship was captured by
*Möwe* at 09:00 on 12 December 1916, in
39°30′N 17°30′E. The two guns were mounted
on the main deck alongside No. 2 hold, one to
port and one to starboard, and *Geier* was
despatched under the command of
Kapitänleutnant Wolf.
**Victims** One Canadian barque (*Jean*, 215grt)
and another small sailing ship, details
unknown.
**Fate** Scuttled at 13:53 on 14 February 1916 off
Ilha da Trindade, in 21°1′S 31°49′W.

## ILTIS

Hilfskreuzer.
Builder: Flensburger Schiffbau-Gesellschaft
(yard no. 254). Equipped at sea by *Wolf*, 1917.
Owner: originally Deutsche
Dampfschifffahrts-Gesellschaft 'Hansa',
Bremen (named *Gutenfels*). Seized in

Alexandria in 1914 and sold in 1915 to the Anglo-Saxon Petroleum Company of London (named *Turritella*).
Launch date: 18 November 1905.
Commissioned: February 1917.
Crew: 1 officer, 27 men and 46 Chinese.
**Dimensions**
Registered tonnage (grt): 5,528.
Full-load displacement: 10,700 tonnes.
Overall length: 135·2 metres.
Waterline length: 128·8 metres.
Beam: 16·8 metres.
Full-load draught: about 6·3 metres.
**Weapons**
Guns: one 5·2cm SK L/55.
Maximum range of main guns: 7,500 metres?
Lesser guns: small-arms only.
Munitions: 200 5·2cm shells and 25 mines.
Armour protection: none.
**Performance**
Powerplant: one vertical three-cylinder triple expansion steam engine, supplied by two boilers. One propeller shaft.
Boiler pressure: 13at (191psi).
Speed, service maximum: 11 knots (2,600ihp).
**Career** Captured on 27 January 1917 by *Wolf* (q.v.), then despatched to lay mines off Aden.
**Fate** Scuttled at 16:50 on 5 March 1917 when challenged by HMS *Odin*, west south-west of Aden (12°26′N 44°12′E).

## LEOPARD

Hilfskreuzer.
Builder: W. Dobson & Company, Newcastle upon Tyne (yard no. 178). Equipped by the Kaiserliche Werft, Kiel, 1917.
Owner: Mackill Steam Ship Co. Ltd, Glasgow (named *Yarrowdale*).
Launch date: 1912.
Commissioned: 19 January 1917.
Crew: 15 officers and 304 men.
**Dimensions**
Registered tonnage (grt): 4,652.
Full-load displacement: 9,800 tonnes.
Overall length: 124·7 metres.
Waterline length: 118·9 metres.
Beam: 15·9 metres.
Full-load draught: about 7·3 metres.
**Weapons**
Guns: five 15cm SK L/40 and four 8·8cm L/45.
Maximum range of 15cm guns: 13,700 metres.
Lesser guns: small-arms only.
Torpedo tubes: two.
Munitions: 600 15cm shells, 450 8·8cm shells and twelve 50cm C/08 torpedoes.
Armour protection: none.
**Performance**
Powerplant: one vertical three-cylinder triple expansion steam engine, supplied by two boilers. One propeller shaft.
Boiler pressure: 12·5at (185psi).
Coal bunkerage: 4,500 tonnes.
Speed, service maximum: 13 knots (2,400ihp).
Range: 26,000 nautical miles at 11 knots.
**Career** Captured in 42°N 18°W by *Möwe* on 11 November 1916, and sent back to Germany under the command of a prize crew. The steamer was then armed and sent out again on a raiding cruise on 16 March 1917, disguised as the Norwegian *Rena*. She was painted black, had white upperworks, and a black funnel with two narrow white bands; 'RENA', the Norwegian flag and 'NORGE' were painted on the sides of the hull. The 8·8cm guns were placed alongside No. 1 and No. 3 holds, with the 10·5cm guns alongside No. 2 and No. 4. The fifth 10·5cm gun was placed on the poop,

where it could be hidden inside a deck house made largely of canvas.
**Fate** At 02:00 on 17 March 1917, *Leopard* was stopped by the armoured cruiser *Achilles* (Captain Frederick Leake RN) and sent west by south to be inspected by men of the Armed Boarding Steamer *Dundee* (Commander Selwyn Day RNR), which carried one 4-inch gun and a 3-pdr. A boarding party was sent over at 02:42 whilst a lengthy series of signals began. As Commander Day became increasingly suspicious, the raider launched two torpedoes which passed aft of *Dundee*. The British steamer immediately opened fire at 1,200 yards, knocking out most of the raider's port guns, and had expended seventy shells before *Leopard* replied. The range had reduced to only five hundred yards and virtually every British shell had hit home. At 04:10, *Achilles* opened fire at 5,300 yards and torpedoed the German ship in the bow. At about 04:35, having taken a dreadful hammering, *Leopard* sank with all hands in 64°54′N 0°22′E. The British lost the boarding party of one officer and five men, taken aboard the raider before the action began.

## METEOR

Hilfskreuzer.
Builder: Ramage & Ferguson Ltd, Leith (yard no. 188). Equipped by the Kaiserliche Werft, Wilhelmshaven, 1915.
Owner: Leith, Hull & Hamburg Steam Packet Company (named *Vienna*).
Launch date: May 1903.
Commissioned: 6 May 1915.
Crew: not known.
**Dimensions**
Registered tonnage (grt): 1,912.
Full-load displacement: 3,640 tonnes.
Overall length: 89·1 metres.
Waterline length: 85·3 metres.
Beam: 11·3 metres.
Full-load draught: about 5·1 metres.
**Weapons**
Guns: see text.
Lesser guns: two 3·7mm machine-cannon and small-arms.
Torpedo tubes: two.
Munitions: 600 8·8cm (?) shells, 374 mines and two 50cm C/08 torpedoes.
Armour protection: none.
**Performance**
Powerplant: one vertical three-cylinder triple expansion steam engine, supplied by two boilers. One propeller shaft.
Boiler pressure: 12·5at (185psi).
Coal bunkerage: possibly 250 tonnes.
Speed, service maximum: 14 knots (2,400ihp).
Range: 5,000 nautical miles at 9 knots.
**Career** Seized in Hamburg when the First World War began, this North Sea packet was equipped for a mine-laying sortie into the White Sea and the Kola Peninsula, disguised as the Russian *Bue* or *Imperator Nikolai II*. Two 8·8cm L/40 guns were mounted on the fore-deck alongside No. 1 hold, close to the foremast. A third gun, possibly 5·2cm-calibre, was placed on top of the deck house aft. Claims that the 8·8cm guns were on disappearing mountings are misleading; they were conventionally shielded, but partially hidden behind the high gunwhales.

*Meteor* was sent out on a second sortie in August 1915 to mine the Moray Firth, under the command of Korvettenkapitän von Knorr. At 05:30 on 8 August, *Meteor* was stopped by

the 1,862grt Armed Boarding Steamer *Ramsey* (Lieutenant-Commander Raby RNR) which carried two 12-pdr guns. The raider immediately opened fire and had soon sunk *Ramsey* with the loss of Raby and more than fifty of his crewmen.
**Victims** One British steamer and one small Norwegian schooner.
**Fate** The return to Germany was threatened by warships of the Light Cruiser Force, despatched from Harwich. Consequently, to save the lives of British captives as well as his own crew, von Knorr scuttled *Meteor* on 9 August 1915 in 55°56′N 6°43′E.

## VICTORIA LUISE

Hilfskreuzer.
Builder: AG 'Vulcan', Stettin-Bredow (yard no. 244). Equipped by the Vulcan yard in Hamburg, 1914.
Owner: Hamburg–Amerika Linie, Hamburg (originally named *Deutschland*).
Launch date: 10 January 1900.
Maiden voyage: July 1901.
Commissioned: never formally accepted.
Crew: 22 officers and 448 men.
**Dimensions**
Registered tonnage (grt): 16,703.
Full-load displacement: 27,350 tonnes.
Overall length: 207·2 metres.
Waterline length: 201·5 metres.
Beam: 20·5 metres.
Full-load draught: about 8·5 metres.
**Weapons**
Guns: four 10·5cm SK C/88 L/40.
Maximum range of main guns: 12,200 metres.
Munitions: 800 10·5cm shells.
Lesser guns: four 3·7cm Hotchkiss revolver cannon and small-arms.
Munitions: 800 10·5cm shells.
Armour protection: on gun shields only.
**Performance**
Powerplant: two vertical four-cylinder quadruple expansion steam engines, supplied by eight boilers. Two propeller shafts.
Boiler pressure: 15at (221psi).
Coal bunkerage: 5,600 tonnes.
Speed, service: 17·5 knots (15,000ihp).
Range: 7,000 nautical miles at 15 knots.
*Note*: originally listed as 16,502grt and capable of 22·5 knots, having gained the Blue Riband for the fastest Atlantic crossing in 1901. Re-engined by Vulcan in 1910–11.
**Career** This ship had been fitted with her guns by 8 August 1914, but trials showed that boilers and machinery were no longer capable of raising enough speed. Consequently, apparently after considering using the ship as a minelayer, the navy returned *Victoria Luise* to her peacetime owners.
**Fate** Converted into the Hamburg–Amerika Linie emigrant ship *Hansa* in 1921 and scrapped in Hamburg in 1925.

## VINETA (I)

Hilfskreuzer.
Builder: Blohm & Voss, Hamburg (yard no. 221). Equipped by Blohm & Voss, 1914.
Owner: Hamburg-Südamerikanische Dampfschifffahrts-AG, Hamburg (named *Cap Polonio*).
Launch date: 25 March 1914.
Commissioned: 8 February 1915.
Crew: not known.
**Dimensions**
Registered tonnage (grt): 20,572.
Full-load displacement: 24,500 tonnes.

Overall length: 200·1 metres.
Waterline length: 193·4 metres.
Beam: 22·0 metres.
Full-load draught: about 8·4 metres.
**Weapons**
Guns: four 15cm SK L/40 and four 8·8cm L/45.
Maximum range of 15cm guns: 13,700 metres.
Lesser guns: small-arms only.
Munitions: 600 15cm shells.
Armour protection: on gun shields only.
**Performance**
Powerplant: two vertical four-cylinder triple expansion steam engines and a low-pressure exhaust turbine, supplied by fourteen boilers. Three propeller shafts.
Boiler pressure: 15at (221psi).
Coal bunkerage: 5,000 tonnes.
Oil bunkerage: 200 tonnes.
Speed, trials: 16·9 knots (17,500ihp).
Speed, service maximum: 15 knots (16,000ihp).
Range: 7,000 nautical miles at 15 knots.
**Career** Cap Polonio was the first major German merchant ship to be fitted with forced-draught water-tube boilers. However, good-quality Welsh steam coal was required to attain the desired eighteen knots in service. Trials run early in 1915 showed that even seventeen knots was unattainable with the poorer fuel available in Germany, and that the boiler-tubes soon clogged. The ship was subsequently returned to her builders, regaining her third (dummy) funnel and full-height masts, but was then laid-up for the remainder of the war. The 15cm guns were placed singly on the centre-line of the superstructure ahead of the foremast, ahead of the bridge, immediately ahead of the mainmast and on the poop. The 8·8cm guns were set into the port and starboard sides of the superstructure beneath the bridge and forward funnel.
**Fate** Ceded to Britain in April 1919 to serve as a troopship, she made one voyage to South Africa and one to Bombay under the management of the Union-Castle Line and the Peninsular & Oriental Steam Navigation Company ('P&O') respectively. Laid-up again in 1920, Cap Polonio was sold back to her original owners in 1921, extensively refitted

and converted to oil firing. She served until the early 1930s, but was then reduced to an accommodation ship in Hamburg-Waltershof and finally went to the breakers in Wilhelmshaven in June 1935.

## VINETA (II)

The raider Möwe (q.v.) operated as Vineta in the Kattegat and Skagerrak in June–August 1916 before reverting to her original name. One Russian (?) merchant ship of 3,226grt is said to have been taken in this period.

## WOLF (I)

Hilfskreuzer.
Builder: Workman, Clark & Co. Ltd, Belfast (yard no. 231). Equipped by the Kaiserliche Werft, Wilhelmshaven, 1916.
Owner: Hamburg–Amerika Linie, Hamburg (named Belgravia).
Launch date: 10 May 1906.
Commissioned: 14 January 1916.
Crew: 16 officers and 345 men.
**Dimensions**
Registered tonnage (grt): 6,648.
Full-load displacement: 12,900 tonnes.
Overall length: 141·1 metres.
Length (bp): 136·8 metres.
Beam: 16·3 metres.
Full-load draught: about 7·8 metres.
**Weapons**
Guns: four 15cm SK L/40.
Maximum range of guns: about 13,700 metres.
Lesser guns: two 3·7cm machine-cannon and small-arms.
Torpedo tubes: two.
Munitions: 600 15cm shells and sixteen 50cm C/08 torpedoes.
Armour protection: none.
**Performance**
Powerplant: one vertical four-cylinder quadruple expansion steam engine, supplied by four boilers. One propeller shaft.
Boiler pressure: 15at (221psi).
Coal bunkerage: 5,900 tonnes.
Speed, trials: 13 knots (3,300ihp).
Speed, service: 11·5 knots (2,800ihp).
Range: 30,000 nautical miles at 10 knots.
**Career** Impressed into navy service at the

beginning of 1916, this merchant cruiser left Hamburg on her first sortie on 26 February. The four guns—two on each beam—were placed behind hinged bulwarks on the foredeck abaft the forecastle break.
Weather conditions became so bad that Wolf was forced aground at the mouth of the Elbe and was too seriously damaged to continue. The ship was towed back to port and de-commissioned.
**Fate** Ceded to France in March 1919, rebuilt, and re-registered in 1922 by Compagnie Générale Transatlantique of Paris as Iowa, the ship went to the breakers in April 1934.

## OTHERS

Gun mountings were built into many of the larger passenger ships, particularly those dating from 1905–14. According to Gröner, Jung and Maass in Der deutschen Kriegsschiffe (vol. 3), they included the following:
**Norddeutscher Lloyd**
Bülow, 8,965grt (1906); Derfflinger, 9,144grt (1907); Goeben 8,792grt (1906); Kaiser Wilhelm II, 19,361grt (AG 'Vulcan', Stettin, 1903); Kronprinzessin Cecilie, 19,360grt (AG 'Vulcan', Stettin, 1907); Lützow, 8,826grt (1907); Prinz Ludwig, 9,687grt (1906); and Yorck, 8,909grt (1906).
**Deutsch Ostafrika-Linie**
Kigoma, 8,156grt (1914).
None of these ships was ever armed. In addition, several large ships lacking gun mounting-points were also considered for the role of merchant cruiser, though nothing more was ever done. They are said to have included Cap Finisterre of Hamburg-Südamerikanische Dampfschifffahrt-Gesellschaft (Blohm & Voss AG, Hamburg, 14,503grt, 1911); George Washington of Norddeutscher Lloyd (AG 'Vulcan', Stettin, 25,570grt, 1909); Kaiserin Auguste Victoria of the Hamburg–Amerika Linie (AG 'Vulcan', Stettin, 24,581grt, 1906); and Prinz Friedrich Wilhelm of Norddeutscher Lloyd (J.C. Tecklenborg AG, Geestemünde, 17,082grt, 1908).
Several fast cargo-ships were impressed for conversion in 1915–16 in addition to Möwe and Wolf, but details are still lacking.

**Right**

Wolf (I), formerly the steamship Belgravia, is seen here in a photograph taken from the dreadnought Ostfriesland in the first weeks of 1916. The raider ran aground on her maiden voyage—before leaving German territorial waters—and was deemed beyond easy repair. She was replaced by the much better-known Wolf (II).

Author's collection.

# 2: VICTIMS OF THE RAIDERS

Note: the data extracted from Lloyd's Registers of Shipping refer to the year of loss. All ships plied under the British flag except where noted. Unless stated otherwise, triple- and quadruple-expansion steam engines had three and four cylinders respectively. Lengths quoted are 'between perpendiculars', unless qualified as overall ('oa') or waterline ('wl') measurements. Tonnages are generally gross registered figures ('grt') for merchant ships or displacement ('td') for warships, and dates accompanying the builder's names represent the year of completion. Owing to restrictions on space, details of ships stopped, but released after examination, have been omitted. Copies of the expanded material may be obtained directly from the author.

## I. SHIPS DESTROYED

**A.B. Johnson** Wilson Bros & Co. Flag: USA. Official number: 107553. Port of registry: San Francisco. Call sign: KQDM. J. Lindstrom, Aberdeen, Washington, 1900; 529grt, 165·3 × 37ft. Wood hull. Schooner rig, four masts. Captured and sunk by *Seeadler* on 14 June 1917.

**Alcantara** British merchant cruiser (Royal Mail Steam Packet Co., London). Official number: 132050. Port of registry: Belfast. Call sign: JFPR. Harland & Wolff Ltd, Glasgow, 1914; 16,034grt, 590(oa) × 65·3ft. Two four-cylinder triple expansion engines and an exhaust turbine, three shafts; seventeen knots. Armament: eight 6-inch and two 6-pdr QF guns. Colours: warship grey overall. Sunk by *Greif*, 29 February 1916.

**Anne de Bretagne** Société Nouvelle d'Armement. Flag: French. Port of registry: Nantes. Call sign: HJCS. A. Dubigeon, Nantes, 1901; 2,063grt, 261·3 × 38·8ft. Steel hull. Barque rig, three masts. Captured and sunk by *Kronprinz Wilhelm* on 21 November 1914.

**Antonin** Ant. Dom. Bordes et fils. Flag: French. Port of registry: Dunkerque. Call sign: HJKN. Ateliers et Chantiers de France, Dunkerque, 1902; 3,071grt, 313·5 × 45ft. Steel hull. Barque rig, four masts. Captured and sunk by *Seeadler* in February 1917.

**Ariadne** Ariadne Steam Shipping Co. (manager: G.P. Sechiardi). Official number: 118462. Port of registry: London. Call sign: VKTF. W. Gray & Co., West Hartlepool, 1904; 3,055grt, 325 × 49ft. Triple-expansion engine by the Central Marine Engineering Works, West Hartlepool, one shaft. Captured and sunk by *Möwe* on 15 January 1916.

**Asnières** Société Anonyme des Longues Couriers Français. Flag: French. Port of registry: Le Havre. Call sign: HKDL. Forges et Chantiers de la Méditerranée, Le Havre, 1902; 3,103grt, 312 × 45·1ft. Steel hull. Barque rig, four masts. Taken and sunk by *Möwe* on 2 January 1915.

**Author** Charente Steamship Co. Ltd (managers: T. & J. Harrison Ltd). Official number: 120877. Port of registry: Liverpool. Call sign: HDJV. Charles Connell & Co. Ltd, Glasgow, 1905; 3,496grt, 350 × 46·2ft. Triple-expansion engine by Dunsmuir & Jackson, Glasgow, one shaft; 10 knots. Funnel: black with three equal bands, white/red/ white. House flag: white, bearing a red cross formy (i.e., with arms broadening progressively towards their extremities) extending to the edges. Captured and sunk by *Möwe* on 13 January 1916.

**Bankfields** Bank Shipping Co. Ltd (managers: W. Just & Co.). Official number: 126823. Port of registry: Liverpool. Call sign: HBRM. W. Pickersgill & Sons, Sunderland, 1905; 3,763grt, 361 × 46·2ft. Triple-expansion engine by G. Clark Ltd, Sunderland, one shaft. Sunk by *Leipzig* on 25 September 1914.

**Bellevue** Bellevue Steam Shipping Co. Ltd (managers: Bell, Bros & Co.). Official number: 105978. Port of registry: Glasgow. Call sign: PFSB. Charles Connell & Co., Glasgow, 1896; 3,814grt, 350 × 45ft. Captured by *Kronprinz Wilhelm* on 4 December and sunk on 20 December 1914.

**Beluga** Flag: USA. Wood hull, barque rig? No details in Lloyd's Register. Captured and sunk by *Wolf* on 11 July 1917.

**Benmohr** William Thompson & Co. Ltd, The Ben Line. Official number: 129416. Port of registry: Leith. Call sign: HWNV. Scott's Shipbuilding & Engineering Co. Ltd, Greenock, 1912; 4,806grt, 403·3 × 51·5ft. Triple-expansion engine, one shaft; 11 knots. Funnel: buff. House flag: a blue anchor on a white rectangle edged in red. Captured and sunk by *Emden* on 16 October 1914.

**Bowes Castle** Lancashire Shipping Co. Ltd (managers: James Chambers & Co.). Official number: 135440. Port of registry: Liverpool. Call sign: JBQN. Sir James Laing & Sons Ltd, Sunderland, 1913; 4,650grt, 385 × 51·7ft. Triple-expansion engine by Richardsons, Westgarth & Co. Ltd, Sunderland, one shaft. Funnel: red with a black top. House flag: red, with a blue 'C' in a white canton. Captured and sunk by *Karlsruhe* on 18 August 1914.

**Brecknockshire** Royal Mail Steam Packet Co. Official number: 136359. Port of registry: Belfast. Call sign: JNRV. Harland & Wolff Ltd, Belfast, 1917; 8,422grt, 470·2 × 60·3ft. Quadruple-expansion engine by builders, one shaft; twelve knots. Funnel: yellow buff. House flag: white, charged with a gold crown on a red ribbon. Laid down in 1914, though work was suspended until 1916. Taken and sunk by *Möwe* on 15 February 1917.

**British Yeoman** Eschen & Minor. Flag: USA. Port of registry: San Francisco. Call sign: LFBJ. Oswald, Mordaunt & Co., Southampton, 1880; 1,953grt, 269·2 × 39·8ft. Iron hull. Barque rig, three masts. Launched as *British Yeoman*, but subsequently renamed *Stefano Razeto*. Reverting to her original name when purchased in the early 1900s by the British Yeoman Ship Co. of Victoria, British Columbia, *British Yeoman* was acquired about 1915 by Eschen & Minor—who had previously managed her—and re-registered. Captured and sunk by *Seeadler* on 26 February 1917.

**Buenos Ayres** B. Scotto Lachianca (sic). Flag: Italian. Official number: 239. Port of registry: Napoli. Call sign: NHRB. Russell & Co., Greenock, 1891; 1,811grt, 252·1 × 40ft. Steel hull. Ship rig, three masts. Captured and sunk by *Seeadler* on 9 February 1917.

**Buresk** Buresk Steam Ship Co. Ltd (managers: Burdick & Cook). Official number: 136673. Port of registry: London. Call sign: JFMK. Richardson, Duck & Co., Stockton on Tees, 1914 (yard no. 638); 4,337grt, 380·1 × 51ft. Triple-expansion engine by Blair & Co. Ltd, Stockton on Tees, one shaft; 10 knots. Funnel: black. Captured by *Emden* on 27 September 1914 and scuttled by the prize crew on 9 November 1914.

**Cambrian Range** Neptune Steam Navigation Co. Ltd (managers: Furness, Withy & Co. Ltd). Official number: 124005. Port of registry; Liverpool. Call sign: HJLR. A. Rodger & Co., Port Glasgow, 1906; 4,234grt, 384·9 × 50ft. Triple-expansion engine by Dunsmuir & Jackson Ltd, Glasgow, one shaft. Funnel: black, with a narrow red band above a broad red one. House flag: 'F' in white on a blue ground. Formerly *Crown*. Taken and sunk by *Möwe* on 9 December 1916.

**Cervantes** Liverpool, Brazil & River Plate Steam Navigation Co. (managers: Lamport & Holt Ltd). Official number: 105301. Port of registry: Liverpool. Call sign: HMVF. D. & W. Henderson & Co., Glasgow, 1895; 4,635grt, 410 × 48·1ft. Triple-expansion engine by builders, one shaft. Funnel: blue, with a black top above a broad white band. House flag: red, with 'L + H' in black on a horizontal white band. Captured and sunk by *Karlsruhe* on 8 October 1914.

**Charcas** New York & Pacific Steam Ship Co. Ltd (managers: Grace Bros.). Official number: 123741. Port of registry: London. Call sign: NJPF. Armstrong, Whitworth & Co. Ltd, Newcastle upon Tyne, 1906; 5,067grt, 402 × 52·3ft. Quadruple-expansion engine by the Wallsend Slipway & Engineering Co. Ltd, Newcastle upon Tyne, one shaft. Funnel: green with a black top. Captured by *Prinz Eitel Friedrich* on 5 December 1914.

**Charles Gounod** Société Nouvelle d'Armement. Flag: French. Port of registry: Nantes. Call sign: HQVC. Ateliers et Chantiers de la Loire, Saint Nazaire, c.1900; 2,199grt, 279·8 × 40·2ft. Steel hull. Barque rig, three masts. Captured and sunk by *Seeadler* on 21 January 1917.

**Chilkana** British India Steam Navigation Co. Ltd. Official number: 136315. Port of registry: Glasgow. Call sign: JGFM. W. Gray & Co., West Hartlepool, 1914; 5,146grt, 400 × 53·5ft. Triple-expansion engine by the Central Marine Works Co., West Hartlepool, one shaft; ten knots. Funnel: black with two narrow white bands. House flag: a white swallow-tail with a red saltire. Captured and sunk by *Emden* on 19 October 1914.

**City of Winchester** Ellerman Lines Ltd (managers: G. Smith & Sons). Official number: 136290. Port of registry: Glasgow. Call sign: JFNP. Earle's Ship Building Co., Hull, 1914; 6,601grt, 449·2 × 56·8ft. Triple-expansion engine by builders; twelve knots. Funnel: buff with a white band beneath a black top. House flag: 'J.R.E.' in white on a blue ground. Captured by *Königsberg* on 6 August and scuttled on 12 August 1914.

**Clan Grant** The Clan Line Steamers Ltd (managers: Cayzer, Irvine & Co. Ltd). Official number: 115683. Port of registry: Glasgow. Call sign: TKBG. William Doxford & Sons Ltd, Sunderland, 1902 (yard no. 296); 3,948grt, 360·4 × 48·1ft. Triple-expansion engine by builders, one shaft; eleven knots. Funnel: black with two narrow red bands close together. House flag: red, with a red lion rampant on a white lozenge extending to the edges of the ground. Captured by *Emden* on 15 October and sunk on 16 October 1914.

**Clan Mactavish** The Clan Line Steamers Ltd (managers: Cayzer, Irvine & Co. Ltd). Official number: 133100. Port of registry: Glasgow.

Call sign: JBQH. Sir W.G. Armstrong, Whitworth & Co. Ltd, Newcastle upon Tyne (yard no. 847), 1913; 5,816grt, 450·1 × 57·1ft. Triple-expansion engine by the Wallsend Slipway & Engineering Co. Ltd, one shaft; twelve knots. Colours: see *Clan Grant*. Seized and sunk by *Möwe* on 16 January 1916.

**Clan Matheson** The Clan Line Steamers Ltd (managers: Cayzer, Irvine & Co. Ltd). Official number: 121305. Port of registry: Glasgow. Call sign: HFQJ. Furness, Withy & Co. Ltd, West Hartlepool, 1906 (yard no. 289); 4,775grt, 400 × 51ft. Triple-expansion engine by Richardsons, Westgarth & Co. Ltd, Hartlepool, one shaft; eleven knots? Colours: see *Clan Grant*. A turret steamer seized and sunk by *Emden* on 14 September 1914.

**Coleby** R. Ropner & Co. Official number: 124274. Port of registry: Stockton on Tees. Call sign: HLKP. Ropner & Son, Stockton on Tees, 1907; 3,824grt, 350 × 50ft. Triple-expansion engine by Blair & Co. Ltd, Stockton on Tees, one shaft. Funnel: black, charged with a red-and-white quartered square. House flag: red and white, with 'R.', 'R.', 'Co.' and '&' in the quarters, reading clockwise from the upper hoist position. The lettering was white or red, to contrast with the background colour. A trunk-deck steamer captured and sunk on 27 March 1915 by *Kronprinz Wilhelm*.

**Condor** New York & Pacific Steam Ship Co. Ltd (managers: Grace Bros). Official number 102781. Port of registry: London. Call sign: NCSD. Joseph L. Thompson & Sons, Sunderland, 1893; 3,053grt, 322 × 42·7ft. Triple-expansion engine by J. Dickinson, Sunderland, one shaft. Colours: see *Charcas*. Seized by *Karlsruhe* on 11 October and sunk on 14 October 1914.

**Conway Castle** The Ship 'Conway Castle' Co. Ltd (managers: R. Thomas & Co.). Official number 101959. Port of registry: London. Call sign: MWHL. W. Pickersgill & Co., Sunderland, 1893; 1,694grt, 258 × 38·3ft. Steel hull. Barque rig, three masts. Captured and sunk by *Dresden* on 27 February 1915.

**Corbridge** Corbridge Steam Ship Co. (managers: J. Hoggarth & Co.). Official number: 128515. Port of registry: Cardiff. Call sign: HRLG. R. Thompson & Sons, Sunderland, 1910 (yard no. 264); 3,687grt, 350 × 50ft. Triple-expansion engine by the North East Marine Engineering Co. Ltd, one shaft; nine knots. Taken by *Möwe* on 11 January and scuttled on 14 January 1916.

**Cornish City** Instow Steam Ship Co. Ltd (managers: William Reardon Smith & Son). Official number: 123680. Port of registry: Bideford. Call sign: HGRV. Joseph L. Thompson & Sons, Sunderland, 1906; 3,816grt, 346 × 49·5ft. Triple-expansion engine by J. Dickinson & Sons Ltd, Sunderland, one shaft; ten knots. Funnel: red, with a black top, a black 'S' and a narrow black band at the base. House flag: red, charged with a black 'S'. Built as *Charlton* for W. & E.S. Lamplough, London. Purchased in 1912, but captured and sunk by *Karlsruhe* on 21 September 1914.

**Dee** Le Nouveau Chantier Ltd. Official number: 89486. Port of registry: Port Louis, Mauritius. Call sign: KDFM. Russell & Co., Port Glasgow, 1885; 1,169grt, 215·2 × 35·1ft. Iron hull. Barque rig, three masts. Captured and sunk by *Wolf* on 31 March 1917.

**Demeterton** Owned jointly by the Carlton Steam Ship Co. Ltd and the Camboy Steam

Ship Co. Ltd (managers: R. Chapman & Sons). Official number: 133557. Port of registry: Newcastle upon Tyne. Call sign: JFQK. Ropner & Sons, Stockton on Tees, 1914; 6,048grt, 415 × 55ft. Triple-expansion engine by Blair & Co. Ltd, Stockton on Tees, one shaft. Funnel: black, with a small white rectangle—quartered diagonally, white and red—between two narrow white bands. House flag: quartered diagonally, white (nearest the hoist) and red. The letters 'R', '&', 'C' and 'S', reading clockwise from the hoist, appeared in red or white to contrast with the background colour. Captured and sunk by *Möwe* on 13 March 1917.

**Diplomat** Charente Steam Ship Co. Ltd (managed by T. & J. Harrison Ltd). Official number: 131457. Port of registry: Liverpool. Call sign: HWQM. Charles Connell & Co. Ltd, Glasgow, 1912; 7,615grt, 470 × 57·2ft. Triple-expansion engine by Dunsmuir & Jackson Ltd, Glasgow, single shaft; twelve knots. Colours: see *Author*. Captured and sunk by *Emden* on 13 September 1914.

**Dramatist** Charente Steam Ship Co. Ltd (managers: T. & J. Harrison Ltd). Official number: 135544. Port of registry: Liverpool. Call sign: JDVF. Charles Connell & Co. Ltd, Glasgow, 1914; 5,415grt, 410·1 × 52·3ft. Triple-expansion engine by Dunsmuir & Jackson Ltd, Glasgow, one shaft; twelve knots. Colours: see *Author*. Captured and sunk by *Möwe* on 18 December 1916.

**Dromonby** R. Ropner & Co. Official number: 112424. Port of registry: West Hartlepool. Call sign: RWPD. Ropner & Sons, Stockton on Tees, 1900; 3,627grt, 330·5 × 46·5ft. Triple-expansion engine by Blair & Co. Ltd, Stockton on Tees, one shaft. Colours: see *Coleby*. Captured and sunk by *Möwe* on 13 January 1916.

**Drummuir** The Ship 'Drummuir' Co. Ltd (managers: Hind, Rolph & Co.). Official number: 86233. Port of registry: Victoria, British Columbia. Call sign: W.H. Potter & Son, Liverpool, 1882; 1,844grt, 270·5 × 39·2ft. Iron hull. Barque rig, four masts. Built for Gillison & Chadwick, but sold in 1900 to Captain John Barneson of Victoria, British Columbia; re-sold to James Rolph & Co. of San Francisco about 1908 and thence to Canadian interests. Captured by *Leipzig* on 2 December and sunk on 6 December 1914.

**Duchess of Cornwall** Robert Moulton Ltd. Official number: 113878. Port of registry: St John's, Newfoundland. Call sign: NTJR. M. Nash, Burgeo, Newfoundland, 1903? 152grt, 105 × 25·6ft. Wood hull. Barque rig, three masts. Captured and sunk by *Möwe* on 6 December 1914.

**Dupleix** Société Anonyme des Armateurs Nantais. Flag: French. Port of registry: Nantes. Call sign: HWRG. Ateliers et Chantiers de la Loire, Saint Nazaire, 1900; 2,206grt, 276·6 × 40·3ft. Steel hull. Barque rig, four masts? Captured and sunk by *Seeadler* on 5 March 1917.

**Eddie** Thomas Turnbull & Son Shipping Co. Ltd (managers: T. Turnbull & Son). Official number: 106101. Port of registry: Whitby. Call sign: HWRP. T. Turnbull & Sons, Whitby, 1895; 2,652grt, 310 × 43ft. Triple-expansion engine by Blair & Co. Ltd, Stockton on Tees, one shaft. Captured by *Möwe* on 16 February and apparently sunk on 17 February 1917.

**Edinburgh** J. Stewart & Co. Official number: 90059. Port of registry: Glasgow. Call sign:

JWPH. Charles Connell & Co., Glasgow, 1885; 1,473grt, 241·7 × 38ft. Iron hull. Barque rig, three masts. Captured and sunk by *Möwe* on 20 January 1917.

**Elsinore** Bear Creek Oil & Shipping Co. Ltd (managers: C.T. Bowring & Co.). Official number: 135530. Port of registry: Liverpool. Call sign: JDQH. Swan, Hunter & Wigham Richardson Ltd, Newcastle upon Tyne, 1913; 6,542grt, 420·5 × 54·6ft. Triple-expansion engine by the Wallsend Slipway & Engineering Co. Ltd, Newcastle upon Tyne, one shaft. Funnel: black, with a red saltire on a white band. House flag: a red saltire on a white ground. Captured and sunk by *Leipzig* on 11 September 1914.

**Encore** Simpson Lumber Co. Flag: USA. Official number: 136612. Port of registry: San Francisco. Call sign: KNCD. A.M. Simpson, North Bend, Oregon, 1897; 651grt, 181·9 × 36·4ft. Wood hull. Barque rig, four masts. Captured and sunk by *Wolf* on 13 July 1917.

**Esmeraldas** Pacific Steam Navigation Co. Official number: 123985. Port of registry: Liverpool. Call sign: HGTB. Sir James Laing & Sons, Sunderland, 1906; 4,678grt, 390 × 50ft. Triple-expansion engine by G. Clark Ltd, Sunderland, one shaft; twelve knots. Funnel: yellow-buff. House flag: a blue cross on a white ground, surcharged centrally with a gold crown. The letters 'P', 'S', 'C' and 'N' appeared in the quarters, reading clockwise from the upper hoist position. Captured and sunk by *Möwe* on 10 March 1917.

**Farringford** Harrogate Steam Ship Co. Ltd (managers: Jenkins Bros). Official number: 106410. Port of registry: Sunderland. Call sign: PKBJ. Joseph L. Thompson & Sons Ltd, Sunderland, 1896; 3,146grt, 325 × 45·4ft. Triple-expansion engine by J. Dickinson & Sons Ltd, Sunderland, one shaft; eleven knots. Taken and sunk by *Möwe* on 11 January 1916.

**Flamenco** Pacific Steam Navigation Co. Official number: 124003. Port of registry: Liverpool. Call sign: HJKC. Sir James Laing & Sons, Sunderland, 1906; 4,629grt, 390 × 50ft. Triple-expansion engine by G. Clark Ltd, Sunderland, one shaft; twelve knots. Colours: see *Esmeraldas*, above. Captured and sunk by *Möwe* on 6 February 1916.

**Floride** Compagnie Générale Transatlantique. Flag: French. Port of registry: Le Havre. Call sign: JGTH. Chantiers et Ateliers de Provence, Port de Bouc, 1907; 6,629grt, 413·2 × 52·2ft. Triple-expansion engine by builders, Marseilles, one shaft. Funnel: red with a black top. House flag: white, with a large ball in the canton and 'CIE. GLE.' above 'TRANSATLANTIQUE', all in red. Captured and sunk by *Prinz Eitel Friedrich* on 19 February 1914.

**Foyle** Mercantile Steam Ship Co. Ltd. Official number: 115800. Port of registry: London. Call sign: THPG. Joseph L. Thompson & Sons Ltd, Sunderland, 1902; 4,147grt, 345 × 48·5ft. Triple-expansion engine by Richardsons, Westgarth & Co. Ltd, Hartlepool, one shaft; ten knots. Captured and sunk by *Emden* on 27 September 1914.

**French Prince** Prince Line Ltd (manager: J. Knott). Official number: 111306. Port of registry: Newcastle upon Tyne. Sir James Laing & Sons Ltd, Sunderland, 1900 (yard no. 577); 4,766grt, 391·5 × 51·2ft. Triple-expansion engine by Blair & Co. Ltd,

Stockton on Tees, one shaft; about eleven knots. Funnel: black, with the Prince of Wales's feathers in white on a broad red band. Built as *Mineola* for the Menantic Steamship Co. Ltd, and registered in 1901 under the ownership of the North Atlantic Steamship Co. Ltd. Purchased by the Prince Line in 1912 as *Bulgarian Prince*; renamed in 1915. Taken and sunk by *Möwe* on 16 February 1917.

**Georgic** Oceanic Steam Navigation Co. (White Star Line). Official number: 105326. Port of registry: Liverpool. Call sign: NWMG. Harland & Wolff Ltd, Belfast, 1895; 10,077grt, 558·7 × 60·3ft. Triple-expansion engines by builders, two shafts. Funnel: buff with a black top. House flag: a red swallow-tail pennant bearing a five-point white star. Captured and sunk by *Möwe* on 10 December 1916.

**Gladys Royle** James Westoll. Official number: 104341. Port of registry: Sunderland. Call sign: NMQC. Short Bros, Sunderland, 1894; 3,268grt, 351·7 × 45·1ft. Triple-expansion engine by W. Allan & Co. Ltd, Sunderland, one shaft. Funnel: black. House flag: a blue 'W' on a white ground, with a small blue anchor in the canton. Captured and sunk by *Seeadler* on 9 January 1917.

**Glanton** Steel, Young & Co. Official number: 104815. Port of registry: London. Call sign: NPHB. Ropner & Son, Stockton on Tees, 1894; 3,021grt, 322·2 × 41·5ft. Triple-expansion engine by Blair & Co. Ltd, Stockton on Tees, one shaft. Captured and sunk by *Karlsruhe* on 18 October 1914.

**Governor** Charente Steam Ship Co. Ltd (managers: T. & J. Harrison Ltd). Official number: 137483. Port of registry: Liverpool. Call sign: JLWN. D. & W. Henderson & Co. Ltd, Glasgow, 1915; 5,524grt, 410 × 52·2ft. Triple-expansion engine by builders, one shaft; twelve knots. Colours: see *Author*. Captured and sunk by *Möwe* on 14 March 1917.

**Guadeloupe** Compagnie Générale Transatlantique. Flag: French. Port of registry: Le Havre. Call sign: JLMV. Chantiers de l'Atlantique, Saint Nazaire, 1906; 6,600grt, 432·6 × 52·3ft. Triple-expansion engine by builders, one shaft. Colours: see *Floride*. Captured and sunk by *Kronprinz Wilhelm* on 9 March 1915.

**Hemisphere** Hemisphere Steam Ship Co. Ltd (managers: W. Thomas, Sons & Co. Ltd). Official number: 106587. Port of registry: Liverpool. Call sign: PRVG. Bartram & Sons, Sunderland, 1897; 3,486grt, 350 × 46·5ft. Triple-expansion engine by J. Dickinson & Sons, Sunderland, one shaft. Captured by *Kronprinz Wilhelm* on 28 December 1914 and sunk on 7 January 1915.

**Highland Brae** Nelson Steam Navigation Co. Ltd (managers: H. & W. Nelson Ltd). Official number: 129153. Port of registry: London. Call sign: HRWC. Cammell, Laird & Co., Birkenhead, 1910; 7,364grt, 413·8 × 56·2ft. Triple-expansion engine by builders, one shaft; thirteen knots. Funnel: red, with a black top above three bands of equal width (white/black/white). House flag: Royal Mail Steam Packet Co. design—see *Brecknockshire*. Taken by *Kronprinz Wilhelm* on 14 January and sunk on 31 January 1915.

**Highland Hope** Nelson Steam Navigation Co. Ltd (managers: H. & W. Nelson Ltd). Official number: 115954. Port of registry: London. Call sign: TSRK. Russell & Co., Port Glasgow, 1903; 5,159grt, 384·4 × 51ft. Triple-expansion engine by Rankin &

Blackmore, Greenock, one shaft; ten knots. Colours: see *Highland Brae*. Captured and sunk by *Karlsruhe* on 14 September 1914.

**Hitachi Maru** Nippon Yusen Kabushiki Kaisha. Flag: Japanese. Official number: 10577. Port of registry: Tokyo. Call sign: LCBS. Mitsubishi Dockyard & Engineering Works, Nagasaki, 1906 (yard no. 188); 6,716grt, 449·6 × 50·1ft. Triple-expansion engines by builders, two shafts; fourteen knots. Funnel: black. House flag: white with two horizontal red bands. Seized by *Wolf* on 26 September and sunk on 6 November 1917.

**Holmwood** F.S. Holland. Official number: 132732. Port of registry: London. Call sign: HWCS. Northumberland Ship Building Co. Ltd, Newcastle upon Tyne, 1912; 4,223grt, 379·9 × 49·1ft. Triple-expansion engine by Richardsons, Westgarth & Co. Ltd, Hartlepool, one shaft. Captured and sunk by *Dresden* on 26 August 1914.

**Horace** Liverpool, Brazil & River Plate Steam Navigation Co. Ltd (managers: Lamport & Holt Ltd). Official number: 105355. Port of registry: Liverpool. Call sign: PDGS. D. & W. Henderson & Co., Glasgow, 1895; 3,335grt, 350 × 45·8ft. Triple-expansion engine by builders, one shaft; ten knots. Colours: see *Cervantes*. Captured and sunk by *Möwe* on 9 February 1916.

**Horngarth** Horngarth Steam Ship Co. Ltd (managers: Turnbull Bros). Official number: 132858. Port of registry: Cardiff. Call sign: HVCW. R. Thompson & Sons Ltd, Sunderland, 1911; 3,609grt, 360·3 × 51·8ft. Triple-expansion engine by Blair & Co. Ltd, Stockton on Tees, one shaft. Captured and sunk by *Seeadler* on 11 March 1917.

**Hurstdale** Lambert Bros Ltd. Official number: 115321. Port of registry: Liverpool. Call sign: TQPF. J. Blumer & Co., Sunderland, 1902; 2,752grt, 314 × 46·5ft. Triple-expansion engine by J. Dickinson & Sons Ltd, Sunderland, one shaft. Funnel: black, with a red triangle on a broad white band. House flag: white bearing a large red triangle, point upward. Captured and sunk by *Karlsruhe* on 23 October 1914.

**Hyades** British & South American Steam Navigation Co. Ltd (managers: R.P. Houston & Co.). Official number: 110588. Port of registry: Liverpool. Call sign: RFTQ. J. Blumer & Co., Sunderland, 1900; 3,352grt, 350·5 × 47ft. Triple-expansion engine by J. Dickinson & Sons Ltd, Sunderland, one shaft; eleven knots. Taken and sunk by *Dresden* on 21 August 1914.

**Indian Prince** Prince Line Ltd (manager: J. Knott). Official number: 129755. Port of registry: Newcastle upon Tyne. Call sign: HRKC. John Readhead & Sons Ltd, South Shields, 1910 (yard no. 414); 2,846grt, 340·4 × 46·3ft. Triple-expansion engine by builders, one shaft; eleven knots? Colours: see *French Prince*. Captured by *Kronprinz Wilhelm* on 4 September and sunk on 9 September 1914.

**Indrani** Indra Line Ltd (managers: T.B. Royden & Co.). Official number: 131440. Port of registry: Liverpool. Call sign: KWBN. Charles Connell & Co. Ltd, Glasgow, 1912 (yard no. 345); 5,706grt, 430·1 × 54ft. Triple-expansion engine by Dunsmuir & Jackson Ltd, Glasgow, one shaft; twelve knots. Captured by *Karlsruhe* on 17 September 1914 and subsequently renamed *K.D.II*; scuttled on 9 November 1914.

**Indus** James Nourse Ltd. Official number:

118440. Port of registry: London. Call sign: VRNL. Charles Connell & Co. Ltd, Glasgow, 1904; 3,413grt, 350 × 43ft. Triple-expansion engine by D. Rowan & Co., Glasgow, one shaft; twelve knots? Funnel: buff, with a circlet of red triangles whose tips touched a black top. House flag: white, with a small blue lozenge on a blue saltire. Captured and sunk by *Emden* on 10 September 1914.

**Invercoe** G. Milne & Co. Official number: 99643. Port of registry: Aberdeen. Call sign: MVTL. A. McMillan & Co., Dumbarton, 1892; 1,421grt, 238 × 46·2ft. Steel hull. Barque rig, three masts. Captured and sunk by *Prinz Eitel Friedrich* on 12 February 1915.

**Isabel Browne** Aug. Troberg. Flag: Russian. Port of registry: Mariehamm. Call sign: TVNK. Built by Russell & Co., Port Glasgow, 1885; 1,315grt, 230·5 × 36·1ft. Iron hull. Barque rig, three masts. Captured and sunk by *Prinz Eitel Friedrich* on 26 January 1915. Often mistakenly listed as 'Isobel Brown' or 'Isobel Browne'.

**Jacobsen** Société Anonyme les Voiliers Dunkerques. Flag: French. Port of registry: Dunkerque. Call sign: JPNR. Ateliers et Chantiers 'Loire', Nantes, 1901; 2,195grt, 276·5 × 40·3ft. Steel hull. Barque rig, three masts? Captured and sunk by *Prinz Eitel Friedrich* on 29 January 1915.

**Jean** (i) Société Anonyme des Armateurs Nantais. Flag: French. Port of registry: Nantes. Call sign: JQBS. Ateliers et Chantiers de la Loire, Saint Nazaire, 1902; 2,207grt, 280·2 × 40·2ft. Steel hull. Barque rig, three masts. Captured by *Prinz Eitel Friedrich* on 11 December 1914 and sunk on 31 December 1914.

**Jean** (ii) J.C. Crosbie. Official number: 116916. Port of registry: Liverpool, Nova Scotia. John S. Gardner, Liverpool. Nova Scotia, 1905; 215grt, 118 × 28·9ft. Wood hull. Schooner rig, three masts. Captured and sunk by *Geier* in January 1917.

**John H. Kirby** W.B. Gillican. Flag: USA. Port of registry: New Orleans. Whitehaven Ship Building Co. Ltd, Whitehaven, 1879; 1,395grt, 240·1 × 36·9ft. Captured and sunk by *Wolf* in November 1917.

**Jumna** Mercantile Steam Ship Co. Ltd. Official number: 115798. Port of registry: London. Call sign: THNK. Bartram & Sons, Sunderland, 1902; 4,152grt, 360 × 46·9ft. Triple-expansion engine by J. Dickinson & Sons Ltd, Sunderland, one shaft. Captured by *Wolf* on 1 March and sunk on 4 March 1917.

**Kaipara** New Zealand Shipping Co. Ltd. Official number: 114630. Port of registry: Plymouth. Call sign: VHTF. John Brown & Co., Clydebank, 1903; 7,392grt, 460·4 × 58·2ft. Two triple-expansion engines by builders, two shafts; thirteen knots. Funnel: yellow-cream. House flag: a red cross on a white ground, with 'N', 'Z', 'Co.' and 'S' in the quarters, reading clockwise from the upper hoist. Captured and sunk by *Kaiser Wilhelm der Grosse* on 16 August 1914.

**Katherine** Chr. Salvesen & Co. Official number: 115167. Port of registry: West Hartlepool. Call sign: WFBJ. Furness, Withy & Co. Ltd, West Hartlepool, 1904; 2,926grt, 325 × 47ft. Triple-expansion steam engine by Richardsons, Westgarth & Co. Ltd, Hartlepool, one shaft; eleven knots. Funnel: red with a blue top above a broad white band. House flag: white, with a red lozenge bearing a white-edged blue cross. Previously owned by the Seaton Shipping Co. Ltd (Sydney, Hogg &

Co.) but sold in 1915. Captured and sunk by *Möwe* on 23 February 1917.

**Kildalton** Kildalton Barque Co. Ltd (managers: J. Hardie & Co.). Official number: 115739. Port of registry: Glasgow. Call sign: TSPV. Ailsa Ship Building Co. Ltd, Troon, 1903; 1,784grt, 261·4 × 39·2ft. Steel hull. Barque rig, three masts. Captured and sunk by *Prinz Eitel Friedrich* on 12 December 1914.

**Killin** Connell Bros Ltd. Official number 124270. Port of registry: Glasgow. Call sign: HMPD. Charles Connell & Co. Ltd, Glasgow, 1908; 3,544grt, 350 × 46·2ft. Triple-expansion engine by Dunsmuir & Jackson Ltd, Glasgow, one shaft; ten knots. Funnel: red with a black top. House flag: a white diamond centred on a halved ground of red and blue. Captured and sunk by *Emden* on 13 September 1914.

**King George** Glasgow King Shipping Co. Ltd (managers: J.A. Walker & Co.). Official number: 124129. Port of registry: Glasgow. Call sign: HJBD. R. Craggs & Sons Ltd, Middlesbrough, 1906; 3,852grt, 350 × 49ft. Triple-expansion engine by Blair & Co. Ltd, Stockton on Tees, one shaft. Captured and sunk by *Möwe* on 8 December 1916.

**King Lud** King Line Ltd (managers: Philipps, Philipps & Co.). Official number: 124273. Port of registry: Stockton on Tees. Call sign: HJRB. Joseph L. Thompson & Sons Ltd, Sunderland, 1906; 3,650grt, 350 × 50·3ft. Triple-expansion engine by Blair & Co. Ltd, Stockton on Tees, one shaft; eleven knots. Funnel: buff with a black top. Captured and sunk by *Emden*, 25 September 1914.

**La Correntina** Houlder Line Ltd (managers: Houlder Bros & Co.). Official number: 131470. Port of registry: Liverpool. Call sign: JBFC. Irvine's Ship Building & Dry Dock Co. Ltd, West Hartlepool, 1912; 8,529grt, 440 × 58·9ft. Triple-expansion engines by Richardsons, Westgarth & Co. Ltd, West Hartlepool, two shafts. Funnel: black, with a white cross formy on a red band. House flag: a white cross formy extending to the edges of a red ground. Captured by *Kronprinz Wilhelm* on 7 October and sunk on 10 October 1914.

**La Rochefoucauld** Société Nouvelle d'Armement. Flag: French. Port of registry: Nantes. Call sign: JVNW. Ateliers et Chantiers 'Loire', Nantes, 1899; 2,200grt, 275·5 × 40·4ft. Steel hull. Barque rig, four masts. Captured and sunk by *Seeadler* on 27 February 1917.

**Lovat** J. Warrack & Co. Official number: 129401. Port of registry: Leith. Call sign: HSKT. Russell & Co., Port Glasgow, 1911; 6,102grt, 405 × 52·2ft. Triple-expansion engine by Dunsmuir & Jackson Ltd, Glasgow, one shaft: about eleven knots. Funnel: black with one white band. Captured and sunk by *Emden* on 11 September 1914.

**Lundy Island** Williams Steam Navigation Co. Ltd (managers: W. Williams & Co.). Official number: 112407. Port of registry: West Hartlepool. Call sign: RJHB. W. Gray & Co. Ltd, West Hartlepool, 1899; 3,095grt, 325·3 × 48·5ft. Triple-expansion engine by the Central Marine Engineering Works, West Hartlepool, one shaft. Captured and sunk by *Seeadler* on 10 March 1917.

**Luxembourg** Compagnie Nationale Belge de Transportation Maritime (Armement Adolf Deppe). Flag: Belgian. Port of registry: Antwerp. Call sign: MBCW. Flensburger Schiffbau-Gesellschaft, 1908; 4,322grt, 383·4 × 52·1ft. Triple-expansion engines by

builders, two shafts; fourteen knots. Funnel: buff. House flag: white, edged in blue, bearing an enrayed roundel (black within yellow within red) flanked by 'A' and 'D' in blue. Formerly named *Helene Manzell* and then *Eberhard*. Captured and sunk by *Möwe* on 4 February 1916.

**Lynrowan** Liver Shipping Co. Ltd (managers: Johnstone, Sproule & Co.). Official number: 124095. Port of registry: Liverpool. Call sign: HLWK. R. Craggs & Son, Middlesbrough, 1907; 3,384grt, 361 × 47·5ft. Triple-expansion engine by Blair & Co. Ltd, Stockton on Tees, one shaft. Captured and sunk by *Karlsruhe* on 7 October 1914.

**Manila** Pacific Freighters Co. Flag: USA. Port of registry: San Francisco. Call sign: KNVS. A.M. Simpson, North Bend, Oregon, 1899; 1371grt, 182·1 × 39·8ft. Schooner rig, four masts. Taken and sunk by *Seeadler* on 8 July 1917.

**Maple Branch** Nautilus Steam Shipping Co. Ltd (managers: F. & W. Ritson). Official number: 118749. Port of registry: Sunderland. Call sign: HCTV. Gourlay Bros & Co. (Dundee) Ltd, 1905; 4,338grt, 380·4 × 48ft. Triple-expansion engines by builders, one shaft. Captured and sunk by *Karlsruhe* on 3 September 1914.

**Maréchal Davout** Société Nouvelle d'Armement. Flag: French. Port of registry: Nantes. Call sign: KCNR. Ateliers et Chantiers 'Loire', Nantes, 1895; 2,192grt, 275·4 × 40·4ft. Steel hull. Barque rig, three masts. Captured and sunk by *Wolf* on 5 December 1917.

**Maria** Holland–Gulf Stoomvart Maatschappij (manager: Jos de Poorter). Flag: Dutch. Port of registry: Rotterdam. Call sign: PKMD. J. Priestman & Co., Sunderland, 1898; 3,804grt, 340 × 48ft. Triple-expansion engine by W. Allan & Co. Ltd, Sunderland, one shaft. Captured and sunk by *Karlsruhe* on 21 September 1914.

**Maroni** Compagnie Générale Transatlantique. Flag: French. Port of registry: Le Havre. Call sign: KFTW. Chantiers et Ateliers de Provence, Port de Bouc, c.1906. 3,109grt, 310·4 × 43·1ft. Triple-expansion engine by builders, one shaft. Colours: see *Floride*. Captured and sunk by *Möwe* on 23 February 1916.

**Mary Ada Short** James Westoll. Official number: 106412. Port of registry: Sunderland. Call sign: PKJC. Short Bros, Sunderland, 1896; 3,605grt, 359·5 × 47·1ft. Triple-expansion engine by W. Allan & Co. Ltd, Sunderland, one shaft. Colours: see *Gladys Royle*. Captured and sunk by *Prinz Eitel Friedrich* on 18 February 1915.

**Matunga** Burns, Philp & Co. Ltd. Official number: 113366. Port of registry: Sydney, New South Wales. Call sign: RSPH. Napier & Miller Ltd, Glasgow, 1900; 1,618grt, 273 × 37·1ft. Triple-expansion engine by Dunsmuir & Jackson Ltd, Glasgow, one shaft. Funnel: black, with a ring of chequering (black and white) edged in white. House flag: divided into near-vertical bands of red, white and blue, with slanted edges and a green thistle on the white band. Formerly *Zweena*. Seized by *Wolf* on 6 August and sunk on 26 August 1917.

**Minieh** Khedivial Mail Steam Shipping & Graving Dock Co. Ltd (manager: Lord Ernest Hamilton). Official number: 73817. Port of registry: London. Call sign: PLGW. D. & W. Henderson, Glasgow, 1876; 2,890grt,

356·7 × 36·2ft. Triple-expansion engine by builders, one shaft; twelve knots. Funnel: black. House flag: white, bordered in red, bearing the company name in Arabic script. Formerly named *Alsatia*. Captured and sunk by *Möwe* on 9 January 1917.

**Monmouth** British warship. First Class Armoured Cruiser of the County or Monmouth class (ten ships). London & Glasgow Shipbuilding Co., Glasgow, 1903; 9,800td, 440 × 66ft. Four-cylinder triple-expansion engines by builders, two shafts; 23 knots. Fourteen 6-inch, ten 12-pdr and three 3-pdr QF guns, plus two 18-inch torpedo tubes. Sunk by *Nürnberg* at the conclusion of the Battle of Coronel, 1 November 1914.

**Mont Agel** Société Générale de Transport Maritime à Vapeur. Flag: French. Port of registry: Marseilles. Call sign: KHRQ. Ateliers et Chantiers de France, Dunkerque, 1911; 4,803grt, 366·5 × 49·1ft. Triple-expansion engine by builders, one shaft. Funnel: black with a broad red band. House flag: quartered diagonally, white, blue, white and red (clockwise from hoist), with 'T' (blue), 'S' (white), 'M' (blue) and 'G' (white) in the quarters. Captured and sunk by *Kronprinz Wilhelm* on 4 December 1914.

**Mount Temple** Canadian Pacific Railway Co. Official number: 113496. Port of registry: Liverpool. Call sign: SPCJ. Armstrong, Whitworth & Co. Ltd, Newcastle upon Tyne, 1901 (yard no. 709); 9,792grt, 485 × 59ft. Triple-expansion engines by the Wallsend Slipway & Engineering Co. Ltd, Newcastle upon Tyne, two shafts; twelve knots. Funnel: buff. House flag: divided into six compartments (two rows of three), alternately white and red. Built for the Beaver Shipping Line, but purchased by Canadian Pacific in April 1903. Captured and sunk by *Möwe* on 6 December 1916.

**Mousquet** French warship. Torpedo-boat destroyer of the Arquebuse class (twenty ships). Ateliers et Chantiers de la Loire, Saint Nazaire, 1902; 298td, 58·2(wl) × 6·4m. Triple-expansion engines, two shafts; 28 knots when new. One 6·5cm and six 4·7cm QF guns, plus two 38cm torpedo tubes. Sunk by *Emden* on 28 October 1914.

**Nantes** Société Nouvelle d'Armement. Flag: French. Port of registry: Nantes. Call sign: KJHW. Ateliers et Chantiers de Normandie, Grand Quevilly, 1900; 2,679grt, 295·4 × 41·1ft. Steel hull. Barque rig, four masts. Captured and sunk by *Möwe* on 25 December 1916.

**Netherby Hall** Ellerman Lines Ltd (managers: Hall Line Ltd). Official number: 120643. Port of registry: Liverpool. Call sign: HFJS. Swan, Hunter, & Wigham Richardson, Newcastle upon Tyne, 1905; 4,461grt, 381·6 × 47·5ft. Triple-expansion engine by the Wallsend Slipway & Engineering Co. Ltd, Newcastle upon Tyne, one shaft; ten knots. Colours: see *City of Winchester*. The 'J.R.E.' flag was flown as a pennant above a blue and white flag, quartered diagonally, with 'HALL' and 'LINE' in blue on the white. Launched as *Netherby Hall* but finished as *Glenearn* for MacGregor, Gow & Co. before reverting to the Hall Line and her original name in 1910. Taken and sunk by *Möwe* on 10 January 1917.

**Niceto de Larrinaga** Miguel de Larrinaga Steamship Co. Ltd (managers: Larrinaga & Co.). Official number: 135433. Port of registry: Liverpool. Call sign: JBLC. Russell &

Co., Port Glasgow, 1912; 5,018grt, 420·2 × 54ft. Triple-expansion engine by D. Rowan & Co., Glasgow, one shaft. Funnel: black, with a black top above a broad yellow band bearing two narrow red bands (one near each edge). House flag: three clasping hands, in red, on a white ground. Captured and sunk by *Karlsruhe* on 6 October 1914.

**North Wales** North Wales Shipping Co. Ltd (managers: H. Roberts & Son). Official number: 122825. Port of registry: Newcastle upon Tyne. Call sign: HDCM. J. Readhead & Sons, South Shields, 1905; 3,691grt, 347·2 × 49·1ft. Triple-expansion engine by builders, one shaft. Captured and sunk by *Dresden* on 16 November 1914.

**Nyanga** Elder Line Ltd (managers: Elder, Dempster & Co. Ltd). Official number: 113423. Port of registry: Liverpool. Call sign: SFBC. W. Dobson & Co., Newcastle upon Tyne, 1900; 3,066grt, 325·7 × 45·2ft. Triple-expansion engine by the North East Marine Engineering Co. Ltd, Newcastle upon

Tyne, one shaft. Funnel: black. House flag: a white swallow-tail bearing a blue cross. Captured and sunk by *Kaiser Wilhelm der Grosse* on 16 August 1914.

**Otaki** New Zealand Shipping Co. Ltd. Official number: 124576. Port of registry: Plymouth. Call sign: HNGJ. William Denny & Bros, Dumbarton, 1908; 9,575grt, 465·4 × 60·3ft. Two triple-expansion engines by builders and one Parsons exhaust-steam turbine, three shafts; fourteen knots. Funnel: cream-yellow. House flag: white, with a red cross and 'N', 'Z', 'S' and 'Co.' in blue in the quarters. Flown beneath a pennant divided vertically red (nearest the hoist), white and blue. Sunk by *Möwe* on 10 March 1917.

**Pegasus** British warship. Third Class cruiser of the Pelorus class (eleven ships). Palmer & Co., Jarrow, 1899; 2,135td, 300 × 36·5ft. Triple-expansion engines, two shafts; 18·5 knots. Eight 4-inch and eight 3-pdr QF guns, three ·303 machine-guns and two 18-inch torpedo-tubes. Sunk by *Königsberg* on 20

September 1914.

**Perce** A Canadian three-masted schooner, 364grt. Captured and sunk by *Seeadler* on 24 January 1917. Not listed in Lloyd's Register.

**Pierre Loti** Société Nouvelle d'Armement. Flag: French. Port of registry: Nantes. Call sign: KQJL. Chantiers Nantais de Construction Maritime, Nantes, 1901; 2,196grt, 277 × 40·4ft. Steel hull. Barque rig, three masts. Captured and sunk by *Prinz Eitel Friedrich* on 27 January 1915.

**Pinmore** Tridonia Ltd (managers: R.D. Braillie & Co.). Official number: 81840. Port of registry: Greenock. Call sign: WPNR. J. Reid & Co., Port Glasgow, 1882; 2,431grt, 310·1 × 43·7ft. Steel hull. Barque rig, four masts. Captured by *Seeadler* on 19 February 1917 and sunk at the end of the month.

**Ponrabbel** Marine Board of Launceston. Port of registry: Launceston, Tasmania. Ferguson Bros (Port Glasgow) Ltd, 1914; 473grt, 155 × 34·2ft. Twin two-cylinder compound engines by builders, two shafts; eight knots. Captured and sunk by *Emden* on 16 October 1914.

**Potaro** Royal Mail Steam Packet Co. Official number: 120704. Port of registry: Belfast. Call sign: HBNS. Harland & Wolff Ltd, Belfast, 1904; 4,419grt, 375 × 48·3ft. Triple-expansion engine by builders, one shaft; twelve knots. Colours: as *Brecknockshire*. Captured on 10 January 1915 by *Kronprinz Wilhelm*, painted grey for use as a scout but sunk on 30 January.

**Pruth** Mercantile Steam Ship Co. Ltd. Official number: 120529. Port of registry: London. Call sign: HCNK. W. Gray & Co., West Hartlepool, 1905; 4,408grt, 360·3 × 50·2ft. Triple-expansion engine by the Central Marine Engineering Works, West Hartlepool, one shaft. Captured and sunk by *Karlsruhe* on 9 October 1914.

**Radnorshire** Royal Mail Steam Packet Co. Official number: 135237. Port of registry: London. Call sign: JCND. Bartram & Sons, Sunderland, 1913; 4,310grt, 385 × 52ft. Triple-expansion engine by J. Dickinson & Sons Ltd, Sunderland, one shaft; twelve knots. Colours: see *Brecknockshire*. Launched for J. Mathias as *Salopian*, but purchased by Royal Mail before completion. Captured and sunk by *Möwe* on 7 January 1917.

**R.C. Slade** Pacific Freighters Co. Flag: USA. Port of registry: San Francisco. Call sign: KQHG. J. Lindstrom, Aberdeen, Washington, 1900; 673grt, 176·6 × 38·7ft. Wood hull. Schooner rig, four masts. Captured and sunk by *Seeadler* on 15 June 1917.

**Rhodanthe** London Marine Steam Ship Co. Ltd (managers: Petersen & Co. Ltd). Official number: 115803. Port of registry: London. Call sign: THQJ. W. Gray & Co., West Hartlepool, 1902; 3,061grt, 325·5 × 47·2ft. Triple-expansion engine by the Central Marine Engineering Works, West Hartlepool, one shaft. Captured and sunk by *Möwe* on 4 March 1917.

**Ribera** Bolton Steam Shipping Co. (managers: F. Bolton & Co.). Official number: 118484. Port of registry: London. Call sign: HBDR. Joseph L. Thompson & Sons Ltd, Sunderland, 1904; 3,500grt, 336 × 49·3ft. Triple-expansion engine by J. Dickinson & Sons Ltd, Sunderland, one shaft; ten knots. Funnel: black. House flag: red, with a red 'FB' on a white lozenge. Captured and sunk by *Emden* on 27 September 1914.

**Rio Iguassu** London-American Maritime &

Trading Co. Ltd (managers: Petersen & Co. Ltd). Official number: 110004. Port of registry: London. Call sign: QKGB. Short Bros, Sunderland, 1898; 3,817grt, 369·5 × 46·1ft. Triple-expansion engine by G. Clark Ltd, Sunderland, one shaft. Sunk by *Karlsruhe* on 22 September 1914.

**Saxon Prince** Prince Line Ltd (manager: J. Knott). Official number: 110336. Port of registry: Newcastle upon Tyne. Call sign: RFTS. Short Bros, Sunderland, 1899 (yard no. 282); 3,471grt, 352·6 × 45·1ft. Triple-expansion engine by T. Richardson & Sons Ltd, Hartlepool, one shaft; ten knots. Colours: see *French Prince*. Captured and sunk by *Möwe* on 25 February 1916.

**Semantha** Akties. 'Semantha' (managers: B.A. Olsen & Son). Flag: Norwegian. Port of registry: Lyngnör. Call sign: WJHG. William Hamilton & Co., Port Glasgow, 1888; 2,280grt, 296·7 × 43·2ft. Steel hull. Barque rig, four masts. Captured and sunk by *Kronprinz Wilhelm* on 3 February 1915.

**Störebror** Akties. 'Excelsior' (managers: S.O. Stray & Co.). Flag: Norwegian. Port of registry: Christiansand. Call sign: WKGL. Alex. Stephen & Sons, Glasgow, 1891; 2,050grt, 284·4 × 41ft. Steel hull. Barque rig, four masts. Captured and sunk by *Wolf* on 4 January 1918.

**Strathroy** Strathroy Steamship Co. Ltd (managers: Burrell & Son). Official number: 129440. Port of registry: Glasgow. Call sign: HPVW. W. Hamilton & Co., Port Glasgow, 1909 (yard no. 207); 4,336grt, 376·6 × 52·3ft. Triple-expansion engine by D. Rowan & Co., Glasgow, one shaft; eleven knots. Captured by *Karlsruhe* on 31 August 1914 and renamed *K.D.I.* (Kohlendampfer I, 'Steam collier 1') on 1 September. Scuttled on 26 September.

**Tamar** Royal Mail Steam Packet Co. Official number: 113904. Port of registry: Middlesbrough. Call sign: TKWJ. Craig, Taylor & Co., Stockton on Tees, 1902; 3,207grt, 331·1 × 46·2ft. Triple-expansion engine by the North East Marine Engineering Co. Ltd, Sunderland, one shaft; fourteen knots. Colours: see *Brecknockshire*. Captured and sunk by *Kronprinz Wilhelm* on 24 March 1915.

**Trabboch** Kyle Transport Co. (manager: Alexander Bicket). Official number: 128025. Port of registry: Liverpool. Call sign: HQPJ. A. McMillan & Sons Ltd, Dumbarton, 1910; 4,028grt, 351·8 × 50ft. Triple-expansion engine by D. Rowan & Co., Glasgow, one shaft; ten knots. Funnel: black. House flag: red, with a white 'K' on a blue lozenge. Sunk by *Emden* on 14 September 1914.

**Trader** London Traders Shipping Co. Ltd (managers: W. Thomas, Sons & Co.). Official number: 120669. Port of registry: London. Call sign: HFQG. R. Craggs & Sons Ltd, Middlesbrough, 1906; 3,608grt, 346·5 × 50·7ft. Triple-expansion engine by the North East Marine Engineering Co. Ltd, Sunderland, one shaft. Captured and sunk by *Möwe* on 13 January 1916.

**Troilus** Ocean Steam Ship Co. (managers: Alfred Holt & Co. Ltd). Official number: 135552. Port of registry: Liverpool. Call sign: FHB. Hawthorn, Leslie & Co. Ltd, Newcastle upon Tyne, 1914; 7,562grt, 455·3 × 56·3ft. Triple-expansion engine by the North East Marine Engineering Co. Ltd, Newcastle upon Tyne, one shaft; eleven knots. Funnel: mid-blue with a black top. House flag: blue,

with a black 'AH' monogram on a white lozenge. Captured by *Emden* on 18 October 1914 and sunk on 19 October.

**Tubal Cain** Rushworth & Atkinson (manager: J.E. Atkinson). Official number: 122769. Port of registry: Grimsby. Call sign: HDWR. Smith's Dock Co. Ltd, North Shields, 1905; 227grt, 120·2 × 22ft. Triple-expansion engine by W.V.V. Lidgerwood, Glasgow, one shaft. A steam trawler captured and sunk by *Kaiser Wilhelm der Grosse* on 7 August 1914.

**Tymeric** Tymeric Steam Ship Co. Ltd (manager: A. Weir & Co.). Official number: 113930. Port of registry: Glasgow. Call sign: SDNR. Russell & Co., Port Glasgow, 1901; 3,314grt, 330·3 × 48·1ft. Triple-expansion engine by J.G. Kincaid & Co., Greenock, one shaft; about ten knots. Funnel: buff with a black top. Captured and sunk by *Emden* on 25 September 1914.

**Unidentified** small sailing ship. Sunk by *Geier* in January 1915.

**Unidentified** Norwegian steamship sunk by *Möwe*, 5 December 1916.

**Union** Ant. Dom. Bordes et fils. Flag: French. Port of registry: Bordeaux. Call sign: LGRN. Built by Russell & Co., Greenock, 1882; 2,183grt, 289·8 × 43ft. Iron hull. Barque rig, four masts. Captured by *Kronprinz Wilhelm* on 28 October and sunk on 20 November 1914.

**Valentine** Ant. Dom. Bordes et fils. Flag: French. Port of registry: Dunkerque. Call sign: LHFF. Chantiers de Normandie, Grand Quevilly, 1901; 3,120grt, 311·2 × 45ft. Steel hull. Barque rig, four masts. Captured by *Leipzig* on 2 November and sunk on 6 November 1914.

**Vandyck** Liverpool, Brazil & River Plate Steam Navigation Co. (managers: Lamport & Holt Ltd). Official number: 131378. Port of registry: Liverpool. Call sign: HTKF. Workman, Clark & Co. Ltd, Belfast, 1911; 10,328grt. Colours: see *Cervantes*. Captured by *Karlsruhe* on 26 October and sunk on 28 October 1914.

**Voltaire** Liverpool, Brazil & River Plate Steam Navigation Co. Ltd (managers: Lamport & Holt Ltd). Official number: 124049. Port of registry: Liverpool. Call sign: HKJR. D. & W. Henderson & Co. Ltd, Glasgow, 1907; 8,618grt, 485·3 × 58·2ft. Triple-expansion engine by builders, one shaft. Colours: see *Cervantes*. Captured and sunk by *Möwe* on 2 December 1914.

**Wairuna** Union Steamship Co. of New Zealand Co. Ltd. Official number: 118495. Port of registry: London. Call sign: HBGL. Armstrong, Whitworth & Co. Ltd, Walker upon Tyne, 1904; 3,947grt, 360 × 47·5ft. Triple-expansion engine by the Wallsend Slipway & Engineering Co. Ltd, Newcastle upon Tyne, one shaft; ten knots. Funnel: red, with a black top and two ultra-narrow black bands. House flag: red, charged with a Union Flag within 'S', 'U', 'Co.' and 'S' in white (reading clockwise from the hoist). Built for W. Peterson Ltd as *Lady Strathcona*, but purchased by the J. Bucknall Steamship Co. in May 1905 (as *Matoppo*) and then sold to the Union Steamship Co. in October. Captured by *Wolf* on 2 June and sunk on 17 June 1917.

**Westburn** James Westoll. Official number: 99626. Port of registry: Sunderland. Call sign: NFBP. Built by Short Bros, Sunderland, 1893; 3,300grt, 351·7 × 45·1ft. Triple-expansion engine by W. Allan & Co., Sunderland, one shaft. Colours: see *Gladys Royle*. Captured by

*Möwe* on 8 February 1916 and subsequently sent into Santa Cruz de Tenerife before being scuttled on 23 February 1916.

**Wilfred M** The Ship 'Wilfred M' Co. Ltd (manager: J. Backman). Official number: 126583. Port of registry: Bridgetown, Barbados. Smith & Rhuland, Lunenburg, Nova Scotia, 1909; 251grt, 116·9 × 30ft. Wood hull. Schooner rig, three masts. Captured and sunk by *Kronprinz Wilhelm* on 14 January 1915. The wreck drifted ashore in April 1915. Often known, erroneously, as 'Wilfred 19'.

**Willerby** R. Ropner & Co. Official number: 124073. Port of registry: Stockton on Tees. Call sign: HWRD. Ropner & Sons, Stockton on Tees, 1912; 3,630grt, 346·5 × 50·8ft. Triple-expansion engine by Blair & Co. Ltd, Stockton on Tees, one shaft. Colours: see *Coleby*. Captured and sunk by *Prinz Eitel Friedrich* on 20 February 1915.

**William P. Frye** A. Sewall & Co. Flag: USA. Official number: 81792. Port of registry: Bath, Maine. Call sign: KPGL. A. Sewall & Co., Bath, Maine, 1901; 3,375grt, 332·4 × 44ft. Steel hull. Ship rig, four masts. Captured by *Prinz Eitel Friedrich* on 27 January and sunk on 30 January 1915.

**Winslow** G.E. Billings. Flag: USA. Official number: 81657. Port of registry: San Francisco. Call sign: KPGB. Hall Bros, Port Blakeley, Washington, 1899; 567grt, 170·4 × 37·6ft. Wood hull. Schooner rig, four masts. Captured by *Wolf* on 16 June and sunk on 22 June 1917.

**Wordsworth** Shakespear Shipping Co. Ltd (managers: Glover Bros). Official number: 136807. Port of registry: London. Call sign: JKHF. W. Gray & Co. Ltd, West Hartlepool, 1915; 3,509grt, 343 × 49ft. Triple-expansion engine by the Central Marine Engineering Works, West Hartlepool, one shaft. Funnel: black. House flag: quartered diagonally in red (hoist) and white, with 'G' and 'B' in blue on the white sections. Captured by *Wolf* on 11 March and sunk on 18 March 1917.

**Zhemchug** Russian warship. Protected cruiser, Izumrud class (two ships). Nevski shipyard, St Petersburg, 1904; 3,103td, 110·9 × 12·2m. Triple-expansion engines, three shafts; 24 knots when new. Eight 12·2cm, six 5cm and two 3·7cm guns and three 45cm torpedo tubes. Sunk by *Emden* on 28 October 1914.

## 2: SHIPS TAKEN

*a) Used as colliers, released or recaptured*
**Exford** Tatem Steam Navigation Co. (managers: W.J. Tatem & Co. Ltd). Official number: 128527. Port of registry: Cardiff. Call sign: HSRW. Craig, Taylor & Co., Stockton on Tees, 1911 (yard no. 144). 4,542grt, 380 × 50ft. Triple-expansion engine by the North East Marine Engineering Co. Ltd, Sunderland, one shaft; twelve knots. Funnel: black, with a white 'T' on a red band. House flag: a white 'T' on a red ground. Captured by *Emden* on 18 October 1914 but recaptured by the armed merchant cruiser *Himalaya* on 11 December 1914. Subsequently renamed *Brendon*, then sold to Italy in 1922 to become *Valnegra*, *Assunzione* and *Santa Elisabetta* before going to the breakers in 1953.

**Farn** Fargrove Steam Navigation Co. Ltd (managers: Farrar, Groves & Co.). Official number: 129135. Port of registry: London. Call sign: HRQD. William Doxford & Sons, Sunderland, 1910 (yard no. 415); 4,393grt,

369·5 × 50ft. Triple-expansion engine by builders, one shaft; about eleven knots. Seized by *Karlsruhe* on 5 October 1914 to serve as *K.D.III.* (Kohlendampfer III, 'Steam Collier 3'). Interned in San Juan de Puerto Rico until reverting to the original owners in April 1917; sunk by *UB31* on 19 November 1917.

**Pontoporos** National Steam Navigation Co. of Greece. Flag: Greek. Port of registry: Andros. William Doxford & Sons Ltd, Sunderland, 1913 (yard no. 462); 4,049grt, 385·8 × 52·1ft. Triple-expansion engine by builders, single shaft; nine knots. Funnel: buff, with a black top above a blue band displaying 'E' on a white circle superimposed on a white saltire. House flag: blue, displaying 'E' on a white circle superimposed on a white saltire. Captured by *Emden* on 9 September 1914, recaptured on 12 October 1914 by HMS *Yarmouth*, returned to her owners, and eventually torpedoed by *UC21* in the Bay of Biscay in August 1917.

### b) Released as prison ships

**Appam** British & African Steam Navigation Co. (managers: Elder, Dempster & Co. Ltd). Official number: 135442. Port of registry: Liverpool. Call sign: JBQV. Harland & Wolff Ltd, Belfast, 1913; 7,781grt, 425·6 × 57·3ft. Quadruple-expansion engines by builders, two shafts; fourteen knots. Colours: see *Nyanga*. Captured by *Möwe* on 15 January 1916 and used to land prisoners in Newport News.

**Cambronne** Ant. Dom. Bordes et fils. Flag: French. Port of registry: Dunkerque. Call sign: HPGD. Laporte et Cie, Rouen, 1897; 1,863grt, 253·3 × 36·7ft. Steel hull. Barque rig, four masts. Captured by *Seeadler* on 21 March 1917, then released to take prisoners into Rio de Janerio.

**Chasehill** Essex Chase Steam Ship Co. Ltd (managers: Meldrum & Swinson). Official number: 98893. Port of registry: London. Call sign: MBVJ. William Doxford & Sons Ltd, Sunderland, 1891; 4,583grt, 383·1 × 48ft. Triple-expansion engine by builders, one shaft. Funnel: black. House flag: apparently a blue cross formy on a white ground. Formerly named *Hawkes Bay*. Captured by *Kronprinz Wilhelm* on 23 February 1915 and used to land prisoners in Pernambuco.

**Gryfevale** Gryfevale Steam Ship Co. Ltd (managers: A. Crawford, Barr & Co.). Official number: 121326. Port of registry: Glasgow. Call sign: HGCQ. Grangemouth & Greenock Dockyard Co., 1906; 4,437grt, 370 × 52·2ft. Triple-expansion engine by J.G. Kincaid & Co., Greenock, one shaft; ten knots. Funnel: black with three equal narrow bands, blue/black/blue. House flag: a large blue 'C' on a white ground. Captured by *Emden* on 26 September 1914, but released as a prison-ship on 28 September and returned to her owners. *Gryfevale* was chased onto the coast north of Cap Blanco by a U-boat on 21 October 1917 and wrecked.

**Hudson Maru** Tatsuma Kisen Goishi Kaisha. Flag: Japanese. Official number: 13897. Port of registry: Kobe. Call sign: LRNV. Sunderland Ship Building Co. Ltd, 1900; 3,798grt, 356 × 45·2ft. Triple-expansion engine by the North East Marine Engineering Co. Ltd, Sunderland, one shaft. Formerly named *Hudson*. Captured by *Möwe* on 2 January and released on 10 January 1917.

**Kabinga** Ellerman & Bucknall Steam Ship Co. Ltd. Official number: 125599. Port of registry:

Liverpool. Call sign: HLCS. Armstrong, Whitworth & Co. Ltd, Walker upon Tyne, 1907; 4,657grt, 400 × 52·1ft. Triple-expansion engine by the North East Marine Engineering Works Co. Ltd, Newcastle upon Tyne, one shaft; ten knots. Funnel: black with a circlet of six white diamonds. House flag: blue, charged with three narrow white diamonds bearing 'E', '&' and 'B' in red. This was flown beneath a blue pennant bearing 'J.R.E.' in white. Captured by *Emden* on 12 September 1914 but released as a prison-ship on 14 September. Sold to the African & Continental Steam Ship Co. Ltd in October 1938 as *Lulca*, then *San Leonardo* of Compania Ligure di Navigatori, Genova; interned in the USA in 1940 and impressed by the US Maritime Commission as *Reigh Court*. Sunk in a collision in June 1943.

**Saint Egbert** British & Foreign Steam Ship Co. Ltd (managers: Rankin, Gilmour & Co.). Official number: 135563. Port of registry: Liverpool. Call sign: JFCT. Russell & Co., Port Glasgow. 1914; 5,596grt, 423·2 × 53ft. Triple-expansion engine by D. Rowan & Co., Glasgow, one shaft; ten knots. Funnel: red, with a black top above three narrow bands (white/red/white). House flag: white, edged top and bottom in red, with a central 'RG' in red. Stopped by *Emden* on 18 October 1914 but subsequently released. Acquired by T. & J. Harrison in December 1917 and renamed *Author* (see above). Scrapped in Italy, 1935.

### c) Sent back to Germany

**Igotz Mendi** Compañia Navigación Sota y Aznar. Flag: Spanish. Port of registry: Bilbao. Euskalduna de Construción Maritima SA, Bilbao, 1916 (yard no. 35); 4,648grt, 385 × 50·2ft. Triple-expansion engine by Blair & Co. Ltd, Stockton on Tees, one shaft; ten knots. Funnel: buff with a red 'SA' monogram. House flag: white, edged in red and charged with a red 'SA' monogram. Seized by *Wolf* on 10 November 1917. Taken back to Germany, but ran aground on the Danish coast on 24 February 1918. Refloated, repaired and returned to Spain in 1919. Renamed *Monte Mulhacen* in 1939 and *José Villalonga* in 1953. The vessel was finally stricken from the

register in 1970 and scrapped in the Far East.

**Yarrowdale** Mackill Steam Ship Co. Ltd (managers: R. Mackill & Co.). Official number: 133049. Port of registry: Glasgow. Call sign: HWBR. W. Dobson & Co., Newcastle upon Tyne, 1912 (yard no. 178); 4,652grt, 390·2 × 52ft. Triple-expansion engine by the Wallsend Slipway & Engineering Co. Ltd, Newcastle upon Tyne, one shaft; thirteen knots. Captured by *Möwe* on 11 December 1916 and sent back to Germany. Converted into the raider *Leopard* (see Appendix I).

### d) Armed at sea to act as raiders

**Ryazan** Volunteer Fleet Association. Flag: Russian. Port of registry: Vladivostok. Call sign: PABJ. Friedr. Schichau AG, Elbing, 1909 (yard no. 831); 3,522grt, 338 × 45ft. Triple-expansion engine by builders, one shaft; sixteen knots with forced draught. Captured by *Emden* on 4 August 1914 and commissioned as the raider *Cormoran* (see Appendix I).

**Saint Theodore** British & Foreign Steam Ship Co. Ltd (managers: Rankin, Gilmour & Co.). Official number: 135461. Port of registry: Liverpool. Call sign: JCHL. W. Hamilton & Co. Ltd, Glasgow. 1913 (yard no. 288); 4,992grt, 405·1 × 52ft. Triple-expansion engine by D. Rowan & Co., Glasgow, one shaft; 12·5 knots. Colours: see *Saint Egbert*. Captured by *Möwe* on 12 December 1916 and pressed into service as the tender/raider *Geier* (see Appendix I); scuttled on 14 February 1917.

**Turritella** Anglo-Saxon Petroleum Co. Ltd. Official number: 136811. Port of registry: London. Call sign: JKFL. Flensburger Schiffbau-Gesellschaft, 1905 (yard no. 254); 5,528grt, 422 × 55ft. Quadruple-expansion engine by builders, one shaft; eleven knots. Funnel: yellow-buff with a black top. House flag: a blue saltire on a white ground, with a central red disc. Built as *Gutenfels* for DDG 'Hansa' of Bremen, but seized in Alexandria in August 1914 and impressed into Admiralty service as *Polavon*. Altered to serve as a tanker in 1915. Captured by *Wolf* on 27 February 1917, renamed *Iltis* (see Appendix I) and scuttled on 5 March.

**Below:** the British India Steam Navigation Company's steamship *Chinkoa*, sister of *Emden*'s victim *Chilkana*—a brand-new ship sunk on her maiden voyage in September 1914. Photograph by courtesy of Laurence Dunn.

# LEGENDS OF WARFARE

## GROUND

# Sherman Tank, Vol. 1

### America's M4A1 Medium Tank in World War II

## DAVID DOYLE

Schiffer Publishing Ltd

4880 Lower Valley Road • Atglen, PA 19310

**Other Schiffer Books by the Author:**

*Grumman J2F Duck* (978-0-7643-5448-9)

*USS Iowa (BB-61)* (978-0-7643-5417-5)

*M40 Gun Motor Carriage and M43 Howitzer Motor Carriage in WWII and Korea* (978-0-7643-5402-1)

Designed by Justin Watkinson
Type set in Impact/Minion Pro/Univers LT Std

ISBN: 978-0-7643-5567-7
Printed in China

Published by Schiffer Publishing, Ltd.
4880 Lower Valley Road
Atglen, PA 19310
Phone: (610) 593-1777; Fax: (610) 593-2002
E-mail: Info@schifferbooks.com
www.schifferbooks.com

For our complete selection of fine books on this and related subjects, please visit our website at www.schifferbooks.com. You may also write for a free catalog.

Schiffer Publishing's titles are available at special discounts for bulk purchases for sales promotions or premiums. Special editions, including personalized covers, corporate imprints, and excerpts can be created in large quantities for special needs. For more information, contact the publisher.

We are always looking for people to write books on new and related subjects. If you have an idea for a book, please contact us at proposals@schifferbooks.com.

# Acknowledgments

This book would not have been possible without the gracious help of many individuals and institutions. Beyond the invaluable help provided by the staffs of the National Archives and the Patton Museum, I am deeply indebted to Tom Kailbourn, Scott Taylor, Steve Zaloga, Dana Bell, Mike Petty, Mike Haines, Mike Canaday, Joe DeMarco, Kurt Laughlin, and Pat Stansell. Special thanks to Allan Cors, Marc Sehring, Brent Mullins for allowing me access to the tanks that they have so masterfully preserved. Their generous and skillful assistance adds immensely to the quality of this volume. In addition to such wonderful friends and colleagues, the Lord has blessed me with a wonderful wife, Denise, who has tirelessly scanned thousands of photos and documents for this and numerous other books. Beyond that, she is an ongoing source of support and inspiration.

# Contents

# Introduction

The M4 Sherman series of medium tanks not only formed the backbone of the US armored force during World War II, it filled the ranks both of the US and Allied nations' armies in the immediate post–World War II era as well. With a cumulative output of nearly 50,000 units, the Sherman was the Western Allies' most widely produced tank during World War II and far exceeded Germany's entire tank production from 1939 to 1945.

The changing world situation, especially in Europe, led the US Army Ordnance Department to issue a contract in August 1940 for the production of 1,000 M2A1 Medium Tanks. To manufacture these tanks, Chrysler was contracted to operate the to-be-constructed Detroit Arsenal Tank Plant. However, German armored victories against a variety of nations proved that the M2A1 was obsolete before the plant would be finished. As a result, Rock Island Arsenal constructed the few M2A1s that were actually built (and that were subsequently used as training tanks), and the new Detroit plant instead would produce the M3 Medium Tank, itself an interim vehicle.

The "General Lee," as the M3 would come to be known, while an improvement over the M2A1, had many shortcomings. Most notably, its 75 mm gun was mounted in a sponson with limited traverse. The secondary weapon, a 37 mm antitank gun, was mounted in a turret with 360-degree rotation. This was because at that time a producible design for the desired turret-mounted larger gun had not been developed. Other shortcomings of the basic M3 design were its riveted construction and tall silhouette, the latter in part due to its radial engine.

During the course of production, some of the M3's shortcomings were addressed, and both welded-hull and cast-hull versions were produced, eliminating the dangerous rivets. On the plus side, the M3 got many things right. The drive train and suspension worked well, and the tank's 75 mm gun provided the United States and Great Britain with desperately needed firepower in North Africa. Perhaps equally important, the family of M3 Medium Tanks gave its manufacturers, Detroit Tank Arsenal, American Locomotive Company, Baldwin Locomotive Works, Pullman Standard Car Company, and Pressed Steel Car Company with much-needed experience building tanks. That so many firms from the railroad industry became involved in tank production was strangely logical. These firms had considerable experience building heavy, mobile equipment, working with heavy steel plate as well as large castings, and many had excess capacity as a result of the Great Depression.

By February 1941, the problem of turret-mounting the 75 mm gun seemed to have been solved, and as a result, a mock-up of a new medium-tank design had begun to take shape at Aberdeen Proving Ground. Designated the T6, the new tank would utilize the lower hull, suspension, and drive train of the M3. A new, cast armor hull and cast turret would be used. The turret would have a ring of 69 inches and a removable front plate to allow easy removal of the 75 mm main gun. By September 1941, an operational pilot of the T6 had been assembled at Aberdeen. Interestingly, this was only six months after the M3 pilot had been completed.

The M2A1 was envisioned as the first mass-produced US medium tank of the post–World War I era. However, observation of the advances in armored combat in early days of World War II in Europe showed the M2A1 to be obsolete. Thus, only a few were built, with the production resources (including at the new Detroit Arsenal Tank Plant) planned for the M2A1 instead being devoted to the M3 Medium Tank. *National Archives*

The M3, with its 75 mm gun, was a marked improvement over the M2A1, but it was recognized from the outset as a stopgap measure pending development of a turret that could mount a 75 mm weapon. The M3, however, not only laid the foundation for the US tank industry but also provided the United States and its allies a badly needed, reliable, heavily armed tank with which to hold the line against Nazi Germany. *Patton Museum*

# CHAPTER 1

# The Direct Vision M4A1

The T6 Medium Tank served as the prototype of the M4A1 Medium Tank, the successor, along with the M4 Medium Tank, to the M3 Medium Tank. This one-off vehicle was assembled at Aberdeen Proving Ground and was completed by September 3, 1941. The vehicle used the same lower hull, running gear, and power train as the M3 Medium Tank but had a cast upper hull and a turret that was larger than that of the M3, mounting a short-barreled 75 mm gun M2. There was a door on each side of the hull, a pistol port with a protectoscope on each side of the turret, and a coaxial .30-caliber machine gun on the left side of the 75 mm gun. There were two counterbalances on the muzzle end of the main gun, to enable the gun's gyrostabilizer to operate correctly. In addition to a socket-mounted .30-caliber machine gun, there were two fixed .30-caliber machine guns protruding though the center of the glacis, which were fired by the driver. The driver and the assistant driver had direct-vision slots, located at the top of the glacis, and the driver had a periscope on his hatch cover. (There was no hatch door for the assistant driver.) This photo of the T6 was taken at Aberdeen Proving Ground on September 16, 1941. *Ordnance Museum*

The T6 design was well-received by inspectors both for the US Army and the British, although a few changes were requested, notably including the deletion of the side doors, and the addition of a hatch in the hull roof above the assistant driver. Somewhat counterintuitively, given the cast hull of the T6, the new tank, dubbed the "General Sherman," was designated M4 when produced with a welded hull, and M4A1 when produced with a cast hull. It was the cast-hull M4A1 version, the subject of this volume, that was the first to enter production. Produced at Lima Locomotive Works in a plant expansion funded by the British government, the first M4A1 was completed in February 1942.

Like the T6, the first M4A1s off the Lima assembly line featured two fixed .30-caliber Browning machine guns in the lower front hull, and a rotating shield on the right turret roof for the gunner's periscope sight. Both these features were quickly eliminated. Incorporated from the M3 was the Continental R975-C1 radial engine, the transmission, and the suspension and tracks.

In short order, Lima's production was augmented by that of Pressed Steel Car Company, beginning in March 1942, and Pacific Car and Foundry, which began delivering M4A1s in May.

The lower hulls of the early Pressed Steel M4A1s were of riveted construction, as they had been with the M3 Lee.

The initial production tanks are referred to as direct-vision tanks due to the vision slits directly in front of the driver and codriver. Even though protected by armored doors, it was revealed that these slits were a significantly vulnerable area, causing them to be eliminated on later production tanks.

The tanks were equipped with a radio mounted in the rear overhang of the turret, an area often referred to as the bustle. The radio was either the SCR 538, SCR 528, or SCR 508, all of which are VHF FM types with a range of about ten miles, and all included an intercom set. The direct-vision Shermans used the so-called low-bustle turret, more properly known as the D50878 turret. The M3 75 mm gun was installed via an M34 combination gun mount, which featured a rotor shield scarcely wider than the gun tube.

The T6 prototype, unlike the M4A1 production tanks, had a gunsight for the assistant driver / bow machine gunner. This sight is visible just above the assistant driver's direct-vision port. The sight was mechanically linked to the .30-caliber bow machine gun. On production M4A1s, this sight was eliminated, and the assistant driver aimed the machine gun by following the trajectory of tracer rounds. The T6 originally was armed with the M2 75 mm gun, but in this photo that piece has been replaced with an M3 75 mm gun, the type used in production M4A1s. *Patton Museum*

Lima Locomotive Works, of Lima, Ohio, had a contract with the British to produce Grant Medium Tanks in a 125,000-square-foot plant built in 1941. However, during that year, the US Army Ordnance Department, which had assumed the contracts for tanks destined for the British, decided to shift production at Lima Locomotive to the M4A1(75) Medium Tank. (The number 75 in parentheses indicated that the tank was armed with a 75 mm gun, as opposed to later M4A1s armed with 76 mm guns.) This photo, taken March 11, 1942, depicts the first M4A1 at Aberdeen Proving Ground, with its original British War Department (WD) number, T-25189, painted in white on the upper hull. The upper hull was cast by the Continental Roll and Steel Company and was delivered to Lima Locomotive Works in November 1941 with side doors installed. At Lima, these doors were removed and steel plates were welded over the openings, as shown here. *Patton Museum*

The first M4A1 Medium Tank is viewed from the right side, with the original WD number, T-25189, present. A departure from the T6 was the absence of a pistol port on the right side of the turret. The left side of the turret retained a pistol port, but without a protectoscope installed in it. Another significant difference between the T6 and the M4A1 was that the latter added an armored cover over the air intake on the engine deck, as well as a prominent splash guard around the air intake cover, which is visible behind the turret. *Patton Museum*

The second M4A1, also produced by Lima Locomotive Works, was transferred to the British and was supplied with placards on the upper hull with the name "Michael," in tribute to Michael Dewar, head of the British Tank Mission to the United States. Initially, this tank was assigned with WD number T-25190. Later, the British assigned it a new WD number, T-74195. "Michael" was delivered with two fixed bow machine guns in addition to the flexible bow gun, and it was armed with the M2 75 mm gun. *Patton Museum*

The rear face of the upper hull of the M4A1, as seen in a right-rear view of "Michael," was of a visibly different design than that of the T6: this feature on the T6 had a straight lower edge, while the M4A1 had a prominent recess or cutout on the bottom. The armored cover for the air intake and its splash guard are also visible. On the turret roof is the commander's hatch, technically called the race assembly, which at this early stage consisted of the hatch ring mounted on a race so it could be freely traversed, and a split hatch cover with a periscope and a grab handle. A socket for mounting an antiaircraft machine gun was part of the hatch ring. Pioneer tools are on the right side of the engine deck. *Patton Museum*

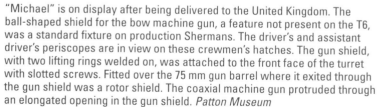

"Michael" is on display after being delivered to the United Kingdom. The ball-shaped shield for the bow machine gun, a feature not present on the T6, was a standard fixture on production Shermans. The driver's and assistant driver's periscopes are in view on these crewmen's hatches. The gun shield, with two lifting rings welded on, was attached to the front face of the turret with slotted screws. Fitted over the 75 mm gun barrel where it exited through the gun shield was a rotor shield. The coaxial machine gun protruded through an elongated opening in the gun shield. *Patton Museum*

"Michael" is seen from the right front while on display in the United Kingdom. Protruding from the right upper front of the turret is the early style of gunner's sight, called a rotor sight, which was the same assembly used on the T6 prototype. Soon, this sight would be deleted, and a periscopic gunsight would be mounted on the right side of the turret roof. On the outboard side of the assistant gunner's hatch is a ventilator hood. On command tanks, this hood and ventilator would be removed, and an antenna for an SCR 506 radio would be mounted there. "Michael" was preserved after World War II and is on display at the Tank Museum at Bovington, UK. *Patton Museum*

An early M4A1 upper hull with direct-vision slots for the driver and the assistant driver is hung suspended above lower-hull assemblies stacked two high. Openings for two fixed bow machine guns are present in the upper hull. The rectangular openings in the floors of the lower hulls are the bottom escape hatches. The rolled, homogenous steel armor of the lower hull was 1.5″ thick on the sides; the forward part of the floor was 1″ thick, while the rear part of the floor was 0.5″ in thickness. *National Archives*

The lower hull of an M4A1 Medium Tank with the bogie assemblies installed has been hoisted up during construction, revealing details of the bottom of the hull. Reinforcing cross members in the form of hat-channel strips are mounted laterally on the bottom of the hull between the center and the rear bogie assemblies. *National Archives*

Power for the M4A1 Medium Tank was supplied by the Continental R975-C1 four-cycle, nine-cylinder, air-cooled radial engine. This engine had a displacement of 973 cubic inches and achieved a maximum of 400 horsepower at 2,400 rpm. The R975-CI weighed 1,137 pounds dry and ran on 80-octane gasoline. Here, an R975-C1 is viewed from the rear, mounted upside down on a stand, showing the engine accessories, exhaust manifold, and intricate wiring harness. The carburetor is at the top of the engine accessories, with the generator and the cranking motor below it. *Patton Museum*

Two workers at Lima Locomotive Works are guiding a Continental R975-C1 radial engine into the rear of an M4A1 Medium Tank hull. Visible in this photo is the light-colored main bracket of the engine mount, attached to the rear of the engine. Note the two exhaust pipes along the lower part of the engine: these will be fastened to the two "pepper-pot" exhausts, similar to those of the M3 Medium Tank, on the rear of the hull. This type of exhaust system was found on approximately the first 100 M4A1s, following which the design of the exhausts was changed to the so-called "fishtail" type, and two air cleaners were mounted in place of the pepper-pot exhausts. *National Archives*

A Lima Locomotive Works M4A1 with the 75 mm gun dismounted is parked between an M3 Lee Medium Tank (left) and an M3 Stuart Light Tank. Ports for fixed bow machine guns, the rotor sight for the gunner, and direct-vision ports mark this M4A1 as an early-production example.
*National Archives*

An early-production, Lima-built M4A1 advances through a thicket at Ft. Knox, Kentucky, in mid-1942. The early final-drive assembly, sometimes referred to as the FDA and also called the differential housing or gearbox cover, had three armored sections that were bolted together. Casting numbers are in raised figures on these sections: 1858 on the right one and E1232 on the center one. The headlight assemblies were removable: plugs for the mounting sockets are dangling from retainer chains. Note the lack of brush guards for the headlights.
*National Archives*

The Pressed Steel Car Company (PSC) plant in the Hegewisch neighborhood of Chicago, Illinois, was the second manufacturer to undertake production of the M4A1 Medium Tank, completing 3,700 examples of the 75 mm gun version between March 1942 and December 1943. A very early, newly completed M4A1 with an M2 75 mm gun is seen here on the assembly line at PSC, with another one visible in the right background. Several M3 General Grant Medium Tanks are under assembly in the left background. *National Archives*

The US Army registration number, W-3014765, is faintly visible on the rear of the sponson of this early-production PSC-manufactured M4A1. Circular protectors with gaps in the front, for the driver's and assistant driver's hatch periscopes, are visible. The bow and coaxial machine guns are dismounted, and the armored ball shield for the bow gun is not installed. A rotor sight is on the upper front right of the turret. The M3 75 mm gun is mounted, and brush guards for the headlights are present. *Patton Museum*

Pressed Steel Car Company M4A1 registration number W-3014927 is shown during tests by the Ordnance Operation, General Motors Proving Ground, on July 9, 1942. The cylindrical object on the top of the hull adjacent to the air intake is a muffler for an auxiliary engine. Fuel tanks have been mounted atop the rear mudguards. Note the wedge-shaped air vents on the grouser-box covers atop the rears of the sponsons. The bogie assemblies are referred to as the D37892 Suspension. They were a vertical-volute design with the track-support roller (or track-return roller) centrally mounted on top of the component called the bogie bracket. Brush guards for the taillights were not installed during production at PSC until later. *Patton Museum*

The same M4A1 in the preceding photo is viewed from above during tests at General Motors Proving Ground on July 9, 1942. A close examination of the photo reveals that expanded-steel grilles were attached to the fronts of the air vents on the grouser-box covers. A clear view is available of details on the engine deck, the turret roof, the front hatches, and the bow. The ventilator on the hull to the right of the turret bustle has been removed and the opening has been protected with masking tape, and the ventilator on the turret has tape on it. The commander's hatch had a two-piece door with a periscope; on the inboard side of the hatch ring is a socket for mounting an antiaircraft machine gun. A vane sight, to help the commander quickly lay the gun on target, is to the right of the gunner's periscope, which by now has replaced the rotor sight. *Patton Museum*

The third manufacturer of the M4A1 Medium Tank was the Pacific Car and Foundry (PCF) plant at Renton, Washington, which completed these tanks from May 1942 to November 1943. Most of the 975 small-hatch M4A1 Medium Tanks produced by PCF were used for training armored units on the West Coast or for equipping combat units in the Pacific theater. Shown here is the first PCF M4A1, registration number W-3060572, armed with an M3 75 mm gun and equipped with a gunner's periscope and tracks with reversible rubber tread links: the T41 type. *National Archives*

The first Pacific Car and Foundry M4A1, registration number W-3060572, is seen from the right front during evaluations at Aberdeen Proving Ground on the same date as the preceding photo, June 9, 1942. A Browning M2 .50-caliber machine gun has been mounted on the commander's hatch ring. T41 tracks are installed on the vehicle. On the driver's and assistant driver's hatch covers, flap covers for the periscopes are open. Otherwise, these periscopes lack guards. The lifting eyes on the bow have pyramidal weld joints, which was a characteristic of early M4A1s produced by PCF. *Patton Museum*

The following series of photographs is of an M4A1 owned by Allan Cors. Manufactured by Pressed Steel Car Company, the hull is serial number 192 and registration number 3014948. It has the direct-vision, small-hatch hull; a gunner's periscopic sight instead of the early rotor sight; a later-type single-piece, cast final-drive assembly; and the later D47527 suspension with offset roller and late-type skid. The rotor shield, or mantlet, is part number D68454, introduced in March 1943, with extended sides and armored "cheeks" to each side of the 75 mm gun barrel, for additional protection to the gun.

The D47527 suspension units include a mix of roller supports: the front and rear ones are of the upswept type, while the center one is the level type with a fittings on the rear to raise the roller. The bogie wheels are also a mixed lot, with stamped-spoke wheels and open-spoke wheels with plugs welded over the openings between the spokes.

The doors in the rear of the hull are open, to the sides of which are the square-type oil-bath air cleaners. (In addition, a cylindrical oil-bath cleaner was used on M4A1s.) The high location of the lifting eyes toward the rear of the turret was a hallmark of turrets produced before late 1942. The air vents on the grouser-box covers were fabricated from welded sheet metal and were box shaped with rounded upper corners.

The arrangement of D47527 bogie units and offset roller types on the left side of the Cors M4A1 is the same as on the right side. The idler wheels on both sides are the solid-disc type, part number C85164.

The number 345 is present in raised figures below the recognition star on the left side of the turret. The sprockets are part number D47366B, designed by the Chrysler Defense Arsenal.

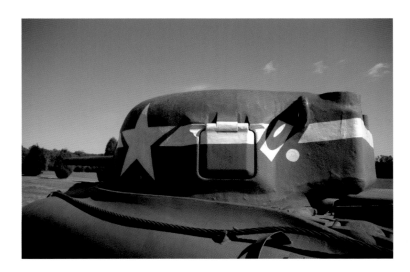

The left side of the turret of the M4A1 with direct-vision, small-hatch hull is viewed close-up, providing a clear view of the pistol port and its hinge on top. An oblong opening on the top of the turret above and to the front of the recognition star was the aperture for a smoke grenade mortar, a feature on later M4A1s. To the upper rear of the rear lifting ring on the turret is a radio antenna bracket, in the form of a cup-shaped recess in the turret armor.

The turret is viewed from the right rear. In the left foreground are a fuel-filler cap and the armored hood of the rear-hull ventilator. Molded into the top of the hull to the sides and the front of the turret is a splash guard, to prevent projectiles and shrapnel from jamming the gap between the bottom of the turret and the turret ring. On the outboard side of the commander's hatch ring is a socket mount, also called bracket, for the antiaircraft machine gun.

The right sprocket, part number D47366B, is depicted. The tracks are identifiable as the T51 type rather than the similar, earlier T41 type, because the rubber treads extend noticeably away from the tips of the sprocket teeth. This is because these treads were thicker than those of the T41, whose rubber treads came about even with the tips of the sprocket teeth.

The right front bogie assembly is shown in detail. Marked vertically in raised figures on the center of the bogie bracket, the large structure with vertical ribs, is "GAD," the foundry mark for Ford Motor Car Company, Dearborn, Michigan, which was a vendor of vertical-volute suspension system (VVSS) bogie assemblies; also marked is the Ordnance part number, D47526A.

The solid-spoked right idler wheel was part number C85164. This replaced the original D37916 open-spoked idler wheels. There are two grease fittings on the wheel, with considerable grease and soil caked around them. The track connectors are part number C55592, characterized by a relatively narrow horn as compared to the similar C100997 connectors.

The right direct-vision port cover is slightly ajar on the M4A1. These ports were found to be vulnerable to enemy fire, and soon after the introduction of the M4A1, measures would be taken to eliminate them.

The final-drive assembly is the early type of single-piece casting, with a rounded nose (later, a version with a sharper, though still rounded, nose was introduced). And the type on this vehicle has single towing eyes, while some types had double towing eyes.

This turret on this M4A1 DV hull has been fitted with an M34A1 gun mount, introduced into production in March 1943. By the following month, it apparently had entirely supplanted the old M34 gun mount. Part of the M34A1 gun mount was the new, widened mantlet, part number D68454, and that part number is present on the lower right of the mantlet. Note how the rotor shield is extended on each side to protect both the telescopic sight and the coaxial machine gun.

In a view of the turret from the front, to the left is the commander's front vane sight, which he used, viewing through his periscope or open hatch, to quickly align the 75 mm gun on a target. Behind the vane is the lid for the gunner's periscope, to the rear of which is the commander's hatch. A grab handle is on one panel of the hatch cover, while the commander's rotating periscope and the rear vane sight are on the other panel. At the center of the turret is the turret ventilator hood, surrounded by an armored splash guard. To the right is the loader's periscope.

In a view taken from the turret roof of the Cors M4A1, in the foreground are the two antenna brackets on the turret roof. Farther to the rear is the engine deck, including part of the air-intake cover and surrounding splash guard; armored fuel-filler covers; and, toward the rear, the air vents for the grouser-box covers. The air vents were often installed to dissipate the gasoline fumes that tended to collect in the grouser boxes.

The assistant driver's hatch and the bow are viewed from above. The periscope holder is on a rotating mount on the hatch cover. Partially hidden by the periscope holder and the hatch cover is the front-hull ventilator hood. To the immediate front of the hatch, the top of the direct-vision port is visible. On the right side of the bow are the ball mount for the bow machine gun, the headlight assembly (a blackout lamp above a service headlight), the brush guard, and the front right lifting ring.

# CHAPTER 2
# The Late Small-Hatch Tanks

The Ordnance Department recognized that the direct-vision (DV) ports in the early, small-hatch M4A1s were vulnerable spots, so two appliqué armor plates were installed on the front of the hull to cover the DV ports on many vehicles. Another solution to the DV problem was a redesigned hull in which the DV ports were eliminated and extensions called hoods were incorporated into the glacis to the front of the driver and the assistant driver. All M4A1 assembly lines discontinued the DV hulls by March 1943. On the top of each hood was a fixed M6 periscope, to be used in conjunction with the periscopes in the hatch covers. This example is equipped with a single-piece final-drive assembly; heavily worn T48 tracks with chevron treads; a relocated siren, moved to the left of center of the glacis in late 1942; and an M3 75 mm gun on M34 combination gun mount. By now, the driver's and assistant driver's hatches had been equipped with coil springs for counterbalancing. *National Archives*

In early 1943, the direct-vision doors were eliminated from the hull casting. Small gaps around those visors had allowed bullet and shell fragments to enter the fighting compartment, injuring crew and risking detonation of ammunition. However, the driver and assistant driver hatches remained rectangular and were mounted via a hinge running parallel to the hull side, as they had been on the direct-vision tanks. All tanks with this hatch arrangement are commonly called "small-hatch" tanks.

At about the same time the direct-vision slots were eliminated, the heavy-duty D47527 vertical-volute suspension system was introduced. When compared to the earlier D37892 suspension, with the return roller mounted directly above the center of the suspension unit, the new arrangement allowed more space within the bogie casting for larger springs, enabling better handling of the weight of the tank.

A single-piece E4186 cast housing for the differential and final-drive assembly was introduced as well. Offering greater rigidity, and hence greater reliability, the single-piece unit began to replace the three-piece design.

New track designs incorporating cleats or chevron patterns to improve traction were developed and incorporated into production. To save scarce rubber, several track designs of all-steel construction were developed as well. Extended track end connectors known as "duck bills" were developed to increase surface area of the tracks, thereby decreasing ground pressure and improving flotation on soft ground. Sand shields were added above the tracks to minimize the amount of dust kicked up by the tank.

Less noticeable was the addition of a blade sight added to the turret roof ahead of the commander, to aid him in traversing the turret quickly to lay the gun on a target. The outer rotor shield casting of the M34 gun mount received ears that protected the recoil area of the gun barrel from small-arms fire. In time, the M34 gun mount was replaced by the new M34A1, with a wider shield that included a direct-vision telescopic gunsight and protected the opening for the coaxial machine gun.

While the M4A1 was a significant improvement over the M3, nevertheless it proved vulnerable to hits, especially in the areas where the main gun ammunition was stowed. To combat this,

M4A1 registration number W-3058661, manufactured at the Lima Locomotive Works, was photographed at Aberdeen Proving Ground on January 12, 1943. It featured the M34 combination gun mount, a single-piece final-drive assembly, fender-mounted siren, bogie assemblies with trailing track-support rollers, an angle-iron step on the center of the glacis, and T54E1 steel-tread tracks.
*National Archives*

Sand shields, or skirts, are fitted onto M4A1 registration number 3037452 and serial number 28922, a product of the Pressed Steel Car Company, during evaluations at Aberdeen Proving Ground on August 12, 1943. On the center and rear bogie brackets is the foundry symbol "HYL," which appears to have been one of several heat-lot codes used by the American Steel Foundries Indiana Harbor Works, East Chicago, Indiana. The front bogie bracket is a different type, with the horizontal casting seam lower down on it. Solid-spoke bogie wheels are installed.
*National Archives*

An Achilles heel of the turret for the 75 mm gun of the early small-hatch M4A1s was a thin area on the right front, which was intended to provide room for the power traverse mechanism. As an expedient until the new turrets with thicker armor in that area were available, appliqué armor was welded over the thin spot. The variant of appliqué armor on this vehicle consists of two plates, bent to conform to the contours of the turret, and with six neatly applied weld beads between the two plates. Presumably the number chalked on the upper hull, 29988, is the serial number, which pertains to an M4A1 from the Lima Locomotive Works. *Patton Museum*

appliqué armor plates were developed. Ultimately, four types of 1-inch-thick appliqué armor kits were developed, most of which were installed at the factories; some, at army depots. The kits included two plates for the right side of the tank, and one for the left. Because the kits were made of flat armor plate, these plates had to be cut, fitted, and welded in order to fit on the curved cast hull of the M4A1.

Ultimately, 6,281 M4A1s were built with the 75 mm gun before production switched to the 76 mm armed variant in December 1943. These tanks served with all US armored units, both army and USMC. Additionally, the British received 942 M4A1s through the Lend-Lease Act.

In the summer of 1943, new-production and existing M4A1s began to be fitted with appliqué armor on the sides of the hull to provide additional protection in areas where ammunition was stored in the sponsons. This M4A1 has appliqué armor toward the front of the hull; it consists of a tall lower plate and a shorter upper plate, designed to conform to the curvature of the hull. This tank was a product of the Pressed Steel Car Company, on the basis of the registration number, 3037783, and the style of the taillight brush guard, a two-piece assembly with the two legs of the arch-shaped piece directly welded to the hull. (Lima brush guards were three-piece, and the arch-shaped main piece of the Pacific Car and Foundry's three-piece brush guard had a 90-degree twist near the bottom of each leg, which was welded to the hull.) Note the .50-caliber machine gun with a dust cover, and the tow pintle and its long mounting bracket on the rear of the lower hull. *Patton Museum*

Appliqué armor is present on the hull of this M4A1 manufactured by the Pressed Steel Car Company, in a photo dated August 4, 1944. There is a travel lock for the 75 mm gun on the glacis, and the siren and brush guard have been moved farther to the left to make room for the lock. A Browning .30-caliber machine gun is mounted on the commander's hatch ring. As manifested by the casting seams and other details, each of the bogie brackets is of a different pattern. This tank is equipped with final drive housing featuring the sharply pointed E8543 casting, which offered better ballistic protection than did the previous E4186 casting. Two sighting vanes are on the turret roof: the original type and a new model, located between the original vane sight and the front lifting eye of the turret. *TACOM LCMC History Office*

The restored small-hatch M4A1 without DV ports featured in the following series of images currently is owned by Brent Mullins. It was manufactured by the Pressed Steel Car Company, and it bears registration number 3037744. The tracks are T48s, with rubber blocks with chevron-shaped grousers, or cleats. The brush guard for the siren on the glacis was in the form of a cross inside an arch, with two rear braces. On the lower center of the glacis is the foundry mark of the General Steel Castings Corporation: a shield, inside which are four stars above the letter *G*.

The pistol port is open on the left side of the turret. Brush guards fashioned from bent, welded metal rods are mounted on the periscopes. Stamped-spoke bogie wheels, part number C85163, and stamped-spoke idler wheels, C85164, are mounted. Sprockets are D47366.

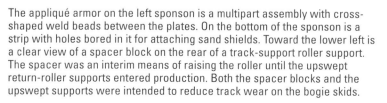

The appliqué armor on the left sponson is a multipart assembly with cross-shaped weld beads between the plates. On the bottom of the sponson is a strip with holes bored in it for attaching sand shields. Toward the lower left is a clear view of a spacer block on the rear of a track-support roller support. The spacer was an interim means of raising the roller until the upswept return-roller supports entered production. Both the spacer blocks and the upswept supports were intended to reduce track wear on the bogie skids.

The left sprocket assembly, part number D47366, is viewed close-up. The rims of the sprockets are fastened to the hubs with hex screws. The inner and outer sprocket rings were interchangeable.

The Mullins M4A1 is parked between two other Sherman tanks. The round, or drum-shaped, style of air cleaners is present. On the rear of the upper hull are a sledgehammer, a wrench for adjusting the idler wheels, and a crank for manually starting the engine. In order to maintain proper track tension, the big wrench was used on the large hex head on the inboard side of each of the idler assemblies, below the air cleaners, to adjust the position of the wheel.

The rear of the Continental R975 engine is seen from a closer perspective. Parts of the main bracket of the engine support, painted black in this instance, are visible. The dark-red cone near the bottom right of the hatch is a nozzle for the fixed fire-extinguisher system.

The rear of the Continental R975 radial engine is visible through the open doors at the rear of the hull. Some new components have been installed for the operability of the vehicle. Toward the bottom of the engine is the black-colored carburetor, with its air ducts. Just below the bottom of the rear overhang of the upper hull are the outlets of the two fishtail exhausts.

The right air cleaner is seen from below. The air cleaners are the oil-bath type, with a cup at the bottom that held oil. Faintly visible on the cup is a line indicating the proper level the oil was to be maintained at. To the left of the air cleaner is the right fishtail exhaust, with louvers visible inside the exhaust outlet.

The Mullins M4A1 is parked to the right of an M4A3E8 at a military reenactment. While there was one area on the left side of the upper hull protected by appliqué armor, there were two appliqué armor assemblies on the right sponson, positioned to protect the 75 mm ammunition storage on that side.

The front-right bogie assembly on the M4A1 has an upswept return-roller support, while the other two bogies have the level-type supports with spacer blocks, to raise the track-support rollers higher.

The M4A1 is seen from the right rear during a reenactment. On the center of the turret bustle is the trademark of the Continental Foundry and Machine Company, of Wheeling, West Virginia, consisting of the letter *W* inside the letter *C*. Pioneer tools are on top of the right sponson: a crowbar, a mattock head and mattock handle, and an axe.

The rear appliqué armor is formed from two plates—a tall lower one and a short upper one—to conform to the curvature of the upper hull. The front appliqué armor is formed from five separate sections: three small, upper ones, and two large ones on the bottom.

The individual plates that constitute the forward-right appliqué armor are shown in detail, along with the weld beads between them. Around the appliqué armor is a welded bead that forms a beveled edge to the armor.

In this view of the center-right VVSS assembly, on the bogie bracket is the trademark of the National Malleable and Steel Castings Company, Cicero, Illinois: the mark is in the form of the letter *H* inside the letter *C*. The tires are marked with their size: 20x9x16. Note the round-headed rivets around the inside of the rim of solid-spoked bogie wheels.

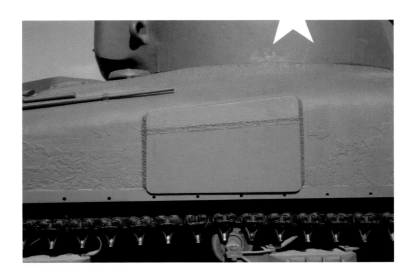

The right-rear appliqué armor is viewed close-up, showing the two plates and the weld beads.

The right idler wheel is the solid-spoke type. On the hubcap, in raised figures, is its part number, A187321. Two grease fittings are on the wheel, opposite from each other.

As viewed from the right side of the M4A1, the armored cover for the engine air intake is mounted on two hinges on its rear. The cover is not flat but has a lateral bend in it. The armored splash guard around the air intake is welded to the forward engine-deck plate. To the right are a fuel-filler cover and the rear-hull ventilator hood.

The trademark of the Continental Foundry and Machine Company, of Wheeling, West Virginia, the letter *W* inside a *C*, is visible on the center of the rear of the turret bustle. An antenna mount is installed on the bracket on the left rear of the turret roof. Footman loops are welded to the bustle, three on top and three near the bottom, for securing equipment with straps.

As seen from the left side, the plate on the engine deck to the rear of the air intake has two hinges on its front, and two grab handles toward the rear. In the right foreground is the cover of the left grouser box, with an air vent with a grille on the front.

The placement of the two rear lifting eyes toward the lower part of the turret bustle, as seen here, was a feature introduced in late 1942, replacing the earlier, higher location for the lifting eyes.

Nearly encircling the bow machine gun mount is a welded-on, tubular mount for a snap-on dust cover for the gun. On the inboard side of the brush guard is a holder and retainer chain for a plug to insert into the headlight socket when the headlight assembly is dismounted.

The small-hatch M4A1 with appliqué armor is viewed head-on during a military reenactment. Fitted across the final-drive assembly is a piece of lumber, to replicate the modification that permitted the tank crew to stow sandbags, or bedrolls, packs, and equipment on the glacis.

The foundry marks cast into the upper-right corner of the final-drive assembly provided some of the facts of production of that part. On the top line is the trademark of American Steel Foundries' Granite City, Illinois, plant, the letter *G* inside an octagon, followed by the part number, E4186. On the second line are "2A," thought to be a pattern number or plant location, and "1187," the part number's serial number. On the third line, "LO" is the type of steel used in the casting, and "BU" is thought to be the subcontractor symbols: in this case, Buick. In addition, the number 851 is stamped in the steel following "BU."

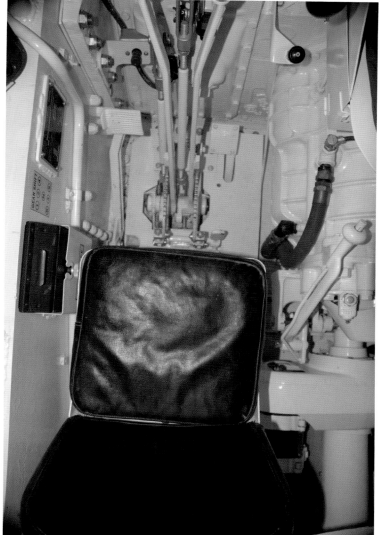

The driver's hatch of the small-hatch M4A1 is viewed from above with the hatch cover open. On the hatch cover are the rotating periscope and a ring-type handle. A rubber gasket for waterproofing is around the perimeter of the hatch opening. To the front of the hatch is the cover for the driver's front periscope. Inside the hatch, the black upholstery of the driver's seat is visible.

Looking down into the driver's compartment, to the left of the driver's seat are a periscope in its storage bracket, and the vehicle's data plate. To the front of the driver's seat are the clutch pedal, the steering-brake levers, and the accelerator pedal. On the driver's right are the transmission, with the gearshift lever next to the seat.

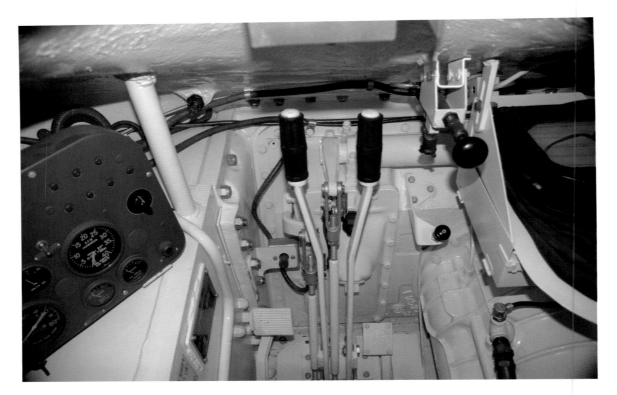

In a driver's-eye view, part of the instrument panel is to the left. The red button to the left of the steering-brake levers is the siren button. The large black knob toward the upper right is part of the fuel primer and strainer assembly. The smaller black knob below the primer handle is part of the hand throttle. Stored above the transmission to the right is a canvas hood and windshield for the use of the driver when operating with his head above his hatch during foul weather.

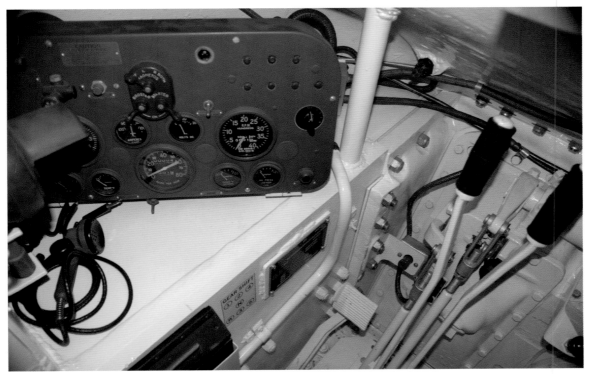

The instrument panel is the D50202 type, with the combination light switch assembly at the upper center, red-colored breaker switches to the upper right, and gauges and indicators on the lower half. At the far left is stored a blackout headlight.

As seen from above the driver's seat, the assistant driver's seat is on the far side, with the transmission and the forward end of the propeller shaft located between the seats. To the far right is the turret basket. On the floor below the assistant driver's seat is the hull escape hatch, its olive drab paint contrasting with the white paint of the interior.

Mounted on the glacis between the driver's and the assistant driver's seats is the hull compass assembly, Ordnance part number D78214, manufactured by Pioneer. Another compass of a different style was mounted in the turret.

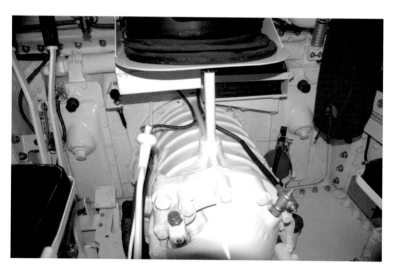

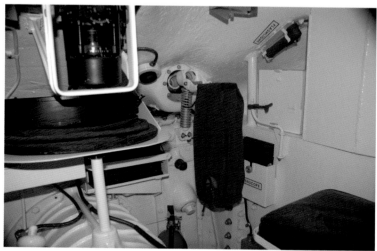

The transmission assembly, center foreground, is bolted to the rear face of the differential assembly. Molded into the top of the transmission case is a socket to hold a support for the rack for the driver's windshield and hood. To the upper right is the spent-casing collector bag for the bow machine gun.

In a view of the assistant driver's compartment from above the rear of the transmission, the spent-casing collector bag and the mount and equilibrator spring for the .30-caliber bow machine gun are at the center. A stowed flashlight and periscope are on the right side of the compartment. Below and partially hidden by the rack for the driver's hood and windshield, the ammunition box for the bow machine gun is on its rack.

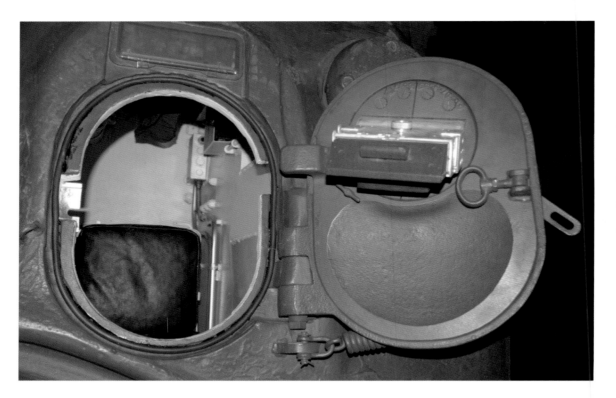

The interior of the assistant driver's hatch cover of the small-hatch, non-direct-vision M4A1 is viewed. An M6 periscope is installed on the rotating mount on the hatch cover. A bean-shaped dome was incorporated into the hatch covers to give the driver and the assistant driver more headroom. A hasp for a padlock juts from the outboard edge of the hatch cover. The lid for the fixed forward M6 periscope is fitted with a piano hinge. Note the eye welded to the hull to hold the equilibrator spring, to the rear of the hinge of the hatch cover.

Looking down through the assistant driver's hatch, to the left are the transmission, driver's hood and windshield, and ammo box for the coaxial machine gun. A nonvintage fire extinguisher is on the floor. The red cap to the front left of the assistant driver's seat is for the transmission oil filler.

The commander's hatch is seen from above. One panel of the split hatch cover holds an M6 periscope, while the other panel is fitted with a grab handle, a latch handle, and cushion to protect the commander's head when inside the hatch. At the top are the .50-caliber machine gun and its cradle. The roof of the turret bustle is to the right.

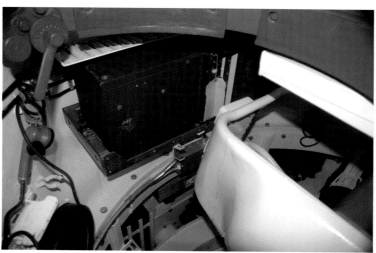

The interior of the turret of the small-hatch, non-direct-vision M4A1 is viewed through the commander's hatch. To the upper right, inside the turret bustle, is part of the radio set. To the lower right is the recoil guard of the 75 mm gun. At the center are two folding seats for the commander; the upper one is for use when he was sitting in the open hatch, and the lower one was for when his hatch was buttoned up. To the lower left is the gunner's seat, with a spare .50-caliber machine gun barrel stored next to it.

More of the radio in the turret bustle is shown. The early M4A1s were equipped either with the SCR 508, SCR 528, or SCR 538 transmitter-receiver radio in the turret bustle. At the top left is the hatch race-lock lever.

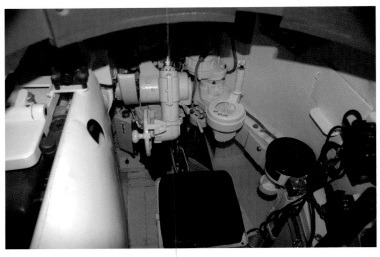

Details on the right side of the turret are shown. Two intercom control boxes and a periscope storage holder are mounted on the turret wall. The black instrument to the left of center is the M19 azimuth indicator, which the commander used to provide the gunner with the azimuth setting to which he was to traverse the gun during indirect-fire missions.

The gunner's station is seen from the right rear of the turret, commander's hatch to the top, with the azimuth indicator to the right of his seat and the M3 75 mm gun and its recoil guard to the left. To the front of the seat are the manual-controls group for the turret, including the manual elevating wheel and gearbox on the left, and the hand-traversing mechanism on the right.

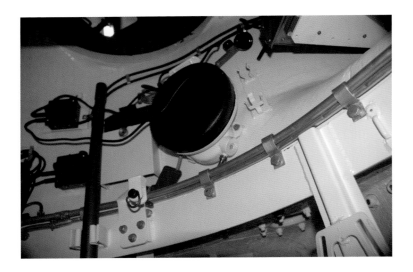

In a view from down in the right side of the turret basket, the commander's hatch is at the top, below which is the commander's upper seat in the stored position. At the top right is the bottom of the radio rack.

The hydraulic traversing equipment (lower left), gunner's power traversing control handle (center), manual elevating wheel (upper center), and gunner's seat (lower right) are the main subjects of this photograph.

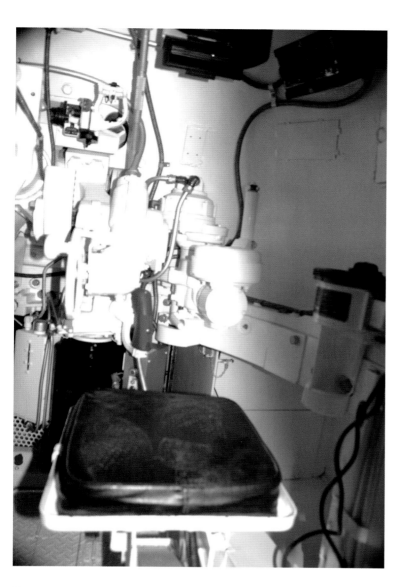

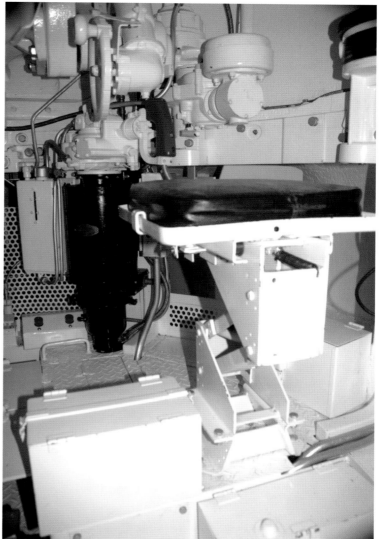

The gunner's seat and manual controls are seen from a different perspective. At the top center is the gunner's periscope, through which he sighted the 75 mm and coaxial guns. To the right of the periscope is a rod that acted as a mechanical linkage from the gun mount to the periscope. A telescopic sight, installed behind an aperture in the right side of the mantlet, also was provided; it is not installed here.

The interior of the turret is viewed from low in the turret basket. The dark-colored object above and to the front of the gunner's seat and below the manual elevating wheel is the gunner's power traversing control handle, which is in the shape of a pistol grip. Below that control handle are elements of the hydraulic traversing mechanism, including an oil reservoir, a motor, a stabilizer oil pump, and a control box.

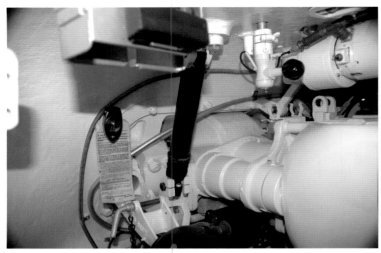

The loader's hatch on the M4A1 was oblong, with a heavy-duty locking bolt on the inside of the hatch cover and a rubber weather seal around the perimeter of the hatch opening. A sprung lock for the hatch cover was mounted on the turret roof and is visible on the far side of the cover. The low-bustle turret of this tank was not originally equipped with this loaders hatch; it was added by the military using a modification kit, a common improvement to these turrets. Inside the hatch, the loader's seat and the left side of the recoil guard of the 75 mm gun are visible. On the side of the 75 mm gun mount is the left recoil cylinder.

In a view of the left front of the interior of the turret from the loader's seat, at the top left is the loader's periscope, to the right of which is the stabilizer cylinder, part of the gyrostabilizer, which acted to keep the elevation of the gun on target while the tank was in motion. Below the periscope are the turret compass, with the instructional tag of the manufacturer, Hull Manufacturing Company of Warren, Ohio, still attached, and the cradle for the coaxial .30-caliber machine gun, including the locking pin. To the upper right is the turret-ventilating blower assembly.

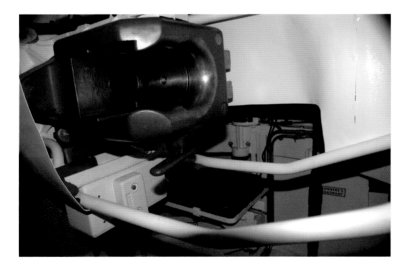

The breech of the M3 75 mm gun is seen from the left rear, with the breechblock open. The breech operating handle is on the underside of the breech. Stamped on the inside of the breach adjacent to the chamber is the gun tube's serial number; "WVT. ARSENAL," a reference to Watervliet Arsenal; and "GUN 75 mm."

Below the platform of the turret basket, and accessed by a hinged door, is space for storing eight rounds of 75 mm ammunition as well as machine gun ammunition. The view is toward the left front, with the driver's steering-brake levers visible through the opening in the turret basket. The metal-colored object with the red arrow on it on the platform in the foreground is the housing for the collector ring, the device through which electrical current is sent from the hull into the turret.

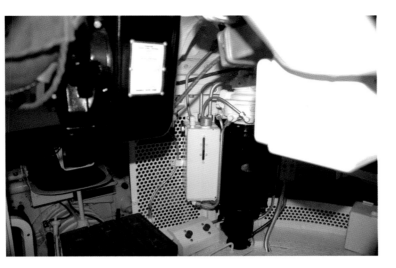

In a view in the left side of the turret basket looking toward the right front of the basket, at the center are elements of the hydraulic traversing system. The white box on the left side of the unit is the oil reservoir; the black object at the center of the unit includes the stabilizer oil pump underneath the larger-sized motor. Partially visible on the right of the unit is a white box with controls for the stabilizer and the 75 mm gun's firing mechanism, as well as the turret master switch and circuit breakers. On the floor to the left of the stabilizer oil pump is a box with electrical foot switches for firing the coaxial machine gun (left) and the 75 mm gun (right). Barely visible to the left of this box is a foot pedal for manually firing the 75 mm gun.

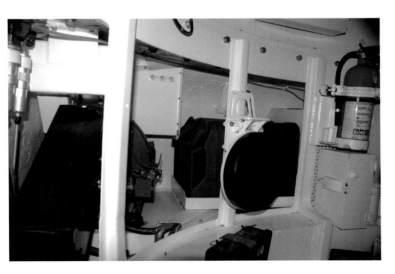

Two five-gallon water containers are stowed in a special rack forward of the auxilliary generator in the left sponson. The loader's seat is folded in the down position, with a first aid kit just below it. Below the modern fire extinguisher in the original bracket is a stowage box for a spare M6 periscope and three spare periscope heads.

## M4A1 Sherman Specifications

| Model | M4A1 | M4A1(76)W |
|---|---|---|
| Weight, lbs. | 66,800 | 70,600 |
| Length* | 230 | 294 |
| Width* | 103 | 105 |
| Height* | 108 | 117 |
| Tread | 83 | 83 |
| Crew | 5 | 5 |
| Max speed | 24 | 24 |
| Fuel capacity | 175 | 175 |
| Range | 120 | 100 |
| Electrical | 24 Neg | 24 Neg |
| Transmission Speeds | 5F<br>1R | 5F<br>1R |
| Turning Radius feet | 31 | 31 |
| Armament Main | 75 mm M3 | 76 mm, M1A1, M1A1C, or M1A2 |
| Armament Secondary | 1 x .50 | 1 x .50 |
| Armament Flexible | 2 x .30 | 2 x .30 |
| **AMMUNITION STOWAGE** | | |
| Main | 90 | 71 |
| .50 caliber | 300 | 600 |
| .30 caliber | 4750 | 6250 |

## Engine Data

| | |
|---|---|
| Engine make/model | Continental R975 C3 |
| Number of cylinders | 9 |
| Cubic-inch displacement | 973 |
| Horsepower | 400 @ 2,400 rpm |
| Torque | 890 @ 1,800 rpm |

## Communication Equipment

M4 Sherman vehicles were provided with SCR 508, SCR 528, or SCR 538 in the rear of the turret. Command tanks also had a sponson-mounted SCR 506. All basic radios were provided with integral interphone.

Flag set M238 and panel set AP50A were also provided

An auxiliary generator rated at 1,500 watts DC, 30 volts, 50 amps, was located in the left rear of the fighting compartment of the M4A1. The generator, typically the Homelite model HRUH-28, was powered by an auxiliary gasoline engine. In this view looking toward the rear, the heater duct is in the foreground, with the auxiliary engine and flywheel coming next, and the generator being located next to the rear corner of the compartment. The generator produced heat, which was sent into the heater duct to warm the fighting compartment. Above the left side of the heater duct are four fuel-shutoff valves.

The radio set installed in this M4A1 appears to be the SCR 528. From left to right are the BC-604 radio transmitter, a storage chest, and a single BC 603 radio receiver. The M4A1s of this vintage also could contain the SCR 508 or the SCR 538, but the SCR 508 had two side-by-side BC 603 radio receivers, while the SCR 538 had only a BC 603 radio receiver with BC 605 interphone amplifier.

Near the end of M4A1 production at Lima Locomotive Works in 1943, small-hatch upper hulls with cast-in, angled-front lifting eyes, or lifting lugs, cast directly into the glacis were introduced to production. The eyes were positioned with their upper legs more inboard than the lower legs. Some researchers believe that Lima Locomotive Works M4A1s acquired these upper hulls from the Pittsburgh Steel Foundry in the final weeks of M4A1 production. In addition, the final LLW-produced M4A1s had a turret with the "low" bustle (i.e., the bottom of the bustle was closer to the engine deck), with no pistol port on the left side. *Patton Museum*

A Lima-built small-hatch M4A1 displays the upper hull with the angled lifting eyes: the right eye is faintly visible to the immediate rear of the right brace of the right brush guard. The turret likely was the type with the thickened left cheek and no pistol port. *Patton Museum*

Another feature of the very late-production Lima small-hatch M4A1s was the incorporation of a rain gutter in the center of the curved upper-rear corner of the upper hull. The two rear lifting eyes also were cast into the upper rear hull and were angled inward at their fronts. *Patton Museum*

# CHAPTER 3
# The Large-Hatch Tank Is Introduced

Research indicates that the final 100 M4A1(75)s made by Pressed Steel Car Company, in December 1943, were equipped with the newly developed large-hatch cast hull, assigned part number E8550. The large-hatch M4A1 hulls would become more associated with the wet-stowage M4A1s with the turret for the 76 mm gun. Here, the nearest vehicle in a column of M4A1(75) Medium Tanks with the E9 extended-suspension modifications, photographed during an Army Day parade at the intersection of Houston Street and North Main Avenue in San Antonio, Texas, on April 6, 1946, is equipped with the large-hatch cast hull. On the final-drive assemblies of the two nearest Shermans are markings for Company A, 66th Armor Regiment, 2nd Armored Division. The rotor shields of the M34 gun mounts have received welded-on "wing" extensions on the right side, and the commander's cupola and pedestal machine gun mount have been installed. Interestingly, this late production date features a three-piece final drive assembly and early M34 gun mount. *Kurt Laughlin*

In the last quarter of 1943, the Sherman family underwent a major design change. The improved models are commonly referred to as "large hatch" tanks, owing to the completely redesigned and larger hatches for the driver and assistantdriver. The redesign was an effort to simplify and speed production, allowing overall Sherman production to be consolidated from ten plants to three, as well as to address shortcomings revealed through combat use.

Pressed Steel Car Company was the first to produce the large-hatch M4A1, and initially the tanks continued to use dry ammunition stowage and were armed with 75 mm guns. However, evidence suggests that fewer than 100 tanks were built in this configuration, before the 76 mm gun and wet ammunition stowage were introduced.

Rather than continuing the use of appliqué armor, the hull casting was thickened in the appropriate areas.

Many of these scarce tanks were ultimately converted to amphibious Duplex Drive tanks for use by US forces in the Normandy invasion.

Pressed Steel Car Company began producing the large-hatch M4A1 with a 76 mm gun in early 1944, with this type being far more common than the large-hatch M4A1 armed with a 75 mm gun. The new gun was installed in a new, larger turret derived from that used in the T23 Medium Tank program.

The first production models were equipped with the M1A1 76 mm gun without a muzzle brake. The tanks featured split hatches for the loader and straight return-roller brackets on the VVSS bogies. Soon the later M1A2 and A3 guns were adopted, as were upswept return-roller brackets,

Internally, the major change incorporated at this time was wet ammunition stowage. Earlier tanks had their ammunition racks in the hull sponsons and were vulnerable to even minor penetrations. The new design moved the ammunition to racks set in the hull floor, which were filled with a solution of water and antifreeze. The intent was to reduce the likelihood of propellant fires in the event of hull side penetration. The tank model designation was changed to reflect both the larger gun and wet ammunition stowage, becoming M4A1(76)W.

The M4A1(76)W was first used in combat during the summer of 1944 by the 2nd and 3rd Armored Divisions.

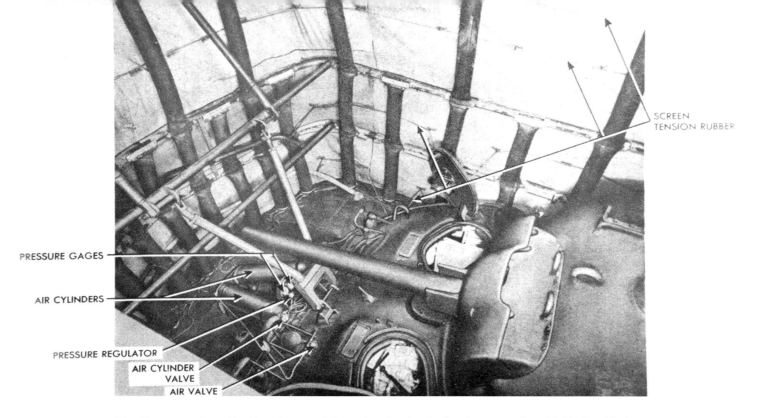

SCREEN
TENSION RUBBER

PRESSURE GAGES

AIR CYLINDERS

PRESSURE REGULATOR

AIR CYLINDER
VALVE

AIR VALVE

The Sherman tank used in this tech-manual illustration showing the flotation screen for a DD (duplex-drive) tank was an M4A1(75) with a large-hatch cast hull. Whereas the surfaces of the driver's and assistant driver's hatches of the small-hatch M4A1s were parallel to the longitudinal centerline of the tank when open, the large hatches were at an angle to the centerline when open, as can be seen here. *Patton Museum*

An M4A1(75) with a large-hatch cast hull rolls along a street in Europe in an undated photograph. The key features in determining the identity of this vehicle are the cast hull, the large driver's hatch, and the turret for the 75 mm gun. This is an amphibious Duplex Drive (DD) tank that has had its flotation screens removed. The power take offs for the propellers are visible on the hull rear inboard of the idler mounts, and the unique idlers of the DD tanks are also visible. *Patton Museum*

In January 1944, in an effort to provide the Sherman tanks with a more powerful main gun, an improved M4A1 with a new turret for the 76 mm gun and other improvements went into production. Usually referred to as the Medium Tank M4A1(76)W, to differentiate it from the M4A1s with a turret for the 75 mm gun, this tank incorporated the turret originally developed for the T23 Medium Tank, armed with an M1A1 76 mm gun on an M62 mount. The "W" in the M4A1(76)W designation stood for wet stowage: the main-gun ammo dry-stowage bins in the sponsons and floor were replaced by storage spaces in the floor with water distributed in them, to reduce the chance of all the ammo exploding in the event of a hit to the tank. The early M4A1(76)W shown here has the new cupola for the commander, with six vision blocks; a round, split hatch for the loader of a type similar tho that used for the commander's hatch in the M4A1(75); and the new, large hatches for the driver and assistant driver. *Patton Museum*

The same early-production M4A1(76)W depicted in the preceding photo is viewed from the left side, with a dust cover over the .50-caliber antiaircraft machine gun. All 3,426 M4A1(76)Ws were produced by Pressed Steel Car Company, with production spanning from January 1944 to July 1945. The large hatches (the driver's is shown open) made it much easier for the driver and the assistant driver to exit than the original small hatches, which were nearly impossible to pass through. *Patton Museum*

The registration number is visible in this third photo of the early M4A1(76)W: 3070871, which was the 375th vehicle of the first production order for 1,130 M4A1(76)W Medium Tanks. The rear of the upper hull of the M4A1(76)W was different from that of the M4A1(75), with a straight lower edge instead of the indented lower edge. A stowage rack has been added to the rear of the upper hull above that new, straight lower edge. On the rear of the turret bustle is another new feature: the hood for the ventilator, which no longer was on the turret roof. New storage brackets for the .50-caliber machine gun when not mounted on the cupola were provided: one attached to the left side of the hood held the cradle and the receiver, while two other brackets jutting from the upper-rear corners of the turret bustle held the gun barrel. *Patton Museum*

Pressed Steel Car Company M4A1(76)W, serial number 38347 and registration number 3070944, produced partway through the first production order, No. T-4166/2, is seen during tests by the Ordnance Operation, General Motors Proving Ground, on April 17, 1944. Cast on the cheek of the turret is its serial number, 535, below which is the number 2, believed to have been the mold number of the manufacturer, Union Steel, which used two different molds for these turrets. *Patton Museum*

As seen in another photo of M4A1(76)W, serial number 38347 and registration number 3070944, this model featured an exhaust deflector in the form of a grille under the rear overhang of the upper hull. The one shown here is the early type; in late 1944 a new exhaust deflector was introduced with an outer frame, for added strength. A storage rack for three spare track links is on each side to the baggage rack on the rear of the upper hull. T48 tracks are installed. A pedestal mount for the .50-caliber antiaircraft machine gun is on the roof of the turret on the left rear of the cupola. *Patton Museum*

This is the 15th M4A1(76)W, registration number 3070511 and serial number 37910, during evaluations by the Office of the Chief of Ordnance, Detroit, on May 1, 1944. Between the brackets for the travel lock for the 76 mm gun is the trademark of General Steel Castings Corporation. Open-spoke bogie wheels are installed, as are sand shields, which, because of their fragile construction, usually were not found on these tanks in operational areas. The 76 mm gun is the M1A1 model with the original style of barrel, which lacked threading on the muzzle end for the installation of a muzzle brake. *Patton Museum*

This tank, registration number 3085062 and serial number 52455, was produced under the second production order for the M4A1(76)W. It was photographed during evaluations by the Ordnance Operation, General Motors Proving Ground, on November 11, 1944. The top of the final-drive assembly where it was bolted to the upper hull had long been a structurally weak feature, and it underwent several improvements. The so-called bolt strip on this final-drive assembly is noticeably thicker than on earlier FDAs. The 76 mm gun is the M1A1C type, which was threaded at the muzzle end to allow for the eventual mounting of a muzzle brake; a collar is screwed on to protect the threading. *National Archives*

The same M4A1(76)W, registration number 3085062, is seen from the left rear at the General Motors Proving Ground on November 11, 1944. The baggage rack on the rear of the upper hull is folded up and secured, and tracks with smooth rubber shoes, apparently T51s, are installed. Interestingly, rearview mirrors have been mounted on the sides of the glacis for the benefit of the driver and the assistant driver. *National Archives*

This M4A1(76)W is on display at Ft. Lewis, Washington. Note the upset return roller. This right-rear view shows the various brackets for holding pioneer tools and other details, such as the style of the right-rear brush guard, the rear lifting eye, and the vertical-volute suspension system. *Mike Petty*

The right idler of the M41(76)W at Ft. Lewis is the solid-spoked type. Above the upper run of track is the welded-on steel strip for holding a sand shield. *Mike Petty*

The ventilator hood on the rear of the turret and the storage brackets for the .50-caliber machine gun on the rear of the turret bustle are seen to good advantage. This rear ventilator was not present on the M4A1(76)W until around the 450th vehicle. The bracket jutting from the left side of the ventilator hood held the machine gun cradle, with the machine gun installed in it. The clamp-type bracket to the extreme left held the barrel support, which is the perforated sleeve at the front of the receiver. *Mike Petty*

The track-support roller support arms are of the upswept type, tilted upward to raise the roller in such manner as to reduce track wear on the skid atop the bogie bracket, to the front of the roller. *Mike Petty*

The casting markings on the final-drive assembly of the Ft. Lewis M41(76)W are on the lower part of the differential housing. They include the trademark of American Steel Foundries, Granite City, Illinois: the letter *G* inside an octagon, to the right of which is the part number, E8543. This is a later-type FDA, with a sharper nose than the original style. Above are the bow machine gun mount, the travel lock, and the mantlet. *Mike Petty*

The turret serial number, 1885, is repeated on the left side of the turret below the number 2. In the foreground is the travel lock for the 76 mm gun. On the upper center of the mantlet is a sprung latch to hold the travel lock in place when not in use. *Mike Petty*

The turret's serial number, 1885, appears at the far left under the number 2. Lifting rings were molded into the upper corners of the mantlet casting. Affixed to the front of the turret and the mantlet are retainers for a dust cover. In the foreground is the assistant driver's large hatch, with the hinge and the periscope guard and lid visible. *Mike Petty*

Details of the brush guard for the left taillight, the left rear lifting ring, and the underside of the turret bustle are visible in this view of the M4A1(76)W at Ft. Lewis, Washington. *Mike Petty*

# CHAPTER 4
# A New Suspension System Is Introduced

The M4A1E8 (76)W was the final development of the cast-hull M4A1 Sherman. Pressed Steel Car Company introduced the horizontal-volute suspension system with the 23-inch-wide track in the third quarter of 1944 and was the sole manufacturer of the type. The key improvement of this model is the "E8" suspension system, which featured horizontal- rather than vertical-volute springs (giving rise to the HVSS abbreviation, versus the VVSS abbreviation used to describe the earlier vertical-volute suspension system). The new HVSS system used dual wheels and a much-wider track, which reduced ground pressure from over 14 psi to about 11 psi and brought with it improved cross-country performance.

The tanks were initially outfitted with an all-steel T66 23-inch-wide single-pin track, but later the T80 dual-pin steel design with a steel chevron-shaped cuff was introduced as well. All the M4A1E8 tanks had the late 7054366 T23 turret with oval loader's hatch.

Production of this, the final M4A1 variant, totaled 1,465 units. Photographic evidence of the M4A1E8 in Europe during World War II is scarce; it is not believed that any of the few that reached the theater saw combat. However, the type did become a mainstay for Army National Guard armor units in the late 1940s and early 1950s. In later years, Israeli forces would convert a large number of surplus cast-hull 76 mm tanks to M51 Ishermans (Israeli Sherman).

Pressed Steel Car Company produced an indeterminate number of M4A1(76)W Medium Tanks with the horizontal-volute suspension system (HVSS) in the final months of World War II; there is evidence that the army accepted over 1,200 of these vehicles in 1945. The HVSS assemblies employed horizontal-volute springs: these are the features visible just above the paired sets of bogie wheels. The HVSS units were wider than the VVSS ones; consequently, wider tracks were required, as well as fenders with support struts. Those mounted on this vehicle, photographed around or after February 11, 1945, are the T66 steel tracks, 23 inches wide, with a pitch (front-to-rear measurement) of 6 inches. All but the last digit of the registration number of this tank is visible: 3012580X, which fell under the first production order in which the M4A1(76)W HVSS Medium Tanks were manufactured, order number T-14608/1. The 76 mm gun is fitted with a muzzle brake; these began to be installed on the Pressed Steel Car assembly line in October 1944. *Patton Museum*

Also produced under production order T-14608/1 was this M4A1(76) W HVSS, registration number 30126231. The tracks are the T80 type, a double-pin design. The track shoes had a steel outer surface with chevron-shaped grousers, and a rubber inner surface. Here, the baggage rack has been folded up onto the rear of the engine deck. *Patton Museum*

Two examples of the M4A1(76)W HVSS are displayed at Camp Atterbury, near Edinburgh, Indiana. These two tanks are the subjects of most of the photographs in this section, with a few exceptions. The tank shown here is equipped with T84 tracks, with rubber track shoes with chevron grousers.

The other M4A1(76)W HVSS at Camp Atterbury, Indiana, is equipped with T66 steel tracks, and the Union Steel–produced turret bears serial number 2451, above which is cast the numeral 1. The outer edges of the fenders were drilled for the installation of sand shields. There were five track-support roller assemblies on each side: the second and the fourth ones had double rollers and are more visible, while the other rollers were single units with smaller diameters and are more difficult to discern; the single units were directly above the bogie assemblies.

The M4A1(76)W HVSS with T84 tracks is viewed from the right rear. On the bottom of the folded-up baggage rack on the rear of the upper hull is a white recognition star and storage brackets for a four-piece bore-cleaning staff. The storage brackets for the .50-caliber antiaircraft machine gun, including the clamp for the gun's barrel support and the clips for the barrel, are intact.

As seen on the M4A1(76)W HVSS equipped with T66 steel tracks at Camp Atterbury, the exhaust deflector is the later type with frame members on the sides for extra strength. The small pipe to the left of the left air cleaner, and above the inboard side of the left track, is the exhaust for the auxiliary-generator engine.

The M4A1(76)W HVSS with T84 tracks at Camp Atterbury is viewed from the left rear. The idler-wheel assembly for the HVSS was part number C135861; the wheel measured 22.5 inches by 6.25 inches.

The turret serial number on the M4A1(76)W HVSS with T84 tracks is 2064, underneath the number 2.

The Camp Atterbury vehicle with T66 steel tracks is seen from the left front. Note the placement of a bracket for a radio antenna on the front left of the turret roof. On the final-drive assembly are dual towing lugs with a step welded to each inboard lug and to the FDA.

This frontal view of the front of the M4A1(76)W HVSS with T66 steel tracks provides a clear view of the shape of the front of the muzzle brake. The relatively sharp nose of final-drive assembly part number E8543 is particularly clear in this image.

As is evident in this photo of the front of the left track assembly, the T66 steel tracks on the Camp Atterbury M4A1(76)W HVSS are in a remarkably good state of preservation.

The M4A1(76)Ws with horizontal-volute suspension system used the same array of sprockets as the VVSS Shermans, except with a wider hub, to accommodate the wider tracks. The right sprocket on the vehicle with T66 steel tracks at Camp Atterbury is the variant with rounded rather than squared tabs where the sprocket is screwed to the hub.

The T84 tracks on the other M4A1(76)W HVSS at Camp Atterbury are in good condition, but with rust on the metal parts and wear to the chevron-style grousers.

The left sprocket assembly is viewed from the rear, showing the wide hub used on the HVSS versions. The hollowed-out track guides at the center of the T66 steel tracks were integral to the track shoes and had a distinct taper, whereas the hollowed-out guides for the T84 tracks with rubber track shoes were bolted on and had far less taper.

The right-front HVSS bogie assembly and part of the right-center one are viewed. Each bogie assembly has two horizontal-volute spring assemblies, side by side but oriented in opposite directions. Above the springs and attached to the tops of the two suspension arms is a shock absorber.

The front-right HVSS bogie assembly is seen in closer detail. Each bogie assembly is mounted on a bogie bracket, which is fastened to the hull. The outboard end of the bogie bracket is the feature below the outboard horizontal-volute spring. The bogie arms, which support the bogie wheels, pivot on the bogie bracket, while the shock absorber fastened to the tops of the bogie arms acted to smoothen the ride.

The rubber tires on the bogie wheels bear the maker's mark "U.S. Tire" and the size, "20½x6¼." Casting numbers are present on the hubcaps, the bogie bracket, and the lower recess on the front (or, in the photo, on the right) bogie arm.

This is one of the larger-diameter, dual-wheel track-support roller assemblies on the Camp Atterbury M4A1(76)W HVSS with the T84 tracks. These rollers are fitted with rubber tires. A good view is available of the inner surfaces of the T84 track shoes and the bolt-on track guides.

A dual track-support roller assembly is viewed from an angle, showing the flange of the roller spindle, which is screwed to the hull. The hollowed-out and tapered design of the guides of the T66 steel tracks is evident.

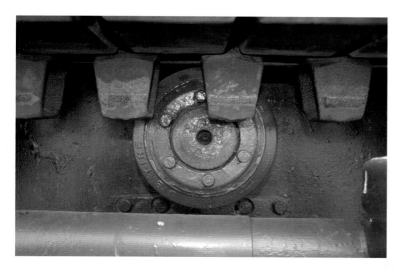

One of the single, smaller-diameter track-support rollers associated with the HVSS suspension system is depicted. These single rollers made contact only with the inboard side of the track. The contrast between the shapes of the T84 track guides, as seen here, and the guides of the T66 track seen in the preceding photo is evident.

The idler wheels of the M4A1(76)W HVSS were equipped with rubber tires. Whereas the T66 steel tracks were linked together with a pin on the front and the rear of each track link, the T84 tracks, shown here, had oval-shaped end connectors, which were secured with a wedge bolt.

The scissors-type brace on the right side of the folding baggage rack (officially called the blanket roll rack) on the rear of the upper hull is depicted. On the rack itself is the right bracket for storing the four screw-together sections of the bore-cleaning staff. A wing nut on a toggle bolt secures each side of the rack in the raised position when not in use.

The left hinge of the air deflector is shown close-up. The retainer rod and wing nut for the left air cleaner are missing.

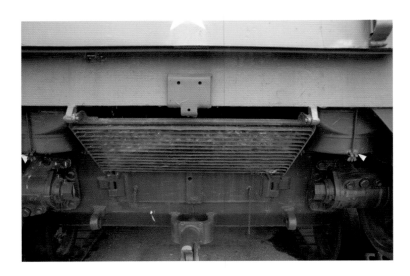

The exhaust deflector is the late type with reinforcing frames on the sides. The deflector is mounted on two top hinges. Partially hidden by the exhaust deflector are the two access doors to the engine compartment, below which are tow lugs and a tow pintle. To the sides are the air cleaners and the idler assemblies.

The tow pintle of an M4A1(76)W HVSS is viewed close-up from the side. It is mounted on a U-shaped bracket that is welded to the lower hull. To the upper left is the left idler assembly.

Another model of tracks used on the M4A1(76)W HVSS was the T80, which are installed on this vehicle. These tracks had a laminated track shoe, with steel outer and inner surfaces with bonded rubber pads between them. A chevron grouser was on the exterior of each track shoe. The air cleaners were highly vulnerable in their exterior positions, and this vehicle has hinged armor plates and shelves for protecting the air cleaners, which Pressed Steel Car began adding to their large-hatch M4A1(76)s in late 1944.

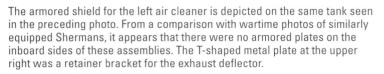

The armored shield for the left air cleaner is depicted on the same tank seen in the preceding photo. From a comparison with wartime photos of similarly equipped Shermans, it appears that there were no armored plates on the inboard sides of these assemblies. The T-shaped metal plate at the upper right was a retainer bracket for the exhaust deflector.

Along the corner between the left side of the lower hull and the floor of the left sponson is the exhaust pipe for the gasoline engine that powered the auxiliary generator. A short strip of steel was welded at an angle above the idler wheel to protect the pipe in that area.

The rear of the turret and the engine deck are the subject of this view of an M4A1(76)W HVSS on display at Camp Atterbury. On the left side of the deck, to the rear of the air intake, is a feature introduced on the large-hatch, wet-stowage M4A1 hulls: a lubricating oil filler cap, surrounded by an armored splash guard. Note the footman loops, for installing retainer straps, on the upper edge of the baggage rack.

The glacis of one of the Camp Atterbury HVSS vehicles is observed from the left side. The headlight is a later replacement item, and a blackout headlight is mounted next to it instead of the specified siren. The bolt strip at the top of the final-drive assembly is noticeably raised. Also in view are the welds holding the lifting eye in place.

The glacis of the M4A1(76)W HVSS with turret serial number 2084 is seen from the left front, allowing a comparison with the previously depicted glacis of the other M4A1(76)W HVSS at Camp Atterbury. The coaxial machine gun barrel is for effect, being a welded-on dummy.

The travel lock for the 76 mm gun barrel and its mounting brackets are shown. Below the travel lock is the trademark of the manufacturer of the cast upper hull, General Steel Castings Corporation: a stylized letter *G* inside a shield with four stars on the top. Also in view are the guards for the periscopes on the driver's and the assistant driver's hatch covers, made of welded steel rods.

Details of the left side of the mantlet on turret serial number 2084 are depicted, along with those of the two large hatches: the ventilator hood between the large hatches, and the guard and lid for the driver's hatch-cover periscope.

Seen here are the faux coaxial machine gun, the left side of the mantlet (including mounting lugs and brackets for the mantlet dust cover), the left lifting ring of the mantlet, and other features, including the large hatches and their accessories, the lids for the driver's and assistant driver's fixed front periscopes, and the travel lock.

Since the protrusion near the front-left corner of the turret roof of the turrets with 76 mm guns was eliminated during production, a ready indicator of an M4A1(76)W HVSS that underwent a postwar rebuild is the presence of a saddle-type mount for a radio antenna in the front-left corner of the turret roof, as seen in the left foreground. The oblong slots for vision blocks on the commander's cupola have been blanked over. In the right foreground is the loader's hatch, with two counterbalance springs visible.

Turret serial number 2451 is viewed from the left side at Camp Atterbury. This photo provides a good sense of the varying textures on the cast hull and the turret for the 76 mm gun.

Turret serial number 2451 is viewed from the right front. On the roof is the gunner's periscope hood, next to which is a pedestal for an antiaircraft machine gun. It is believed that Pressed Steel Car began installing the brackets and lugs for mounting a mantlet cover on its M4A1(76)W HVSS Medium Tanks in the first few months of 1945.

This turret for a 76 mm gun, not stored at Camp Atterbury, bears the serial number 3516 on the turret. This is a relatively late-production turret; researchers have reported observing Union Steel turrets of the type installed on PSC M4A1(76)W HVSS Medium Tanks only up to serial number 3623.

On the same turret shown in the preceding photo, the area between the turret roof and the mantlet is seen, with the front lifting eye of the turret in the foreground. Remnants of the holders for the canvas dust cover for the mantlet are present.

Although there is rust and scaling paint present on the roof of the turret of this surviving M4A1(76)W HVSS, many of the small, more fragile fittings are still intact, such as the folding travel lock for the .50-caliber machine gun, the hold-open latch for the commander's cupola cover, and the guard for the loader's periscope. The vane sight on the inboard side of the aperture for the gunner's periscope is broken, but its base is still attached to the roof.

This detail shot shows the right half of a mantlet cover installed on an M4A1(76)W HVSS. The cover helped prevent dust and moisture from infiltrating around the opening between the turret and the mantlet. Inboard of the direct-sight aperture on the mantlet is the number 5434.

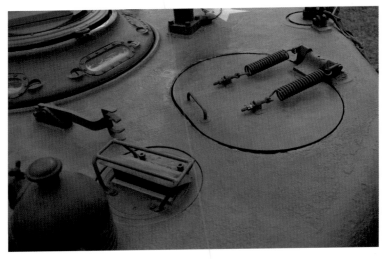

The cupola on this restored M4A1(76)W HVSS is fitted with two rings, one on the cupola cover and one on the hatch rim, for installing a padlock. A periscope and a grab handle were mounted on a rotating disk on the hatch cover. Around the cupola were six vision blocks: 3-inch-thick blocks of laminated glass that were proof against .50-caliber machine gun fire at 100 yards and provided the commander with 360-degree vision around the tank.

In a view from the left front of the turret of an M4A1(76)W HVSS, in the left foreground is a spotlight, with the loader's periscope, the folded-down travel lock for the .50-caliber machine gun, and the loader's hatch with two coil counterbalance springs. Note the contrast between the perfectly smooth surface of the loader's hatch and the textured surface of the turret roof.

The interior of the cupola hatch cover, with the periscope not mounted, is viewed. On the cupola cover inside the perimeter of the rotating disk with the periscope is a brass azimuth ring, with degrees of azimuth marked off, to give the commander a reference when sighting through the periscope. A grab ring is on the hatch cover.

The spotlight is viewed close-up, in the folded-down position. Next to it is the loader's periscope with the protective lid raised. The periscope was mounted on a round, rotating base and was protected by a guard made of welded metal rods, bolted to the rotating base.

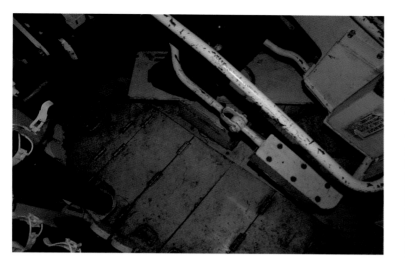

In a view down through the loader's hatch of an M4A1(76)W HVSS, the recoil guard of the 76 mm gun is at the upper right, and 76 mm ready rounds are in holders to the left. On the floor or platform of the turret basket are hinged panels with grab handles, for accessing ammunition stored below.

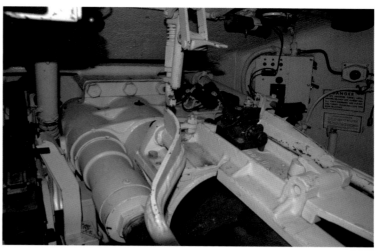

The olive drab instrument mounted on top of the recoil guard to the right of center is the gunner's elevation quadrant, used for setting the elevation of the gun during indirect fire or for coordinating the true elevation of the piece with the gunsight. At the upper center is the interior travel lock for the 76 mm gun.

The recoil guard, 76 mm gun breech (left), and other details, such as a binoculars holder (upper center), stored spotlight (right), and various storage boxes, are viewed through the loader's hatch.

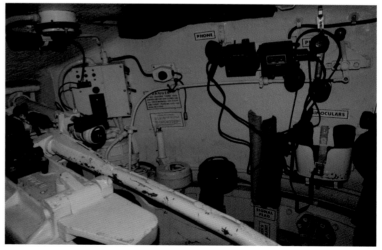

As viewed from the loader's position in the turret of an M4A1(76)W HVSS, to the immediate right of the 76 mm gun is the gunner's telescopic sight. Other features include the power traversing control and the azimuth indicator (center); intercom control boxes, hand phones, headsets, binoculars holder, and stowed signal flags; and, toward the upper right with a red knob on it, the commander's traversing control. The commander used this control to slew the turret and its 76 mm gun onto a target.

# CHAPTER 5
# Remanufactured Tanks

Beginning in August 1944, weary M4A1 (and M4 and M4A3) tanks, previously used for training, were shipped to Chrysler's plant in Evansville, Indiana, and to International Harvester for remanufacturing. Chrysler's Detroit Tank Arsenal undertook a similar program with M4A2s, which were destined for the British, and the Chester, Richmond, and Lima Tank Depots (the latter of which is NOT the same as the Lima Locomotive Works tank plant), as well as the Montreal Locomotive Works, which remanufactured M4s and M4A3s. In total, 5,434 M4-series tanks were remanufactured.

At the end of the remanufacturing process, the tanks were the equivalent of a new tank, and many of these tanks were sent to Europe in 1945 for use after the heavy losses US forces suffered during the Battle of the Bulge. The remanufacturing program ended in April 1945.

During the final months of World War II, the Army implemented a program to remanufacture some 2,200 M4A1 Medium Tanks. This work, conducted from September 1944 to May 1945, entailed modernizing the tanks with the various modifications and changes that had been instituted since production began. This Lima-built M4A1, registration number 3058342, built under production order T-3208 and accepted by the US Army in October 1942, was photographed after being remanufactured by Chrysler at its plant in Evansville, Indiana, during evaluations by the Ordnance Operation, General Motors Proving Ground, on November 11, 1944. It had add-on fenders to provide clearance for duckbill extended end connectors (used for improving flotation on soft ground) to be installed on the outboard sides of the tracks; appliqué armor; repositioned siren and brush guard; and steel tracks with chevron grousers.
*National Archives*

The same M4A1, registration number 3058342, is viewed from the left rear after modernization, showing the new brackets on the rear of the turret bustle for storing the .50-caliber machine gun when not in use. A gun cradle with ammunition-box holder is mounted in the storage bracket, and angle-iron brackets for holding the gun barrel and a separate clamp for holding the barrel support on the receiver of the machine gun are present. A folded-up baggage rack is on the rear of the upper hull; below it, extra armor has been welded onto the rear of the upper hull during the remanufacturing process. The turret serial number is 2748. *National Archives*

This recently remanufactured M4A1, registration number 3058722, was photographed on January 18, 1945; it had been accepted in December 1942. It was appointed similarly to the remanufactured M4A1 in the two preceding photographs, including the addition of fenders and widened mudguards, and still had the original commander's split hatch. The weld beads between the two appliqué armor panels on the hull, and on the turret, were much smoother and more subtle than the welds on the preceding M4A1. The mantlet on this turret and the one on the preceding remanufactured M4A1, part of the M34A1 gun mount, replaced the original, narrow rotor shields. *Patton Museum*

In a left-rear view of Lima Locomotive Works–built, Chrysler-remanufactured M4A1, registration number 3058722, on January 18, 1945, the rear face of the upper hull has had the additional armor welded on, and storage brackets for the .50-caliber machine gun have been mounted on the rear of the turret bustle. On this turret, the pistol port has been dismounted and the opening has been plated over. On the center of the rear of the turret bustle is the trademark of General Steel Castings Corporation. The taillight brush guards are the distinctive Lima Locomotive Works type, with a 90-degree twist on each leg of the arched part of the guards. *Patton Museum*

This Lima Locomotive Works M4A1, registration number 3038692, was accepted in September 1943 and was remanufactured as an M4A1E9, with the VVSS bogie assemblies spaced out from the lower hull and wide fenders and mudguards installed to allow clearance for installing duckbill extended track connectors on both sides of each track assembly. The upper hull is one of the ones that Lima Locomotive Works installed on its final run of small-hatch M4A1s: note the angled-front lifting eyes cast into the glacis. The turret now has a commander's cupola replacing the original split hatch. *Patton Museum*

The same M4A1E9, registration number registration number 3038692, is viewed from the left rear. Note the curved and relatively rough weld beads where the additional armor plate has been installed on the rear face of the upper hull. Storage brackets for the .50-caliber machine gun were mounted on the rear of the turret bustle during the remanufacturing process. *Patton Museum*

The following section of color photographs depicts a Pacific Car and Foundry M4A1 Medium Tank, registration 3060668, accepted in October 1942 and later rebuilt as an M4A1E9, with VVSS bogie assemblies spaced out from the hull to accommodate duckbill extended track connectors on both sides of each track. The M4A1E9s were intended as an expedient to give the tank better flotation and performance on soft ground and snow until wider tracks could be brought into production and distribution. These photos were taken over a period of time, with some showing the vehicle in fresh paint; others, in a different, more faded paint and markings scheme.

The bogie assemblies have the horizontal, not upswept, track-support roller arms, with spacer blocks on the rears of the arms to raise the rollers. The bogie wheels are a mix of concave solid disk (part number D52861) and open spoke with plates welded over the openings (part number D38501).

The welded-on additional armor under the bottom of the rear face of the upper hull, a characteristic of the remanufactured M4A1s, is present and may be seen below the sides of the baggage rack. Also installed, and still present, are the brackets on the rear of the turret bustle for storing the .50-caliber machine gun.

Casting numbers on the upper right of the final-drive assembly are displayed. The top row indicates the maker, American Steel Foundries, Granite City, Illinois, and the part number, E4186. The second row has "2B," the meaning of which remains under debate, and the serial number of the FDA, 792. On the bottom line are "LO," for the type of steel armor used, and "BU," evidently a subcontractor mark indicating that the assembly was manufactured for Buick.

Even the appliqué armor on the turret had foundry markings on it, near the top of the left plate. Next to the appliqué armor are casting marks for the turret. An intact vane site remains in place on the front of the turret roof.

On the left side of the mantlet is the trademark of the maker, National Roll and Foundry, of Avonmore, Pennsylvania: a large *V*, inside which is *NR* over *F*. Below the trademark is the part number of the mantlet, D68454. Near the bottom is 751, the serial number, and below the coaxial machine gun aperture is a raised surface in the shape of a shield, with a number stamped on it.

The casting marks on the turret are the number 4, apparently a mold number; the part number, D50878, which pertains to the 75 mm low-bustle turrets, followed by the trademark of Union Steel Castings; and the serial number of the turret, 3026.

The M4A1E9 displayed at Fort Leonard Wood is viewed from the left front with a light dusting of snow on it. The brush guards are still present on the glacis, but the headlight assemblies and the siren have been removed. A full complement of duckbill extended end connectors are present, at least on the outboard sides of both sets of tracks.

The left side of the rear of the lower hull is in view, showing weld beads for the left engine-access door hinges, the triangular doorstop between the hinges, the bracket on the door for the exhaust deflector, the tow eye, and the joints in the hull armor. To the upper left is the bottom of the round air cleaner.

The taillight brush guards are in the particular style of M4A1s assembled by Pacific Car and Foundry, with a 90-degree twist toward the bottom of each leg of the main, arched part of the guard, to provide flat surfaces to weld to the hull. Details of the baggage rack also are available, including its three hinged mountings on the hull above the rack.

As part of the E9 suspension upgrade, this spacer was added that shifted the mounting point of the idler assemblies to the rear of the tank, as well as moving it four inches outboard. The right idler assembly is shown, along with details of the armor plates above the idler assembly, and the bottom of the right air cleaner at the top center.

# CHAPTER 6
# Into Combat

The M4A1 first saw combat with British forces at the Battle of El Alamein ("al-'Alamayn") in October 1942. Following the devastating British loss at Tobruk, these tanks had been transferred to the Commonwealth by the US Army, which had been using the tanks for training in the United States. The M4A1s, along with a few M4A2s, were hastily withdrawn from training and placed aboard ships sailing for North Africa in July 1942. Of the 318 Shermans sent, 252 were available for El Alamein.

Also in the North African campaign, the cast-hull Shermans also equipped the US 2nd Armored Division in North Africa. The US 1st Armored Division used the radial-powered M4A1 and M4 from the time they arrived in Tunisia, and then into Italy up to the capture of Rome, at which time they began to be augmented by the V-8-powered M4A3.

The radial-powered, cast-hull M4A1s remained in service with the US Army through World War II, with the 3rd and 4th Armored Divisions taking the type into Normandy. From there the tanks saw combat across Europe as well as in the Pacific.

Although the larger, better-armed, and better-armored M26 Pershing Medium Tank had entered production and combat service prior to the end of World War II, the Sherman nevertheless continued to compose the bulk of the US Army's medium-tank force for many years. However, the active army preferred a uniform fleet of Ford GAA-powered tanks such as the M4A3, rather than the radial-engine-equipped M4 and M4A1. Accordingly, the M4A1 was largely relegated to National Guard units or was provided to liberated and allied nations struggling to rebuild their armies following the war.

In July 1942 an early M4A1 is poised at the brink of a steep slope during evaluations of the tank's performance capacities at the Lima factory proving ground in Ohio. The twin fixed machine guns in the bow, characteristic of very early M4A1s, are visible. *Library of Congress*

The same M4A1 has started to roll down the steep slope at the Lima proving ground. The M4A1 was capable of negotiating a maximum grade of 60 percent. Note the rotor gunsight on the turret and the omission of the assistant driver's periscope mount.
*Library of Congress*

Two early Pressed Steel Car M4A1 Medium Tanks are participating in an Army Day parade in Louisville, Kentucky, on April 6, 1942. In the foreground is the first M4A1 produced by PSC: serial number 5 and registration number 3014761. The other tank is PSC M4A1, serial number 10 and registration number 3014766, and that registration number is very faintly visible on the sponson, in the distinctive "railroad font" style that PSC used at that time. *National Archives*

A small-hatch, M4A1 DV (direct vision) and an M3 Medium Tank are parked side by side at a fueling station at Ft. Knox, Kentucky, in June 1942; another M3 is parked behind the Sherman. No vane sight is present on the turret roof. *Library of Congress*

The commander of a small-hatch M4A1 DV, marked DR-A6 on the final-drive assembly, waves a signal flag during a training exercise at the Armored Force School, at Ft. Knox, in June 1942. The bogies remain the early type with the track-support roller mounted above the bogie bracket. *Library of Congress*

The commander of an M4A1 with the 13th Armored Regiment, 1st Armored Division, is maintaining watch through binoculars during the latter part of the Battle of Kasserine Pass, Tunisia, on February 24, 1943, which was the day after Gen. Rommel canceled the German offensive. The M4A1 has the early-style VVSS bogie assemblies and box-type air cleaners. The left rear mudguard is missing. *National Archives*

This mud-camouflaged 1st Armored Division M4A1 command tank, named for Maj. Jim Simmerman, was photographed in Tunisia in February 1943. The tank is equipped with a second radio, as evidenced by the aerial mounted in the opening for the front-hull ventilator. *Patton Museum*

An ever-versatile small-hatch M4A1 is being put to work as a tow vehicle for a half-track through a sandy draw during the first day of the Battle of Sidi Bou Zid, Tunisia, on February 14, 1943. The smooth-rubber track shoes on this M4A1 were not very effective on sand or soft ground. *National Archives*

The full sand shields are being put to good use on this early-production M4A1 of the 1st Armored Division operating near the al-Qaşrayn ("Kasserine") pass in western Tunisia. This tank, which wore yellow turret markings in this February 1943 scene, is unusual in having the sand shields. While they were designed to reduce dust churned up while operating in dry areas, they blocked access for track and suspension maintenance and were often removed in the field. *Patton Museum*

This M4A1 at a depot in Wahrân ("Oran"), Algeria, in 1943 features the heavy-duty vertical-volute suspension system (VVSS) with the trailing return roller. This arrangement provided more room in the bogie housing for large volute springs than did the earlier design, which had the return roller directly over the suspension. *National Archives*

The unique design of the taillight guard is characteristic of M4A1s built by Lima Locomotive Works. *National Archives*

In the spring of 1943, engineers have constructed a ferry craft from pontoons and steel treadway bridge sections for crossing the Colorado River at Yuma, Arizona, and an M4A1 Medium Tank is being transported on it. The tank is equipped with the D47527 VVSS bogie assemblies, with the track-support rollers on arms extending from the top rear of the bogie brackets. *US Army Engineer History Office*

A column of M4A1 Shermans assemble along the shore at Binzart ("Bizerte"), Tunisia, in preparation for Operation Husky, the invasion of Sicily, in early July 1943. The tanks are painted in a disruptive camouflage scheme of Earth Yellow over the standard Olive Drab. Large, wide surrounds have been applied encircling the white stars. In the background, a Higgins PT boat has been beached for repairs. *Naval History and Heritage Command*

A recovery crew is preparing to pull a small-hatch M4A1 nicknamed "Bull o' the Woods" out of a gully next to a bridge near Acerno, Italy, on November 2, 1943. The tank slid off the road during a dark night. The turret but not the left sponson is equipped with appliqué armor. Flanking the recognition star on the turret bustle are the number 1 and the number 6. A cable has been rigged from the tank to a derrick, out of view on the roadway above. *National Archives*

Members of a small-hatch M4A1 Medium Tank crew from the 13th Armored Regiment pose for their photo as a soldier hands a newspaper to the crewman on the engine deck, in the Capua area of Italy on November 29, 1943. This vehicle, registration number W-3058979, was built by Lima Locomotive Works and was accepted in April 1942. It has the original style of VVSS bogie assemblies. Two sections of spare tracks are secured to the glacis. The crewmen have painted the bottom of the 75 mm gun barrel white in an effort to countershadow the barrel, to deceive enemy gunners as to the type of gun, and a white band was previously painted neatly around the barrel. *National Archives*

An M4A1 of the 13th Tank Battalion approaches Riolo, Italy, in the winter of 1944–45. On the right turret side, a first-aid kit has been stowed for ready access. Ahead of the commander's cupola is a hoop, which serves as a guard for an additional sight used when the tank is employed in an indirect-fire role, common in the mountainous terrain. *Patton Museum*

Mechanics of the 87th Ordnance Company (Heavy Maintenance, Tank) are making repairs to several Sherman tanks, including an M4A1 parked next to a mobile workshop, in the Presenzano area of Italy on January 10, 1944. The tracks are off the M4A1. Note the step made of angle iron welded to the glacis between the driver's and assistant driver's hoods. *National Archives*

The crew of this Marine Corps tank training in Australia has removed the headlights and stored them in the interior, and the bow machine gun has been protected by the foul-weather cover. The tank rides on T49 three-bar cleat steel tracks and is equipped with the M34A1 gun mount. *National Archives*

"Sloppy Joe" was the nickname of M4A1 turret number 13, with the USMC's 603rd Light Tank Company, photographed next to another M4A1 on Manus Island, Papua New Guinea, on March 24, 1944. The hull is a small-hatch example, and the turret has the low bustle, with a split-door commander's hatch. *National Archives*

These tanks, attached to the 1st Marine Division, are shown along a beach following the Arawe battles on March 27, 1944. All four tanks are equipped with the T49 three-bar, cleat-style track. *Patton Museum*

Shanghai Lil, an Army M4A1, carries infantry inland from the beach at Humboldt Bay in southern New Guinea, April 22, 1944, as part of Gen. MacArthur's push toward the Philippines. *Patton Museum*

Evidently it was popular for M4A1 crews of the 13th Armored Regiment, 1st Armored Division, in Italy to rig long sections of spare track on the glacis, for extra protection from antitank projectiles and for a ready supply of tracks in the event of detonating a mine. This example is taking position next to a giant haystack in the Anzio area of Italy on April 27, 1944. Of interest is the small shield that has been placed over the coaxial machine gun: a modification dating to late 1942. Curiously, another late 1942 modification, the addition to armored "cheeks" to the rotor shields, is not present on this tank.
*National Archives*

An armored column, including at least five M4A1 Medium Tanks, from the 760th Tank Battalion, Fifth Army, is advancing on the main street in Formia, Italy, on May 19, 1944. They have the early commander's hatches with the split hatch covers, and all have the T48 tracks with rubber track shoes with chevron grousers. Two retainer racks for equipment and baggage have been welded to the engine deck of the tank in the left foreground, while the other tanks have considerable heaps of bedrolls, boxes, and other equipment on their engine decks. *National Archives*

An M4A1 nicknamed "Weenie One" moves out past several other Shermans and a T2 Tank Recovery Vehicle outside Le Ferierre, Italy, on May 25, 1944. It is known only that "Weenie One" was assigned to a Company G in an unidentified battalion or regiment in the 1st Armored Division. This tank apparently had two additional camouflage colors applied in addition to the base color of Olive Drab. The turret bears serial number 2421. The sprocket assembly is the D47366 variant with the solid, "economy" sprockets. *National Archives*

M4A1s from the 41st Division have just landed at Arawa, on Wakde Island, Dutch New Guinea, on May 17, 1944, and are lined up preparatory to moving inland. At least the first two tanks are equipped with T49 tracks, which had grousers running the width of each steel track shoe: one long grouser and two shorter ones with a gap between them. The T49 tracks are frequently seen in photos of Sherman tanks operating in the South Pacific and the South West Pacific Area, as well as in Italy. The lead vehicle has a small-hatch hull. *National Archives*

An M4A1 moves along a road near Mokmer Strip on Biak, New Guinea. Located less than 100 yards from the beach, the airfield was a hard-fought prize won by the US Army in May 1944. *National Archives*

Members of the 752nd Tank Battalion are performing sentry duty in their small-hatch M4A1 at a crossroads in a town near Pisa, Italy, in or around August 1944. The siren is missing from its trapezoidal brush guard on the glacis. Appliqué armor is on the turret but not the hull, and the rotor shield for the 75 mm gun mount has the "cheek" armor. On the right mudguard is a large wine jug. T54E1 steel tracks with chevron grousers are installed on the VVSS suspension. *National Archives*

In a photo taken at nearly the same time as the preceding one, the same tank shown in that photo is on the right, along with another small-hatch M4A1, guarding an intersection in a town near Pisa, Italy. The wine jug is still on the right mudguard, and a tree branch is on the left mudguard of the closer Sherman. The other M4A1 has the original-style VVSS bogie assemblies. Both tanks have the small shield for the coaxial machine gun, a late 1942 modification. *National Archives*

The M4A1 on the right and the welded-hull M4 on the left, assigned to the 752nd Tank Battalion in Italy, are armed with the M17 7.2-inch multiple rocket launchers, nicknamed the "Whizbang." These launchers held twenty 7.2-inch rail-launched rockets, each of which was housed in an armored enclosure; a hydraulically operated armored flap protected the front of the launchers. The rocket mounts had an elevation of +25 to –5 degrees. These rockets were primarily used against obstacles at relatively close range. *National Archives*

During the US Army's first year of combat in World War II, its lessons learned included the need for tanks fitted with bulldozer blades, for clearing obstructions while protecting the crew from enemy fire. The solution was the so-called tankdozer, which was effected by installing the M1 Bulldozer kit on Sherman tanks equipped with VVSS. Here, a small-hatch M4A1 tankdozer with appliqué armor is filling in a roadway over a bombed-out bridge in Lonlay-l'Abbaye, France, on August 15, 1944. *National Archives*

A Culin hedgerow-cutter-equipped M4A1 races through the streets of Aubencheul-au-Bac, France, on September 2, 1944, as liberated French people look on. Developed by Sgt. Curtis Culin and fabricated in the field, typically from discarded German beach obstacles, the hedgerow-cutting devices were added to the differential cover of Sherman tanks. These devices allowed the tanks to penetrate the thick-foliage Normandy hedges without riding up the brush and thereby exposing the thin armor of the hull bottom. This tank is equipped with a wide M34A1 gun mount and full set of appliqué armor, typical of those seen during the battle of Normandy and the breakout from the beachhead. All of the national star markings, viewed as a bull's-eye for the enemy, have been obscured. *National Archives*

A camouflage-painted, small-hatch M4A1 tankdozer with M1 Bulldozer kit, attached to the 16th Engineer Battalion, 1st Armored Division, is clearing a road over a blown bridge in Italy on September 12, 1944. The registration number, 3058559, pertains to an M4A1 manufactured by Lima Locomotive Works. All the return-roller arms on the VVSS bogie assemblies are the type with the horizontal top, with no spacer blocks to raise the rollers. The dozer blade was 48 inches high and 124 inches wide, and the entire M1 Bulldozer kit weighed 7,100 pounds. *National Archives*

The M4A1 armed with a 76 mm gun began to be fielded just prior to "Operation Cobra," the late July 1944 breakout from the Normandy beachhead. While the 76 mm gun was an improvement over the previous 75 mm gun in tank-to-tank combat, it was still inadequate to deal with German Panther or Tiger tanks head on. These two early-production M4A1(76)W tanks were knocked out in the streets of Schevenhutte, Germany, in September 1944. *Patton Museum*

199452

An early-production M4A1 nicknamed "Hang It N" from the 751st Tank Battalion is positioned to guard a strongpoint on a road outside Porreta Terme, Italy, on December 6, 1944. The tank has the narrow rotor shield and the original type of VVSS bogie units. The crewman on the turret, Pvt. Donald E. Hill, has rigged an umbrella over his hatch to make the guard duty in the drizzling rain more bearable. The taillight brush guards are of the distinctive type used by Lima Locomotive Works, with a 90-degree twist partway up each leg of the main piece, and the bottoms bent at a 90-degree angle and welded to the hull. *National Archives*

On December 11, 1944, armored vehicles of the 752nd Tank Battalion are proceeding along a slope only 500 yards from the enemy lines, in the area of De Dusi, Italy. The first and fourth vehicles are M4A1s, while the second and third are M18 Hellcat Tank Destroyers. Farther back is a T2 Tank Recovery Vehicle parked next to a Sherman, evidently an M4A1, with a turret for a 76 mm gun. The M4A1 in the foreground has a dust cover over the bow machine gun mount, and a shield over the coaxial machine gun. As a field modification, racks have been mounted on the fronts of the two nearest M4A1s to hold liquid containers, knapsacks, helmets, and other gear. *National Archives*

Accompanied by a large-hatch M4A1(76)W, elements of the 38th Infantry Regiment, 2nd Infantry Division, cross a Bailey bridge erected on the foundations of a destroyed bridge over the Roer River at Heimbach, Germany, on March 3, 1945. The Sherman was likely with the 741st Tank Battalion, which was the 2nd Infantry Division's assigned tank battalion at that time. The loader's hatch was the early, split type, and the left hatch cover is open. Duckbill extended end connectors are installed on the outboard sides of the tracks, with a damaged or missing duckbill visible here and there. *National Archives*

Just over a half hour after engineers began construction of this treadway bridge, a small-hatch M4A1 from Company A, 741st Tank Battalion, 2nd Infantry Division, is crossing over it, at Dümpel, Germany, on March 9, 1945. Chicken wire rigged to steel cables is attached to the turret and the hull for emplacing tree branches for camouflage. What appear to be steel track links are stacked on the glacis, and a Culin hedgerow cutter, for hacking through the hedgerows encountered in Normandy, is on the bow. This tank was the last surviving tank to have landed in Normandy on D-Day with the 741st. *National Archives*

A mixed column of M4A1 and M4A3 tanks roll into Moers, Germany, on March 24, 1945. The tanks, assigned to the 771st Tank Battalion, all have sandbag supplemental armor on their front plates. The unit markings have been hand painted on the differential covers below their original position, because the original positions have been covered by the sandbags. All other markings on the tanks appear to have been overpainted. Many of the tanks have duckbill extended track end connectors for improved cross-country performance. *National Archives*

This M4A1(76) tank has been field-modified through the addition of two additional layers of armor plate to the hull front. To support the armor against the contours of the cast hull, brackets have been welded in the upper corners. In another field modification, the commander's vision cupola and the split loader's-hatch installations have been reversed, with the commander now having the split hatch. The tank, assigned to the 3rd Armored Division, was photographed near Korbach, Germany, on March 30, 1945.
*National Archives*

The M4A1 Medium Tanks were highly dependable, relatively durable, and, perhaps most importantly, available in vast numbers, but all too often they proved to be no match in a duel with German tanks, mines, and artillery. These two Shermans, an early, small-hatch M4A1 in the foreground and an M4 in the background, were knocked out, back to back, along a road at Campoleone, Italy, where they were photographed after the end of the war in Europe, in May 1945. Note the upside-down recognition star inside a circle on the glacis of the M4A1. Lying on the ground in the right foreground is one of the M4A1's final-drive shaft covers. *National Archives*